Special Advocates in the Adversarial System

The last twenty years have seen an unprecedented rise in the use of secret courts or 'closed material proceedings' largely brought about in response to the need to protect intelligence sources in the fight against terrorism. This has called into question the commitment of legal systems to long-cherished principles of adversarial justice and due process. Foremost among the measures designed to minimise the prejudice caused to parties who have been excluded from such proceedings has been the use of 'special advocates' who are given access to sensitive national security material and can make representations to the court on behalf of excluded parties. Special advocates are now deployed across a range of administrative, civil and criminal proceedings in many common law jurisdictions including the UK, Canada, New Zealand, Hong Kong and Australia.

This book analyses the professional services special advocates offer across a range of different types of closed proceedings. Drawing on extensive interviews with special advocates and with lawyers and judges who have worked with them, the book examines the manner in which special advocates are appointed and supported, how their position differs from that of ordinary counsel within the adversarial system, and the challenges they face in the work that they do. Comparisons are made between different special advocate systems and with other models of security-cleared counsel, including that used in the United States, to consider what changes might be made to strengthen their adversarial role in closed proceedings. In making an assessment of the future of special advocacy, the book argues that there is a need to reconceptualise the unique role that special advocates play in the administration of justice.

John Jackson is Professor of Comparative Criminal Law and Procedure at the School of Law, University of Nottingham, UK and is a qualified barrister.

Special Advocates in the Adversarial System

John Jackson

Routledge
Taylor & Francis Group
LONDON AND NEW YORK

First published 2020
by Routledge
2 Park Square, Milton Park, Abingdon, Oxon OX14 4RN

and by Routledge
605 Third Avenue, New York, NY 10017

First issued in paperback 2020

Routledge is an imprint of the Taylor & Francis Group, an informa business

British Library Cataloguing-in-Publication Data
A catalogue record for this book is available from the British Library

Library of Congress Cataloging-in-Publication Data
Names: Jackson, John D., 1955- author.
Title: Special advocates in the adversarial system / John Jackson.
Description: Abingdon, Oxon; New York, NY: Routledge, 2020. |
Includes index.
Identifiers: LCCN 2019009490 | ISBN 9781138242012 (hardback) |
ISBN 9781315278773 (ebook)
Subjects: LCSH: Defense (Criminal procedure) | National security–
Law and legislation | Ex parte communications–Great Britain. |
Criminal defense lawyers–Great Britain. | Official secrets–Great Britain.
Classification: LCC KD8358 .J33 2020 | DDC 345.41/05044–dc23
LC record available at https://lccn.loc.gov/2019009490

ISBN 13: 978-0-367-72685-0 (pbk)
ISBN 13: 978-1-138-24201-2 (hbk)

Typeset in Galliard
by Deanta Global Publishing Services, Chennai, India.

For my mother

Contents

Foreword

Closed material proceedings, in which one party can rely on evidence not shown to the other, present a fundamental challenge in any adversarial system. They have, however, been considered necessary in an increasingly wide variety of contexts, principally in response to terrorist and other national security threats, since 2001. Special advocates, the security-cleared lawyers who represent the interests of the excluded party, are supposed to provide in these proceedings what the European Court of Human Rights called 'a substantial measure of procedural justice'.

Some of us who have worked as special advocates have attempted, over the years, to throw a little light on how closed material procedures work in practice. On a few occasions, we have given evidence to parliamentary committees, responded to consultations and published modest contributions to the academic literature. One of our aims has been to provide the beginnings of an evidence base for a proper analysis of the extent to which special advocates can, and cannot, meaningfully contribute to the fairness of closed material proceedings.

But even if anyone had the time or inclination to piece to together these scraps, they would hardly provide much in the way of a comprehensive or illuminating account of the topic. Large parts of the picture would remain fuzzy and incomplete. It would be putting it too high to say, as Josef K's interlocutor did in Kafka's *The Trial*, that, because of the secrecy of the proceedings, 'all we know about these earlier cases are just legends'. But it would be hard not to conclude that the secrecy of the proceedings is, to an outsider, a serious obstacle to a complete understanding of them.

Professor John Jackson has not, however, been deterred. Not only has he made coherent sense of the case law and other publicly available sources. Not only has he produced a perceptive comparative analysis placing the United Kingdom's experience alongside that of other jurisdictions from the common law world and beyond. His real insight comes from the research material he has gathered himself. His quantitative data give the most accurate indication to date of the extent of the use of closed material procedures of different kinds. In addition, and uniquely, he draws on detailed interviews with a large proportion of the lawyers with experience of closed material proceedings in the UK. These interviews with special advocates, open lawyers, government counsel and judges provide a more comprehensive and balanced account of the role of the special advocate than any published work to date.

Special Advocates in the Adversarial System will be an invaluable resource to academic commentators seeking to study and understand this topic. It will provide a wealth of insights to seasoned practitioners in the national security field. It should also be compulsory reading for any special advocate, any lawyer working with or against a special advocate and any judge embarking for the first time on litigation involving a closed material procedure. Most importantly, it will do what special advocates themselves never could: provide a comprehensive and authoritative factual underpinning for any proposal for reform. Sunlight, it is said, is the best of disinfectants. This book will open the curtains.

Martin Chamberlain QC

Acknowledgements

Throughout the course of the research project which led to this book, I have been most fortunate to secure assistance, encouragement and support from many quarters. My first thanks must go to the British Academy and the Leverhulme Trust for awarding me a Senior Fellowship which enabled me to conduct most of the fieldwork for the research in the academic year 2015–16. The British Academy and the Leverhulme Trust also awarded me a small grant during 2015–17 which funded my travel to interview special advocates in Ottawa and Toronto and security-cleared lawyers and federal prosecutors in New York. I would also like to thank the University of Nottingham for enabling me to employ research assistants and for granting me study leave in the first semester of the academic year 2017–18.

In research which aims to shed light on practices that have not been widely scrutinised, it is vitally important to obtain the goodwill and cooperation of those on the ground who have direct experience of them. I would like to thank all the special advocates, government counsel, open counsel and the judges and commissioners who generously gave up their time to be interviewed on the work of special advocates. In order to preserve their anonymity, I have used the masculine gender to refer to all interviewees. It would have been impossible to carry out this research without their cooperation.

From my first approach until the very end, the Special Advocates' Support Office (SASO) has been exceedingly supportive of the research. The Office initially helped me to reach out to special advocates and government counsel and it responded patiently to numerous queries throughout the duration of the research. The lead lawyers, Tom Bullmore and Steven Winder, were particularly helpful. I would also like to thank the Attorney General's Office for answering a number of queries relating to the appointment of special advocates, and the Special Immigration Appeals Commission (SIAC) Office for answering queries relating to the database of open SIAC decisions, which can be viewed on the SIAC website. I first came across special advocates in my role as a Parole Commissioner in Northern Ireland, and I would like to thank the Chief Commissioner, Christine Glenn, for her support for the project and for allowing me to refer to the Parole Commissioners' *Guidance on Confidential Information Cases*. I would also like to thank HH Judge Roberts for facilitating a visit to the Parole Board. Further afield, I would like to thank Keith Wilkins QC, then senior counsel to the Special Advocate Program in Canada, for facilitating a very useful visit to Ottawa in March 2016 and allowing me to attend parts of a training session for Canadian special advocates.

A number of academic colleagues and practitioners provided advice and assistance on various aspects of the project. I would particularly like to thank Ron Allen, Stephen Bailey, Iain Cameron, John Campbell, Jim Cohen, David Cole, Laura Donohue, Sean Doran QC, HH Judge Enright, Peter Duff, Lindsay Farmer, John Feerick, Jordi Ferrer, Craig Forcese, Zach Goldman, Bruce Green, Lissa Griffin, David Jenkins, Maya Lester QC, Kevin McGinty, Simon McKay, Michele Panzavolta, Stephen Parkinson, Martha Rayner, Kent Roach, Jimmy Scholes, Asbjørn Strandbakken, Cees van der Eijk, Natalie Wortley and Simon Young. I would also like to thank Charlotte Fallenius for her help in translating certain Swedish materials on 'privacy' advocates, Sebastian Walker for providing invaluable research assistance in examining open decisions on the SIAC database and Cerys Gibson for assistance in the presentation of the tables.

I was able to benefit from valuable feedback on presentations delivered at a number of seminars and workshops while the research was in progress. In particular, I would like to thank participants for their comments at the following events: staff seminars at the University of Strathclyde in December 2015 and at the University of Sussex in March 2016; a training session for special advocates organised by the Special Advocates Program at the Ministry of Justice in Ottawa in March 2016 and a seminar at Cornerstone Chambers, London organised by SASO in November 2016; the Gerald Gordon Seminar in Criminal Law, University of Glasgow in June 2016; the Society of Legal Scholars Conference: Criminal Justice Section, University of Oxford in September 2016; a seminar on Secret Justice at the Centre for Criminal Law, University College London in November 2016; a symposium in honour of Clive Walker, University of Leeds in November 2017; a postgraduate seminar at the Faculty of Law, University of Göttingen in January 2018; a session on secret justice at the International Association for the Study of Forced Migration Conference, University of Macedonia in July 2018; and a Criminal Justice Discussion Group Seminar on Procedural Innovation at the University of Nottingham in November 2018.

Towards the later stages of the research, a number of individuals were most generous in giving up their time to read and comment on draft chapters of the book. I am most grateful to the following for their comments: Tom Bullmore, Martin Chamberlain, Yvonne McDermott Rees, Graham Hudson, Sebastian Walker, Steven Winder and Adrian Zuckerman. Particular thanks are due to Paul Roberts who read and commented on the entire draft. Needless to say, I take sole responsibility for any errors or omissions contained in the final text.

I would like to thank the editorial and production staff at Routledge for bringing the book to speedy fruition.

Finally, I would like to acknowledge the constant support of my family. The book is dedicated to my mother with whom I discussed some of my early ideas about the project before she sadly suffered a stroke.

John Jackson
University of Nottingham
25 February 2019

Table of cases

Australia

Canada

Court of Justice of the European Union

England and Wales

European Court of Human Rights

Hong Kong

International Criminal Court

New Zealand

Northern Ireland

Scotland

Special Tribunal for Lebanon

United States

Abbreviations

ABA	American Bar Association
AGO	Attorney General's Office
CHIS	Covert Human Intelligence Source
CIPA	Classified Information Procedures Act 1980
CJEU	Court of Justice of the European Union
CMP	Closed Material Proceeding
CPR	Civil Procedure Rules
CSIS	Canadian Security Intelligence Service
CSO	Court Security Officer
ECHR	European Convention on Human Rights
ECtHR	European Court of Human Rights
EU	European Union
FISC	Foreign Intelligence Surveillance Court
FP	Federal prosecutor
GC	Government counsel
GCHQ	Government Communications Headquarters
HCCAC	House of Commons Constitutional Affairs Committee
ICC	International Criminal Court
IPT	Investigatory Powers Tribunal
IRPA	Immigration and Refugee Protection Act 2001
J	Judge
JCHR	Joint Committee on Human Rights
OC	Open counsel
PII	Public interest immunity
POAC	Proscribed Organisations Appeal Commission
SA	Special advocate
SAP	Special Advocate Program
SASO	Special Advocates' Support Office
SCC	Security-cleared lawyer
SCIF	Secure Compartmented Information Facility
SIAC	Special Immigration Appeals Commission

SIRC	Security Intelligence Review Committee
SSHD	Secretary of State for the Home Department
STL	Special Tribunal for Lebanon
SVAP	Security Vetting Appeals Panel
TPIM	Terrorism Prevention Investigation Measure

1 Introduction

Over the last number of decades, there has been considerable literature devoted to the increasing focus on managing risk in Western democracies, which has coincided with the development of technologies which can be used to impose increased scrutiny on 'risky' individuals. Within the criminal justice system, attention has been drawn to a paradigm shift away from the 'old penology', with its focus on identification, prosecution, punishment and treatment of offenders, towards a 'new penology' which is concerned with managing risk and 'risky' individuals in terms of the danger they pose.[1] Quite a lot of the literature has focused on how the police have shifted away from bringing offenders to trial after they have committed offences to focusing on surveillance and intelligence to probe knowledge of populations and to assess and manage risk.[2] Notions of preventive justice are not new.[3] The police have had a longstanding interest in taking preventive measures which are independent of the adjudication process.[4] The courts too have a long history of attaching importance to measures of preventive justice. But it would seem that within the last quarter of a century, a growing concern across Western societies with safety and security has led to a preoccupation with managing risk. Events such as 9/11 seem to have helped to drive a perception that we are all a lot less safe than we used to be, even though there is incontrovertible evidence that we are in fact safer than ever before.[5] In fact, the number

1 M Feeley and J Simon, 'Actuarial Justice: The Emerging New Criminal Law' in D Nelken (ed), *The Futures of Criminology* (Sage 1994) 173.

2 R Ericson and K Haggerty, *Policing the Risk Society* (OUP 1997); A Edwards and G Hughes, 'The Preventive Turn and the Promotion of Safer Communities in England and Wales' in A Crawford (ed), *Crime Prevention Policies in Comparative Perspective* (Willan 2009).

3 M Dubber, 'Preventive Justice: The Quest for Principle' in A Ashworth, L Zedner and P Tomlin (eds), *Prevention and the Limits of the Criminal Law* (OUP 2013) 47. See also A Ashworth and L Zedner, *Preventive Justice* (OUP 2014).

4 E Miller, 'A Fair Cop and a Fair Trial' in J Jackson and S Summers (eds), *Obstacles to Fairness in Criminal Proceedings* (Hart 2018) 239.

5 S Pinker, *The Better Angels of Our Nature: Why Violence Has Declined* (Viking 2011).

of attacks and deaths from terrorism, at least in Western Europe, is down significantly from 20 to 40 years ago.[6]

This preoccupation with the calculation of risk and the prevention of harm has had a number of ramifications. One of these is that it has expanded the scope for criminalisation in a number of different ways.[7] Ashworth and Zedner have highlighted a number of different kinds of preventive measures across the criminal justice process, as well as in areas such as mental health and immigration.[8] These pose a challenge to what they have called the 'liberal conception' of criminal justice, whereby the purpose of the criminal law is to censure and sentence those who have committed wrongs, rather than to criminalise on the basis of character and risk.[9] Outside the criminal justice system, civil orders made in civil proceedings, but known as 'hybrid' orders because of the criminal sanctions that are imposed when they are breached, subject individuals to a number of wide-ranging constraints. Control orders, now known as TPIMs (terrorism prevention and investigation measures), for example, impose wide-ranging conditions on persons deemed to be a security risk such as curfew, tagging, reporting requirements and restrictions on access to computers or communications equipment.

The shift to secret adjudication

Apart from the ramifications for the criminal law and individual liberty,[10] a heightened concern for security and safety is also changing the way in which adjudication has traditionally been managed in both civil and criminal processes. Adjudicative practices in common law systems are commonly characterised as 'adversarial', in contrast to the 'inquisitorial' process in civil law countries. Although these have not always been helpful labels to describe the differences between common law and civil law procedural systems, adversarial systems have long been associated with certain core values such as open and natural justice, which require that proceedings are heard in public in the presence of the parties and that the judge knows nothing that is not known to the parties.[11] But these core values are challenged when 'intelligence' starts to be used in judicial processes

6 See the University of Maryland's Global Terrorism Database: https://www.start.umd.edu/gtd/. Although the number of civilian deaths arising from terrorism has increased globally since 2011, the vast majority of these deaths in 2015 (74%) were confined to five countries: Iraq, Afghanistan, Nigeria, Sudan and Pakistan.

7 N Lacey, *In Search of Criminal Responsibility: Ideas, Interests, and Institutions* (OUP 2016) 47.

8 Ashworth and Zedner (n 3).

9 A Ashworth and L Zedner, 'Defending the Criminal Law: Reflections on the Changing Character of Crime, Procedure, and Sanctions' (2008) 2 *Criminal Law and Philosophy* 21.

10 For the dangers involved in trading off individual liberty against heightened concerns about security, see J Waldron 'Security and Liberty: The Image of Balance' (2003) 11 *Journal of Political Philosophy* 191.

11 Although it has been claimed that there is a conceptual distinction between the ideas of natural justice and open justice, there are intimate connections between the two, not least the idea that open justice helps to instil discipline in the professionals to each play their part

as evidence. So long as a distinction was maintained between the role of the intelligence services, which was to inform government about risk, and the role of the police whose job was to collect evidence for the courts after a crime has been committed, the courts could be immunised from intelligence.[12] But once these roles became blurred, the courts became exposed to intelligence as evidence and measures needed to be taken to protect the sources of such information.

The growing global trend in the use of secret evidence has been particularly evident in national security law.[13] Focusing specifically on this context, the New Zealand Law Commission has posed the dilemma in terms of finding solutions along a continuum between two extremes.[14] At one extreme, there are the ordinary traditional court processes committed to open and natural 'adversarial' justice – full disclosure of the evidence to both the public and the accused – which fails to address the need to protect national security interests. At the other extreme is a closed, inquisitorial model where national security information is protected by being heard only by the decision-maker in a secret hearing, without the affected person being present or represented. Somewhere between these fully open and fully closed models, there are a number of options of 'partial disclosure', which can range from an order excluding the public from access to the court to restricting the person affected by the proceedings from the process as well. The Commission devoted the bulk of its report to considering which of these partial models should be adopted, and it is a measure of how far we are drifting away from the traditional open court process that the fully open model is not even considered a feasible option.

Looking at the UK, even in criminal trials where protections for those accused of criminal offences should be at their greatest, there are now a number of measures that judges can apply to restrict open and natural justice. First of all, there are in camera hearings removing the public from the trial. It has for some time been the case that any part of a trial involving offences against the Official Secrets Act 1920 may be held in camera.[15] But a new precedent seemed to be set a few years ago when a trial judge in a terrorist case ruled that the entire trial be held in camera with the public and media excluded. On an appeal lodged by media groups, the Court of Appeal modified the judge's order somewhat, but the bulk of the trial was carried out in secret and the jurors, the lawyers, the accused and

---

in delivering fairness or natural justice. See J Jaconelli, *Open Justice: A Critique of the Public Trial* (OUP 2002) 32–39.

12 See K Roach, 'The Eroding Distinction between Intelligence and Evidence in Terrorist Investigations' in N McGarrity, A Lynch and G Williams (eds), *Counter-Terrorism and Beyond: The Culture of Law and Justice after 9/11* (Routledge 2010) 48.

13 See eg T Hickman and A Tomkins, 'National Security Law and the Creep of Secrecy: A Transatlantic Tale' in L Lazarus, C McCrudden and N Bowles (eds), *Reasoning Rights: Comparative Judicial Engagement* (OUP 2014) 135.

14 New Zealand Law Commission, *National Security Information in Proceedings* (NZLC IP38, 2015) [6.41].

15 Official Secrets Act 1920, s 8(4). See Jaconelli (n 11) 139.

certain 'accredited' journalists allowed to be present were legally bound not to reveal its contents.[16] Second, a number of witness protection measures have been developed which in one way or another prevent the defendant from having full access to the way the evidence is presented – for example, the evidence may be given behind screens, or by a video-link, or, with voices electronically modified, the defence may even be prevented from knowing the identity of the witness.[17] These measures can conflict in varying degrees with principles linked to open and natural justice such as the right to confrontation recognised by the common law for centuries and an essential element of a fair trial.[18] Perhaps most troubling from the point of view of natural justice are public interest immunity (PII) hearings held in the absence of defendants and their counsel, where prosecutors claim that they should be exempted in the public interest from having to make disclosure to the accused of material that would otherwise be disclosed to him. Considered a rarity back in 1989,[19] such hearings are now much more common than they used to be.[20] The difficulty for the defence is that they do not know what the undisclosed material is and cannot therefore make a reasoned objection to the prosecutor's claim, so the judge is tasked with making decisions on the basis of one-sided argument. Sometimes the defence do not even know that an application is being made to the judge at all.[21] We shall see that this is one area where a special counsel may be appointed to play a role akin to that of a special advocate by putting arguments on behalf of the defence.

It is not just criminal trials that have been affected by the need to protect sensitive information and the safety of witnesses. There is now a whole range of situations outside the criminal arena where non-governmental parties may be excluded in so-called 'closed material procedures' (CMPs). The most important aspect of the principle of natural justice has been said to be that every party has a right to know the full case against them and the right to test and challenge that case fully.[22] In criminal proceedings, it is not (yet) possible to withhold any of the evidence the prosecution intends to rely upon at trial against the defendant.[23] Yet that is precisely what can happen in closed material procedures when 'closed material' is withheld from parties on the ground it contains information that the government claims would be damaging to national security or would

16 See *Guardian News and Media Ltd v AB & CD* [2014] EWCA Crim 1861. An appeal to have the reporting restrictions lifted was rejected by the Court of Appeal in *Guardian News and Media Ltd and Erol Incedal* [2016] EWCA Crim 11 (9 February 2016).

17 See eg Youth Justice and Criminal Evidence Act 1999, Part II, Ch I; Coroners and Justice Act 2009, Part III, Ch II.

18 *R v Davis* [2008] UKHL 36, [2008] AC 1128.

19 A Zuckerman, *The Principles of Criminal Evidence* (OUP 1989) 300–01.

20 P Roberts and A Zuckerman, *Criminal Evidence* (2nd edn OUP 2010) 323.

21 See *R v Davis, Rowe and Johnson* [1993] 1 WLR 613.

22 *Bank Mellat v HM Treasury* (No 1) [2013] UKSC 38, [2014] AC 700 [3] (Lord Neuberger). See also *Re D (Minors)(Adoption Reports: Confidentiality)* [1956] AC 593, 615.

23 D Corker and S Parkinson, *Disclosure in Criminal Proceedings* (OUP 2009) [5.15]. See *Kanda v Government of Malaya* [1962] AC 322, 337 (Lord Denning).

otherwise be harmful to the public interest if it were disclosed, and is then used in a closed hearing from which the affected party and their lawyers are excluded. Not all the evidence in cases where CMPs are deployed will necessarily be withheld from affected parties – only that which would harm the public interest. The proceedings will invariably have both 'open' and 'closed' elements. But there is the potential for the outcome of the case to be decided entirely on the closed elements. This is an altogether more drastic erosion of the principles of open and natural justice than when defendants are excluded from public interest immunity hearings. Indeed, a closed procedure has been described as the 'very antithesis' of a PII procedure, which can apply in both civil and criminal proceedings.[24] Closed procedures are concerned with the use of information that has been *included* as evidence in the case but has been kept secret from one of the parties, while PII procedures are concerned with whether information should be *excluded* from the case. It is because CMPs constituted such an erosion of the principles of natural and open justice that a majority of the UK Supreme Court in *Al Rawi v The Security Service* considered that the courts had no 'inherent jurisdiction' to authorise a CMP in a civil claim at common law.[25]

Yet CMPs have continued to expand on a statutory basis throughout the UK. Having begun life in the relatively obscure setting of the Special Immigration Appeals Commission (SIAC), which was established in 1997 to hear a small number of immigration and asylum cases where the Home Secretary's decision was based on national security concerns, these proceedings have proliferated across such a large variety of different types of proceeding that they have come to be described as a 'parallel justice system' for cases the government claims are related to national security.[26] After 9/11 in particular, their use expanded to cases involving counter-terrorism measures, including preventive detention, control orders (now TPIMs), proscription of terrorist organisations, and domestic asset freezing orders. They can also apply in parole hearings, employment disputes (including security vetting), care proceedings, and now, under the Justice and Security Act 2013, in any proceedings (other than those in a criminal cause or matter) before the High Court, the Court of Session, the Court of Appeal, or the Supreme Court.[27]

The 'parallel justice system' of closed procedures has meant having to get used to a whole new terminology associated with secret hearings. Terms such as 'open

24 *Al Rawi v The Security Service* [2011] UKSC 34, [2012] 1 AC 531 [41] (Lord Dyson).
25 *Al Rawi v The Security Service* [2011] UKSC 34, [2012] 1 AC 531.
26 Amnesty International, *Left in the Dark: the Use of Secret Evidence in the United Kingdom* (Amnesty International 2012) 7.
27 Justice and Security Act 2013, s 6(11). Judicial review of a decision made in a criminal case (eg a decision not to prosecute) has been held by a majority of the Supreme Court to constitute a decision made in a criminal cause. See *Belhaj v DPP* [2018] UKSC 33, [2018] 3 WLR 435.

material' and 'closed material', 'redaction',[28] 'gisting',[29] and a 'core, irreducible, minimum entitlement'[30] have become common currency in CMPs. We have also had to become acquainted with national security principles which have the effect of keeping information in the dark. The 'control principle', for example, requires that in all intelligence exchanges between intelligence agencies, the originator of the material remains in control of its handling and dissemination.[31] Another that is frequently applied in the national security context is the 'NCND' (Neither Confirm Nor Deny) principle which has been the response of successive governments and intelligence services when faced with claims or speculation about sensitive security matters such as whether someone is an undercover agent.[32] These principles, and much of the terminology associated with CMPs, jar with the principles of openness and fairness associated with adversarial justice. This book does not attempt to provide a guide to or a critique of CMPs.[33] It rather focuses on one particular feature that has been described as 'an attempt to resolve the conflict between due process and national security',[34] and that is the use of special advocates who are lawyers with security clearance appointed to represent the interests of parties who have been excluded from CMPs.

Understanding the role of special advocates

Special advocates were first introduced alongside the closed procedures established under the Special Immigration Appeals Commission Act 1997 (the SIAC Act) for dealing with national security issues, and they have become a feature of most CMPs established since then. Although it has been claimed that this Act

28 The term used for concealing sensitive details in open material disclosed to individuals.
29 The term used for providing a summary of closed material to an individual whenever it is possible to summarise that material without disclosing information contrary to the public interest. See Ministry of Justice, *Justice and Security Green Paper* (Cm 8194, 2011) Glossary.
30 The term used to indicate the minimum amount of information that may have to be disclosed to an excluded party in order to comply with minimal standards of fairness. See *Roberts v Parole Board* [2005] UKHL 45, [2005] 2 AC 738 [68] (Lord Woolf).
31 See Ministry of Justice (n 29) 9. The need to uphold the control principle was central to the government's case for abolishing the *Norwich Pharmacal* jurisdiction in any case concerning the disclosure of sensitive information. See Justice and Security Act 2013, s 17(2). Under this jurisdiction, the courts may disclose information where there has been wrongdoing by a third party and the information is required to seek justice.
32 Ministry of Justice (n 29), Glossary. See *Re Freddie Scappaticci* (2003) NIQB 56. Note, however, that NCND is not a legal principle. See *Mohamed and CF v SSHD* [2014] EWCA Civ 559 [20]: 'It is not simply a matter of a governmental party to litigation hoisting the NCND flag and the court automatically saluting it'. See also JUSTICE, *To 'Neither Confirm nor Deny': Assessing the Response and its Impact on Access to Justice* (JUSTICE 2017).
33 For an anthropological critique of the closed procedures adopted in one particular secret trial, see J Campbell, 'Guilt by Association: Contrasting views on the fairness of "secret trials" of "terrorists"' in J Simeon (ed), *Terrorism and Asylum* (Brill Njihoff 2019).
34 J Ip, 'The Rise and Spread of the Special Advocate' [2008] PL 717, 741.

was the first statutory provision for the use of secret evidence by a British court,[35] secret evidence has in fact been used in 'quasi-judicial' proceedings before then. In the aftermath of the introduction of internment without trial in Northern Ireland in 1971, following the rise in paramilitary violence which it was claimed could not be contained by the criminal process, judicial hearings were convened to review detentions, and parts of the hearing could be held in the absence of the detainee or his legal representative in the interests of public safety or the safety of any persons.[36] In many ways, these proceedings can be seen as the 'forerunner' of the 'open' and 'closed' elements that are to be seen in SIAC and in other cases involving CMPs.[37] The one difference, however, is that there was no special advocate appointed to probe the material presented in the closed sessions.

The 'judicial' detention arrangements in Northern Ireland were eventually phased out on the grounds that they were totally at odds with common law adversarial procedures.[38] The special advocate system introduced under the SIAC Act was, by contrast, hailed by parliamentarians as the solution to the adverse human rights ruling by the European Court of Human Rights (ECtHR) in *Chahal v UK*[39] that had held that the secretive arrangements for reviewing the detention of persons pending deportation were in breach of Article 5(4) of the European Convention on Human Rights (ECHR).[40] This points to a paradox underlying the special advocate system. On the one hand, the system is central to the claim that CMPs are capable of delivering procedural fairness.[41] On the other hand, it is this very claim to procedural fairness that justifies and legitimises the use of closed procedures which appear to flout principles that are central to the adversarial system. In other words, the more special advocates are used, the more CMPs become normalised within the adversarial system.

Yet, as special advocates themselves have said on a number of occasions, they operate under a number of disadvantages in CMPs which call into question the claim that CMPs are capable of delivering procedural fairness.[42] One special

35 JUSTICE, *Secret Evidence* (JUSTICE 2009) [80].

36 Detention of Terrorists (Northern Ireland) Order (1972 No 1632 NI 15) Arts 14–17, later incorporated in the Northern Ireland (Emergency Provisions) Act 1973. For a description of the procedures, see K Boyle, T Hadden and P Hillyard, *Law and State: The Case of Northern Ireland* (Robertson 1975) 59–61; R J Spjut 'Internment and Detention without Trial in Northern Ireland 1971–1975: Ministerial Policy and Practice' (1986) 49 MLR 712.

37 D Bonner, *Executive Measures, Terrorism and National Security* (Ashgate 2007) 93–94.

38 Lord Gardiner, *Report of a Committee to consider, in the context of civil liberties and human rights, measures to deal with terrorism in Northern Ireland* (Cmnd 5847, 1975) [152]–[54].

39 *Chahal v UK* (1996) 23 EHRR 413.

40 See HC Deb 30 October 1997, vol 299, col 1057 (Mr Mike O'Brien).

41 See Ministry of Justice (n 29) [2.2].

42 See eg House of Commons Constitutional Affairs Committee, *The Operation of the Special Immigration Appeals Commission (SIAC) and the Use of Special Advocates* (HC 2004-05, 323-1) Ev 53-61 and *Response to Green Paper Consultation from Special Advocates* (2011). See also M Chamberlain 'Special Advocates and Procedural Fairness in Closed Proceedings' (2009) 28 *Civil Justice Quarterly* 314 and 'Update on Procedural Fairness in Closed

advocate, who later became a High Court judge, has said that the public should be left in no doubt that what is happening has nothing to do with the traditions of adversarial justice as we have come to understand them.[43] Lord Steyn, a former Law Lord, went further and described the special advocate procedure, where special advocates are imposed on the prisoner and his legal representatives who know nothing of the case against them, as undermining the very essence of elementary justice.[44] In his view, they bore a striking resonance to the situation of Joseph K in Kafka's masterpiece *The Trial* where 'all who appeared before the Court as Advocates were in reality merely in the position of hole-and-corner Advocates'.[45]

This book aims to augment our understanding of the role that special advocates play within the different procedural contexts in which they operate. The study advances understanding on three different levels. First of all, on the empirical level, it aims to inform debate on the contribution that special advocates make by examining the different types of special advocates, how they are chosen and supported, what professional obligations they owe to excluded parties, how their position differs from that of ordinary counsel, and what challenges they face in their professional work. Although there have been previous surveys on the work of special advocates in the UK,[46] this study expands on previous studies by incorporating the experiences not only of special advocates themselves but of other professional participants in special advocate cases to obtain a rounded view of the work that they do.[47] The study draws on the views expressed by special advocates before various parliamentary committees and public consultations, as well as on interviews with special advocates and other professionals involved in special advocate cases such as judges or commissioners, government counsel, and so-called

Proceedings' (2009) 28 *Civil Justice Quarterly* 448. Special advocates have emphatically commented that while the use of special advocates may attenuate the procedural unfairness entailed by CMPs to a 'limited extent', even with the involvement of special advocates, CMPs remain 'fundamentally unfair'. See *Response to Green Paper* (2011) [2(4)]. This response was signed by 57 out of the list of 69 that were then appointed to the special advocate list.

43 Joint Committee on Human Rights, *Counter-Terrorism Policy and Human Rights: 28 Days, Intercept and Post-Charge Questioning* (HL 2006-07, 157, HC 2006-07, 394) [210].

44 *Roberts v Parole Board* [2005] UKHL 45, [2005] 2 AC 738 [88].

45 ibid [95] citing F Kafka, *The Trial* (Penguin 1953) 128.

46 An early survey by JUSTICE conducted two face-to-face, four written and two telephone interviews with special advocates. See in particular, E Metcalfe 'Representative but nor Responsible: the use of special advocates' (2004) 1 *Justice Journal* 11, 35–38. A later survey, carried out by Craig Forcese and Lorne Waldman after the Canadian Supreme Court in *Charkaoui v Canada (Citizenship and Immigration)* 2007 SCC 9, [2007] 1 SCR 350 struck down the security certificate system in Canada, interviewed 11 UK special advocates. See C Forcese and L Waldman, *Seeking Justice in an Unfair Process* (University of Ottawa 2007).

47 Cf Amnesty International (n 26). For this report Amnesty International conducted interviews with 25 barristers and solicitors who acted in cases where CMPs had been used, but although they convened a meeting with three special advocates, their report did not focus directly on the role of special advocates.

'open counsel' who have represented parties excluded from closed procedures and who were themselves not allowed to be present in such procedures.[48]

The aim here was not to make a definitive assessment of the extent to which special advocates provide a measure of procedural fairness to individuals in closed procedures, as there are obvious difficulties in making such an objective assessment in the absence of being able to view and report on what goes on in closed procedures. One of the advantages commonly claimed for open justice is that the general public and the media are able to observe court proceedings, which is linked to broader arguments for transparency and accountability in a democratic society.[49] Open justice in a similar way enables the researcher to assess how justice is done, and its absence correspondingly inhibits such an assessment being made.[50] Any assessment of what goes on in closed procedures is inevitably a very pale alternative to the kind of assessment that can be made of open proceedings. But what can be achieved by probing the views of participants who have acted in different closed procedures is to bring to light their interpretation of how they see justice being done and, in particular, what impact special advocates have on what would otherwise be a very one-sided process.

Second, there is a comparative and international element to the research which aimed to examine how special advocates and other security-cleared counsel have operated in other countries. Although special advocates originated in the UK, there has been an important comparative and international aspect to their development.[51] First of all, the apparent endorsement by the ECtHR in *Chahal* of a similar security-cleared counsel arrangement in Canada gave the UK government the encouragement it needed to go down the special advocate route.[52] Second, the Court's apparent approval of the system in subsequent decisions has given them an international human rights pedigree which has helped to normalise the

48 Between the period November 2015 and July 2017, I interviewed 18 UK special advocates or former special advocates (four in Northern Ireland), seven open counsel (three in Northern Ireland), seven government counsel (two in Northern Ireland) and six judges or commissioners involved in special advocate cases (two in Northern Ireland). I also interviewed two officials who worked in the Attorney General's Office.

49 R Goss, '"To the Serious Detriment of the Public": Secret Evidence and Closed Material Procedures' in Lazarus and others (n 13) 121.

50 One former special advocate has commented that, to some extent, it will always be difficult for those who have not participated in closed hearings to understand how they are conducted. See M Chamberlain 'Special Advocates' (n 42) 315. The author who has participated in closed hearings in his capacity as a Parole Commissioner and Sentence Review Commissioner in Northern Ireland considered seeking security clearance in order to observe a number of closed procedures. While this might have added to the author's understanding of them, there would still be the difficulty of communicating this to readers and the general public.

51 See D Jenkins 'There and Back Again: The Strange Journey of Special Advocates and Comparative Law Methodology' (2011) 42 *Columbia Human Rights Law Review* 279.

52 ibid 313–14, citing the British Home Office Minister, Mike O'Brien, who introduced the scheme in the House of Commons.

CMP phenomenon.[53] The argument that can be made in defence of their use is thus that they not only help to make closed procedures fairer, but that they are compatible with international standards of procedural fairness, thereby deepening the paradox whereby procedures that are offensive to core adversarial values can at the same time be justified as fair. Third, notwithstanding the distaste for closed procedures, other common law countries have begun to establish their own special advocate systems to varying degrees: first Canada, and now also New Zealand, Hong Kong and Australia. The US, by contrast, has had a longer history of using security-cleared counsel to represent their clients in closed procedures. What is interesting to probe here are the similarities and differences between these different systems. Interviews were conducted for this study with special advocates and security-cleared counsel in Canada and the US, as well as with others involved in such cases.[54] It is also interesting to consider why other jurisdictions have not felt the need to introduce special advocates. Although provision is made for special counsel in the Special Tribunal for Lebanon,[55] they have yet to become a feature of the emerging international criminal justice landscape.

A third dimension to the research has been to examine, within the normative framework of the adversarial tradition, the degree to which the use of special advocates or security-cleared counsel systems is acceptable, drawing on the different processes in which they operate and on the different models and practices to be seen within the UK and other common law systems. Now that special advocates and cleared counsel systems have been established, attention has shifted away from *whether* they should be used to *what* are the best practices that are adopted in the different countries in which they operate. In one such study of cleared counsel in the US, the UK and Canada, Cole and Vladeck considered those features of each system that appeared to maximise fairness to individuals who had been deprived of their liberty without unduly jeopardising security concerns.[56] They took their cue from the principle established by the Canadian

53 E Nanopoulos 'European Human Rights Law and the Normalisation of the "Closed Material procedure": Limit or Source?' (2015) 78 MLR 913.

54 Between March 2016 and July 2017, four special advocates and the senior counsel to the special advocate programme were interviewed in Ottawa and Toronto and six security-cleared counsel, two federal prosecutors, and a US judge who had experience of the Foreign Intelligence Security Court (FISC) were interviewed in New York.

55 STL RPE 119. A visit to the Special Tribunal for Lebanon (STL), sitting in The Hague, was carried out in July 2016 in order to discover how special counsel who are expressly mentioned in the rules are being deployed. Interviews were carried out with two STL prosecutors and one STL defence lawyer.

56 D Cole and S I Vladeck, 'Navigating the Shoals of Secrecy: A Comparative Analysis of the Use of Secret Evidence and "Cleared Counsel" in the United States, the United Kingdom and Canada' in Lazarus and others (n 13) 161, 171. See also D Cole and S I Vladeck, 'Comparative Advantages: Secret Evidence and "Cleared Counsel" in the United States, the United Kingdom and Canada' in D Cole, F Fabbrini and A Vedaschi (eds), *Secrecy, National Security and the Vindication of Constitutional Law* (Edward Elgar 2013).

Supreme Court in *Canada v Charkaoui*[57] that since the use of secret evidence so directly compromises the fundamental fair trial principle that individuals should be able to see and confront the evidence used against them, those compromises should be 'minimally intrusive'. From this principle, they adopted the prescription that where one nation has demonstrated that practices more conducive to fair processes can be undertaken without unduly compromising security, other nations should be required to adopt those measures as well, or at a minimum, meet a heavy burden of justifying why such procedures would not be practicable in their jurisdiction.

Cole and Vladeck's study focused on the specific context of the procedures that should operate when persons risk losing their liberty. This study considers the impact of special, security-cleared advocacy more broadly upon local procedural traditions across the different adversarial systems in which they operate. New literature has recently been emerging on common law comparativism which emphasises the differences between common law adversarial systems.[58] Of course, local tradition or culture can be used as an unprincipled device for opposing reform.[59] But in considering practices, it is important at least to be aware of what obstacles might lie in seeking to have them implanted across different legal cultures. As such, the aim has been less to make policy prescriptions based on 'best practice' and more to understand how such practices are likely to be received within different procedural cultures. The methodology in this sense is more interpretivist than positivist.[60]

A particular practice may be more 'fair' in terms of being less restrictive on rights than other practices, but if it is undermining well-established traditions there will be difficulties in getting it accepted. A more fundamental question is whether such a practice should be prescribed. Some practices can over time be shed if they are seen to be obsolete and resistant to best or better practice. Traditions can be adapted when they are not required to sacrifice underlying values. But if the best practice is at odds with fundamental core values undermining the tradition, there are questions about whether it ought to be followed. Glenn has argued that the identity of a tradition is best thought of in 'triptych' form.[61] The overall identity of a tradition constitutes its total information base and includes many internal dissenting elements. There is within this a 'leading' or primary version of the tradition which at any given time appears accepted as its truest version. But there are also the underlying or basic elements without which no other elements would stand, and when there is a challenge to these elements, the tradition can become more fundamentally undermined.

57 *Charkaoui v Canada (Citizenship and Immigration)* 2007 SCC 9, [2007] 1 SCR 350.
58 See eg J Hunter and P Roberts (eds), *Criminal Evidence and Human Rights: Reimagining Common Law Procedural Traditions* (Hart 2012).
59 See J Jackson 'Playing the Culture Card in Resisting Cross-Jurisdictional Transplants (1997) 5 *Cardozo Journal of International and Comparative Law* 51.
60 See D Nelken, *Comparative Criminal Justice: Making Sense of Difference* (Sage 2010) 40–42.
61 H P Glenn, *Legal Traditions of the World: Sustainable Diversity in Law* (5th edn OUP 2014) 39.

One of the reasons why their lordships in *Al Rawi v Security Service* felt that they could not endorse CMPs in civil proceedings without parliamentary approval was because they undermined fundamental tenets of justice. In his judgment, Lord Kerr sought to make a distinction between features of an adversarial system and fundamental features of a fair trial, when he said that the right to know the case against you is:

> not merely a feature of the adversarial system of trial, it is an elementary and essential pre-requisite of fairness ... the key nature of this right and its utter indispensability to the fairness of the proceedings must occupy centre stage in the debate as to whether it may be compromised.[62]

Making a similar point, Lord Hope made a distinction between choices as to how the conduct of the courts' business (for which one could read the 'adversarial system') may be simplified or made less expensive or easier to understand, and choices that cut across absolutely fundamental principles such as the right to a fair trial, the right to be confronted by one's accusers, and the right to know the reason for the outcome which the court has for centuries held the line in defending.[63]

When it is asked why these principles are worth defending, the answer is arguably not just to preserve a particular procedural tradition or system but to preserve the fundamental value of a fair process on which the legitimacy of decisions depends.[64] Hampshire has remarked upon the fact that each particular institution has its own procedures for deciding between rival conceptions of what is substantially just and fair, and these come and go in history, but there is one general feature of the processes of decision that has been preserved over time: 'that contrary claims are heard'.[65] An unjust procedure, violating this necessary condition of procedural fairness, is unjust always and everywhere without reference to any distinct conception of the good.[66] Roberts has more recently drawn attention to the fundamental bond that courts owe to the procedures that they operate.[67] As he puts it, questions of substantive law do not engage the courts' institutional preconditions of existence in quite the same way.[68] A court that enforces an unjust law might still be regarded as a properly constituted tribunal, but a court which fails to secure fair trials with due process is a 'self-parody and corruption of the core commitments which qualify judicial institutions *as judicial*'.[69]

62 [2011] UKSC 34, [2012] 1 AC 531 [89]–[90].
63 ibid [72].
64 For more on the relationship between truth finding, due process and legitimacy, see I Dennis, *The Law of Evidence* (6th edn Sweet & Maxwell 2017) 52–63.
65 S Hampshire, *Justice is Conflict* (Princeton University Press 2000) 16–17.
66 ibid 17.
67 P Roberts 'The Priority of Procedure and the Neglect of Evidence and Proof: Finding Facts in International Criminal Law' (2015) 13 *Journal of International Criminal Justice* 479.
68 ibid 487–88.
69 ibid 488 (italics in original).

In fairness to Cole and Vladeck, we shall see that they do raise questions about whether the use of cleared counsel or special advocates is 'inescapably flawed' by pointing out how many of the secret processes undermine key adversarial values of open and natural justice.[70] Before we come to such normative questions, we must return to the question of how special advocates have come to play an increasingly important role in adversarial systems. Chapter 2 considers the origin of special advocates, and Chapter 3 charts the large number of procedural contexts in which they can, and do, operate within the UK. Chapter 4 then considers how they have been migrating to other legal systems. The following chapters then consider a number of particular issues. Chapter 5 considers how special advocates are appointed, the training they receive once appointed, and the support they obtain once they become engaged in actual cases, drawing comparisons between different special advocate systems. An important question here is not only how special advocates gain competence in their role, but also how they have managed to create a sense of identity and community among themselves as their role has developed. Chapter 6 then considers the ethical challenges presented by special advocacy and whether these undermine the adversarial tradition. This involves considering whether the kind of advocacy involved in closed procedures is considerably different from 'ordinary' advocacy. As in the case of ordinary advocates, special advocates act in the interests of the parties they represent, but they do so in a different capacity from ordinary advocates in that they do not 'act' for the parties whose interest they represent and do not owe them a duty of care. The effect is to sever the normal professional–client relationship, whereby counsel are instructed by their clients through solicitors. Chapter 7 looks specifically at one particular issue that has been said to undermine the ability of special advocates to represent the interests of excluded parties, and that is the restrictions that have been placed upon their communications with excluded parties and their legal representatives. The chapter first considers the communications that take place before special advocates gain access to closed material and then how communications are regulated after this point, again drawing comparisons between the UK system and other systems in these respects. Chapter 8 then looks at one of the key functions that special advocates perform and that is in relation to disclosure. Two distinct processes are examined: first of all, the way in which they obtain disclosure to closed material, and, second, their role in advocating for greater disclosure of 'closed' material to be given to the excluded party. Chapter 9 then considers the representation function of special advocates, which consists of representing the interests of the excluded party in a closed hearing. As has been said, there are limits to what can be said about how effective special advocates are in exercising this role, but the views of practitioners involved in closed hearings are canvassed on how significant they consider this role to be. Chapter 10 widens the discussion by looking at the use of other models of security-cleared counsel as a means of providing a measure of procedural fairness: the 'own counsel' security-cleared

70 Cole and Vladeck, 'Navigating the Shoals of Secrecy' (n 56) 174–76.

model and the 'tribunal counsel' or 'amicus curiae' model. Once again, the aim is not necessarily to come to conclusions on which model should be adopted across the board but rather to highlight which models might be most appropriate for the different contexts in which national security information is used. This leads on to the final chapter, Chapter 11, where an assessment is made about the future of special advocates' role within the adversarial system, highlighting the different processes in which they have been used. It will be argued that there is nothing in the special advocates' role per se which undermines the adversarial system as a whole, but that it is important to have regard to their particularised contributions in the different procedural settings involving closed procedures in assessing whether they constitute a net gain to judicial administration.

2 The origin of special advocates

Although special advocates were originally introduced in the UK, the last chapter highlighted the importance of European human rights law in providing the impetus for the special advocate system and later giving it legitimacy across different areas of practice. In *Chahal v UK*,[1] Mr Chahal, an Indian Sikh, and members of his family made a number of human rights claims against the UK's decision to deport him to India because of his alleged involvement in terrorist activities in support of Sikh separatism. The ECtHR ruled that if Mr Chahal were returned to India, there would be a real risk that he would be subjected to treatment contrary to Article 3 of the ECHR and that his order for deportation would give rise to a violation of Article 3. The Court also ruled that his detention pending deportation was a breach of Article 5(4) of the ECHR because he was unable to have the legality of his detention determined by a court. The only means available to him to appeal the deportation order was to make representations to a panel known as the 'Three Wise Men' whose role was merely to advise the Home Secretary.[2] When Mr Chahal later brought judicial review proceedings, the Secretary of State invoked national security considerations as grounds for the decision to deport and detain him, and the court's powers of review were limited. Although the ECtHR accepted that the use of confidential information may be unavoidable where national security is at stake, it ruled that this did not mean that national authorities can be free from effective control by the domestic courts when they choose to assert that national security and terrorism are involved.[3] In a passage that appeared to give the green light to the special advocate system, the Court pointed to the example of Canada where a more effective form of judicial control had been developed through the use of security-cleared lawyers. This illustrated that there are 'techniques which can be employed which both accommodate legitimate security concerns about the nature and sources of intelligence information and yet accord the individual a substantial measure of procedural fairness'.[4]

1 (1997) 23 EHRR 413.

2 For a detailed description of these procedures, see L Lustgarten and I Leigh, *In From the Cold: National Security and Parliamentary Democracy* (OUP 1994) 183–191.

3 (1997) 23 EHRR 413 [131].

4 ibid.

The example the Court was referring to was brought to its attention by a number of human rights organisations and was described as follows:

> Under the Canadian Immigration Act 1976 (as amended by the Immigration Act 1988) a Federal Court judge holds an in camera hearing of all the evidence, at which the applicant is provided with a statement summarising, as far as possible, the case against him or her and has the right to be represented and to call evidence. The confidentiality of security material is maintained by requiring such evidence to be examined in the absence of both the applicant and his or her representative. However, in these circumstances, their place is taken by a security-cleared counsel instructed by the court, who cross-examines the witnesses and generally assists the court to test the strength of the State case. A summary of the evidence obtained by this procedure, with necessary deletions, is given to the applicant.[5]

It has been pointed out that the ECtHR's reference to the use of security-cleared counsel in Canada was misleading.[6] Under the immigration scheme in Canada at that time,[7] there were two types of security certificate proceedings leading to the detention and deportation of a non-citizen: the grounds for issuing certificates against permanent residents were reviewed by the Security Intelligence Review Committee (SIRC) and certificates issued against foreign nationals were reviewed by the Federal Court.[8] Security-cleared counsel were appointed by the SIRC when the Minister for Immigration and the Solicitor General of Canada referred to it permanent residents whom they considered to be inadmissible to Canada on national security grounds or other grounds such as involvement in serious criminality or organised crime. These counsel primarily acted for the Committee in a manner akin to the role of counsel to a Commission of Inquiry or a public inquiry.[9] Their role has been identified as threefold: to assist the members of the Committee in the conduct of the proceedings; to assist and liaise with the named person or their counsel to further their interests (which can involve negotiating with counsel for the Canadian Intelligence Service on what evidence can be disclosed); and to cross-examine government witnesses in

5 ibid [144].

6 See D Jenkins, 'There and Back Again: The Strange Journey of Special Advocates and Comparative Law Methodology' (2011) 42 *Columbia Human Rights Law Review* 279. See also N Phillips, 'Closed Material', *London Review of Books*, 17 April 2014.

7 See Immigration Act 1985.

8 A detailed account of these procedures is provided in I Leigh, 'Secret Proceedings in Canada' (1996) 34 *Osgoode Hall Law Journal* 113.

9 C Forcese and L Waldman, *Seeking Justice in an Unfair Process: Lessons from Canada, the United Kingdom and New Zealand on the Use of Special Advocates* (University of Ottawa 2007) 9. For the role of counsel to an inquiry, see L Blom-Cooper, *Public Inquiries: Wrong Roads on Bloody Sunday* (Hart 2017) 105.

closed hearings.[10] But the SIRC was not a court; it was a Committee charged with making a recommendation to the Governor-in-Council on whether there were reasonable grounds for concluding that the named person was inadmissible and if it considered that there were, the Governor-in-Council could then direct the Minister to issue a security certificate to that effect. As an advisory body, it was similar in function to the advisory 'Three Wise Men' procedure that the ECtHR found incompatible with the ECHR, although its recommendations along with the decisions of the Governor-in-Council were reviewable on judicial review grounds in the Federal Court.[11] The Federal Court itself reviewed whether a security certificate was reasonable when it was issued by the Minister and the Solicitor General against a foreign national who was *not* a permanent resident. The Court could hold ex parte in camera hearings to consider the national security information presented by the government, but there was no security-cleared counsel used to cross-examine witnesses.[12]

Despite the somewhat misleading depiction by the ECtHR of their use in Canada, the idea of using security-cleared counsel in judicial proceedings proved appealing to the UK government as a workable compromise between the demands of national security and fairness that would provide an effective response to the *Chahal* judgment. The UK was under pressure to act, as there was also a ruling from the European Court of Justice which suggested that EU nationals had a right of appeal against exclusion and deportation decisions taken on grounds of national security with a minimum context of fairness including the fair hearing standards of the ECHR.[13] As mentioned in the last chapter, the Government's legislative response came in the form of the Special Immigration Appeals Commission Act 1997 which established the Special Immigration Appeals Commission (SIAC). This was a new judicial body charged with hearing appeals in immigration and asylum cases where the Secretary of State certified that his or her decision was taken wholly or partly in reliance on information which should not be made public in the interests of national security or of the relationship between the UK and another country, or otherwise in the public interest. Since 2001, the Commission has been a superior court of record. It sits in three member panels of whom one must have high judicial office (a High Court judge) and another must be a legally qualified member of the Asylum and Immigration Tribunal.[14] The third member is a lay member who will normally be a person with experience of national security matters and be familiar with the

10 See Leigh (n 8) 163.

11 See Jenkins (n 6) 301.

12 It seems that the Federal Court could also become involved under s 38 of the Canada Evidence Act where the government and SIRC could not agree on what information to disclose to the person to be deported. See Jenkins (n 6) 299–300.

13 *R v SSHD, ex p Shingara and Radiom Reference for preliminary ruling* [1997] ECR I-03343. See also N Blake, 'The UK Experience of Special Advocates' (paper delivered at the Danish Institute for Human Rights, Copenhagen, May 2009).

14 SIAC Act 1997, sch 1.

kind of evidence that is likely to be presented in such cases. The Commission was innovative because it operates in both open sessions where the appellant and his legal representatives may be present and in closed sessions where they are excluded. Under Rule 4 of the Commission's rules, the Commission is under a duty to 'secure that information is not disclosed contrary to the interest of national security, the international relations of the UK, the detection and prevention of crime, or in any other circumstances where disclosure is likely to harm the public interest'.[15] But undoubtedly the most innovative aspect of the Act was the provision in section 6 for the appointment of 'a person to represent the interests of the appellant' in any proceedings before the Commission from which the appellant and any legal representative of his are excluded. Although the Act does not refer in terms to such persons being 'special advocates', this was the term used by the Minister introducing the Bill in Parliament and is the term used in the Rules made under the Act.[16]

The special advocate concept

The special advocate scheme that came to be deployed in the UK was different in character from the system of security-cleared counsel used in the Canada at the time, although, as we shall see, it was the UK model that later came to be adopted in Canada. Under the original Canadian system, the security-cleared counsel appointed by SIRC to assist it in its review were either employees of SIRC itself or were legal agents appointed to act on behalf of SIRC.[17] The idea of a court or tribunal appointing counsel to assist it by putting arguments that might not otherwise be put is not a new one. The notion of a 'devil's advocate' dates back to canon law; at common law, an amicus curiae (or 'friend of the court') has long been used to assist the court where a party was absent or where the court needed specialist legal expertise.[18] The role of the amicus, now known as an 'advocate to the court', is usually limited to where there is a point of law that has to be decided by the court on a matter of public interest on which the parties may not be able to adduce relevant argument.[19] Security-cleared counsel in the Canadian system had a broader role. They were appointed to cross-examine witnesses and not merely to present argument, and they were given a specific task of representing the interests of the non-citizen. But as SIRC's own counsel, their job was primarily to assist the Committee.[20]

15 SIAC (Procedure) Rules 2003 (SI 2003/1034).

16 See originally SIAC (Procedure) Rules 1997 (SI 2003/1034), r 7. See now SIAC (Procedure) Rules 2013 (SI 2013/2995), rr 34–36.

17 Forcese and Waldman (n 9) 7–8.

18 See JUSTICE, *Secret Evidence* (JUSTICE 2009) [321]–[22]. On the role of the 'devil's advocate', see M Damaška, *The Faces of Justice and State Authority* (Yale UP 1986) 163.

19 Lord Goldsmith, 'Advocate to the Court' (2002) 32 *Family Law* 228.

20 Leigh (n 8) 162–63.

This was the model that seemed to be preferred by the UK government when it first proposed the SIAC Bill.[21] At the Second Reading in the House of Lords the government originally proposed that the Commission would be able to appoint a person – a counsel – to:

> help it in its examination of the security evidence, and in particular to look at that evidence as if on behalf of the defendant. The Commission would then give the appellant as full a summary as is possible in the circumstances of any evidence taken in its absence.[22]

This proposal met with little resistance except on the issue of the amount allocated for the legal costs of such counsel (£1,000 per year), Lord Lester of Herne Hill suggesting that this surely was a mistake and the figure should be £10,000 or higher.[23] On this issue almost everyone in the debate spoke, and winding up for the government, Lord Williams of Mostyn observed that it was a topic that seemed to be one of enormously gratifying interest to their noble lordships. He conceded that £1,000 may be an under-estimate but the numbers of cases involving such counsel were likely to be 'very small indeed'.[24] Their use was, of course, being debated in the context of the pre-9/11 world when security issues loomed less large.

Only Lord Thomas of Gresford objected to the idea of the Commission appointing counsel to represent the excluded party. He alluded to the principle that where a court or tribunal deals with the liberty of the subject, he should be told the substance of the allegation against him. Lord Thomas asked on what basis the Commission was to appoint its own counsel – was the person appointed to take and follow the appellant's instructions and to have confidentiality and the benefit of legal professional privilege?

When the Bill moved to the Committee stage a few weeks later, Lord Williams announced that some further thinking had been going on regarding the role of the person appointed to help the Commission in its examination of the security evidence and that certain amendments were needed. For the first time, the term 'special advocate' was used to refer to this person and a number of statements were made about this role.[25] To ensure the independence of a special advocate, it was considered more appropriate if the person were to be appointed by the Attorney General. The role of the special advocate would be to represent the interests of the appellant in those parts of the proceedings from which he and his legal representative are excluded. That would probably mean that the special advocate

21 The parliamentary history is recounted in J Jackson, 'The role of special advocates: Advocacy, due process and the adversarial tradition' (2016) 20 *International Journal of Evidence and Proof* 343, 348–49.

22 HL Deb 5 June 1997, vol 580, col 736 (Lord Williams of Mostyn).

23 ibid col 743 (Lord Lester of Herne Hill).

24 ibid col 751 (Lord Williams of Mostyn).

25 HL Deb 23 June 1997, vol 580, col 1437 (Lord Williams of Mostyn).

would have to be present throughout the proceedings. Finally, in answer to Lord Thomas's question, the special advocate would not have a client relationship with the appellant. Lord Williams said that we do not judge the situation to be workable on any other basis. When asked where such a person would come from, he said that it would have to be the same sort of security-vetted person as one who prosecutes for the Treasury in important, delicate national security matters.

The idea that the counsel would act for the Commission therefore disappeared and it has since been stressed that the role of the special advocate is not the same as an amicus curiae.[26] The person would instead be independently appointed but such a person would not act like ordinary counsel in a client relationship with the appellant. The amendment to the Bill specifically stated that the 'person appointed shall not be responsible to the person whose interests he is appointed to represent'.[27] To emphasise the special nature of the role, such a person, while acting in the interests of the appellant, would be appointed from the ranks of those who had acted for the government as Treasury counsel. This solution met with acceptance, Lord Lester saying that the amendment was a 'fair compromise' and it was carried.[28]

By the time the Bill came before the Commons, the amendment had been fully incorporated into the Bill. To illustrate how rarely it was thought necessary to invoke the special advocate procedure, the Home Office Minister, Mr O'Brien, said that, leaving aside the Gulf War cases, in the six years before *Chahal*, there had been only six cases involving the deportation of foreign nationals on security grounds.[29] Mr O'Brien explicitly made the point that 'there will not be the lawyer-client relationship, where the special advocate is required to disclose all information to the client'.[30] He added further confusion to the role of the special advocate, however, by likening it to a person appointed by a court to represent a minor or child or someone with a psychiatric problem.[31] That person does not take instructions from the client and is not obliged to do what the client says. It has been pointed out, however, that this analogy is unsound because even litigation friends or guardians ad litem owe a duty to those they represent.[32] Under the Act, however, the special advocate is not responsible to the person he represents, not because that person has some disability, illness or is too young, but because the government has entirely severed the relationship between lawyer and client. Special advocates are in a 'no man's land' where they appear to be responsible

26 See eg *SSHD v AHK* [2009] EWCA Civ 287 [37](ix). See also M Chamberlain, 'Special Advocates and Amici Curiae in National Security Proceedings in the United Kingdom' (2018) 68 *University of Toronto Law Journal* 496.

27 See now SIAC Act 1997, s 6(4).

28 HL Deb 23 June 1997, vol 580, col 1438 (Lord Lester of Herne Hill).

29 HC Deb 30 October 1997, vol 299, col 1053 (Mr Mike O'Brien MP).

30 ibid col 1056.

31 ibid cols 1070–71.

32 JUSTICE (n 18) [342].

to no one, neither acting on behalf of the client nor the court.[33] It has been suggested that to say the special advocate will not be responsible to the person whose interests he is appointed to represent tends to go against the 'grain of the rule of law'.[34] We shall later come to examine how the ethical role of the special advocate differs from that of ordinary counsel, but we next need to consider exactly how it was envisaged that special advocates would represent the interests of appellants in closed sessions where appellants are not permitted to be present.

Acting in the interests of the appellant

The SIAC (Procedure) Rules set out a detailed picture of how special advocates are to operate which has acted as a template for the operation of all closed procedures involving special advocates. The Special Advocates' Support Office (SASO) which consists of a small team of lawyers and administrators who provide legal and administrative support to special advocates has also prepared a Special Advocates' *Open Manual* which contains a helpful summary of the procedures.[35] It is important from the outset to note that any use which the Secretary of State wishes SIAC to make of closed material is contingent upon the appointment of a special advocate. There would also seem to be a principle that the party seeking to depart from the normal procedures of open justice (normally the government) should pay the costs of the special advocates and SASO.[36] We will consider the appointment processes later, but if no special advocate is appointed, the Secretary of State may not rely on closed material.[37] It is this link between closed procedures and special advocates which has made their role so controversial, but we shall see that the notion of an advocate being appointed to represent the interests of an individual who is unable or unwilling to act on his own behalf is one that is expanding to other contexts.

Once a special advocate is appointed and has reviewed the open material, she and a member of SASO's open team will usually meet the appellant and/or her legal representative to discuss the open material which has been served in the case.[38] But a fundamental aspect of the SIAC procedures and the other statutory procedures providing for special advocates in the UK is that once the closed material is served upon the special advocate, the special advocate must not communicate any longer with the appellant or her representative (often referred to

33 Ip considers that special advocates occupy 'an interstitial space' somewhere between an amicus curiae and an ordinary legal representative. See J Ip, 'The Rise and Spread of the Special Advocate' [2008] *PL* 717, 735.

34 HC Deb 30 October 1997, vol 299, col 1037 (Mr David Winnick MP).

35 SASO, *A Guide to the Role of Special Advocates & the Special Advocates' Support Office* (2nd edn, Government Legal Department 2019), Part IV.

36 ibid [101] referring to *Re R (Closed Material Procedure; Special Advocates Funding)* [2017] EWHC 1793 (Fam).

37 SIAC (Procedure) Rules 2003 (SI 2003/1034), r 37(2).

38 SASO (n 35) [57].

as the 'open representative'), unless specifically authorised by the Commission to do so.[39] As we shall see, this has been one of the constant criticisms that has been made of the system, not least by special advocates themselves, as it means that they cannot take instructions on an informed basis from the excluded party.[40] The appellant and her open representatives may continue to send information in writing to the special advocate if they wish, but the problem is that any instructions may be unhelpfully uninformed as to key points in the case. The receipt of closed material is known colloquially as 'going into closed' and marks the beginning of what can be a long period of 'purdah' for special advocates who are screened off from engaging in any communication with the one person whose interests they are required to represent. This restriction on communication is one of the most controversial rules in the UK system, but it is a rule on which the government has remained firm.[41]

Along with the closed material, the Secretary of State is required to serve on the special advocate a statement of reasons for objecting to its disclosure and 'if and to the extent that it is possible to do so without disclosing information contrary to the public interest, a statement of the material in a form which can be served on the appellant'.[42] This acts as the trigger for the special advocate to exercise the first important function that she can perform in the interests of the appellant, known as the 'disclosure' function,[43] namely to prepare submissions, known as Rule 38 submissions under the SIAC Rules, on whether any of the closed material should be classified as open and therefore disclosed to the appellant. There follows what can be a protracted period of to-ing and fro-ing between the special advocate and the Secretary of State's counsel to try to reach agreement on what material can be made open and if agreement is not reached, a 'disclosure' hearing will take place for the Commission to rule on any outstanding issues. The Secretary of State cannot, however, be required to disclose closed material that the Commission rules should become open, nor be required to provide a summary of the material that the Commission has directed should be made. This is an important principle which applies in other courts and tribunals that handle secret information as well. It gives some comfort to intelligence services that information which is disclosed to government counsel, special advocates and the court, material that may be highly sensitive, perhaps emanating from foreign intelligence services, will not go any further. Instead, the Commission may direct that the Secretary of State may not rely in the proceedings on that material or on that which is required to be summarised, or if the material is exculpatory or

39 ibid, r 36(2).

40 See eg House of Commons Constitutional Affairs Committee (HCCAC), *The Operation of the Special Immigration Appeals Commission (SIAC) and the Use of Special Advocates* (HC 2004-05, 323-21) Ev 53–61 and *Response to Green Paper Consultation from Special Advocates* (2011).

41 Ministry of Justice, *Justice and Security Green Paper* (Cm 8194, 2011) [2.28]–[2.36].

42 SIAC (Procedure) Rules 2003 (SI 2003/1034), r 37(3).

43 HCCAC (n 40) [58].

supports the appellant's case, may direct that the Secretary of State shall not rely on any points in relation to it or shall make such concessions or take such further steps as the Commission may specify.[44] Any further material which the Secretary of State decides to disclose in the light of the Commission's rulings is then served on the appellant.

Once all the open and closed material has been served, the case is then ready for hearing and the special advocate's second important function comes into play. Known as the 'representation' function,[45] it is to represent the appellant's interests in the closed parts of the hearing. The hearing consists of both an open part and a closed part. The open hearing takes place first and this is where the appellant and her open representatives are able to participate. Although the special advocate will not usually contribute substantively, she attends the open part because this presents an opportunity to see how the case for the appellant is put and may give her some guidance on possible cross-examination topics from the lines of questioning pursued by the appellant's counsel.[46] At this open stage, the Secretary of State's witnesses will often be screened from public view to preserve their anonymity.[47] According to the *Open Manual*, they will only answer questions in cross-examination to the extent that they are able to do so in open court.[48] Should the answer to that question be based on closed material, their answer will be that they cannot answer the question in open court. Special advocates will then be able to follow up such questions in the closed part of the hearing. The appellant and her open representatives withdraw for the closed part of the hearing and at this point the special advocate takes over the representation of the appellant's interests.[49] In theory, in the closed part of the hearing it appears that the special advocate can take advantage of all the procedural opportunities that are open to counsel in any ordinary proceedings: she may adduce evidence, including calling witnesses, cross-examine witnesses and make whatever submissions she wishes.[50] As we shall see, the practice is rather different.

The SIAC rules do not make provision for how exactly the open and closed hearings should proceed, merely saying that the Commission may, in addition to giving directions at a directions hearing as to the order in which documents should be served, give directions relating to the conduct of proceedings.[51] The order in

44 SIAC (Procedure) Rules 2003 (SI 2003/1034), r 38(9). Similar provisions apply in the High Court where CMPs are held but the Court considers that closed material should not be withheld. See CPR r 76.29(7) (control orders), r 79.26(7) (asset-freezing and financial restriction orders), r 80.25(7) (TPIMs) and r 82.14(9) (closed procedures under the Justice and Security Act 2013).

45 HCCAC (n 40) [58].

46 SASO (n 35) [84].

47 ibid [85].

48 ibid [85].

49 ibid [86].

50 SIAC (Procedure) Rules 2003 (SI 2003/1034), r 35.

51 ibid.

which the open and closed hearings normally proceed is set out in the first edition of the SASO *Open Manual* and reproduced in Figure 2.1 below.[52] The proceedings begin with the open hearing consisting of an opening statement by each party, the Secretary of State's open evidence followed by the appellant's evidence. The closed hearing then proceeds with the Secretary of State's closed evidence. At this point, there may be submissions by the special advocate for some of the evidence in closed to be made open and the Commission will make a ruling on this. The hearing then goes back into open for closing speeches by the parties and finally into closed for the closing submissions of the Secretary of State and the special advocate.

Another way to proceed, which appears to be the manner in which parole hearings involving open and closed evidence are held in Northern Ireland, is for the open evidence of the Secretary of State to be followed by the closed evidence of the Secretary of State.[53] There would then be a decision made as to whether anything in closed may be made open. The appellant would then give her open evidence followed by the open submissions of Secretary of State and the appellant. The proceedings then finally go into closed again for the closing submissions of the Secretary of State and the special advocate. These standard procedures do not always apply in judicial review proceedings involving closed procedures and here the open case may be concluded in its entirety before the closed case begins.[54]

The judgments that are issued by SIAC and other courts and tribunals in which there are closed procedures are also normally in two formats, open and closed, although it may not be necessary for there to be a closed judgment because courts are mindful of the need to keep in closed only that which can harm the national interest and to give open reasons so far as possible.[55] There is a danger in this latter event that the closed evidence may in fact have inadvertently influenced the decision without the tribunal having to set out its reasoning in relation to the closed evidence. Closed judgments are handed down in the normal way but will only be made available to the Secretary of State, the special advocate and the SASO closed team.[56] The SIAC rules provide that the Commission must serve its open determination first on the Secretary of State and the special advocate before serving it on the appellant.[57] This 'undesirable process', as described by the Court of Appeal,[58] is to enable the judgment to be checked by the Secretary of State to

52 SASO, *A Guide to the Role of Special Advocates and the Special Advocates Support Office* (Treasury Solicitor 2006) 32.

53 See Parole Commissioners for Northern Ireland, *Guiding Principles and Procedures in Confidential Information Cases* (on file with author).

54 SASO (n 35) [88].

55 ibid [90].

56 ibid [93].

57 SIAC (Procedure) Rules 2003 (SI 2003/1034), r 48(2).

58 *R (Binyam Mohamed) v Secretary of State for Foreign and Commonwealth Affairs* [2010] EWCA Civ 65 [217]. In this case the applicant sought disclosure of material which the UK government had in its possession relating to his detention and torture by or on behalf of the

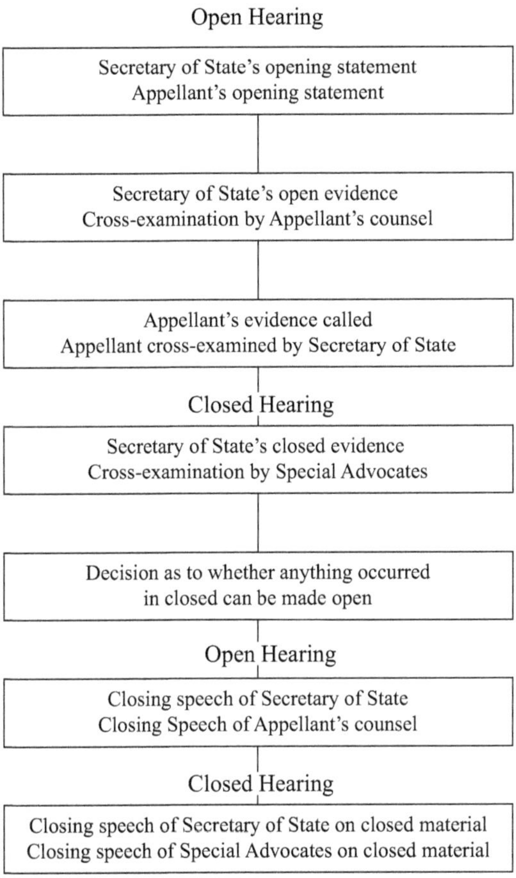

Figure 2.1 Standard procedure for open and closed hearings.

see that closed matters have not been inadvertently disclosed in the judgment. If the Secretary of State considers that notification to the appellant of any matter contained in the open judgment would cause information to be disclosed contrary to the public interest, an application may be made to the Commission to

US in order to prepare his defence against criminal charges in the US. There was considerable argument over the publication of seven paragraphs in the Divisional Court's judgment which the UK government said would seriously harm the intelligence-sharing arrangements between the UK and the US. The Court of Appeal considered that the procedure enabling one party to the litigation to seek to edit the court's judgment on public interest grounds, although no doubt 'important and necessary in public interest cases which concern national security', was on one view 'an intrinsically undesirable process'. For further analysis of the litigation in this case, see T Hickman and A Tomkins, 'National Security and the Due Process of Law' (2011) 64 CLP 215.

amend the judgment.[59] A degree of adversariality is preserved by permitting the special advocate to make representations against such an application, and if need be, a closed hearing may be heard to determine the issue.

At this closing stage of the proceedings, when judgment is about to be issued, the special advocate's disclosure function comes back into play. It is important to note that there is a wider role here than simply making representations on the Secretary of State's objection to parts of the open judgment being disclosed. The SIAC rules also provide an opportunity for the special advocate to apply to amend both the open and the closed judgment on the ground that the closed judgment contains material the disclosure of which would *not* be contrary to the public interest.[60] It can be argued that this is a very important part of the special advocate's role and would seem to provide a justification for letting the Secretary of State and the special advocate have first sight of the open judgment, based not only on national security grounds but also on grounds of due process. It is a well-established common law principle that not only has one the right to know the case against one but that one has the right to be given the full reasons for the outcome of proceedings.[61] In *Bank Mellat v HM Treasury*,[62] where secret evidence was used in an appeal by an Iranian bank against the imposition of sanctions on account of its alleged support for Iran's nuclear weapons programme, the Supreme Court emphasised the importance of the judge who has relied on closed material in a closed judgment saying in the open judgment as much as can properly be said about the closed material he has relied upon. By letting the special advocate, as well as the Secretary of State, have first sight of the open judgment, there is an opportunity for the special advocate as well as the Secretary of State to make submissions on what should, as well as what should not, be disclosed in the open judgment, with the potential for the appellant to be given fuller reasons for the decision than he or she might otherwise have been given.

Finally, special advocates may become involved in appeals or judicial reviews against judgments or court orders. This can happen in two ways.[63] First of all, the special advocate may consider that there are closed grounds of appeal. As they are not a party to proceedings, special advocates may not themselves lodge

59 SIAC (Procedure) Rules 2003 (SI 2003/1034), r 48(3).
60 ibid, r 47(5) (emphasis added).
61 See eg *English v Emery Reimbold & Strick Ltd* [2002] EWCA Civ 605, [2002] 1 WLR 2409, [16]: 'Justice will not be done if it is not apparent to the parties why one has won and the other has lost' (Lord Phillips MR). Cited in *Al Rawi v The Security Service* [2010] EWCA Civ 482 [16] (Lord Neuberger MR). See also *R (Binyam Mohamed) v Secretary of State for Commonwealth Affairs* [2010] EWCA Civ 65, where Lord Neuberger said that there was a very strong presumption that a court's judgment should be available for all to see and that absent good reason, 'it is axiomatic that a litigant should be able to see all the reasoning of the court in his case' [134].
62 *Bank Mellat v HM Treasury* (No 1) [2013] UKSC 38, [2014] AC 700 [69].
63 SASO (n 35) [94]–[96].

an appeal and must rely on the open representatives to do so. If the open representatives do not intend to appeal the open judgment, the special advocate must inform the open representatives, after getting authorisation to do so, that there are closed grounds of appeal so as to require them to lodge an appeal. Secondly, the Secretary of State may wish to bring its own appeal on closed material or resist an appeal being brought by the open representatives. In this event the special advocate will need to consider the closed material and take part in the appeal.

Rolling out the use of special advocates within SIAC

The SIAC framework sets the benchmark for how special advocates participate in closed procedures. As we have seen, at the time it was considered that they would be deployed in a very limited number of cases and this view seemed to be vindicated by the fact that in its first four years of operation, SIAC only heard three cases, all involving appeals against deportation. In all three cases, the appeals were successful. In the first appeal, SIAC was not convinced that the appellant Mr Rehman who was alleged to have been involved with an Islamic terrorist organisation, was a threat to national security, although this ruling was reversed by both the Court of Appeal and the House of Lords on the ground that SIAC had interpreted the meaning of 'national security' too narrowly and had applied a standard of proof that was too high.[64] In the second two cases, the appeals were allowed on the grounds that the appellants would face a real risk of torture if returned to India.[65]

SIAC's jurisdiction and the use of special advocates dramatically changed, however, in the climate after 9/11 when it was given jurisdiction to hear appeals against the powers given to the Home Secretary under Part 4 of the Anti-Terrorism, Crime and Security Act 2001 to detain foreign nationals who could not be deported or removed from the UK on the basis of reasonable suspicion that they were 'international terrorists' and therefore a threat to national security. In the words of one commentator, SIAC was 'thrust into the legal front-line of the UK's post-September 11 counter-terrorism efforts'.[66] SIAC heard a number of appeals under the Act using closed procedures and in contrast to the SIAC appeals heard before 2001, in every case, bar one, the Secretary of State's certification that the detainee was a suspected international terrorist was upheld.[67] Although special advocates had few successes in these cases, their presence was used to meet challenges that were mounted against the use of closed procedures. In the view of the Court of Appeal, the special advocate system provided

64 *SSHD v Rehman* [2000] 3 All ER 778 (CA) and [2001] UKHL 47, [2003] 1 AC 153 (HL). For a full analysis of the SIAC ruling and the appeal judgments, see JUSTICE (n 18) [91]–[100].

65 *SSHD v Mukhtiar Singh* July 2000 (unreported), *SSHD v Paramjit Singh* July 2000 (unreported).

66 Ip (n 33) 722.

67 See JUSTICE (n 18) [106].

a 'substantial degree of protection' and that, looking at the proceedings as a whole, there was no contravention of Article 6 of the ECHR.[68] When SIAC's jurisdiction in these cases came to an end in 2004, it was not as a result of any successful challenge to closed procedures but as a result of a ruling by the House of Lords that indefinite detention of foreign nationals under the Act was discriminatory and incompatible with Article 14 of the ECHR.[69]

This successful challenge to what has been called the 'internment' regime established under the 2001 Act[70] did not mean that SIAC returned to hearing only a trickle of cases. This time it was the terrorist attacks on the London Underground which killed 52 people on 7 July 2005 which gave the impetus for further use of closed procedures within SIAC. In his famous press conference where he declared that 'the rules of the game are changing',[71] the Prime Minister, Tony Blair, announced that there would be a new approach to deportation orders, which in practice meant that the government would seek diplomatic assurances that deportees would not be subjected to ill-treatment by the countries to which they were returned. Deportation orders were made against a number of foreign nationals, and in the SIAC appeals, closed evidence was used to show not only that these individuals were a national security risk but also that it was safe for them to be deported on the basis of assurances given in secret negotiations between the UK and the countries where they were to be sent.

The counter-terrorist context has continued to ensure that SIAC hears a steady stream of cases. In 2002, the jurisdiction of SIAC was further widened by the Nationality, Immigration and Asylum Act 2002 to enable it to hear appeals against a removal of citizenship by the Secretary of State where the Secretary of State again certifies that the decision was taken in reliance on information which should not be made public. By 2011, the government revealed that SIAC had been used in around 70 cases since December 2001, 10 individuals had been deported and another 11 had left voluntarily.[72] Some of these 70 cases involved deprivation of citizenship proceedings, others were immigration decisions to exclude individuals from the UK and a number of other individuals had been detained or put on strict bail conditions for a period of time, restricting their opportunity to engage in terrorist or criminal activity. Since then, SIAC's jurisdiction has been extended to hear applications on judicial review grounds challenging decisions which do not carry a right of appeal in relation to exclusion, naturalisation and refusal of citizenship where the Secretary of State again

68 *A, X and Y v SSHD* [2003] 2 WLR 564 [57].
69 *A v SSHD (No 1)* [2004] UKHL 56, [2005] 2 AC 68.
70 See Amnesty International, *Left in the Dark: the Use of Secret Evidence in the United Kingdom* (2012) 14.
71 Press conference, 5 August 2005.
72 Ministry of Justice (n 41) [1.20].

certifies that the decision was made in reliance on information that should not be made public.[73]

No-one in the parliamentary debates that gave approval to the special advocate system used in SIAC envisaged that they could or would be extended to a large number of other types of proceedings. But as we shall see in the next chapter, this is exactly what has happened. A special kind of lawyering introduced in response to the judgment in *Chahal* for a limited purpose within the immigration context has developed within CMPs to become an established part of the legal landscape in a range of different types of civil and criminal proceedings. This expansion can in part be explained as one of the consequences of the 'war on terror' whereby a measure used in one policy field (immigration) has become used in another (counter-terrorism).[74] This is certainly what happened within SIAC. But we shall also see that special advocates have in fact been used in non-terrorist contexts as well as terrorist contexts and have extended their reach into areas beyond national security where secret evidence is used. Not for the first time, a measure that was first justified as exceptional in one context has spread beyond its original boundary to become normalised.[75]

73 Justice and Security Act 2013, s 15, introduced after the High Court ruled that it could not hold CMPs in ordinary judicial review proceedings to hear the Secretary of State's full reasons for refusing to grant certain individuals naturalisation. See *AHK v SSHD* [2012] EWHC 1117 (Admin).

74 See C C Murphy, 'Counter-Terrorism and the Culture of Legality: the Case of Special Advocates' (2013) 24 *King's Law Journal* 19, 24.

75 Ip uses two examples to illustrate how exceptional measures can spread beyond their original boundaries and become normalised. See Ip (n 33) 738–39. First of all, the US use of harsh interrogation techniques in the 'war on terror' was first limited to the interrogation of high value detainees but came to be employed more widely in Guantánamo, Iraq and Afghanistan. See also J Margulies, *Guantánamo and the Abuse of Presidential Power* (Simon Schuster 2006) chs 2 and 4. Secondly, legislation curtailing the right of silence introduced in Northern Ireland to combat the 'wall of silence' that the police faced when questioning terrorist suspects migrated to England and Wales and has since migrated to other jurisdictions such as the Republic of Ireland and New South Wales. See Y Daly and J Jackson, 'The Criminal Justice Process: from questioning to trial' in D Healy, C Hamilton, Y Daly and M Butler (eds), *The Routledge Handbook of Irish Criminology* (Routledge 2016) 280.

3 The rise of special advocates in the UK

In this chapter, we attempt to chart the use that has been made of special advocates in the UK. In January 2010, the Joint Committee on Human Rights (JCHR) was informed by the Minister of State at the Home Office that although there are some contexts in which the use of special advocates is provided for by legislation, in addition the courts have an inherent jurisdiction to request that the relevant law officer consider appointing special advocates.[1] It was consequently difficult to provide a comprehensive list of all these contexts. However, the Minister went on to list 21 different contexts in which special advocates had been or may be used, stressing that in many proceedings, they are not used routinely and in some cases, they had not yet been used at all.[2] As we shall see, the passage of the Justice and Security Act 2013 has since opened up the potential for their use in many more types of civil proceedings. It will be convenient to consider, first of all, how Parliament has rolled out their use in a variety of different contexts before going on to consider the circumstances in which the courts have invoked their inherent jurisdiction to use them. We will then review how human rights law has reacted to their use and show how it has continued to provide legitimacy for them. Finally, we will consider the number of cases in which they have actually been used.

Parliamentary expansion beyond SIAC

Although SIAC was the first body to use special advocates in the UK, it was not long before provision was made for them to be used in a range of other judicial proceedings where national security information was involved. As with SIAC in its early days, their use may be seen in the light of a progressive 'human rights' movement to judicialise review procedures which had hitherto remained within the executive's realm. But as we shall see, it was not long before they were used as part of a counter-terrorist strategy that made significant inroads into individuals'

1 JCHR, *Counter-Terrorism and Human Rights (Sixteenth Report): Annual Renewal of Control Orders Legislation 2010* (2009-10, HL 64, HC 395) 50.
2 ibid 50–52.

rights. Interestingly, it was in Northern Ireland where Parliament next authorised the use of special advocates within a context where the Belfast/Good Friday Agreement,[3] together with the newly enacted Human Rights Act 1998, was requiring that public bodies complied fully with human rights law. The ECtHR had already referred to the need to balance carefully national security concerns and fairness in *Tinnelly & Sons Ltd v UK*,[4] where a discrimination claim concerning tenders for a contract with Northern Ireland Electricity Services was ousted by a national security certificate which conclusively certified that the decision not to grant the contract to the applicants was 'an act done for the purpose of safeguarding national security'. The Court held that the issue of the certificate by the Secretary of State constituted a disproportionate restriction on the applicants' right of access to a court or tribunal which was a breach of Article 6 of the ECHR. The right of access to a court could not be displaced by the '*ipse dixit* of the executive'.[5] In phrasing reminiscent of *Chahal v UK*,[6] the Court noted that:

> in other contexts it had been found possible to modify judicial procedures in such a way as to safeguard national security concerns about the nature and sources of intelligence and yet accord the individual a substantial degree of procedural justice.

The Court referred to the fact that the applicants had drawn attention to the SIAC procedures and the appointment of a special advocate.[7] With this implicit endorsement of the special advocate system and the precedent of SIAC, it was not surprising that the government acted to establish a Tribunal to which claimants could bring appeals against national security certificates.[8] Rules were made for the withholding of information from the claimants, for proceedings to be held in the absence of the claimant and for regulating the functions of those who might be appointed to represent the interests of the claimant when the claimant and his legal representative were excluded.[9]

At around the same time, provision for special advocates was also made in a number of enactments dealing with prisoner releases in Northern Ireland. In order to implement a key component of the Belfast/Good Friday Agreement, the Northern Ireland (Sentences) Act 1998 provided for prisoners serving sentences for scheduled offences committed during 'the Troubles' to apply to a new body, the Sentence Review Commissioners, for early release if they were able to meet certain statutory conditions. Schedule 2 to the Act empowers the Secretary of State to make rules providing, amongst other things, for the withholding of

3 *Agreement Reached in the Multi-Party Negotiations* (Cm 3883, 1998).
4 *Tinnelly & Sons Ltd v UK; McElduff v UK* (1998) 27 EHRR 249.
5 ibid [77].
6 (1997) 23 EHRR 413.
7 ibid [78].
8 Northern Ireland Act 1998, s 91.
9 See Northern Ireland Act Tribunal (Procedure) Rules 1999 (SI 1999/2131).

evidence or information about a prisoner, the holding of hearings in the absence of the prisoner and any legal representative and the appointment of a person 'to represent the prisoner's interests' when he and his legal representatives are excluded.[10] Under the rules, 'damaging information' may be withheld from the prisoner and his representative where disclosure would be likely to be contrary to the interests of national security or to have adverse effects on the health, welfare or safety of any persons.[11] Similar rule-making powers were given to the Secretary of State pursuant to Schedule 2 to the Life Sentences (NI) Order 2001 (SI 2001/2564) which made provision for a new independent body, known as the Life Sentence Review Commissioners, to deal with tariff and release decisions in respect of life prisoners. This new body was deemed necessary in order to comply with a series of decisions of the ECtHR which required life sentence prisoners seeking release to have their case reviewed by an independent court in accordance with Article 5(4) of the ECHR.[12] European case law also inspired the need for provision to be made for judicial review when a prisoner's licence was revoked.[13] On 13 January 2003, the Secretary of State issued a 'Written Statement' delegating his functions under the Northern Ireland (Remission of Sentences) Act 1995 by providing for the appointment of independent Commissioners to hear representations from prisoners and for a special advocate to be appointed to safeguard the interests of the prisoner when there is 'damaging information' which cannot be disclosed to the prisoner.[14] Later, when Parole Commissioners replaced Life Sentence Commissioners and were given duties to consider the release and recall of a wider range of prisoners, it was also considered necessary to make provision for closed procedures and the appointment of special advocates in cases where 'confidential information' was withheld.[15]

Hot on the heels of the ECtHR decision in *Tinnelly* prohibiting conclusive national security certificates issued by ministers in the context of a discrimination claim, the UK Government acted to remove the power of ministers to issue conclusive national security certificates in race discrimination claims in the rest of the UK but at the same time permitted them to make rules for the exclusion of claimants from judicial hearings and for the appointment of special advocates.[16]

10 See Northern Ireland (Sentences) Act 1998 (Sentence Review Commissioners) Rules 1998 (SI 1998/1859).

11 ibid, r 22(1).

12 See eg *Thynne, Gunnell and Wilson v UK* (1991) 13 EHRR CD 135; *Hussain v UK* (1996) 22 EHRR 1; *Stafford v UK* (2002) 35 EHRR 32. See Criminal Justice Review Group, *Review of the Criminal Justice System in Northern Ireland* (HMSO 2000) [12.64].

13 *Waite v UK* (2002) 36 EHRR 1001.

14 See *Roberts v Parole Board* [2005] UKHL 45, [2005] 2 AC 738 and *Re McClean* [2005] UKHL 46, [2005] NI 490 for a full description of these procedures. See also J Jackson, 'Evidence and Proof in Parole Hearings: Meeting a Triangulation of Interests' [2007] Crim LR 417.

15 See Criminal Justice (NI) Order 2008 (SI 2008/1216), sch 4 [4] and Parole Commissioners' Rules (NI) 2009 (SI 2009/92), rr 9, 19.

16 Race Relations (Amendment) Act 2000, ss 7 and 8, amending Race Relations Act 1976, s 67A(2).

More broadly, the power of ministers to certify conclusively that acts were done on grounds of national security in employment disputes involving the Crown was also removed. Instead, Ministers were given the power to direct that special procedures should apply in Crown employment proceedings excluding the applicant and his legal representatives, and employment tribunals were given a general power to order that applicants and their legal representatives be excluded in cases involving national security and for the appointment of special advocates to represent the applicants' interests in such cases.[17] Outside the employment context, provision was also made for the appointment of special advocates in planning inquiries to represent the interests of persons prevented from hearing or inspecting evidence as a result of a ministerial direction that the evidence concerns matters of national security and that its disclosure would be contrary to the national interest.[18]

Once again, however, it was the use of special advocates in the counter-terrorism field that received the most attention and was regarded as most controversial. Provision was, first of all, made for the appointment of special advocates to represent the interests of organisations or individuals in appeals before specialist tribunals against decisions of the Secretary of State to proscribe terrorist organisations or deny persons access to dangerous substances. The Proscribed Organisations Appeal Commission (POAC) and the Pathogens Access Appeals Commission set up to hear these appeals provide remedies that were previously denied to organisations and persons affected by these decisions.[19] When the 'internment' powers under the Anti-Terrorism, Crime and Security Act 2001 depriving foreign nationals of their liberty were struck down by the House of

17 See Employment Relations Act 1999 s 41 and sch 8 (amending s 10 of the Employment Tribunals Act 1996) and Employment Tribunals (Constitution and Rules of Procedure) Regulations 2004 (SI 2004/1861), sch 2. See also Industrial Tribunals (Constitution and Rules of Procedure)(Regulations) (NI) 2005 (SI 2005/150), sch 2. The procedure for CMPs within the employment tribunal is now contained in the Employment Tribunal (Constitution and Rules of Procedure) Regulations 2013 (SI 2013/1237). Appeals to the Employment Appeals Tribunal are governed by the Employment Appeal Tribunal Rules 1993 (SI 1993/2854), r 30A. Note also that in 1997, a non-statutory body, the Security Vetting Appeal Panel (SVAP), was established giving civil service staff an independent avenue of appeal where their security clearance has been refused or withdrawn and providing for the appointment of special advocates to represent their interests in such appeals.

18 Planning and Compulsory Purchase Act 2004, s 80 (amending s 321 of the Town and Country Planning Act 1990) and Planning (National Security Directions and Appointed Representatives) (England) Rules 2006 (SI 2006/1284) and Planning (National Security Directions and Appointed Representatives) (Wales) Regulations 2006 (SI 2006/1387).

19 See, respectively, Terrorism Act 2000, s 4 establishing the Proscribed Organisations Appeal Commission and Proscribed Organisations Appeal Commission (Procedure) Rules 2001 (SI 2001/443) and the Court of Appeal (Appeals from Proscribed Organisations Appeal Commission) Rules 2002 (SI 2002/1843); Anti-Terrorism, Crime and Security Act 2001 s 70 and sch 6 establishing Pathogens Access Appeals Commission and Pathogens Access Appeal Commission (Procedure) Rules 2002 (SI 2002/1845) and the Court of Appeal (Appeals from Pathogens Access Appeal Commission) Rules 2002 (SI 2002/1844).

Lords, the government's response – apart, as we have seen in Chapter 2, from pursuing diplomatic assurances from states to which deportees were to be sent – was to enable the Home Secretary under the Prevention of Terrorism Act 2005 to make control orders restricting the liberty of any person whom he or she reasonably suspected of being 'involved in terrorist-related activity'.[20] Those subject to 'non-derogating' orders which were not considered severe enough to trigger Article 15 of the ECHR were entitled to have the Home Secretary's decision reviewed in the High Court and SIAC-style procedures were authorised providing for the non-disclosure of evidence and for closed proceedings with the appointment of special advocates to represent their interests.[21] Although falling short of restrictions on liberty that were considered in breach of Article 5, the type of restrictions that could be imposed was nevertheless significant, including, typically, a combination of curfews between 8 and 16 hours a day; forced relocation to another city or town; electronic tagging; restrictions on visitors, meetings with others, employment, movement and communication; bans on the use of mobile phones and the internet; and restrictions on having a bank account or other financial restrictions.[22] These restrictions were arguably punitive in their effect,[23] yet they could be imposed without the safeguards available to those charged with actual criminal offences. The provision of a special advocate was deemed a sufficient counterbalancing measure for the lack of knowing the full case against a person. This was also the first time that the use of special advocates was authorised in the ordinary courts, a step that can be seen as a significant 'normalisation' of the special advocate procedure.[24] To cater for the inroads into normal High Court procedures, moreover, the Civil Procedure Rules had to be amended so that the civil litigation 'overriding objective' of enabling the Court to deal with cases justly was to be read and given effect in a way which was compatible with the Court's duty to ensure that information is not disclosed contrary to the public interest.[25]

The government lost no time in subjecting those who had been indefinitely detained under the 'internment' procedures to these non-derogating control orders and over the lifetime of the Prevention of Terrorism Act (2005–11),

20 Prevention of Terrorism 2005, s 1.

21 ibid sch Control Order Proceedings, etc [7] and the Civil Procedure Rules (CPR) Pt 76. Derogating control orders could only be imposed by the High Court on application by the Home Secretary: Prevention of Terrorism Act 2005, s 1(4).

22 Amnesty International, *Left in the Dark: the Use of Secret Evidence in the United Kingdom* (Amnesty International Publications 2012) 24.

23 L Zedner, 'Preventive Justice or Pre-Punishment: the Case of Control Orders' [2007] *CLP* 174, citing the view of the JCHR that although the non-derogating orders would appear to be civil orders intended as an alternative to prosecution, in substantive terms in most, if not all cases, they amount to a determination of a criminal charge against an individual who is the subject of an order.

24 J Ip, 'The Rise and Spread of the Special Advocate' [2008] PL 717, 724.

25 CPR, r 76.2(1)(2).

52 people were subject to them.[26] The orders were subjected to considerable criticism. In 2010, the JCHR came to the view that they were no longer sustainable for a number of reasons based on the unjustifiable interferences with people's liberty that they entailed, the unfairness of the process and reservations about whether they were effective in disrupting terrorism compared with other means of achieving the same end.[27] After a further review announced by the incoming Coalition Government in 2010, the orders were abolished, only to be replaced with TPIMs under the Terrorism Prevention and Investigation Measures (TPIMs) Act 2011. Although these new measures differed from control orders in raising the threshold for imposition from 'reasonable suspicion' to 'reasonable belief', by ending the involuntary relocation requirements and limiting the lifetime of the new TPIMs to two years, they continued to impose significant restrictions on the affected individual. They were immediately dubbed 'control orders lite' and later additional powers were introduced under the Counter-Terrorism and Security Act 2015 to enable the Secretary of State once again to require subjects to reside in another location.[28] Most importantly, the 2011 Act did little to change the powers of review and the use of closed hearings and the special advocate system remained intact.[29]

SIAC-style procedures involving special advocates were also introduced into the High Court for applications to set aside asset-freezing measures taken by the Treasury against persons under domestic sanction schemes or under international UN orders. The need for some independent review of asset-freezing measures with a right to be heard was emphasised by the Court of Justice of the European Union (CJEU) in *Kadi* where the Court refused to uphold the UN Security Council's listing of the applicants on account of their alleged association with the Al-Qaeda network which had been implemented by EU Regulation 881/2002 in circumstances where the applicant had no opportunity to contest the measures directed against him and his right to be heard had been violated.[30] Although it made no reference specifically to special advocates, the Court did refer to the passage in *Chahal* where the ECtHR stated that there were techniques which could accommodate legitimate security concerns and the need to accord individuals a sufficient measure of procedural justice.[31] In a Treasury paper issued before the UK procedures were enacted, the government had emphasised the

26 D Anderson, *Final Report of the Independent Reviewer on the Prevention of Terrorism Act 2005* (Home Office 2012) 5.

27 JCHR (n 1).

28 Counter-Terrorism and Security Act 2015, s 16.

29 See Terrorism Prevention and Investigation Measures Act 2011, sch 4 [10] and CPR pt 80. Note, however, that the Counter-Terrorism and Security Act 2015, s 20 (1) amended the requirement for the Secretary of State to be satisfied of involvement in terrorism from 'reasonably believes' to 'on the balance of probabilities'.

30 (Joined cases C-402/05P and C-415/05P) *Kadi v Council of the EU and the Commission* [2008] 3 CMLR 41, [2008] ECR-I 6351, 3 September 2008.

31 ibid [344].

importance of asset-freezing as part of the international community's counter-terrorist effort and to use 'closed source' evidence in asset-freezing cases where there were operational reasons to impose a freeze but insufficient open source evidence available.[32] However, it gave an assurance that in order to ensure the fairness of any court challenge to the imposition of a freeze, it would introduce a procedure for the appointment of special advocates to represent the interests of applicants in respect of the closed evidence.[33] Within the UK, persons affected by asset-freezing measures may appeal or apply to have them reviewed by the High Court which is governed by special rules which provide for limited open disclosure, closed proceedings and special advocates.[34] The provision for closed procedures combined with special advocates in the asset-freezing legislation is one more example of the High Court having to implement procedures which may have to depart from the overriding objective of dealing with cases justly in the interests of national security,[35] 'a frank acknowledgement', according to the Independent Reviewer on Terrorism, 'that the interests of national security and of justice are not completely reconcilable'.[36]

But it was the momentous step taken under the Justice and Security Act 2013 to permit closed material procedures to be used in any form of civil litigation where there is material which it would be damaging to national security to disclose that set the scene for special advocates to be used in all types of civil proceedings involving national security in the UK, with the Civil Procedure Rules again having to be modified to ensure that such material is not disclosed.[37] The genesis of the Act is to be found in the Supreme Court case of *Al Rawi v Security Service*[38] where six former detainees in Guantánamo Bay had brought a claim for damages in tort on the ground that the Security Service and other organs of the state had been complicit in the detention and ill-treatment of them by foreign authorities. In defending the claims, the government proposed that instead of claiming PII for sensitive material which would have the effect of ruling it out of consideration by the court, the court should receive the material and consider it on its merits without it being seen by the claimants, but with special advocates representing the interests of claimants in closed hearings. As we have seen, a majority of the Supreme Court concluded that in the absence of statutory authority, the courts had no common law power to order a CMP in a civil claim.[39]

32 HM Treasury, *The Financial Challenge to Crime and Terrorism* (HMSO 2007) [2.33].

33 ibid.

34 See Counter-Terrorism Act 2008, ss 66–68, Terrorist Asset-Freezing Etc Act 2010, ss 26–29 and CPR, Pt 79.

35 See CPR, r 79.2(1)(2).

36 D Anderson, *First Report on the Operation of the Terrorist Asset-Freezing Etc Act 2010* (The Stationery Office 2011) [4.17].

37 See CPR Pt 82, r 82.2(1)(2).

38 *Al Rawi v The Security Service* [2011] UKSC 34, [2012] 1 AC 531.

39 ibid. Lords Clarke and Mance and Lady Hale considered that there could be circumstances where a CMP might be appropriate.

The government's response to the *Al Rawi* decision was to issue a Green Paper in which it proposed that CMPs should be generally available in civil proceedings, arguing that it was *fairer* in terms of outcome to seek to *include* relevant material, rather than *exclude* it from consideration altogether, and that the public interest is best served altogether by enabling as many cases as possible to be determined by the courts.[40] The government's particular concern was that without the availability of a CMP, it would either have to disclose closed evidence that was helpful to its case or withhold it via PII, and withholding it meant losing the case and paying damages. With both sides able to present their case fully to the court, albeit in closed procedures, it would be less likely that cases would have to be dropped or settled, as was the case in the Guantánamo litigation, or struck out by the court.[41] In *Carnduff v Rock*,[42] the Court of Appeal considered that a claim by a police informer who sought to recover payment for information he supplied to the police could not be litigated consistently with the public interest and should be struck out, as the determination of the claim would have required the disclosure of sensitive information. The Green Paper adverted to the special advocate system which was provided for in legislation in 14 different contexts of civil proceeding and stated that the contexts in which CMPs were already used had proved they were capable of delivering procedural fairness, the effectiveness of the special advocate system being central to this.[43]

The proposals met with much criticism,[44] not least from special advocates themselves who disputed the claim that CMPs were fair and effective in the contexts in which they had been used, citing Lord Kerr's view in *Al Rawi* that the special advocate system should never be regarded as an acceptable substitute for the compromise of the fundamental right to be informed about the case

40 Ministry of Justice, *Justice and Security Green Paper* (Cm 8194, 2011) [2.2] (emphasis in original).

41 ibid [2.3].

42 [2001] EWCA Civ 680, [2001] 1 WLR 1786.

43 Ministry of Justice (n 40) [2.37] and [2.3]. When the paper was published, the JCHR asked the government to clarify what the specific statutory provisions in question were. The Ministry of Justice's memorandum in response identified 14 contexts in which there was statutory provision for closed procedures but some of these do not provide for special advocates. For example, production hearings under sch 5 to the Terrorism Act 2000 and pre-charge detention hearings under Pt III of sch 8 to the Terrorism Act 2000 provide for closed hearings but not for special advocates. Similarly, as the memorandum states, there is no express provision for special advocates in closed procedures in the Information Rights Tribunal established under the Freedom of Information Act 2000 to consider whether material is exempt from disclosure without disclosing that material to the requestor. See JCHR, *Justice and Security Green Paper Written Evidence* Q 1 [9]–[10] (28 March 2012).

44 See the wide-ranging criticism of the proposals in JCHR, *The Justice and Security Green Paper: Twenty-fourth Report of Session* (2010-12, HL 286, HC 1777); Amnesty International (n 22) 31–38; and the various responses to the Green Paper at: <http://webarchive.nationalarchives.gov.uk/20140911100336/http://consultation.cabinetoffice.gov.uk/justiceandsecurity/responses-to-the-consultation> archived 11 September 2014.

against you and drawing attention to serious difficulties with the present system.[45] Notwithstanding such criticism, the government pressed ahead to enact its proposals. During the parliamentary process, however, a number of amendments were put down to ensure that closed procedures could only be considered in rare and exceptional cases, under full judicial control and where absolutely necessary.[46] One of the amendments that was made was to restrict the range of public interests that could justify a CMP to national security (unlike in other CMPs where a broader range of public interests can justify withholding material). This gives rise to the possibility of PII proceedings taking place in parallel with a statutory CMP if, for example, there is material the disclosure of which would be damaging to international relations, but not national security.

Under the scheme in the 2013 Act, there is a two-stage process which must be undertaken before any material can be deployed in a CMP.[47] At the first stage, a party (which need not be the government) applies for a declaration under section 6 of the Act that the proceedings are proceedings in which a closed material application *may* be made to the court. Only if this gateway is opened is it possible for a closed material application to be made under section 8 of the Act by which it is determined whether certain material should be disclosed and deployed in open or in closed procedure. The court can only make a section 6 declaration on two conditions: where a party would be required to disclose sensitive material the disclosure of which would be damaging to national security were it not for the possibility of a PII claim; and where it is in the interests of the 'fair and effective administration of justice' to make a declaration.[48] The requirement under the scheme whereby it is for the court and not for the government to make a declaration permitting a CMP has had the effect of giving special advocates a particularly important role in making submissions to the court on whether such a declaration should be made, as hearings on this question themselves take place in a closed procedure.[49]

In their interpretation of section 6, the courts have resisted submissions that declarations should only be made as a last resort and have held that there is no reason to give the statutory provisions a narrow or restrictive construction.[50] The latest figures that are available for the use of closed procedures from 25 June 2013 to 24 June 2017 indicate that over the course of these four years,

45 *Response to Green Paper Consultation for Special Advocates* [15]–[17]. See *Al Rawi v The Security Service* [2011] UKSC 34, [2012] 1 AC 531 [94] (Lord Kerr).

46 For discussion of the various parliamentary amendments, see A Tomkins 'Justice and Security in the United Kingdom' (2014) 47 *Israel Law Review* 305. For the role played by a former Supreme Court justice in the parliamentary procedure, see N Phillips, 'Closed Material', *London Review of Books*, 17 April 2014.

47 For a detailed review of the procedures, see A Zuckerman, *Zuckerman on Civil Procedure* (3rd edn Sweet & Maxwell 2013) 938–943.

48 Justice and Security Act, s 6(4)(5).

49 ibid s 11(2), CPR, r 82.23(3). The general functions of the special advocate are listed in CPR r 82.10.

50 See *McGartland and Asher v SSHD* [2015] EWCA Civ 686 [35]; *R (Sarkandi) v Secretary of State for the Foreign and Commonwealth Affairs* [2015] EWCA Civ 687 [58].

41 applications were made for a CMP under section 6 (some for more than one claimant in a case) and 27 declarations in response to applications were made by the courts under section 6.[51] The figures do not disclose how many applications have been refused by the courts as opposed to being withdrawn by the parties. However, it appears that there have to date been very few cases where a section 6 application has been refused (as opposed to withdrawn).[52]

The applications have been divided between cases where judicial review is sought against the imposition of restrictive measures such as freezing of assets or revocation of passports and civil claims where damages are sought for alleged government wrongdoing. Examples of the latter have included allegations of complicity in unlawful detention and ill-treatment by foreign powers of the kind alleged in the *Al Rawi* case,[53] or allegations by alleged informants that they have not been adequately protected.[54] There would also seem to have been a rise in the number of cases where the government is defending claims arising out of alleged wrongdoing during the Northern Ireland conflict.[55] Civil liberty organisations suspicious that CMPs under the 2013 Act are being used to prevent exposure of government wrongdoing continue to keep a watchful eye over the kinds of cases where section 6 applications are being made.[56]

Expansion beyond express parliamentary approval

Although a majority of the Supreme Court in *Al Rawi* was of the view that there was no inherent common law power to order CMPs in the ordinary civil courts, there are a number of instances where courts and tribunals have had special advocates appointed without any express statutory authority for doing so, using their 'inherent jurisdiction' to regulate their own procedure or reasoning that there was an implied statutory authority for doing so.[57] In fact, 12 of the 21 contexts listed by the government in 2010 where special advocates had been or were able

51 See the annual reports on the use of closed procedure which must be prepared by the Ministry of Justice under Justice and Security Act 2013, s 12. The latest is to be found in Ministry of Justice, *Report on use of closed procedures (from 25 June 2016 to 24 June 2017)* (HMSO 2017). Note that six applications made during this last reporting period were not decided within this period.

52 Email correspondence between the author and SA20 and SA5 (23 and 24 November 2018). For one example where an application was refused, see *XYZ; HTF; ZMS v Ministry of Defence* [2017] EWHC 547 (QB).

53 See eg *CF v The Security Service* [2013] EWHC 3402 (QB); *R (K, A and B) v Secretary of State for Defence* [2016] EWHC 1261 (Admin), [2016] EWCA Civ 1149.

54 See eg *McGartland and Asher v SSHD* [2015] EWCA Civ 686.

55 Of the 25 applications made in the reporting periods June 2015–June 2016 and June 2016–June 2017, nine were in respect of claims made in Northern Ireland.

56 See O Boycott and I Cobain, 'Secret Court Case Application Numbers More Than Double in a Year', *The Guardian* (London, 16 October 2015).

57 On 'inherent jurisdiction', see I H Jacob, 'The Inherent Jurisdiction of the Court' (1970) 23 CLP 23.

to be used related to non-statutory arrangements. There would seem to be three types of cases where this has happened. First of all, there are cases where there is already a statutory basis for CMPs in the lower courts or tribunals and special advocates are appointed to act in higher appellate courts in cases where rulings arising out of closed hearings have been appealed. Secondly, there are cases where special advocates have been appointed in order to enhance the procedural fairness of existing closed procedures. Thirdly, and more controversially, there are cases where CMPs have been ordered and special advocates appointed in a new situation without express statutory approval for doing so.

To come to the first category of case, appeals against closed rulings, in *Rehman v SSHD*,[58] the first appeal against a SIAC case, the Court of Appeal accepted that it may be necessary to hear submissions in the absence of Mr Rehman and his counsel in order to dispose justly of the appeal, and a special advocate was appointed despite the absence of any statutory backing for this to be done. But there has been a reluctance within the higher judiciary to consider closed evidence and hold closed hearings. In *SSHD v AF*,[59] where as we shall see the House of Lords set out a test to meet the disclosure requirements of Article 6 of the ECHR, Lord Brown considered that now the proper approach had been declared as definitively as possible, it should never again be necessary for the Court of Appeal as opposed to first instance judgments, to consider closed material or hold closed hearings or itself deliver closed judgments.[60] Lord Hope considered that the Court of Appeal might have to do so but, in his view, it would be hard to imagine any circumstances in which scrutiny of such material by the Supreme Court would ever be necessary or appropriate.[61] In *Bank Mellat v HM Treasury (No 1)*[62] a reluctant majority of the Supreme Court did, however, for the first time consider a closed judgment in a closed hearing with special advocates being appointed. In this case, the courts below had an express power to conduct a CMP under Part 6 of the Counter-Terrorism Act 2008 which is concerned with asset-freezing, but the Supreme Court had no such power. The Court, however, considered that a power to hold a CMP was implicit in its statutory powers under the Constitutional Reform Act 2005 to hear appeals in 'any' order or judgment of the Court of Appeal and a power to 'determine any question necessary … for the purposes of doing justice on any appeal to it under any enactment'. The Court held that a determination by the Supreme Court on a basis different from that required and adopted in the courts below would have been self-evidently unsatisfactory, risk injustice and, in some cases, be absurd. Similar reasoning was applied in *R (Haralambous) v Crown Court at St Albans*[63] where the Supreme

58 *SSHD v Rehman* [2000] 3 All ER 778 [31]–[32].
59 *SSHD v AF (No 3)* [2009] UKHL 28, [2010] 2 AC 269.
60 ibid [121]. This was also Lady Hale's view, ibid [106].
61 ibid [88].
62 *Bank Mellat v HM Treasury (No 1)* [2013] UKSC 38, [2014] 1 AC 700.
63 *R (Haralambous) v Crown Court at St Albans* [2018] UKSC 1, [2018] AC 236.

Court held that the High Court can conduct a CMP and rely on information that is not disclosed to an interested party when there is a judicial review of the legality of a search warrant issued after a statutory ex parte hearing held in the magistrates' court in the absence of the interested party. The same applied to a judicial review of an order made by the Crown Court to retain unlawfully seized material which relied on undisclosed information.

In *Bank Mellat*, the Supreme Court emphasised that an appellate court should be asked to conduct a closed hearing only if it is strictly necessary for fairly determining the appeal and that initiation of a CMP should be avoided if at all possible.[64] The reluctance of the appellate courts to examine closed material and hear from special advocates has been criticised on the ground that if the public interest justifies the use of CMPs at first instance even though they represent a fundamental derogation from the foundational right of every litigant to know the case against him, it is important that appellate courts should stand ready to scrutinise the fairness of the procedures adopted by the court below, and not to do so is inimical to the proper exercise of the appellate function.[65] A refusal by the appellate courts to do this would certainly appear to compound the unfairness of CMPs still further. Not only is a party to the litigation unable to see the closed material and any closed ruling against him, but there is then no mechanism whereby there can be scrutiny of whether the first instance court or tribunal came to a decision which was open to it. Ironically, this is one instance where fairness would seem to demand the use of closed material and special advocates.

The second type of case where special advocates have been appointed in the absence of statutory authority has been where it has already been established that the public interest requires that evidence may be withheld from one of the parties to the proceedings. In these instances, it can be argued that special advocates are being appointed to enhance the fairness of proceedings rather than to reduce protections that were already provided for. The first example where special advocates were appointed in this type of case was in public interest immunity (PII) proceedings. It is well established that the courts have a power to inspect closed material for which PII is claimed in order to decide whether the material should be disclosed or not.[66] The point has already been made that if the judge rules that the material should not be disclosed, it cannot be used in the subsequent proceedings. Nevertheless, the very fact that an ex parte application is made for PII in the absence of a party challenges the adversarial principle that both parties to the contest should participate in the proceedings. Once again, the ECtHR provided the springboard for the use of special advocates when it was argued in *Jasper v UK*

64 *Bank Mellat v HM Treasury (No 1)* [2013] UKSC 38, [2014] 1 AC 700 [70].

65 M Chamberlain, 'Update on Procedural Fairness in Closed Proceedings' (2009) 28 *Civil Justice Quarterly* 448, 452; M Chamberlain, 'Special Advocates and Amici Curiae in National Security Proceedings in the United Kingdom' (2018) 68 *University of Toronto Law Journal* 496, 508–10.

66 See eg *Conway v Rimmer* [1968] AC 910.

and *Fitt v UK* that special advocates should have been used in a criminal case where the defendants had notice of the PII application but were unable to view the material.[67] Although a bare majority of the Grand Chamber considered that the existing procedures satisfied Article 6 and that a special counsel procedure was not necessary,[68] a substantial minority considered that adequate compensatory measures for the lack of an adversarial procedure had not been put in place and strongly hinted that appointing special counsel to represent the interests of the defence in circumstances where neither the accused nor his legal advisors can be present may be a sufficient counterbalancing procedure.[69] The idea of using special counsel in ex parte proceedings was then enthusiastically championed by Auld LJ in his *Review of Criminal Courts* in 2001.[70] He envisaged that these counsel would make submissions, first of all, on the relevance of the undisclosed material if, and to the extent that, it had not been resolved in favour of disclosure by the judge; secondly, on the strength of the claim to public interest immunity; then, thirdly, on how helpful the material might be to the defence; and finally, generally to safeguard against the risk of judicial error or bias. In Auld LJ's view, special counsel would restore some adversarial testing of the issues hitherto absent in the determination of often critical and finely balanced PII applications.

The decision of the ECtHR in *Edwards and Lewis v UK*[71] increased the pressure for special advocates to be appointed still further when the ECtHR ruled that the ex parte PII procedure did not meet the requirements of Article 6 of the ECHR in two entrapment cases where the trial judge rejected the claims of entrapment after seeing undisclosed prosecution evidence in the course of the PII proceedings. The ECtHR distinguished this case from *Jasper*. In that case, the Court considered it decisive that, in finding no violation of Article 6, the material which was withheld from the defence and was found to be subject to PII formed no part of the prosecution case whatever and was never put to the jury. In the present cases, however, it was the judge, not the jury, who determined the substantive issue of entrapment, and the material that he had ruled should not be disclosed to the defence may nevertheless have been relevant to the issue. In one of the cases, it was revealed that the evidence produced to the trial judge in the ex parte hearings included material that suggested that the applicant had been involved in drug-dealing prior to the events that led to his arrest and prosecution. The defence were not informed of the content of this undisclosed evidence and were thus denied an opportunity to counter this allegation. In the other case, the nature of the undisclosed evidence was not revealed but the Court considered that it was possible that it too was damning to the defence. In these

67 *Jasper v UK* (2000) 30 EHRR 441; *Fitt v UK* (2000) 30 EHRR 480.

68 *Jasper v UK* (2000) 30 EHRR 441 [55]; *Fitt v UK* (2000) 30 EHRR 480 [48].

69 See the dissenting opinions of Judges Palm, Fischbach, Vajic, Thomassen, Tsatsa-Nikolovska and Traja in *Jasper* and *Fitt*.

70 Lord Justice Auld, *Review of the Criminal Courts of England and Wales* (Stationery Office 2001) ch 10 [191]–[97].

71 *Edwards and Lewis v UK* (2005) 40 EHRR 24.

circumstances, the Court did not consider that the procedure complied sufficiently with the requirements to provide adversarial proceedings and equality of arms with the result that there was a violation of Article 6.

The Court did not consider whether the appointment of a special advocate would provide a sufficient counterbalancing measure to fill the missing adversarial element, but it cited Auld LJ's recommendations on special counsel in some detail and this was a strong implication of the decision. The decision led the appellants in *R v H and C*[72] to argue that it was incompatible with Article 6 of the ECHR for a trial judge to rule on his own on a PII application where the undisclosed material may be relevant to any disputed issue of fact he has to decide. The Court of Appeal considered that the trial judge should invite the Attorney General to appoint special counsel in those few exceptional cases whether the material is so sensitive that the defence cannot be informed that a PII hearing is to take place or where the judge considers that the material is so highly prejudicial that he or she ought not to make a ruling without the benefit of further adversarial comment upon it.[73] On appeal, the House of Lords refused to place trial judges in this 'strait jacket' but nevertheless ruled that the appointment of special advocates may be necessary to ensure that the contentions of the prosecution are tested and the interests of the defendant protected in cases of 'exceptional difficulty'.[74] Earlier in his judgment, Lord Bingham accepted that there was as yet little express sanction for the appointment of a special advocate or special counsel to represent, as an advocate in PII matters, a defendant in an ordinary criminal trial, but 'novelty is not itself an objection'.[75] He mentioned a number of ethical problems which we will examine later and practical problems of delay, expense and of continuing review but ultimately concluded, in a passage that has been much cited in later cases where the courts have had to consider the appointment of special advocates, that:[76]

> None of these problems should deter the court from appointing special counsel where the interests of justice are shown to require it. But the need must be shown. Such an appointment will always be exceptional, never automatic; a course of last and never first resort. It should not be ordered unless and until the judge is satisfied that no other course will adequately meet the requirement of fairness to the defendant.

Although Lord Bingham's judgment was confined to criminal cases, this is a passage that has been much cited in other contexts where the question arises whether a special advocate should be appointed in the absence of statutory

72 *R v H and C* [2003] EWCA Crim 2847 (CA), [2004] UKHL 3, [2004] 2 AC 135 (HL).
73 *R v H and C* [2003] EWCA Crim 2847, [33](v).
74 [2004] UKHL 3, [2004] 2 AC 135 [33], [36].
75 ibid [22]. It is interesting to note that statutory provision has since been made for the appointment of special advocates in Scotland. See Criminal Justice and Licensing (Scotland) Act 2010, ss 151 and 152.
76 ibid.

authority for doing so.[77] Thus in *SSHD v AHK*,[78] the Court of Appeal accepted that it may also be permissible to appoint a special advocate in civil proceedings involving PII applications. This was an appeal against a judge's direction to appoint a special advocate to make submissions about whether there could be further disclosure to applicants who had been refused a detailed explanation of the Home Secretary's reasons for refusing them naturalisation. The Court of Appeal held that a special advocate should be appointed where it is just, and therefore necessary, to do so in order for the issues to be determined fairly. It is, for example, likely to be just where there may be 'significant issues and/or a significant number of documents', but the position may be different where there are 'very few documents and the judge can readily resolve the issues by reading them'.[79] All would depend upon the circumstances, but it was important to bear in mind the claimant's point of view and the difficulties facing the claimant in effectively challenging the case against him and whether the appointment of a special advocate might assist the claimant in meeting the Secretary of State's case and the court in arriving at a fair conclusion.[80] What is unclear from the judgment is whether the appointment of the special advocate was limited to assistance in PII applications or whether it also related to assistance in determining the merits of the case in a closed procedure where the judge had access to the closed material. In *Al Rawi*, Lord Dyson gave explicit approval to the use of special advocates in civil cases to '*enhance the PII process*' but appeared to question the assumption in *AHK* that the judge had the power to order a CMP to determine the merits of the case.[81] The Justice and Security Act now, of course, gives courts the power to order a CMP.

Beyond the area of PII applications, there are also other situations where Parliament has provided that closed procedures may be required and special advocates have been appointed in the absence of parliamentary authority to enhance the fairness of the proceedings. Specialist tribunals such as the Information Tribunal dealing with appeals from the Information Commissioner have agreed to the appointment of special advocates in closed proceedings.[82] But following *H and C*, the courts have tended to limit their request for appointment to cases where it is considered necessary in the interests of justice. In *Malik v Manchester Crown Court*,[83] for example, the Divisional Court considered whether the appointment of a special advocate was necessary in Crown Court proceedings where a production order had been made against an investigative journalist

77 See eg *Malik v Manchester Crown Court* [2008] EWHC 1362 (Admin); *Murungaru v SSHD* [2008] EWCA Civ 1015.

78 [2009] EWCA Civ 287.

79 ibid [37] iv) c).

80 ibid [37] iv) d).

81 *Al Rawi v The Security Service* [2011] UKSC 34, [2012] 1 AC 531 [49], [58] (emphasis in original).

82 See eg *CAAT v Information Commissioners and the Ministry of Defence* [2008] UKIT EA_2006_0040.

83 [2008] EWHC 1362 (Admin).

pursuant to Schedule 5 of the Terrorism Act 2000. Following *H and C*, the Court said that the court can request the appointment of a special advocate where the interests of justice require it; however, the need for such an appointment must be shown and such an appointment will be exceptional, never automatic, and a course of last resort. Factors to bear in mind included the seriousness of the issue the court had to determine; the fact that the entitlement to disclosure is not an absolute right; whether, even in a procedure which is entirely ex parte, the absent party is afforded a sufficient measure of procedural protection by the obligation on the party present to lay before the court material which undermines or qualifies his case or would assist the absent party; and whether the special advocate is likely to be able to further the absent party's case. The Court concluded that such an appointment was not necessary in the instant case, as the client could fully explain to the court how such an order would impact on him and he would not have been in a position to give the special advocate instructions on the issues which were affected by the closed material.

Another example of a closed hearing that may take place under the Terrorism Act 2000 is where the court is considering whether to extend a person's detention.[84] Closed hearings in these circumstances have been challenged on the ground that they are incompatible with the requirement for an adversarial hearing under Article 5(4) of the ECHR.[85] In *Duffy*,[86] the Northern Ireland High Court considered that in each case it was for the court to make a judgment about the extent of procedural protection required under Article 5 and referred to a range of tools available to it to do this, including in exceptional cases the appointment of a special advocate. In *Sher v UK*,[87] the ECtHR considered that Article 5(4) could not preclude the holding of a closed hearing to allow the court to consider confidential information provided the authorities disclose adequate information to enable the applicants to know the nature of the allegations against them. In this case, the applicants had been notified of the allegations against them in accordance with Schedule 8 to the Terrorism Act and had been given reasons for the withholding of certain information. The judge was able to ensure that no material had been unnecessarily withheld. Furthermore, the Terrorism Act did not preclude the appointment of a special advocate and the judge could have made such an appointment if it was necessary in the interests of justice. In the event, the applicants had not requested such an appointment. Although the applicants' claims failed, mention of the fact that they could have requested the appointment of a special advocate is likely to encourage defendants in future to make such requests, for example, where applications are made ex parte before

84 Terrorism Act 2000, sch 8 [33](2)(3).

85 Cf, however, *Ward v PSNI* [2007] UKHL 50, [2007] 1 WLR 3013 where there was no discussion of the compatibility of the provisions of sch 8 with art 5 ECHR.

86 *Re Duffy* [2011] NIQB 16 [35].

87 [2015] ECHR 920.

trial for search warrants or surveillance warrants.[88] Another situation where it has been deemed appropriate to have a special advocate appointed to represent the interests of the defendant is where an ex parte application is made for a witness anonymity order and it is necessary to test the criteria for the making of the Order.[89]

Finally, there are other situations where it has long been recognised that the public interest requires that it may be necessary to exclude parties from the proceedings. In *SSHD v MB*,[90] where the use of secret evidence in control order proceedings was being challenged, Lady Hale gave examples of cases concerning children and mental health patients. Where the whole object of the proceedings was to promote the best interests of a child, there may be exceptional circumstances in which disclosure of some of the evidence would be so detrimental to the child's welfare as to defeat the object of the exercise.[91] In recent years, the question has arisen whether special advocates should be involved when a local authority or the police (as parties) wish to withhold sensitive information in family cases. In *Re T (Wardship: Impact of Police Intelligence)*,[92] special advocates were appointed, possibly for the first time in family proceedings, to represent the interests of the father and grandparents of a child in a closed hearing where the police were resisting the disclosure of intelligence which pointed to the father having taken out a contract to have the mother murdered. The wardship court considered that it had a duty to investigate that allegation so as to inform any subsequent decision about the child's welfare, and it appointed special advocates to assist in the disclosure process which eventually led to the great bulk of the material for which PII was claimed being disclosed. In relation to that which remained undisclosed, the special advocates also conducted 'a process of cross-examination and submission designed to test the material and enable the court to see any weakness there may be in its evidential value'.[93]

In a later case, however, the President of the Family Division decided that special advocates were not required in a case where the court had to decide whether to set aside a Forced Marriage Protection Order and material was being withheld from the defendants.[94] Bearing in mind the strictures of Lord Bingham in *H and C* that the use of special advocates is a matter of last, as opposed to first, resort, Wall LJ considered that it should usually not be necessary in a forced

88 Cf *R (Haralambous) v Crown Court at St Albans* [2018] UKSC 1, [2018] AC 236.

89 *R v Mayers* [2008] EWCA Crim 2989, [2009] 1 WLR 1915. See Criminal Evidence (Witness Anonymity) Act 2008 re-enacted in Coroners and Justice Act 2009, ss 86–96. AG's Guidelines refer to their appointment on an exceptional basis: see AGO,*Guidelines on the Prosecutor's Role in applications for Witness Anonymity Orders: Criminal Evidence) Witness Anonymity) Act 2008* (2012).

90 [2007] UKHL 46, [2008] 1 AC 440 [58].

91 ibid. See *Re D (Minors)(Adoption Reports: Confidentiality)* [1996] AC 593.

92 [2009] EWHC 2440 (Fam).

93 ibid [30].

94 *Chief Constable and A v YK, RB, ZS, SI, AK and MH* [2010] EWCA Fam 2438.

marriage case for a special advocate to assist on issues of disclosure. There had to be something a special advocate could do which cannot properly be done by the judge. He also considered that special advocates were not needed to help resolve any issues of fact which may arise on the closed evidence. The judge did not, however, rule out the need for special advocates in certain family proceedings. In a later case in which a blanket ban on the disclosure of confidential information was imposed in care proceedings, it was considered that in order to fully protect their rights under Articles 6 and 8 of the ECHR, there was a need for a special advocate to represent the interests of the parents in relation to continuing and future disclosure and in the testing of the closed evidence at the subsequent trial.[95] It would seem clear that, although no provision has yet been made for making a declaration under section 6 of the Justice and Security Act in respect of proceedings in family courts,[96] special advocates have now become an established feature in such proceedings, albeit in exceptional cases. Guidance issued by the President of the Family Division states that special advocates are usually appointed because a public body that is party to litigation, often a local authority or the police, resist disclosure of sensitive documents.[97] A special need must be identified and the Court should determine which party shall pay the costs of the special advocate.[98]

In this second category of cases where special advocates have been appointed in the absence of express statutory authority, it is considered that they are necessary to *enhance* procedural fairness in situations where closed procedures have already been established either under statute or as a result of a well-established public interest. There remain questions to be asked as to whether the appointment of special advocates even in such circumstances does *enough* to ensure procedural fairness where rights under the ECHR are engaged and we will return to this. But at least in these cases, special advocates are being appointed to enhance, not reduce, procedural fairness. More controversial have been cases which we have characterised as coming within a third category, which is where special advocates are appointed in situations where courts or tribunals take it upon themselves to *reduce* procedural rights by ordering a CMP and requesting the appointment of a special advocate without express parliamentary approval. This was exactly what a majority of the UK Supreme Court in *Al Rawi* considered they could not

95 *BCC v FZ* [2012] EWHC 1154 (Fam).

96 In particular, CPR Pt 82 does not apply to family proceedings and CPR Pt 82 is not otherwise incorporated into the FPR 2010. See *Commissioner of the Police of the Metropolis v A Local Authority* [2016] EWHC 2400 (Fam) [92]–[93].

97 See President of the Family Division, *The Role of the Attorney General in Appointing Advocates to the Court or Special Advocates in Family Cases* 26 March 2015. See also President of the Family Division, *Radicalisation Cases in the Family Courts* 8 October 2015.

98 See *Re R (Closed Material Procedure: Special Advocates Funding)* [2017] EWHC 1793 (Fam) where the court ruled that the police should be required to fund the special advocate as they were the owners of the closed material who wished to ensure that the court saw it in a closed session procedure.

do in conventional civil litigation. However, in the Court of Appeal, a distinction was made between an ordinary civil claim where the judge is sitting as an 'arbiter' between the parties (sometimes called a 'lis inter partes') and other civil proceedings involving a 'substantial public interest', where the courts may have more leeway to order a CMP.[99] In *Roberts v Parole Board*,[100] the House of Lords was seriously split over whether the Parole Board was within its powers to withhold material relevant to the appellant's parole review in order to protect the safety of the source of the material and instead deploy a special advocate to represent the interests of the prisoner. We have seen that parliamentary approval was expressly given to the Northern Irish bodies to do this, but although there were rules permitting the English and Welsh Parole Board to direct that material be withheld from the prisoner and his legal representative,[101] there was nothing that expressly gave approval for the Board to make a decision adverse to the prisoner without disclosing the case against him.

Their lordships spoke of a triangulation of interests to be balanced: the Board's ultimate purpose to protect the public, the prisoner's interest in fairness, and the human rights interests of the informants who provided information.[102] The disagreement was a reflection of how these interests were to be balanced; the majority taking the view that the interests of the public and the human rights of the informant had to prevail over those of the appellant, such that the Board had the power to invoke the special advocate procedure.[103] Lords Bingham and Steyn disagreed, with Lord Steyn expressing in strong terms the view that the special advocate procedure struck at the root of the prisoner's right to a basically fair procedure and that if such departures were to be introduced, it must be done by Parliament.[104] Even assuming the Board had the power to invoke the special advocate procedure, there remained a second question, which was whether, if the hearing went ahead as planned, the procedure met the requirements of Article 5(4) of the ECHR which requires that reviews of detention be decided by a court meeting 'to the largest extent possible the basic requirements of a fair trial'.[105] The majority of the Law Lords took the view that it was premature to rule on the fairness of the procedure until the case in hand had been heard and it could not be said in advance that the outcome was unfair, but there seemed to be a consensus that there may well be cases where the procedures would not be sufficiently

99 *Al Rawi v The Security Service* [2010] EWCA Civ 482 [67] (Lord Neuberger MR). Note though that in the Supreme Court Lord Clarke questioned this distinction, considering there was no principled basis for distinguishing between ordinary civil claims and others. See *Al Rawi v The Security Service* [2011] UKSC 34, [2012] 1 AC 531 [166]–[69].

100 [2005] UKHL 45, [2005] 2 AC 738.

101 See Parole Board Rules 2004, r 6(3).

102 See Jackson (n 14).

103 The Parole Board Rules now make express provision for the appointment of a special advocate. See Parole Board Rules 2016, r 8(6)(d).

104 [2005] UKHL 45, [2005] 2 AC 738 [93].

105 See *Garcia Alva v Germany* (2003) 37 EHRR 12 [39].

fair. This takes us back to the question whether there are circumstances where the use of special advocates may not adequately satisfy human rights law.

Special advocates and human rights law

We have already seen that notwithstanding the erosion of basic principles of open and natural justice involved in special advocate procedures, the ECtHR did much to encourage them with its implicit endorsement of such procedures as providing a substantial measure of procedural fairness in *Chahal*, *Tinnelly* etc.[106] The decisions of the ECtHR have had an influential bearing on domestic human rights challenges in the UK to the use of CMPs and special advocates, as the domestic courts have recognised the ECtHR as the authoritative source of the ECHR's correct interpretation.[107] Thus in 2009, the House of Lords unanimously held that SIAC's use of closed procedures and special advocates in considering the deportation of three men on the ground that each was a danger to national security was compatible with the ECHR.[108] Unlike *Chahal*, in this case the appellants whom the Secretary of State wished to deport were on bail, so no question arose as to whether their rights under Article 5 were engaged. A majority of the Law Lords followed the ECtHR in holding that deportation proceedings do not engage Article 6 and so there was no requirement to disclose evidence to the appellant where this was considered contrary to the public interest.[109] The one Law Lord who considered that Article 6 might apply considered that the SIAC rules struck a fair balance between the public interest and the need for a fair hearing.[110] Reliance was placed upon the fact that the rules made provision for the special advocate to draw SIAC's attention to shortcomings in the evidence and invite the Commission to call for additional evidence.[111] As an 'expert' Tribunal, SIAC could be expected to make a realistic appraisal of the closed material in the light of the special advocate's submissions.

In *SSHD v MB*,[112] where the appellants challenged control orders made by the Secretary of State under the Prevention of Terrorism Act 2005, the Law Lords accepted that control orders affected civil rights and that Article 6 was engaged in the proceedings, but they did not consider that they amounted to a criminal

106 See also *Al-Nashif v Bulgaria* (2003) 36 EHRR 37 [97].
107 *R (Ullah) v Special Adjudicator* [2004] UKHL 26, [2004] 2 AC 323 [20] (Lord Bingham).
108 *RB (Algeria) v SSHD* [2009] UKHL 10, [2009] 2 AC 110.
109 See *Maaouia v France* (2000) 33 EHRR 1037 [35] holding that the decision whether or not to authorise an alien to stay in a country of which he is not a national does not entail any determination of his civil rights.
110 *RB (Algeria) v SSHD* [2009] UKHL 10, [2009] 2 AC 110 [103] (Lord Phillips).
111 ibid [104].
112 [2007] UKHL 46, [2008] 1 AC 440.

charge.[113] A starting point even when Article 6 is engaged whether in the civil or criminal context, however, was that the entitlement to disclosure of relevant evidence is not an absolute right. Even in a criminal case, the ECtHR has said that there may be competing interests, such as national security or the need to protect witnesses at risk of reprisals or keep secret police methods of investigation of crime, which must be weighed against the rights of the accused, although there will not be a fair trial unless any difficulties caused to the defendant are sufficiently counterbalanced by the procedures that are followed by the judicial authorities. Most of the Law Lords appeared to accept that the appointment of a special advocate would usually provide a sufficient safeguard even where controlees (the persons subject to control orders) were unable to see much of the evidence against them. But with the exception of Lord Hoffmann, who agreed with the Court of Appeal that in principle the special advocate process provided sufficient safeguards to satisfy Article 6, they followed *Roberts* in considering that it would not *always* provide a fair trial. Lord Bingham was the most specific in indicating when it would not do so. He contrasted the ordinary case where a client will brief his advocate on how to meet the case against him with the special advocate case where the client does not know the case against him and the special advocate who does know what it is cannot seek instructions without the Court's permission, which is rarely given. In *Roberts*, Lord Woolf had accepted the applicant's argument that there was a 'core, irreducible, minimum entitlement' for him to be able effectively to test and challenge any evidence which decisively bore on the legality of his detention. Lord Bingham said that he did not see how the requirements of procedural fairness would be met if a person entitled to a fair hearing, in a situation where an adverse decision could have severe consequences, were denied such knowledge, in whatever form, of what was said against him as was necessary to enable him, with or without a special advocate, effectively to challenge or rebut the case against him.

It was this test that the ECtHR developed when it issued its landmark decision in *A v UK*[114] on whether the closed procedures that SIAC had operated in the appeals of those who had been detained indefinitely under the Anti-Terrorism, Crime and Security Act 2001 were compatible with the ECHR. Remarkably, despite numerous references to the special advocate system, this was the first occasion when the ECtHR had to decide explicitly whether to endorse a special advocate system that had been put into effect. The Court took as its starting point that there was an urgent need to protect the population of the UK from terrorist attack, to obtain information about Al-Qaeda and to maintain the secrecy of the sources of such information. However, balanced against these public interests was the applicants' right to procedural fairness and in view of the dramatic impact of

113 Lord Bingham saw great force in the argument that non-derogating control orders must in substance constitute a criminal charge given that any past or present terrorism-rated activity is likely to be criminal, but accepted that such orders were preventive in purpose and not punitive or retributive. ibid [19]–[24].

114 *A v UK* (2009) 49 EHRR 29.

the lengthy deprivation of liberty on the applicants' fundamental rights, Article 5(4) of the ECHR must import 'substantially the same fair trial guarantees as Article 6 (1) in its criminal aspect'.[115] This meant that as much information about the allegations and evidence against each applicant must be disclosed as was possible without compromising national security. As regards the special advocate procedure, the Court considered the two major roles that special advocates can play in closed procedures: the disclosure role and the substantive representation role. In relation to the former, it considered that the special advocate could provide an important additional safeguard through questioning the State's witnesses on the need for secrecy and through making submissions to the judge regarding the case for additional disclosure.[116] The Court further considered that the special advocate could perform an important role in counterbalancing the lack of a full, open adversarial hearing by testing the evidence and putting arguments on behalf of the detainee during the closed hearings. It then, however, laid down a principle of minimal disclosure by adding that 'the special advocate could not perform this function in any useful way unless the detainee was provided with sufficient information about the allegations against him to enable him to give effective instructions to the special advocate'.[117] The Court went on to clarify how this principle was to be applied:[118]

> While this question must be decided on a case-by-case basis, the Court observes generally that, where the evidence was to a large extent disclosed and the open material played the predominant role in the determination, it could not be said that the applicant was denied an opportunity effectively to challenge the reasonableness of the Secretary of State's belief and suspicions about him. In other cases, even where all or most of the underlying evidence remained undisclosed, if the allegations contained in the open material were sufficiently specific, it should have been possible for the applicant to provide his representatives and the special advocate with information with which to refute them, if such information existed, without his having to know the detail or sources of the evidence which formed the basis of the allegations. … Where, however, the open material consisted purely of general assertions and SIAC's decision to uphold the certification and maintain the detention was based solely or to a decisive degree on closed material, the procedural requirements of Article 5(4) would not be satisfied.

We shall consider later how easy it is to apply this principle of minimal disclosure, which has become known as *A*-type disclosure.[119] At one level, this

115 ibid [217].
116 ibid [219].
117 ibid [220].
118 ibid.
119 *Home Office v Tariq* [2011] UKSC 35, [2012] 1 AC 452 [88] (Lord Brown). See further Chapter 8 of this book.

important qualification to the special advocate procedures may be seen as a welcome affirmation of due process principles, setting minimal disclosure as a 'baseline' requirement and stressing the importance of giving the subject a basis on which to meet the allegations against him. But the judgment was very case-specific in its reference to this standard of disclosure and appeared to send out two signals which have arguably done much to entrench the special advocate system as being capable of guaranteeing sufficient fairness across a wide spectrum of closed judicial proceedings. First of all, in cases like *Chahal*, the ECtHR seemed to suggest that special advocates could be used as a technique to raise the level of procedural protection up to a standard that had hitherto been lacking. But in *A v UK*, the ECtHR seemed to be endorsing their use, albeit conditioned on minimal disclosure, as a counterbalancing measure to *lower* the level of procedural protection below that which had been previously guaranteed to those subjected to lengthy deprivation of liberty, namely a right to be given full disclosure of the case against them. Secondly, the fact that the ECtHR was highlighting that the special advocate system needed to be buttressed with at least a minimal level of disclosure to those entitled to substantially the same fair trial guarantees as Article 6 in its criminal aspect suggested that the special advocate system alone, without the minimal disclosure standard, might be an adequate safeguard for other closed judicial procedures that do not carry the same or similar consequences as criminal trials.[120] Rather than making minimal disclosure to the individual the bedrock counterbalancing measure of any closed procedure, the special advocate system seemed to become the bedrock counterbalancing procedure and the only remaining issue then was whether a minimal disclosure standard was also necessary in order to satisfy Article 5(4) or Article 6.

This was indeed exactly the issue that came to the forefront in domestic UK law after *A v UK* was decided.[121] Although the decision in *MB* clearly indicated that the domestic courts had already accepted that the special advocate procedure could be compatible with Article 6, the ECtHR appeared to put this beyond doubt and the jurisprudence shifted towards the question whether *A*-type disclosure was additionally required in Article 6 proceedings, assuming CMPs and special advocates could be used. The first evidence of this new approach was seen soon after *A* was decided in *Secretary of State for the Home Department v AF*,[122] where in the light of the decision in *A v UK*, the Law Lords had to decide whether *A*-type disclosure applied in control order cases. It is a measure of the respect with which the House of Lords regarded rulings from the Grand Chamber of the ECtHR that none of their Lordships – even Lord Hoffmann who went so far as to say that the decision in *A* was wrong – contemplated refusing to

120 E Nanopoulos, 'European Human Rights Law and the Normalisation of the "Closed Material procedure": Limit or Source?' (2015) 78 MLR 913, 926.

121 For further discussion see J Jackson, 'Justice, Security and the Right to a Fair Trial: Is the Use of Secret Evidence Ever Fair?' [2013] PL 720.

122 *SSHD v AF* [2009] UKHL 28, [2010] 2 AC 269.

follow it. Counsel for the Secretary of State argued that account could be taken of the fact that control orders are less severe than lengthy detention, but their lordships did not think there was room for such a distinction and it was held that the controlled person must be given sufficient information about the allegations against him to give effective instructions to the special advocate. That was the 'bottom line, or the core irreducible minimum … that cannot be shifted'.[123]

The Law Lords in *AF* were not required to consider whether *A*-type disclosure was necessary in other civil proceedings that are subject to the fair trial guarantees of Article 6. It was pointed out that the Grand Chamber in *A* had made it clear that non-disclosure cannot go so far as to deny a party knowledge of the essence of the case against him, at least where he is at risk of consequences as severe as those normally imposed under a control order. The Court of Appeal subsequently held that financial restrictions imposed on UK financial institutions prohibiting them from dealing with Bank Mellat, an Iranian-based bank, affected the bank's civil rights and that *A*-type disclosure applied to this case.[124] But what about other cases where the consequences may not be as severe? This issue came to a head in *Home Office v Tariq*[125] where the respondent had alleged unlawful discrimination against the Home Office for withdrawing his security clearance. The UKSC was required to decide two issues. The first issue was whether the CMP provided for in the legislative scheme of the Employment Tribunal was in principle compatible with Article 6 of the ECHR and with EU law which was relevant in the case because the UK had given effect to an EU Directive on employment equality which implemented the principle of equal treatment in employment and occupation. The second issue was whether Article 6 required that in a civil case, such as the respondent's, *A* or *AF*-type disclosure or 'gisting', as it is also sometimes called, was required. Not surprisingly, given the previous experience of CMPs involving special advocates, the justices had little difficulty dealing with the first issue and unanimously held that the rules providing for a CMP struck the right balance between justice and security.[126] Particular attention was given to the counterbalancing effects of scrutiny by an independent court and the testing of closed material by a special advocate.[127] Lord Mance considered a number of concerns about special advocates raised by Mr Tariq's counsel relating to their role, powers and lack of supervision, which we will examine in detail later in Chapter 5, but ultimately concluded that these concerns were unfounded and not such as to render the whole CMP unfair.[128]

The justices therefore concluded unanimously that the holding of a CMP with provision for the appointment of special advocates was compatible with

123 ibid [81] (Lord Hope).
124 *Bank Mellat v HM Treasury* [2010] EWCA Civ 483.
125 *Tariq v Home Office* [2011] UKSC 35, [2012] 1 AC 452.
126 Lord Hope said that he found 'the second issue more troublesome than the first' ibid [77].
127 ibid [142] (Lord Dyson) and [78] (Lord Hope).
128 ibid [42]–[59].

Article 6 and EU law. The second issue, however, proved more difficult to determine. A majority of their lordships (by 8 to 1) disagreed with the Court of Appeal which had held that in all circumstances in which Article 6 in its civil dimension was engaged, *AF* gisting was required. A number stressed the different context of this case from *A* and *AF* where the fundamental rights of the individual were being severely challenged.[129] Reference was made to the second *Kadi* decision[130] where the General Court of the EU stressed that the applicant had not been given even the most minimal access to the evidence against him when he was given a brief narrative summary as to why he had been listed under the United Nations Security Council's sanctions system. But in Lord Mance's words, 'detention, control orders and freezing orders impinge directly on personal freedom and liberty in a way to which Mr Tariq could not be said to be exposed'.[131] His lordship also referred to the reasoning in *R (AHK) v SSHD (Practice Note)*[132] where the Court of Appeal distinguished detention cases such as *A v UK* from a refusal to grant British citizenship on the ground that in the former case the consequences are much more serious.[133] In his dissenting judgment, however, Lord Kerr queried why if *A*-type disclosure applied in challenges to freezing orders, it should not extend to property cases more generally and why then property rights should be distinguished from employment rights, as loss of livelihood may be just as devastating as having one's assets frozen.[134] This suggests that it is not easy to draw a bright line on the question whether an individual's personal freedom is affected. Apart from the stakes for the individual affected, another factor mentioned that is relevant in this context is the consequence of *A*-type disclosure for national security. Lord Dyson, for example, examined a number of ECtHR decisions which he said supported the proposition that in surveillance and security vetting cases an individual is not entitled to full Article 6 rights if to accord him such rights would 'jeopardise the efficacy of the surveillance or security vetting regime itself'.[135]

The decision in *Tariq* that where closed procedures are authorised under statute, there is no absolute rule that whenever Article 6 in its civil aspect is engaged there must be *A*-type disclosure only served to open up more argument as to when this type of disclosure would be required. The position is complicated by the fact that there may also be rights which arise under EU law which do not involve civil rights and obligations under Article 6 of the ECHR but which are subject to the fair trial guarantees of Article 47 of the Charter of Fundamental Rights of the EU.[136] It would seem, however, that in all respects other than scope, the guarantees in Article 47 of the Charter apply in the same way as Article 6 of

129 ibid [27] (Lord Mance), [81] (Lord Hope), [88] (Lord Brown), [144] (Lord Dyson).
130 *Kadi v Commission of the EU* Case T-85/09 [2011] 1 CMLR 697.
131 [2011] UKSC 35, [2012] 1 AC 452 [27].
132 [2009] EWCA Civ 287, [2009] 1 WLR 2049.
133 [2011] UKSC 35, [2012] 1 AC 452 [27].
134 ibid [133].
135 ibid [158]. See eg *Kennedy v UK* (2011) 52 EHRR 4.
136 OJ (2012 C326/02).

the ECHR.[137] In *ZZ (France) v SSHD*,[138] the CJEU endorsed a test very similar to *A*-type disclosure where it had to rule on the extent of disclosure that should be given in a case where SIAC had ruled that an EU national should be denied entry into the UK. The Court ruled that where state security stands in the way of communicating the full grounds on which the decision was based, the parties concerned must at least be informed of the 'essence' of the basis for refusing entry, a decision that was later endorsed by the English Court of Appeal.[139]

It would seem in the cases since *Tariq* which are governed by either Article 6 of the ECHR or Article 47 of the EU Charter that there is a spectrum rather than a hierarchy of disclosure.[140] *A* or *AF*-type disclosure or the disclosure rendered in *ZZ* is reserved for cases which concern what have been called 'objectively high level rights', such as liberty, or the most important rights conferred upon EU citizens, such as free movement.[141] So *A*-type disclosure is necessary in decisions to revoke or deny bail or apply restrictive bail conditions to aliens pending a determination of their immigration status.[142] It has also been accepted that in parole cases in Northern Ireland where a person's liberty is at stake, the affected prisoner must be given *A*-type disclosure of the case against her.[143] For cases which are not at this end of the spectrum, which may include civil claims or judicial reviews where a declaration is sought for a CMP under the Justice and Security Act, there would seem to be a sliding scale of disclosure which can range from simply giving the applicant an outline of the grounds against her (as in one case where a Syrian national in the UK was refused a travel document[144]) to cases such as *Tariq* where something more than this but less than the gist or essence of the grounds may be required.[145] In *R (Haralambous) v Crown Court at St Albans*, the Supreme Court held that the issue of a search warrant authorising a search of premises and seizure of documents involved merely a 'short-term invasion of property' and any

137 *Explanations relating to the Charter of Fundamental Rights*,OJ (2007 C303/02) cited in *Kiani v SSHD* [2015] EWCA Civ 776 [17].
138 *ZZ (France) v SSHD* (Case C-300/11) [2013] QB 1136.
139 *ZZ (France)* v *SSHD* [2014] EWCA Civ 7. See also *MR v SSHD* [2016] EWHC 1622 (Admin), 3 CMLR 42 (concerning revocation of an individual's passport).
140 See eg *Kiani v SSHD* [2015] EWCA Civ 776, *AZ (Syria) v SSHD* [2017] EWCA Civ 35, *K, A and B v Secretary of State for Defence* [2017] EWHC 830 (Admin).
141 *AZ v SSHD* [2017] EWCA Civ 35 [29]–[30] (Burnett LJ).
142 *R (CART) v Upper Tribunal, R (U) v SIAC* [2009] EWHC 3052. See also *R (BB) v SIAC* [2011] EWHC 336 (Admin).
143 See eg *Re Corey* [2012] NIQB 56, [2012] NICA 57. In *Brady v UK* App no 37536/08 (ECtHR 22 May 2012) the applicant challenged the Sentence Review Commissioners' decision to determine the case on damaging information which was not disclosed to the prisoner. In settling the case, the UK government made a unilateral declaration accepting that, having regard to *A v UK*, it is generally necessary for a prisoner to be provided with sufficient information to enable a special advocate to be given effective instructions.
144 *AZ (Syria) v SSHD* [2017] EWCA Civ 35.
145 See also *Kiani v SSHD* [2015] EWCA Civ 776; *K, A and B v Secretary of State for Defence* [2017] EWHC 830 (Admin).

gist of relevant information did not need to be supplied to any person claiming to be affected by the warrant.[146]

Of course, to complicate things further, there are also a number of other cases which do not engage Article 6 ECHR or Article 47 EU Charter rights at all, such as the deportation of aliens.[147] In these cases if the disclosure of information is contrary to the interests of national security in any respect, that determines the issue. But for the cases where these rights are engaged, it would seem there is a balance to be struck between the significance of the material from the claimant's point of view in terms of meeting the case against him or making his case, and the effect of disclosure on the interests of national security. It appears that the fact that a special advocate is available is itself part of the calculus used to determine where the balance should be struck. In a number of cases, emphasis has been put on whether the special advocate can test the material without needing to take instructions from the applicant on it. Thus in *Tariq*, it was said that there was real scope for the special advocate to test the issue of discrimination without obtaining instructions on the facts from the claimant. In a later case, claimants brought actions against the UK government for failing to protect them sufficiently when they were allegedly acting as covert human intelligence sources for the UK in Afghanistan.[148] One of the core claims was that there was or should have been a policy for the protection, relocation and compensation of such agents, but it was considered that these were issues on which the instructions of the claimants were irrelevant because the special advocates could handle them without the need for any disclosure to the claimants. The special advocate's role thus becomes pivotal to what disclosure will be ordered and central to what disclosure the claimant will get. Exactly what the special advocate can do in the closed procedures to test the material becomes a vital part of the equation in considering whether the limitation on the individual's general entitlement to full disclosure of relevant evidence under Article 6 is effectively counterbalanced. Once again, we see the special advocate system satisfying human rights demands for disclosure that in its absence could not be otherwise met, with the consequence that the government would be put to its election whether to defend the case giving full disclosure of all relevant evidence or not to defend the case at all. The system would seem to serve as the linchpin in the balance between national security and adequate disclosure, satisfying human rights demands and instrumental in permitting national security cases to run at all.

UK caseload

In the UK, we have seen a rise in the types of cases in which closed procedures and special advocates may be deployed both within and beyond the national

146 *R (Haralambous) v Crown Court at St Albans* [2018] UKSC 1 [64], [2018] AC 236.
147 *RB (Algeria) v SSHD* [2009] UKHL 10, [2010] 2 AC 110.
148 *K, A and B v Secretary of State for Defence* [2017] EWHC 830 (Admin).

security context without being imperilled by human rights law, provided some disclosure is made to the absent party which is proportionate to the interests at stake. We began this chapter by referring to the government's claim that in many of 21 different contexts in which CMPs and special advocates were able to be used, they were in fact used only on rare occasions and in some cases not at all.[149] That was before the enactment of the Justice and Security Act 2013 which has broadened the scope of CMPs to include all types of civil proceedings. It is important therefore to get a picture of the overall numbers of cases involving special advocates and of the types of cases in which special advocates have actually appeared. In response to a Freedom of Information request, the Special Advocate Support Office (SASO) which, as we shall see in Chapter 5, provides support for special advocates has provided figures for the number of cases that it opened in the calendar years 2010 until 2014. Table 3.1 shows the number of cases opened during this period and also the number of cases opened from January 2015 until April 2018 provided to the author.[150] It can be seen that although there appears to have been a dip in the numbers of cases involving special advocates in 2013 and 2014, the numbers in recent years have risen again and have indeed exceeded the numbers in 2010–12.

SASO did not compile a breakdown of the types of cases involving special advocates until April 2015. Table 3.2 shows the kinds of cases that it opened from April 2015 until the end of March 2018. The rise in cases using special advocates during these years would seem to be attributable mainly to the large number of naturalisation cases which we have seen were transferred from the High Court to SIAC under the Justice and Security Act and the number of private damage claims against the government in England and Wales and Northern Ireland which the government has sought to defend by applying for CMPs under

Table 3.1 Number of special advocate cases opened (2010–18)

2010	38
2011	25
2012	28
2013	14
2014	23
January–April 2015	8
April 2015–March 2016	68
April 2016–March 2017	54
April 2017–March 2018	44

Source: SASO.

149 JCHR (n 1).
150 From 2015 SASO began to collate numbers on a cycle from April to March rather than on the basis of a calendar year.

Table 3.2 Types of special advocate cases opened (April 2015–March 2018)

	April 2015–March 2016	*April 2016–March 2017*	*April 2017–March 2018*
Proscribed organisation	1		
Exclusion		1	3
Naturalisation	49	9	2
Deportation	1	1	
Deprivation of citizenship/ settled status		4	19
Travel documents	1		
Passport revocation		1	2
Refusal of citizenship			1
Asset freezing/sanctions	1	1	
Financial restriction		3	
Private law damages	2 (+3 NI)	7 (+7 NI)	3 (+7 NI)
Control order/TPIMs	2	6	2
Other judicial review		4	4
Vetting	1	3	
Employment	2	3	
Care/family proceedings	2	4	1
Parole	3		
Total	68	54	44

Source: SASO.

the 2013 Act. It is too early to predict what effect this Act will have in the longer term and whether the surge in private damage claims where applications are made for CMPs will continue. Even if we take these cases and naturalisation cases out of the equation, there is still over the three years a sufficient flow of different types of cases (14 in 2015–16, 36 in 2016–17 and 32 in 2017–18) to justify the conclusion that there is not only a potential for special advocates to be used widely, but that they are actually being used across a broad spectrum of cases.

Finally, Table 3.3 below shows the courts and tribunals in which these cases were heard. Although it can be seen that special advocates have migrated from their original use in SIAC into many other kinds of judicial proceedings, the majority of cases involving special advocates (54%) continues to be heard in SIAC.

On top of these cases, it should be noted that SASO does not provide support to special counsel who are appointed to act in the interests of defendants in criminal cases. Figures provided to the author by the Attorney General's Office reveal that from the beginning of 2014 until the end of 2016, special counsel were appointed in only two cases, one a criminal appeal and one a trial.[151] It would

151 Email communication from Attorney General's Office to the author, 5 April 2017.

Table 3.3 Courts/tribunals in which special advocates appeared (April 2015–March 2018)

SIAC	90
High Court	20 (+17 NI)
Administrative Court	19
Family Court	7
POAC	1
SVAP	4
Employment Tribunal	5
Parole Commissioners	3
Total	166

Source: SASO.

seem that judges in these cases are adhering strongly to Lord Bingham's admonition that judges' use of special advocates should be very exceptional. This is also borne out by considering that the vast majority of cases opened by SASO from 2015 to 2018 were cases where statutory provision is made for special advocates. In this sense, they remain largely a statutory innovation and, although their use has been endorsed by human rights law, as we have seen in *Al Rawi*, there has been little enthusiasm for embedding them into the heart of the common law. This raises questions about their long term future, to which we will return at the end in Chapter 11. For now, however, we must take up the story of their development beyond the shores of the UK and consider what use has been made of them in other countries.

4 Migration beyond the UK

In this chapter we examine the way in which the special advocate system that has developed in the UK has been exported to other Commonwealth countries and what consideration has been given to them on the European continent and within the international criminal tribunals. It is not perhaps so surprising that special advocates have migrated beyond the UK. First of all, as we have seen, the ECtHR has given its blessing to the system, provided it is combined with an appropriate level of disclosure to the excluded party commensurate with the interests at stake. Although the ECtHR's jurisdiction is limited, of course, to Europe, as the most developed human rights court across the globe it has proved immensely successful in influencing the direction of human rights law in other domestic and international jurisdictions as well.[1] Secondly, the fact that special advocates originated in the UK is in itself significant, as the UK has long exported national security and anti-terrorist laws particularly to Commonwealth countries.[2] The spread of the special advocate system to Canada, New Zealand, Hong Kong and Australia may be seen as yet another example of this phenomenon.

Canada

It is convenient to start with Canada as Canada has to date gone further than any other country outside the UK to develop a special advocate system. At first glance, however, it is perhaps surprising that the UK special advocate system should have been imported into Canada, for as we have seen, Canada had

1 See C McCrudden, 'The Pluralism of Human Rights Adjudication' in L Lazarus, C McCrudden and N Bowles (eds), *Reasoning Rights: Comparative Judicial Engagement* (OUP 2014) 3, 7 stating that the ECtHR is 'clearly influential beyond Europe in the development of the interpretation of international human rights law'.

2 See eg K Roach, 'The post 9/11 Migration of Britain's Terrorism Act 2000' in S Choudhry (ed), *The Migration of Constitutional Ideas* (CUP 2006) 374; K Roach, 'Sources and Trends in Post 9/11 Anti-terrorism Laws' in B Goold and L Lazarus (eds), *Security and Human Rights* (OUP 2007) 228. Kent gives as examples the UK's broad definition of terrorism in the Terrorism Act 2000, offences against terrorist speech, control orders and extended periods of preventive arrest.

already developed its own system of security-cleared counsel before the Security Intelligence Review Committee (SIRC) which was distinctive from the special advocate system developed in the UK.[3] It will be recalled that under this system, counsel were appointed by SIRC to assist the Committee in its conduct of the proceedings. Part of this assistance involved probing the government's position and furthering the interests of permanent residents or 'named persons' whom the government wished to exclude from Canada on security grounds. As counsel to the Committee, however, they were in a different position from UK special advocates whose *sole* function is to represent the interests of excluded parties. Any representational role that SIRC counsel undertook, on the other hand, was subservient to their role of assisting the Committee in the discovery of the truth.[4] As a consequence of their position, they were given full access to the intelligence files on the named persons and could communicate with them and their counsel throughout the process, even after they had access to the secret file.

Whatever its merit as a model for dealing with national security information in immigration cases and its potential for use in other cases, however, SIRC's role in immigration proceedings, along with its use of security-cleared lawyers, was abolished in 2002 by the Immigration and Refugee Protection Act 2001 (IRPA) and replaced instead by the process that had been used by the Federal Court to review security certificates issued against nonresident foreign nationals. This system reduced the procedural protections available to resident aliens in a number of respects, most importantly depriving them of a counsel who could actively argue for greater disclosure to them, advance arguments on their behalf and cross-examine government witnesses. Instead, judges were left to consider the security evidence alone in ex parte in camera hearings, forced to play the 'double role' of impartial decision-maker, while at the same time assuming adversarial responsibilities of probing the evidence as best they could without any input from the named person.[5]

In a landmark judgment in *Charkaoui v Canada*,[6] the Supreme Court unanimously held that the security certificate procedure adopted by the Federal Court unjustifiably violated section 7 of the Canadian Charter of Rights and Freedoms which guarantees the right to life, liberty and security of the person, and the right not to be deprived thereof except in accordance with the principles of fundamental justice. The Court held that while the deportation of a non-national in the immigration context may not in itself engage section 7, features associated with deportation such as detention in the course of the certificate process or the prospect of deportation to torture could do so. According to the Court, the principle

3 See Chapter 2.

4 G Hudson and D Alati, 'Behind Closed Doors: Secret Law and the Special Advocate System in Canada' (2018) 44 *Queen's Law Journal* 1, 28.

5 C Forcese and L Waldman, *Seeking Justice in an Unfair Process* (University of Ottawa 2007) 12.

6 *Charkaoui v Canada (Citizenship and Immigration)* 2007 SCC 9, [2007] 1 SCR 350.

of 'fundamental justice' has a number of facets. It comprises the right to a hearing and requires:

> that the hearing be *before an independent and impartial magistrate*. It demands a *decision by the magistrate on the facts and the law*. And it entails *the right to know the case put against one*, and *the right to answer that case*.[7]

The Court held that the latter two conditions were not satisfied in this case. Although the judges adopted a '*pseudo*-inquisitorial role and sought seriously to test the protected documentation and information', they had no power to independently investigate the facts in the manner of 'true inquisitorial judges' and were 'not in a position to compensate for the lack of informed scrutiny, challenge and counter-evidence that a person familiar with the case could bring'.[8] Such scrutiny was the whole point of the principle that a person whose liberty is in jeopardy must know the case to meet. The fairness of the procedure rested entirely on the shoulders of the designated judge but:

> Those shoulders cannot by themselves bear the burden of assuring, in fact and appearance, that the decision on the reasonableness of the certificate is impartial, is based on a full view of the facts and law, and reflects the named person's knowledge of the case to meet.[9]

The Court acknowledged that section 7's protection may not be as complete as in a case where national security constraints do not operate, but if section 7 were to be satisfied, either the affected person must be given the necessary information or a 'substantial substitute' for that information must be found.[10] Moreover, the security certificate system could not be saved by section 1 of the Charter which permits rights violations where justified in a free and democratic society. It considered that a violation of section 7 rights is particularly difficult to justify due to their fundamental nature. Although the Court recognised that the protection of Canada's national security and related intelligence sources constituted a pressing and substantial objective, the fact that there were less intrusive alternatives to the security certificate system Parliament had chosen meant that the system did not minimally impair the rights of noncitizens.

Unlike the ECtHR in *Chahal*, the Supreme Court then proceeded to highlight a number of less intrusive alternatives to the security certificate system without favouring any particular one. We shall consider the various alternatives canvassed by the Court later when we consider different models of security-cleared

7 ibid [29] (emphasis in original).
8 ibid [51], [64].
9 ibid [64].
10 ibid [61].

systems.[11] For now, it is enough to note that although the Court mentioned the special advocate system as one of these alternatives, it stopped well short of endorsing such a model. It observed that the UK's special advocate system resembled the Canadian SIRC model, each providing for special counsel to objectively review closed material with a view to protecting the named person's interest. But it was also alert to the differences between the two models. In particular, it drew attention to three important disadvantages faced by special advocates which were mentioned by the House of Commons Constitutional Affairs Committee (HCCAC) in its report in 2005, namely that they cannot take instructions from the appellant once they have seen the confidential information, that they lack the resources of an ordinary legal team for the purpose of conducting a full defence and that they had no power to call witnesses.[12] At the same time, the Court referred to the fact that SIAC had commented favourably on the assistance provided by special advocates, referring to one particular case where the 'rigorous cross-examination' of the government's evidence by the special advocate had satisfied it that the government's assertions were unsupported by the evidence.[13]

Despite its review of a wide range of less intrusive alternatives, it was the special advocate procedure closely modelled on the UK system that was favoured by the Canadian Parliament when it came to respond to the Supreme Court's judgment and amend IRPA.[14] This system was already in the forefront of parliamentarians' minds as two parliamentary committees conducting a three-year review of anti-terrorism legislation at the time of the *Charkaoui* decision in 2007 had recommended using special advocates in the security certificate context and in other national security proceedings where the government presents secret information on an ex parte basis.[15] It was somewhat ironic, however, that it was the foreign UK special advocate model that was chosen rather than any of the 'made in Canada' models that had been shown to work in Canada and that this model was approved in particular over the SIRC model that was referred to, albeit inaccurately, by the ECtHR in *Chahal*.[16] It has been argued that of all the alternatives suggested by the Supreme Court, Parliament selected the one that does the worst job in ensuring fair treatment of the affected person.[17] This was not perhaps

11 See Chapter 10.

12 *Charkaoui v Canada (Citizenship and Immigration)* 2007 SCC 9, [2007] 1 SCR 350 [83], citing HCCAC, *The Operation of the Special Immigration Appeals Commission (SIAC) and the Use of Special Advocates* (2004-05, HC 323-1) [52].

13 ibid [84] citing *M v SSHD* SIAC SC/17/2002, 8 March 2004 [10].

14 See An Act to amend the Immigration and Refugee Protection Act (Certificate and Special Advocate) and to Make a Consequential Amendment to Another Act 2008.

15 House of Commons, Subcommittee on the Review of the Anti-terrorism Act, *Rights, Liberty, Security: A Comprehensive Review of the Anti-Terrorism Act and Related Issues* (March 2007) 78–81; Senate of Canada, Special Senate Committee on the Anti-Terrorism Act, *Fundamental Justice in Extraordinary Times* (February 2007) 30–31.

16 J Ip, 'The Rise and Spread of the Special Advocate' [2008] PL 717, 728.

17 K Roach, '*Charkaoui* and Bill C-3: Some Implications for Anti-Terrorism Policy and Dialogue between Courts and Legislatures' (2008) 42 *Supreme Court Law Review* (2d) 281, 305.

so surprising, as the legislature may have an incentive to pick the procedural mechanism that is the least generous to the affected individuals and the most compatible with the interests of the government.[18]

The special advocate's role is set out in the legislation as one of protecting the interests of the permanent resident or foreign national when information or other evidence is heard in their absence.[19] As in the UK, the special advocate is not a party to the proceeding and the relationship between the special advocate and the named person is 'not one of solicitor and client'.[20] Interestingly, there is a further provision which is not to be found in the UK rules, which states that communications between special advocates and named persons are protected as if they were subject to solicitor–client privilege.[21] Crucially, however, the Canadian legislation followed the UK in forbidding special advocates from communicating with any persons once they have received the secret material unless they can obtain the judge's authorisation, subject to any conditions the judge considers appropriate.[22] As in the UK, provision is made for the special advocate to exercise both a disclosure and a substantive representational function. Under the legislation, special advocates may challenge, first, the Minister's claim that the disclosure of information or other evidence would be injurious to national secrecy or endanger the safety of any persons; and, secondly, the relevance, reliability and sufficiency of secret evidence.[23] The legislation goes on to state that special advocates may make oral and written submissions on undisclosed information and evidence and may cross-examine witnesses who testify in closed hearings.[24]

While many features of the UK special advocate system have been transplanted into the Canadian system, one point of contrast is that, unlike in the UK, there has been a reluctance to extend the system beyond the immediate immigration context of security certificates. Although special advocates were imported directly into the Federal Court rather than, as first happened in the UK, into a specialist court such as SIAC, there has been no legislative appetite for further extension. The parliamentary committees into terrorism legislation had recommended that special advocates had a role to play in proceedings under section 38 of the Canada Evidence Act 1985 (which are somewhat analogous to PII applications made by the government in the UK for sensitive information not to be disclosed in the public interest) and under provisions for the listing of terrorist organisations and the deregistering of charities because of alleged involvement in terrorism.[25] However, the government did not implement these recommendations.

18 ibid.
19 IRPA, s 85.1(1).
20 ibid, s 85.1(3).
21 ibid, s 85.1(4).
22 ibid, s 85.4(2).
23 ibid, s 85.1(2).
24 ibid, s 85.2.
25 Roach (n 17) 331.

Consequently, the statutory use of special advocates has to date been much more restricted in Canada than in the UK.

This is not to say, however, that there is a lack of demand for the security-cleared work that special advocates do. IRPA also imported the secret certificate procedure into hearings before the Immigration and Refugee Board (IRB) and, although it is not mandatory to do so, special advocates have been appointed in such hearings.[26] Amici curiae are appointed in section 38 hearings before the Federal Court as well as other hearings such as judicial reviews of IRB hearings, SIRC decisions on no-fly list designations and passport revocations, and in Canadian Security Intelligence Service (CSIS) warrant applications before the Federal Court.[27] Although the role of amici has traditionally been limited to assisting the court on matters of law, increasingly, those who have acted as special advocates are being appointed as amici in these cases and are assuming a much more independent adversarial role, akin to that of a special advocate.[28] One special advocate who confirmed this in an interview said that the order making the appointment spells out what particular role they should play and what conditions are attached to any communications they have with counsel for the named person.[29]

Given that the Supreme Court in *Charkaoui* refused to endorse the special advocate system as its favoured Charter-proof less intrusive alternative qualification on the right of non-citizens to meet the case against them, it was inevitable that the system would be challenged eventually before the Supreme Court, just as the UK special advocate system came to be challenged eventually before the ECtHR. In 2014, the Supreme Court held in *Canada v Harkat*[30] that the amended IRPA regime was constitutional and did not violate the right of named persons to know and meet the case against them or the right to have a decision made on the facts and the law. According to the Court, two of the central principles that guided the scheme were: (1) that the designated judge was given a broad discretion to ensure not only that the record supports the reasonableness of the ministers' finding of inadmissibility but also that the overall process is fair; and (2) that the participation of special advocates in closed hearings was intended

26 See IRPA, s 86.

27 Hudson and Alati (n 4) 11.

28 ibid 66–67. For discussion of the advantages that the special advocate can bring to section 38 hearings, see J Norris, 'Reforming the Bifurcated Process under Section 38 of the Canada Evidence Act' (2018) 68 *University of Toronto Law Journal* 511. The Supreme Court has also referred to the possible use of a special advocate in criminal trials where judges have to decide upon the effect of a section 38 non-disclosure order on the accused's right to a fair trial. See *R v Ahmad* 2011 SCC 6, [2011] 1 SCR 110 [47]. In the light of a National Security Green Paper issued in 2016, the Department of Justice has proposed that select superior trial judges be given statutory jurisdiction to adjudicate national security privilege claims under s 38. See Government of Canada, *Our Security, Our Rights* (National Security Green Paper 2016).

29 SA15, 8 March 2016.

30 *Canada (Citizenship and Immigration) v Harkat* 2014 SCC 37, [2014] 2 SCR 33.

to be a 'substantial substitute' for personal participation by the named person in those hearings.[31] A crucial question that we have seen exercised the ECtHR in determining the compatibility of the special advocate system with the ECHR was whether the special advocate scheme allowed for this intention to become a reality. One difference between the Canadian legislation and the UK system is that IRPA requires the disclosure of a summary of information or other evidence to the named person that enables them to be reasonably informed of the case against them, although the statute goes on to say that this does not include 'anything that, in the judge's opinion, would be injurious to national security or endanger the safety of any person if disclosed'.[32] Under the SIAC rules and other rules of court providing for CMPs in the UK, by contrast, the government is only required to provide a summary to the extent that this is possible without disclosing information contrary to the public interest, although as we have seen a gist may be required where 'objectively high level rights' are engaged.[33] The Supreme Court considered that being 'reasonably informed' meant the named person personally receiving sufficient disclosure to be able to give instructions to his public counsel and meaningful guidance to his special advocates to allow them to challenge the information and evidence relied upon by the minster in the closed hearings.[34] Indeed, 'the named person's ability to answer the case hinged upon the effectiveness of the special advocate which in turn depended on the special advocates being provided with meaningful guidance and information'.[35] The Court referred to the decision of the House of Lords in *AF* in this respect and added that 'the named person need not only be given sufficient information about the allegations against him, but also about the evidence on the record.'[36] Although IRPA was silent as to what should happen where there is an 'irreconcilable tension' between the requirement that the named person be 'reasonably informed', on the one hand, and the imperative that sensitive information not be disclosed, on the other, the Court considered that in this event the Minister must withdraw the information or evidence whose non-disclosure prevented the named person from being reasonably informed.[37]

While the Supreme Court validated the constitutionality of the amended IRPA scheme by emphasising the importance of sufficient disclosure requirements to the named person that drew largely upon the standards set by the ECtHR and the British House of Lords in *AF*, the Court was not simply content to import features of the UK special advocate system into Canada. The Supreme Court went on in addition to graft onto the IRPA model further procedural protections to enhance the effectiveness of the special advocate system which, as we

31 ibid [46] and [47].
32 See IRPA, s 83(e).
33 See eg SIAC (Procedure) Rules 2003, r 37(3).
34 *Canada (Citizenship and Immigration) v Harkat* 2014 SCC 37, [2014] 2 SCR 33 [56].
35 ibid.
36 ibid.
37 ibid [58]–[59].

shall see, have gone beyond the UK system, such as reading in a presumption in favour of continued communication between the special advocate and the named person after the special advocate has seen the secret information.[38] In this manner, the Court nudged the process more in the direction of what critics of the special advocate system have been calling for both in Canada and the UK.[39] It would also be wrong to base any comparison between the two systems purely on the statutory rules and on doctrine. We have seen that the Supreme Court attached importance to judicial discretion and the statute itself states that a special advocate may exercise with the judge's authorisation any other powers that are necessary to protect the interests of the permanent resident or foreign national.[40] Graham and Alati have argued that although the broad parameters of their engagement and role have been set out in statute, the fairness of certificate proceedings depends more on informal social practices and norms than on doctrine with key variables including judicial discretion, customary practices and relations of trust among judges, special advocates, government lawyers and CSIS.[41] Although the number of special advocates in Canada is small, practitioners have accumulated considerable experience of the role over the years and, as in the UK, they have formulated their own position on significant issues. When the government proposed further amendment to IRPA in 2015, for example, relating to the information that should be given to the court and the special advocate, special advocates supplied their own brief to the Bill.[42] Practices have developed which we shall see diverge from UK practice. This illustrates Graham and Alati's point that to the extent that it has ever developed in secret hearings, fairness has been the product of discretion and custom, not formal law. The main features of the UK's special advocate system may have been imported onto Canadian soil, but there are distinctive aspects of the Canadian system that have been developed to give it its own 'made-in-Canada' brand.

Other common law developments

While special advocates in Canada have accumulated considerable experience since they were introduced in 2008, their deployment in other common law countries has to date been more limited. They have, however, been appointed in the immigration context in both New Zealand and Hong Kong, and legislation has recently been enacted in Australia to enable them to be deployed in the context of control orders. Special advocates were appointed for the first time in New Zealand after an Algerian citizen, Ahmed Zaoui, sought a review of the

38 Chapter 7.

39 See C Forcese and K Roach, *False Security: The Radicalisation of Canadian Anti-terrorism* (Irwin 2015) 68.

40 IRPA, s 85.2(c).

41 Hudson and Alati (n 4).

42 Forcese and Roach (n 39) 69.

decision by the Director of the New Zealand Security Intelligence service to issue him with a security certificate.[43] In litigation arising out of this review, Zaoui won the right to be given a non-classified summary of the allegations against him but he was not permitted to see the classified information.[44] The Inspector General of Intelligence and Security conducting the review appointed two special advocates to represent Zaoui's interests in relation to the classified security information which could not be disclosed to him or his counsel. The special advocates were able to argue for greater disclosure of this information and to make submissions and cross-examine witnesses during the closed hearings from which Zaoui and his counsel were excluded. But like their counterparts in the UK, they were unable to communicate with Zaoui and his counsel once they had access to the classified information. In the event, Zaoui's review was never completed as the security risk certificate was subsequently withdrawn.

A special advocate was appointed for the first time in Hong Kong in 2004 after a Sri Lankan national, known as PV, was served with a removal order and placed in detention by the Director of Immigration under Hong Kong's Immigration Ordinance on the ground that he was a 'threat to the peace, order and security' of Hong Kong. When PV applied for a judicial review challenging the lawfulness of the removal order and for bail pending a resolution of the application, the judge ruled that documents containing information on which the Director had acted were protected by PII.[45] But the judge then took the unusual step of seeking the consent of both PV and the Director of Immigration to the appointment of a special advocate and then asking the Secretary of Justice for one to be appointed. The judge's reasoning was based on the fact that the consequence of his non-disclosure order meant that PV's counsel was unable to advocate his case as to why he should no longer be detained which placed him in an invidious position. The judge also said that without a special advocate, he would be deprived of the benefit of submissions made in the interests of PV. Citing *R v H and C*,[46] the judge considered that it was therefore in the interests of justice that a special advocate should be appointed, although he considered that the appointment had to be acceptable to the Director and to the applicant. The Secretary of Justice then approved a number of counsel so that PV would be entitled to a choice. The special advocate who was appointed then took instructions from the applicant before seeing the documents in question and thereafter took no further instructions from him. After hearing submissions from both counsel for the Director and the special advocate, the judge decided to grant bail to the applicant.

This was one of the rare cases where a special advocate has been appointed in Hong Kong. In a later case, the same judge held that he did not need a special

43 Ip (n 16) 729. See also J Ip, 'The Adoption of the Special Advocate Procedure in New Zealand's Immigration Bill' [2009] *New Zealand Law Review* 207, 217.

44 See *Zaoui v Attorney General* [2004] 2 NZLR 339.

45 See *PV v Director of Immigration* HCAL 45/2004.

46 *R v H; R v C* [2004] UKHL 3, [2004] [2004] 2 AC 135.

advocate to be appointed when four applicants challenged decisions refusing them permission to enter Hong Kong because they had been placed on a watch-list.[47] In this case the judge was asked to consider the appointment of a special advocate to assist the judge in determining the public interest immunity application that had been made in respect of certain documents and the judge took the view that in deciding the application, the court would be doing no more than discharging a 'time-honoured' duty of weighing competing interests.[48] The judge added that the present case was not so exceptional as to warrant the adoption of a special advocate procedure. This was not a case where the liberty of the subject was at stake or where an applicant faced deportation or extradition. Judges have refused requests to appoint special advocates in other cases and the Court of Appeal has said it will not interfere unless the judge exercises his discretion wrongly and, citing English authority, that there are cases where the judge can readily resolve disclosure issues without the assistance of a special advocate.[49]

Hong Kong has not yet legislated for the use of special advocates. In 2003, the government put forward a Bill proposing that appeals against the proscription of organisations by the Secretary for Security in the interest of national security could be heard in the absence of the appellant and his counsel and making provision for the appointment of a legal practitioner to act in the interest of the appellant.[50] The Bill was subsequently withdrawn from the Legislative Council. In New Zealand, there has also been some discussion as to whether special advocates should be used in the context of designating an entity as a 'terrorist' entity under the Terrorism Suppression Act 2002.[51] The first statutory provision for special advocates came when changes were made to New Zealand's immigration legislation in 2009. Under the legislation, the courts and the newly established Immigration and Protection Tribunal are obliged to safeguard the confidentiality of classified information and must hold a closed hearing where classified information is involved.[52] The special advocate's role is then to represent the person who is the subject of a decision or proceedings involving classified information.[53] In particular, a special advocate may lodge or commence proceedings on behalf of the person, make oral submissions and cross-examine witnesses at any closed hearing and make written submissions to the Tribunal or the court as the case may be.[54]

47 *Chyi v Director of Immigration* HCAL 32/2003.
48 ibid [101].
49 *Epoch Group Ltd v Director of Immigration* HCMP 52/2011. See *SSHD v AHK* [2009] EWCA Civ 287 [37]–[38].
50 See L Feng, 'The Appeal Mechanism under the NS Bill: A Proper Balance between Fundamental Human Rights and National Security?' in F Hualing, C J Peterson and S N M Young (eds), *National Security and Fundamental Freedoms: Hong Kong's Article 23 under Scrutiny* (Hong Kong University Press 2005) 331.
51 Ip (n 16) 730–731.
52 See Immigration Act 2009, ss 242–244, 252–256.
53 ibid, s 235(1).
54 ibid, s 263(2).

There are some differences that are worth noting from the UK system. First of all, in a change from an earlier version of the Bill which stated that the role of the special advocate is to represent the interests of the appellant in any proceedings involving classified information, the Bill as enacted states that the role of the special advocate is to 'represent' the 'person' who is the subject of decisions or proceedings involving classified information.[55] This is different from the role in the UK and Canada where it is stated to be to represent the 'interests' of the affected person. It is unclear whether this then means that the special advocate is in a professional relationship with the affected person. Clearly, affected persons cannot choose whoever they wish to be their special advocate. Special advocates must have the appropriate security clearance, and a list of special advocates must be maintained by an agency designated by the Prime Minister for the purpose of recognising special advocates.[56] The affected person must be given the names of at least three candidates to choose from. If he or she does not appoint a special advocate, the Department of Immigration must make arrangements for one to be available on his or her behalf.[57] It has been suggested that, given the other provisions in the Bill, this apparent difference in the nature of the representation provided by the special advocate will not make much difference in practice.[58] If special advocates represent the affected person, it is clearly a very different kind of representation from the norm. As in the UK and Canada, special advocates are under a strict obligation not to disclose any classified information and they are prohibited from communicating with the affected person once they are given access to the classified information unless this is authorised.[59] The Act also protects special advocates from liability for any act done or omitted to be done in good faith in his or her capacity as a special advocate.[60]

A more significant difference is that there is no reference in the Act to the special advocate undertaking the disclosure role that we have seen is undertaken in both the UK and Canadian systems. Under the Act, in proceedings before the Tribunal or a court which involve classified information, the chief executive of the relevant agency must develop and provide for approval to the Tribunal or court a summary of the allegations arising from the classified information, and the Tribunal or court may rely on the classified information only to the extent that the allegations arising from the information can be summarised without disclosing the classified information.[61] This goes further than the SIAC rules in the UK which we have seen do not require any summary to be given to the affected person, although this is subject to cases where *A*-type disclosure is required. Curiously, however, the New Zealand legislation goes on to state in relation to

55 See Ip, (n 43) 223–224.
56 Immigration Act 2009, s 264.
57 ibid, s 265(5)(7).
58 Ip, (n 43) 224.
59 Immigration Act 2009, s 267(3).
60 ibid, s 268(3).
61 ibid, s 242(2)(3); s 256(2)(3).

proceedings before the Tribunal that 'to avoid doubt, a special advocate may not be involved in the process of approving, amending, or updating a summary (including an updated summary)'.[62] It has been pointed out that the consequence of this is that a special advocate is unable to argue for greater disclosure, whether by gisting or other means, which is, of course, a role that they play in the UK and Canada.[63] The New Zealand Law Commission, however, has stated that the special advocate may advocate for greater disclosure at a preliminary hearing by trying to get material declassified in the first place.[64]

The idea of using special advocates in a range of different proceedings is attracting interest in both Australia and New Zealand. Even though they have been rarely used in practice, the Australian courts themselves have considered that there are powers at common law to have special counsel appointed in certain circumstances – for example, in determining PII claims in criminal proceedings or in considering criminal intelligence for the purpose of security licence applications.[65] Certain states have also established 'Public Interest Monitors' who play a role analogous to that of a special advocate by making submissions and questioning witnesses when applications are made for search warrants and surveillance warrants.[66] Unlike special advocates, Public Interest Monitors act in the public interest more generally, as do Public Interest Advocates whose role is to make submissions in relation to applications for 'journalism information warrants'.[67] The Public Interest Monitor in Queensland also has a role in making submissions and adducing evidence in relation to the confirmation of an interim control order or the revocation or variation of a confirmed control order.[68] The use of special defence counsel or special advocates has subsequently been an issue of debate and consideration in a number of different contexts relating to the use and disclosure of national security information, including the use of special counsel in closed hearings held under the National Security Information Act 2004 to consider non-disclosure security certificates issued by the Attorney General.[69] Most recently, special advocates have been introduced into Australia's control order hearings to act in the interests of affected parties when they have been excluded

62 ibid, s 142(7).
63 Ip, (n 43) 233–234.
64 New Zealand Law Commission, *National Security Information in Proceedings* (NZLC IP38 2015) [6.73].
65 See eg *R v Lodhi* [2006] NSWSC 586.
66 In Queensland, the Public Interest Monitor is governed by the Police Powers and Responsibilities Act 2000, the Crime and Corruption Act 2001 and the Telecommunications Interception Act 2009. Victoria has created a PI Monitor under the Public Interest Monitor Act 2011.
67 See the Telecommunications (Interception and Access) Act 1979.
68 See Criminal Code s 104.14, 104.19 and 104.23.
69 See Law Council of Australia, *Inquiry into the Operation of the National Security Information (Criminal and Civil Proceedings) Act 2004* (2013).

from such hearings.[70] The Independent National Security Legislation Monitor favoured the UK special advocate model over the Public Interest Monitor model on the ground that the Public Interest Monitor's role is not to advocate for a party and they risk being seen by the affected parties as 'part of the government bureaucracy, not to be trusted'.[71] In his view, it was important that the advocate should unequivocally argue for the result most favourable to the potential controlee without consideration of either the 'public interest' or the 'best interests' of the party.[72] The special advocate system that has been introduced is very similar to the UK model with restrictions on communications between the special advocate and the excluded party after the special advocate is apprised of the withheld sensitive information and with a minimal requirement that the affected party is given notice of the allegations on which the control order request was based.

In New Zealand, the use of special advocates was extended in 2013 to proceedings relating to the interception duties of network operators under the Telecommunication (Interception Capability and Security) Act where the court is provided with relevant classified security information.[73] More recently, the New Zealand Law Commission conducted a first principles review of the way in which national security information is used in criminal, civil and administrative proceedings and it recommended the appointment of special advocates in a wide range of closed procedures.[74] First of all, it recommended that special advocates should be appointed in preliminary hearings in civil proceedings and appeals and reviews of administrative decisions involving national security information. Their purpose here would be to challenge claims that the information cannot be disclosed and to advocate for the affected party on how the information should be used, including whether the court should exclude the information that cannot be disclosed or whether the court should make an order that part of the substantive case be heard under a closed procedure, akin to the CMPs that may be ordered in the UK under the Justice and Security Act 2013. Secondly, it recommended that in civil proceedings and appeals and reviews of administrative decisions where the court orders that part of the substantive hearing be heard as a closed procedure, the special advocate will represent the excluded party's interests during the closed portion of the case. Finally, in relation to criminal proceedings, it recommended the appointment of a special advocate to represent and protect the

70 Counter-Terrorism Legislation Amendment Act (No 1) 2016 making provision for the use of special advocates in control orders under the National Security Information (Criminal and Civil Proceedings) Act 2004.

71 R Gyles, *Control Order Safeguards – (INSLM Report) Special Advocates and the Counter-Terrorism Legislation Amendment Bill (No 1) 2015* (Independent National Security Legislation Monitor 2016) [7.1].

72 ibid.

73 Telecommunication (Interception Capability and Security) Act 2013, s 105.

74 See New Zealand Law Commission, *National Security in Information Proceedings* (NZLC IP38, 2015); New Zealand Law Commission, *The Crown in Court: A review of the Crown Proceedings Act and national security information proceedings* (NZLC R135, 2015).

interest of the defendant during any closed pre-trial hearing on disclosure where the prosecution has withheld national security information. The subject of the Commission's inquiry was national security information and it did not consider whether special advocates should have a role in cases that do not involve national security. Nevertheless, its endorsement of the special advocate system in such a broad range of cases involving national security is a sign that special advocates are becoming a focus of increasing interest in other common law jurisdictions apart from the UK and Canada, reinforcing the need for a closer look, which we take in the chapters that follow, into their appointment, ethical duties and effectiveness.

European continental and international criminal law applications

Special advocates have thus far played less of a role in civil law systems where secret evidence is kept from excluded parties. There would appear to have been little discussion of them in the consideration that has been given to the use of CMPs at the European level within the EU. In the *Kadi*[75] decisions, the Court of Justice of the European Union (CJEU) referred to the need for the applicants to be given some measure of procedural justice when they were listed under the UN sanctions regime, but no reference was made to the special advocate system.[76] In these cases, the CJEU did not have to consider the question of how it would treat the use of intelligence information presented to them, but the decisions prompted discussion of this issue and in 2014, the European Council came up with new procedural rules which make an exception to the 'adversarial principle ... under which all information and material must be fully communicated between the parties'.[77] Under the new rules, the Council may submit material to the court whose disclosure would 'harm the security of the EU or its Member States or the conduct of their international relations' without disclosing it to another party and the Court may base its judgment on such information after taking into account the fact that the other party has not been able to make its views on it known.[78]

75 (Joined cases C-402/05 and C-415/05) *Kadi v Council of the EU* [2008] ECR-I 6351; (Case T-85/09) *Kadi v Commission of the EU* [2011] 1 CMLR 697.

76 They were referred to, without being explicitly endorsed by, the Advocate General in her Opinion in (C27/09 P) *French Republic v People's Mojahedin Organization of Iran*, Opinion of AG Sharpston, 14 July 2011, fn 89, in the context of considering whether the General Court of the EU should be able make use of confidential information. See also C Murphy, 'Secret Evidence in EU Security Law: Special Advocates before the Court of Justice?' King's College London, Centre of European Law, Working paper 02/2012; C Murphy, 'Secret Evidence in EU Security Law: Special Advocates before the Court of Justice?' in D Cole, F Fabbrini and A Vedaschi (eds), *Secrecy, National Security and the Vindication of Constitutional Law* (Edward Elgar 2014) 1.

77 Rules of Procedure of the General Court, Art 64. The new rules came into effect on 1 July 2015.

78 See ibid, Art 105 (8).

It has been suggested that the new rules appear to diverge from Article 6 of the ECHR as interpreted by the ECtHR which requires an 'irreducible minimum level of disclosure and from the decisions of the CJEU in *Kadi* and *ZZ* which require disclosure of the essence of the grounds'.[79] But for our purposes what is interesting to note is the lack of any provision for special advocates under the new rules. In giving evidence to the House of Lords Select Committee on the EU, the British Minister for Europe explained that the special advocate system was not one that other member states have used and it 'never really caught fire as a suggestion in the discussions at European level'.[80] There would obviously be a number of logistical issues for the CJEU to deal with before such a system could be imported successfully into the supranational legal order of the EU, not least the problem of where EU special advocates would come from.[81] Aside from these issues, there is presently little prospect of governments of member states being prepared to disclose information of the sensitivity deployed in CMPs in the UK to judges of the CJEU, let alone to special advocates.[82] The lack of interest in the special advocate system may also be attributable to a view that procedural protection is better focused on what can be disclosed to the excluded party and that any questioning of witnesses in a closed hearing can be conducted adequately by the court, without the need for an extra layer of representation by a counsel who has access to the closed material. Many member states, after all, come from an 'inquisitorial' tradition where judges are used to adopting a much more 'hand-on' approach than in common law jurisdictions.

In a survey conducted for the European Parliament in 2014 on the use of intelligence information within the justice systems of a number of EU member states, it was found that there was a growing reliance on intelligence information in judicial proceedings, but amongst the countries surveyed, only the UK appears to have resorted to special advocates.[83] In the focus group meetings organised by the study which consisted of civil society organisations and legal practitioners, it was acknowledged that while special advocates might have advantages, they did not seem to work at a practical level due to not being in possession of the appropriate materials.[84] Some European countries have, however, begun to adopt special advocate systems. European human rights law would seem to have been influential in the decision to introduce a special advocate system into the

79 See M Lester, 'Draft European Rules Propose Secret Hearings', *European Sanctions Blog*, 6 April 2014.

80 House of Lords Select Committee on the EU, *Inquiry on Plans for New Court Rules and Conduct of EU Sanctions,* Evidence, 2 March 2015 (Mr David Lidington MP).

81 See Murphy (n 76).

82 I owe this point to Martin Chamberlain.

83 D Bigo, S Carrera, N Hernanz and A Scherrer, *National Security and Secret Evidence in Legislation and before the Courts: Exploring the Challenges* (European Parliament 2014). Report for the European Parliament's Committee on Civil Liberties, Justice and Home Affairs. The countries surveyed were the UK, France, Germany, Spain, the Netherlands and Sweden.

84 ibid 85.

Danish Immigration Act in 2009.[85] In an earlier judgment, the Danish Supreme Court had held that the failure of the authorities to substantiate their assessment that an alien was a danger to national security when he was detained with a view to deportation was in breach of Article 5(4) of the ECHR.[86] The new process imports a judicial process similar to SIAC in the UK by requiring that special advocates do not discuss the case with the alien or the alien's counsel once the security information has been transmitted to them. This system has itself been challenged on the basis of the ECtHR decision in *A v UK*[87] that affected persons must be provided with sufficient open material to challenge the allegations against them.[88] But the special advocate system has remained intact and seems to have secured a firm foothold in immigration proceedings.

Certain Scandinavian countries have also resorted to the use of special advocates in certain criminal cases. In both Denmark and Norway it is mandatory to appoint special counsel from a restricted list where applications are made by the prosecution in the absence of the defence for the non-disclosure of certain kinds of sensitive information.[89] Unlike the UK, it appears that they are appointed in all cases where disclosure may be restricted and not just in 'exceptional cases'. Such counsel are required to take care of the accused's interests and to make submissions in respect of the application. As in the UK, such counsel cannot contact the accused and must respect the confidentiality of the sensitive information. They also have the right to appeal any court order refusing disclosure to the ordinary defence counsel. In Denmark, special advocates chosen from the same restricted list are also used to represent parties who have been targeted for certain surveillance measures such as telephone-tapping or bugging.[90] Such advocates are not permitted to approach the persons subject to investigation because the measures being proposed are secret, but they are given access to the entire file and the right of presence at all hearings and may lodge an appeal against a court order. A similar system of 'privacy' advocates was introduced in Sweden in 2004 when warrants are being sought for telephone-tapping, bugging and camera surveillance.[91] The idea was to introduce a 'contradictory process' into the court

85 See Aliens (Consolidation) Act No 785 of 10 August 2009, pts VIIa and b. See J E Rytter, 'Terrorist Threats and Judicial Deference' in D Jenkins, A Jacobsen and A Henriksen (eds), *The Long Decade; How 9/11 Changed the Law* (OUP 2014) 229, 235–236. See also Ministry of Justice, *Justice and Security Green Paper* (Cm 8194, 2011) App J.

86 Danish Supreme Court, 2 July 2008, in *Ugeskrift for Retsvæsen* 2008, 2394 et seq.

87 *A v UK* (2009) 49 EHRR 29.

88 Danish Supreme Court, 24 June 2011, in *Ugeskrift for Retsvæsen* 2011, 2695 et seq.

89 Administration of Justice Act 1916, s 729c (Denmark), Criminal Procedure Code, s 100a (Norway). For commentary see respectively L B Langsted, P Garde and V Greve, *Criminal Law in Denmark* (3rd edn Djoef Publishing 2011) [282a]; A Strandbakken, 'Disclosure of Evidence by the Prosecution' in H Müller-Dietz, E Müller and others (eds), *Festchrift für Heike Jung* (Nomos 2007).

90 Administration Act 1916, ss 784, 785. See Langsted et al, ibid [313].

91 See Statens Offentligu Utredninger, *Hemliga tvangsmedem mot allvarliga brott* (2012) [9.5.1].

hearings to ensure that the interests of suspected individuals were protected.[92] Finally, beyond the surveillance context, an innovative procedure was introduced in Norway some years ago for taking evidence in a judicial hearing very shortly after sexual or violent offences have been reported whereby witnesses under 16 or who have a mental disability are questioned by a trained police interviewer in the presence of a defence lawyer.[93] These hearings may take place before there is any identified defendant who has been charged and a lawyer is then appointed to represent the defence's interests in anticipation of future proceedings.[94]

The idea of special advocates representing the interests of absent parties without receiving instructions from them is not then unknown in continental European systems or at least in Scandinavian ones. Such an idea may not in fact be so alien to the continental tradition as the common law tradition. In a number of continental criminal proceedings, for example, defence counsel does not 'represent' the accused person but is only an adviser to the accused and may be appointed against her will in order to protect her interests where the accused does not want to be assisted by counsel.[95] A number of jurisdictions also permit trials to be conducted in absentia and counsel are then appointed to represent the interests of the absent accused.[96] To see how analogous the role of such a counsel is to the role of special advocates, one can look to the Special Tribunal for Lebanon (STL) which permits trials to be conducted in absentia on certain conditions.[97] If the absent accused fails to appoint a defence counsel, defence counsel will be assigned by the Defence Office to represent the 'interests and rights' of the accused but, congruent with a special advocate, not to act on the instructions of the accused.[98] In order to preserve the right of such an accused to a retrial, should she later be arrested or voluntarily come forward to be tried, the appointed counsel shall, again like a special advocate, not have any contact with the in absentia accused and, if contacted, shall refuse to discuss any element of the case with the accused and refer her to the head of the Defence Office to receive independent legal advice.[99]

92 ibid [9.5.2].

93 Criminal Procedure Regulations of 2 October 1998 no 925. Since 2008 the interviews have taken place at 'Barnahus' ('Child House') sites.

94 For a detailed description of these procedures, see Scottish Courts Service, *Evidence and Procedure Review Report* (2015) [2.48]–[2.62].

95 W Wohlers, 'The Role of Counsel in Criminal Proceedings' in J D Jackson and S J Summers (eds), *Obstacles to Fairness in Criminal Proceedings: Individual Rights and Institutional Forms* (Hart 2018) 127, 145.

96 S Trechsel, *Human Rights in Criminal Proceedings* (OUP, 2005) 254. The Committee of Ministers of the Council of Europe adopted a resolution governing such trials in Res (75) 11 of 21 March 1975.

97 STL Statute, art 22. See also STL RPE 6.

98 ibid, art 22(2)(c).

99 Code of Professional Conduct for Defence Counsel and Legal Representatives of Victims before the Special Tribunal for Lebanon, stl/cc/2012/03, art 8(E).

International criminal courts and tribunals have followed the continental tradition of appointing counsel to represent the interests of the accused even when the accused has insisted on representing herself, adopting what Wohlers has described as a model of 'hybrid' representation.[100] They have also appointed counsel as amici curiae to ensure that a particular defence perspective is presented during the trial or appeal phase of a case.[101] The only example where the rules specifically authorise the appointment of a special counsel in relation to sensitive information, however, appears in the STL.[102] The appointment may be triggered only in a very specific situation when the Pre-Trial Judge is notified by the Prosecutor under Rule 118(C) of the existence of information affecting the security interests of a state or international entity which was provided to the Prosecutor on a confidential basis and which, in the Prosecutor's view, contains exculpatory material. If the Prosecutor has not managed to obtain the consent of the information provider to disclose the information, Rule 119 then empowers the Prosecutor or the Defence to apply to the President to appoint a special counsel to provide advice to the Pre-Trial Judge in the performance of his functions under Rule 118(C) and, if the President agrees, he shall appoint a special counsel from a confidential list of persons who have been approved by the entity providing the confidential information. The special counsel will then review the information that the provider has not consented to being disclosed and the list of counterbalancing measures proposed by the Prosecutor. Rule 119 goes on to state that after reviewing the information and the counterbalancing measures proposed by the Prosecutor, the special counsel shall advise the Pre-Trial Judge of the 'counterbalancing measures that are the most appropriate to protect the rights of the accused to a fair trial under the circumstances' and the Pre-Trial Judge shall issue any appropriate order in this regard.[103] The procedure is somewhat analogous to the procedures that govern PII applications in the UK where we have seen that the trial judge may ask for a special counsel to be appointed in exceptional circumstances, with the important difference that, while the special counsel is able to view the totality of the confidential information, the Pre-Trial Judge is unable to do so.[104] It appears that the role of the special counsel is to assist the Pre-Trial Judge in the exercise of his duties and is not therefore one of exclusively representing the interests of the Defence.[105] Nevertheless, this would appear to be a large part of the raison d'être for the appointment of a special counsel. The rule is silent on whether there can be any contact between the special counsel and the

100 Wohlers (n 95) 142. See C Jalloh, 'Self-representation and the use of assigned, standby and amicus counsel' in L Carter and F Pocar (eds), *International Criminal Procedure: The Interface of Civil Law and Common Law Legal Systems* (Edward Elgar 2013) 125.

101 Jalloh ibid 130.

102 See STL RPE 119.

103 STL RPE 119(C).

104 This is stressed in the Explanatory Memorandum to the STL RPE (2012) [37].

105 See *Prosecutor v Ayyash*, STL-11-01/T/PRES, F2235, Public Redacted Versions of 'Application for Appointment of Special Counsel Pursuant to Rule 119(A)', 5 November 2015.

Defence and the question arises whether the Defence could provide the special counsel with information on an ex parte basis in order for the special counsel to understand the importance of the material to the Defence.[106]

It does not appear that there has been any case in which special counsel have actually been engaged by the STL. In one case, the defence made an application for the appointment of a special counsel when the Defence had been given a redacted version of a document consisting of an interview with a prosecution witness who had since died.[107] The application related to earlier submissions by the Defence requesting the Pre-Trial Judge to resolve a disclosure matter concerning this document under Rule 118(C). The Prosecution submitted, however, that the Prosecutor was not performing its functions under Rule 118 because it had reviewed the contents of the document and concluded that there was no exculpatory information in it. The Pre-Trial Judge then ruled that the disclosure request was unfounded on the basis of Rule 118 and the President dismissed the application to him for the appointment of a special counsel as moot on the ground that before he could consider its merits, the Pre-Trial Judge had to be performing his Rule 118(C) functions.[108]

This case illustrates the exacting nature of the conditions that must be satisfied under the Rules before a special counsel may be appointed, but it would appear that there is nothing that would prevent their appointment outwith the Rules should a judge consider it necessary to do so in the interests of justice. Interestingly, the judges in the ICC have appointed independent counsel to protect privileged communications on the defence side, specifically between defence counsel and the accused, where the prosecution are seeking access to such communications in the course of investigating whether there have been potential offences against the administration of justice under Article 70 of the Rome Statute of the ICC.[109] The independent counsel were tasked with reviewing and identifying those elements of the communications which might be relevant to the Prosecutor's investigations and delivering them to the Prosecutor whilst maintaining strict confidentiality with respect to those elements that were

106 See the competing views of the prosecution and defence in *Prosecutor v Ayyash* STL-11-01/T/PRES, F2235, Public Redacted Versions of 'Application for Appointment of Special Counsel Pursuant to Rule 119)A)', 5 November 2015 and Prosecution Response to Sabra Application for Appointment of Special Counsel pursuant to Rule 119(A), 2 October 2015.

107 *Prosecutor v Ayyash* STL-11-01/T/PRES, F2235, Public Redacted Versions of 'Application for Appointment of Special Counsel Pursuant to Rule 119(A)', 5 November 2015.

108 See, respectively, *Prosecutor v Ayyash* STL-11-10/T/P/PTJ, F2287, Decision relating to the Request for a Document by the Sabra Defence, 26 October 2015, *Prosecutor v Ayyash* Decision on Application for Appointment of Special Counsel Pursuant to Rule 119(A), 30 October 2015.

109 See eg *Situation in the Central African Republic*, No ICC-01/05, Decision on the Prosecutor's 'Request for Judicial Order to Obtain Evidence for Investigation under Article 70', 29 July 2013, *Prosecutor v Bemba*, No ICC-01/05-52-Red2, Decision on the Prosecutor's 'Request for Judicial Order to Obtain Evidence for Investigation under Article 70', 3 February 2014.

not relevant to the investigation. Access to all the communications in question was given exclusively to the independent counsel and not to the Defence, the single Judge, or even to the Prosecutor. This is an interesting example of what might be considered to be a 'reverse' special advocate procedure whereby independent counsel are deployed in effect to represent the interests of the prosecution, but at the same time they have to protect the rights of the Defence in ensuring that any disclosure of information is limited to that which comes within a well-recognised exception to the privileged nature of lawyer–client communications, namely those that are made 'in furtherance of crime'.[110]

This example illustrates the flexibility that is given to judges within the international legal order to come up with an ingenious variant of the special advocate procedure in order to do justice to the parties. The role of special counsel or independent counsel within the international tribunals is more akin to that of an amicus curiae than that of a special advocate in the strict sense, whose role is exclusively to represent the interests of a party that has been excluded from a hearing. The international tribunals have shown that they can import solutions from each other's jurisdictions as well as from domestic jurisdictions, and it will not be surprising if, over time, they come to deploy the special counsel procedures provided for in the STL and extend them to other situations. We must now return to examine the core role of the special advocates in the UK where they have been most commonly deployed and look in more detail at the practices that have emerged there.

110 This exception to or delimitation of the privilege has long been recognised at common law. See *R v Cox and Railton* (1884) 14 QBD 153.

5 Appointment and support

We have seen that a key facet of the special advocate's role is that the advocate acts in the interest of the party who is excluded from the proceedings, but it was not envisaged that the advocate would be in a lawyer–client relationship with that party. This severance of the lawyer–client relationship is manifested in a number of ways and raises important questions. First of all, appellants are prevented from choosing whoever they wish to be 'their' special advocate, although as we shall see, they have some say in being able to choose someone from the list of special advocates. This raises the question of who should be ultimately responsible for appointing special advocates. Secondly, the excluded party is unable to give instructions to the special advocate once the special advocate receives the closed material and there is no instructing solicitor, acting on the client's behalf, to give instructions. This raises questions of competence and accountability. Who is responsible for instructing special advocates to enable them to act in the excluded party's interests and for supporting the special advocates during the case? As we shall see, one of the perennial concerns raised by special advocates has been their isolation from the party they are unable to communicate with and from a team of lawyers who can support them. A further question is to whom are they accountable? While ordinary counsel owe duties to the court and to their professional association, they also owe duties to their client. But when the lawyer–client relationship is severed, to whom are they ultimately accountable? Should they be bound by some ethical code that is different from that of an ordinary counsel? We shall come to these issues in the next chapter (Chapter 6). This chapter will focus upon the issues of appointment and support.

Appointment of special advocates

Early concerns

Special advocate appointments are made by the relevant Law Officer, who is the Attorney General in proceedings before the courts in England and Wales, the Advocate General for Northern Ireland in respect of proceedings in Northern Ireland, and the Lord Advocate for Scotland in respect of Scottish proceedings.[1]

1 See eg Special Immigration Appeals Commission (SIAC) Act 1997, s 6(2).

Some of the special advocates spoken to in this research said that they were appointed under what one special advocate described as the 'old extremely dubious recruitment programme'[2] whereby the Treasury Solicitor identified a number of people who were thought appropriate whose names were then submitted to the Attorney General who approved the list. Those on the list were then required to be cleared to 'developed-vetted' level which is the highest level of UK security clearance.[3] The procedure then was that when a special advocate needed to be appointed, the Treasury Solicitor would make a recommendation to the Law Officers which would then be considered by them.[4] In practice, it seems that at first many, but not all, special advocates were chosen from the civil panel of juniors to the Crown who are approved to undertake government work and some of them would already have been developed-vetted.[5] One special advocate said that the whole system was 'incredibly informal' to begin with and recruitment was 'very much a tap on the shoulder'.[6] He said he was asked because he was on the government panel, although he also did claimant work. Another said that he was probably 'fingered' originally because he had already been 'developed-vetted' for the purposes of other government work.[7] It is true that at the beginning two QCs in particular were chosen who had out-and-out claimant experience, but that did not seem to be the general pattern and most came from a 'panel background'.[8] According to one special advocate, the general perception at the beginning amongst the claimant solicitors was that special advocates were 'stooges of the government', with the result that there was a considerable amount of distrust of them.[9]

Various steps were subsequently taken to allay this perception. In their evidence to the House of Commons Constitutional Affairs Committee (HCCAC) which considered the use of special advocates in SIAC in 2005, special advocates considered that from the perspective of the appellant, special advocates were selected at the discretion of a law officer who was a member of the executive which had authorised their detention; in these circumstances, it would not be surprising if the appellant had little or no confidence in his special advocate.[10] They submitted

2 SA12, 14 January 2016.
3 Presentation by SASO to Information Meeting organised by the Crown Solicitor's Office, Belfast, June 2016. Checks are carried out on all areas of a person's life that could lead to vulnerability to 'improper influence' or otherwise render someone unsuitable.
4 See House of Commons Constitutional Affairs Committee (HCCAC), *The Operation of the Special Immigration Appeals Commission (SIAC) and the Use of Special Advocates* (HC 2004-05, 323-1) Oral evidence, 8 March 2005, Ev 33 (Lord Goldsmith).
5 ibid Ev 49.
6 SA12, 14 January 2016.
7 SA5, 25 November 2015.
8 In giving evidence before the HCCAC, the Attorney General stated that not all counsel on the Special Advocates list were members of such panels and there were Queen's Counsel such as Nick Blake QC and Andrew Nicol QC who were leading members of the Bar in their field with 'good "claimant" experience and expertise'. See HCCAC (n 4) Ev 80 (Lord Goldsmith).
9 SA12, 14 January 2016.
10 HCCAC (n 4) Ev 57.

that there was no reason in principle why appellants should not be allowed to choose their special advocates from a panel of security-cleared advocates and that this was in fact the practice that had developed in SIAC cases.[11] Following a meeting with special advocates on 7 March 2005, the Attorney General agreed that an appellant should be able to select from a security-vetted panel of counsel the person she would like to act as her special advocate.[12] This means that at least the appellant has some say over who should represent her interests. The SASO *Open Manual* states that the relevant Law Officer will always take into account the preference of the open representatives, but there is no absolute right on the part of the excluded party to a special advocate of their choice.[13] Factors that the Law Officers will take into account include the nature and complexity of the proceedings, the level of expertise required and the level of counsel instructed by the opposing side. There are also two further constraints on the excluded party's choice. The first is that there must be no conflict with any other appeal in which that special advocate is acting and the second is that the special advocate must not have had prior access to relevant closed material, as otherwise she would not be in a position to speak to the appellant or her legal representative even at the outset of the case. We will return to these issues later in the chapter.

Another concern expressed in the early days was that the pool was limited largely to lawyers with expertise in administrative law. This limited the supply of special advocates able to do the work, but such lawyers also had a limited skill-set. In an early survey, almost all special advocates agreed with the suggestion of Lord Carlisle, the independent statutory reviewer of Part 4 of the Anti-Terrorism, Crime and Security Act 2001, that the pool should be 'widened well beyond those with detailed knowledge of administrative law'.[14] This was because SIAC cases were more 'fact-intensive' and involved greater cross-examination than most administrative law proceedings. In their evidence to the HCCAC in 2005, the special advocates submitted that from their experience, the principal requirement for a special advocate in proceedings before SIAC was the ability to absorb and analyse information that may be in voluminous documents and to cross-examine effectively on the basis of this material. Such abilities were not confined to public law practitioners. While public law issues did sometimes arise in relation to closed material, the nature of the work also required skills which those such as criminal lawyers or those with experience of handling witnesses in civil cases would be equally, if not better, qualified to perform.[15]

11 ibid Ev 57.
12 HCCAC (n 4) Ev 77.
13 SASO, *A Guide to The Role of Special Advocates & the Special Advocates' Support Office* (2nd edn Government Legal Department 2019) [25].
14 See E Metcalfe, '"Representative but nor Responsible": the use of special advocates in English law' (2004) 1 *Justice Journal* 11, 28.
15 HCCAC (n 4) Ev 57.

More transparent procedures

After his meeting with special advocates in March 2005, the Attorney General agreed to strengthen the existing panel by recruiting more special advocates with experience of handling witnesses in civil cases and also criminal lawyers. Advertisements were placed in professional journals and a fairer and more transparent process was put into operation to recruit special advocates with a wider range of experience.[16] A special advocate is now typically appointed for an initial 10 year period, with the possibility of renewal, upon application to the Attorney General.[17] In their survey in August 2007, Forcese and Waldman reported that the panel was drawn from three main areas of legal expertise: immigration, criminal law and human rights law. Some special advocates were experienced civil litigators.[18] The special advocates on the panel had an average of 18 years of experience since being called to the Bar.[19] In February 2016, there were 40 special advocates on the England and Wales panel (21 senior counsel and 19 junior counsel) and their collective experience reflected a variety of different clients (by no means only the government) in the broad areas of public law and criminal law.[20] Figure 5.1 shows that special advocates in this panel have quite a high level of experience in terms of years since their call to the Bar: on average 24 years (with the most junior having 16 years' experience and the most senior 40). The current panel of special advocates in England and Wales stands at 38.[21]

One of the open counsel interviewed who had experience of working with special advocates said that in his view the people who are selected to appear as special advocates are of an extremely high standard. Obviously, he said he did not know what happens in closed proceedings but:

> They are completely committed to the task of assisting as much as they can, in terms of discussion with them, calling them up, meeting with them before they see the closed material, attempting to brief them and give them answers to the kind of questions that they think they will need to know to maximise the chances of them being able to help in the closed.[22]

He said he felt able to work very well with them and he did not consider that they were somehow 'partis pris' or even neutral. They were there to help him achieve the right results. One former special advocate said he believed that

16 *Government Response to the Constitutional Affairs Select Committee into the Operation of the Special Immigration Appeals Commission (SIAC) and the Use of Special Advocates* (2005, Cm 6596) 6.

17 SASO (n 13) [22].

18 C Forcese and L Waldman, *Seeking Justice in an Unfair Process* (University of Ottawa 2007) 26.

19 ibid 25.

20 Email communication from SASO to the author, 23 February 2016.

21 Email communication from SASO to the author, 12 July 2018.

22 OC5, 2 February 2016.

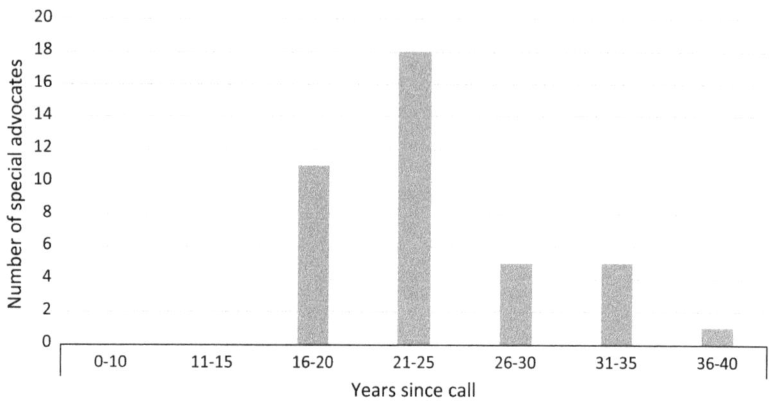

Figure 5.1 Experience levels of special advocates in England and Wales in 2016.

although certain claimant solicitors still remained incredibly hostile to the system of special advocates, there was much more trust in special advocates themselves.[23] This was partly because over the years, special advocates had proved themselves to be independent of government. They had given evidence as a group to parliamentary committees and been vocal in making demands of the Attorney General saying they had to have proper facilities, training and support, none of which would have happened if the special advocates had not demanded it of government.

Finally, it is worth noting, however, that the procedures in place for the appointment of special counsel to act in the interest of defendants in criminal cases would not seem to be as transparent as those in place for the appointment of special advocates. First of all, perhaps because their appointment is rare, there does not appear to be a list of special counsel for which there is an open competition. In giving evidence to the HCCAC, the Attorney General, Lord Goldsmith, said that it was not normally necessary for such advocates to be developed-vetted in the manner in which special advocates were. He said that in the criminal cases where special counsel are occasionally called for, there was not normally a security issue: more likely the issue was one of the identity of informers. In these circumstances, he said he had made an arrangement with the Chairman of the Bar and leaders of the circuit together with First Treasury Counsel, whereby they would identify people whom they regarded as competent to do this work, from whom a choice could then be made in a given case.[24] It is to be noted that in some of

23 SA12, 14 January 2016.

24 HCCAC (n 4) Ev 34. It has since been confirmed that an ad hoc panel of special counsel was set up by the then Attorney General Lord Goldsmith. Candidates for the panel were

these cases, the nature of the PII claim may be of such a kind that the defendant is never made aware of the claim and so would not be in position to make a choice as to which counsel she wished to act as special counsel. As we have seen, the demand for special counsel is low and no further panel selection exercise has taken place.[25] Instead, the practice has been for special counsel to be appointed from criminal practitioners on the special advocate panel taking account of: their experience (both in relation to criminal law and closed material proceedings); their seniority; the level of security clearance required; and availability. This may seem to be a sensible arrangement given that a significant number of special advocates have considerable criminal law experience. At the same time, since special counsel in criminal cases do not need to be developed-vetted, this practice restricts defendants' choice as to whom they would like to act for them as special counsel in those cases where defendants are made aware that special counsel is to be appointed.

Given that special counsel are now chosen from the special advocate panel, there remains the question of why special counsel are not simply renamed special advocates and brought within the support of SASO.[26] The principal reason given by the Attorney General's Office – which retains overall responsibility for the appointment of special counsel as well as special advocates – is the need for criminal law experience and expertise in the handling of requests for special counsel.[27] The work involves liaising with the judiciary and advising the Attorney General on the appointment of special counsel in the context of issues arising from complex and sensitive criminal litigation. It is also more cost-effective to have the casework handled by a small number of people within the Attorney General's Office. In light of the fact that special counsel are now chosen from the special advocate panel, however, it would seem that when there is a recruitment exercise, there should be some acknowledgement of the fact that those who are recruited on to the panel may be asked to act as special counsel in criminal cases in addition to acting as a special advocate in civil cases.[28]

Finally, a role has also developed for a special advocate to act as a PII advocate in civil cases in parallel with, or instead of, an application for a section 6

---

identified by the Attorney General in consultation with the Bar Council, the Criminal Bar Association and representatives of the London and South Eastern Circuit. Those who were considered suitable were sent a letter by the Attorney General's Office, asking if they were willing to be a member of the panel. Email communication from the Attorney General's Office to the author, 18 February 2018.

25 Email communication from the Attorney General's Office to the author, 8 February 2018.

26 SASO's *Open Manual* states that it does not deal with the appointment of special counsel: SASO (n 13) [3].

27 ibid.

28 The Attorney General's Office has indicated that it will be engaging with SASO and the special advocate panel to highlight the approach in relation to special counsel and consider how best to ensure it is made clear in any future special advocate recruitment exercise. Email communication to the author, 8 February 2018.

declaration under the Justice and Security Act 2013.[29] Section 6(7) of the Justice and Security Act 2013 provides that the court must not consider an application for a declaration by the Secretary of State under section 6 unless it is satisfied that she has considered whether to make a claim for PII in relation to the material on which the declaration is based. Again, as with special counsel, PII advocates might not need the same level of security clearance as special advocates. The level of clearance required is determined by the classification of the material subject to the PII application. Although PII advocates may be appointed from the special advocate panel, if the PII material is not closed material which can only be viewed by those who have been developed-vetted, there seems no reason why the choice of PII advocate should be restricted to the special advocate panel.

Northern Ireland

Until recently there was not a particularly well-developed system for appointing special advocates in Northern Ireland. One open counsel who had experience of working with special advocates in England and Northern Ireland said that Northern Ireland was going through what had happened in England and Wales ten years ago.[30] There was naturally still a lot of distrust on the part of solicitors about the role of the special advocate and, unlike England and Wales now, there was a perception that special advocates came from a government background, 'gamekeepers' rather than 'poachers', to use the language of one open counsel who had experience of special advocates in Northern Ireland. According to this advocate:

> Part of the problem lies, I feel, in the fact that special advocates are typically from a certain type of work background as opposed to having experience in the field, one might say. This is a major problem for a couple of reasons. First, in doing a certain type of work only, there is the risk of carrying a certain level of bias into the job at hand however professional the special advocate. Secondly, and perhaps more importantly, if their job background is dealing with the white collar fellow professional, there is the risk that they have not acquired the skill set that is necessary to gain the trust of the excluded person who will invariably be from a diametrically opposite background to the client with whom they typically deal.[31]

One counsel who had acted as a special advocate in Northern Ireland said he had no idea how he came to be appointed. He was approached by the Advocate General's Office and had no idea how his name went into the hat. This counsel

29 SASO (n 13) [152].
30 OC4, 15 January 2016.
31 OC2, 3 November 2015.

had a background in representing the government.[32] Another counsel who used to act as a special advocate again said he had no idea why he was asked, but he speculated that it may have had something to do with the fact that he had acted for both the prosecution and defence and therefore might be perceived as more acceptable to the excluded party than someone who had only done Crown work.[33] He said that an important feature of the system from its inception was that the excluded party was given an opportunity to object to the appointment of the person earmarked for appointment, although this did not amount to a veto of the appointment. As in England and Wales, the appointment system developed by permitting excluded parties to choose from a list of special advocates called to the Northern Ireland Bar. But until recently, the number of special advocates based in Northern Ireland was limited to five (two QCs and three juniors)[34] and it seemed that reliance was placed in a number of cases on special advocates in England who were called to the Northern Ireland Bar.[35]

A major recruitment exercise was conducted in 2016 on the basis of a competition open to both self-employed barristers and solicitor-advocates of at least five years advocacy experience. Applicants had to have experience in practice of representing: either public bodies or litigants in proceedings against the government or other public bodies; criminal law work; or employment tribunal work. The numbers on the list have now vastly increased. As at 16 June 2017, there were 27 special advocates called to the Bar of Northern Ireland (14 QCs and 13 juniors), although it is noteworthy that eight on the list are special advocates based in England who have been called to the Northern Ireland Bar.[36] Figure 5.2 shows that, as in England and Wales, they have quite a high level of experience in terms of years since call to the Bar, on average 23 years (with the most junior having 12 years' experience and the most senior 41). The current panel of special advocates in Northern Ireland stands at 23.[37]

Whether these revised requirements will give excluded parties and their solicitors greater confidence in special advocates will depend, however, not just on the range of experience such advocates have but on their assessment of how the special advocate might assist them in the closed hearing. One open advocate with experience of practising in both England and Wales and Northern Ireland said that the client base in special advocate cases was different in each jurisdiction.[38] In many of the English cases, the clients found themselves marooned in the UK, often seeking asylum and were very reliant on what lawyers told them. In Northern Ireland, the clients were firmly rooted in their community with a very clear perception of what kind of lawyer they wanted to represent them.

32 SA2, 4 November 2015.
33 SA1, 3 November 2015.
34 Email correspondence from SASO to the author, 23 February 2016.
35 Five interviewees came into this category.
36 Email correspondence from SASO to the author, June 2017.
37 Email communication from SASO to the author, 12 July 2018.
38 OC4, 15 January 2016.

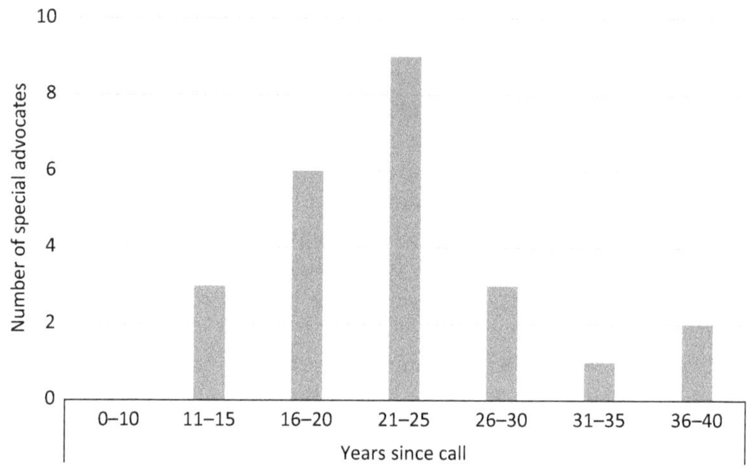

Figure 5.2 Experience levels of special advocates in Northern Ireland in 2017.

Conflicts of interest and tainting

The first edition of the SASO *Open Manual* states that conflicts of interest in the usual sense do not arise, since a special advocate owes no duty to the person whose interests he represents.[39] However, the manual goes on to stipulate that:

> A Special Advocate should be careful that no situation arises in which there could be any perception of anything other than absolute independence on his part. Special Advocates should therefore carefully consider whether any matter in which they have acted previously would lead to a perceived conflict of interest if they were to act for a particular Appellant as a Special Advocate. Likewise, Special Advocates should carefully consider perceived conflicts of interest before accepting instructions in future proceedings. An issue of specific concern is the risk of inadvertent disclosure of closed material, were a Special Advocate to act for another party in future proceedings where there was an overlap of issues.[40]

As there are no guidelines in this area on when such 'conflicts' may arise, the manual exhorts special advocates to ensure that they consider these issues at all stages and bring any possible problems to the attention of SASO as soon as possible.

In the absence of guidelines, it would seem that the question of whether there is a 'conflict of interest' is largely down to special advocates to regulate themselves. However, the new edition of the *Open Manual* envisages a situation where

39 SASO, *Special Advocates: A Guide to the Role of Special Advocates and the Special Advocates Support Office* (Treasury Solicitor 2006) [113].

40 ibid.

an 'information owner', defined as a party who has possession and/or control of closed material, asserts that a special advocate cannot be considered for nomination due to a conflict of interest.[41] In this event, they will provide reasons for reaching this decision and the special advocate will then take a view, bearing in mind their professional duties and obligations more generally. If the special advocate believes that there is no conflict of interest, the information owner may raise the issue with the Bar Council or the Bar of Northern Ireland for determination.

Issues of conflict of interest do not seem to have arisen in practice. One question is how broadly a 'conflict of interest' is to be interpreted. The manual refers specifically to a situation where there is a risk of inadvertent disclosure of closed material where a special advocate acts for another party in future proceedings. This seems to relate more to the issue of 'tainting' which is discussed below. But is it a conflict of interest for a special advocate to be acting as a special advocate in one national security case and then to act for the government or indeed for open counsel in another national security case? It would seem that being admitted to the list of special advocates does not preclude a special advocate from acting for the government in some capacity. Indeed it appears that many special advocates appear regularly both for and against the government in civil cases and for both prosecution and defence in criminal cases.[42] One special advocate disclosed that he was asked to be on the panel but he had to wait for five years before getting any work.[43] He believed this was because he continued to do immigration work for the government and any appellant would not be happy with someone from this background acting in his interests. In time he got work because a solicitor he had done work for recognised that he was very well qualified to represent his client. Another counsel who has since come off the panel said that it was important that special advocates continue to do other work and do not become hived off as a special kind of counsel who does not engage in other cases.[44] In practice, open representatives considered they were able to make informed decisions as to who would act well in the interests of their client based on the reputation that special advocates had built up in acting in other non-special advocate cases.

The need to maintain the confidentiality of closed material can lead to special advocates becoming 'tainted' as a result of being privy to closed information when they were involved in previous national security cases. Tainting does not only affect the cases the special advocate can appear in again as a special advocate. Another situation where tainting can arise is where a special advocate who has acted in a closed hearing is then asked to act as open counsel in another related case. For example, it has been suggested that a barrister performing special advocate work in a case involving deportation to Algeria may as a result of becoming privy to closed information relating to the question whether the appellant might

41 SASO (n 13) [55]–[56].

42 See letter from Angus McCullough QC and Martin Chamberlain to the Chairman of the JCHR, 2 October 2012, available at: <https://www.parliament.uk/documents/joint-committees/human-rights/A_McCullough_and_M_Chamberlain.pdf> accessed 10 May 2019.

43 SA3, 25 November 2015.

44 SA12, 14 January 2016.

be tortured become precluded from representing as open counsel a similarly situated Algerian where this same question is engaged.[45]

The first edition of the *Open Manual* explains how tainting can arise:

> The Government has relied on 'generic material' where a number of individuals are associated with a particular group. As a result, once a Special Advocate has acted for an Appellant, or a group of Appellants, in a case where generic material has been relied upon, he is 'tainted' and cannot subsequently act for further individuals, or groups of individuals, in a case where the same generic material is relied upon unless:
>
> (a) The Appellant is prepared to accept that there will be no open period during which he can meet the Special Advocate and discuss the allegations; or
> (b) In a case where lead and junior Special Advocates have been appointed, the tainted Special Advocate works with an untainted Special Advocate who is able to meet the Appellant.[46]

The rationale behind the bar is clearly to prevent any inadvertent leakage of closed material. In giving evidence to the HCCAC, one special advocate explained how exactly tainting can occur.[47] He said that in any particular case, there may be generic evidence that can apply to a group of cases and then there is specific evidence that deals with a particular appellant:

> The generic evidence affects all the people who may be part of a so-called 'link network' and once you have been instructed in one of these cases, you cannot get involved in another case involving another appellant where the generic evidence may be relevant unless the solicitor is happy for you not to meet with the appellant.[48]

In practice, it would seem that tainting seems to occur on a country-specific basis, so that special advocates who have seen closed information in relation to, say, Algeria are 'tainted' in relation to future Algerian cases. One special advocate said that if he has been involved in a case involving Algeria he would not act in an Algerian case again, but in taking a case relating to a new country, say, Sudan, you cannot be sure that you will not become aware of relevant information that you have been exposed to in a previous case. In the early days when the number of special advocates was quite small, there was a danger that the pool of special advocates could become exhausted through tainting. One special advocate giving evidence to the HCCAC reported that he got a case where the pool of advocates

45 Forcese and Waldman (n 18) 30.
46 SASO (n 39) [112].
47 HCCAC (n 4) Ev 7-8 (Mr Ian MacDonald QC).
48 ibid.

had run out and the only reason he was able to act was because the solicitor was happy that he should not go and see the appellant beforehand.[49] It seems that now that there is a much larger list of special advocates, there is less of a danger of the list becoming exhausted.

The second edition of the *Open Manual* sets out a procedure for avoiding tainting whereby SASO will ask the information owner to perform a 'tainting check' on a special advocate whom the excluded party or his open representative have requested to be appointed:

> 50. Where an Information Owner asserts that a Special Advocate is tainted, they will inform SASO and provide reasons. SASO will then check the basis for the assertion to ensure that no administrative error has occurred.
>
> 51. Where SASO and/or the Special Advocate do not accept the Information Owner's assertion, SASO will request a review. To the extent that it is possible to do so, an indication of the reasons that a Special Advocate is considered to be tainted will be shared with the Special Advocate, the excluded party and the OPEN representatives.
>
> 52. If an internal review does not resolve the question of tainting, disputed cases can ultimately be escalated to the Attorney General's Office. The Attorney General will then make a final determination on the tainting issue and notify the interested parties accordingly. Ultimately, the Attorney General has the final say, as with appointments more generally.[50]

In Sweden, the privacy advocates who operate in surveillance cases are under strict obligations not to accept a commission to work in this capacity if there is a significant risk of a conflict of interest emerging whereby information in the case might be relevant to some other case in which they are or may become involved. This applies also to cases in which colleagues in the same firm may become involved. Because it is forbidden to divulge the names of those who have been subject to coercive measures, however, lawyers in the same firm may not be aware that a colleague has been involved in a case as a privacy advocate and problems will not be noticed until a conflict has emerged. Consequently, it has been the practice for lawyers working mainly in criminal law to avoid acting in this capacity, and instead it has been lawyers who work mainly in the commercial or civil field who have taken on this role. This raises a question as to how well-qualified they are to conduct this work but a report which examined the role of privacy advocates considered that these lawyers were able to draw on considerable experience and professional expertise and may have previously been active in defence work.[51]

49 ibid.

50 SASO (n 13).

51 See Statens Offentliga Utredninger (SOU), *Hemliga tvångsmedel mot allvarliga brott* (SOU 2012).

In practice, it seems that a relaxed approach is taken towards tainting in Canada where a small cadre of five persons has done the bulk of the work in certificate proceedings. It appears that the government has objected to the appointment of special advocates on two occasions.[52] In one case, the objection related to two special advocates who had acted as open counsel for named persons and were serving as outside counsel for them in an inquiry. The objection was dropped when the special advocates agreed to withdraw as outside counsel. In the other case, the government filed an objection before the Federal Court of Appeal relating to the appointment of two special advocates to one named person and the Court of Appeal allowed the original motion to permit two special advocates, this being the standard practice in Canada.

Attorney General or Court?

In England and Wales, the Attorney General has traditionally been responsible for the appointment of amici curiae, and as head of the Bar might appear better placed than the courts to determine which lawyer would be best suited to the task of acting as a special advocate.[53] None of the special advocates who were interviewed took issue with the fact that they had been appointed by the Attorney General, even though the Attorney General is the government's principal legal adviser who may be and indeed, in certain SIAC proceedings in the past has been, in the position of arguing the government's position against an excluded party. In the survey conducted by JUSTICE in 2004, none of the special advocates thought that the current arrangements for appointment were especially unsatisfactory.[54]

Although in practice giving responsibility to the Attorney General for the appointment of special advocates does not seem to have caused any difficulty, there is the question whether in some cases a perception might arise that there is a conflict of interest between the Attorney General's function in representing the government and in these same cases taking responsibility for the appointment of counsel whose function is to represent the interests of the opposing party. In his oral evidence to the HCCAC, the Attorney General revealed that in cases relating to Part 4 of the Anti-Terrorism, Crime and Security Act 2001, where the Attorney General had a personal involvement in representing the Government in the proceedings, it was the Solicitor General who approved the recommendation of the Treasury Solicitor as to whom should be appointed.[55] The issue of conflict of interest in the Attorney General's role came up directly in relation to

52 G Hudson and D Alati, 'Behind Closed Doors: Secret Law and the Special Advocate System in Canada' (2018) 44 *Queen's Law Journal* 1, 43.

53 See JUSTICE, *Secret Evidence* (JUSTICE 2009) [397].

54 Metcalfe (n 14) 35.

55 HCCAC (n 4) Ev 33.

the appointment of special counsel in *R v H and C*[56] where the House of Lords sanctioned their appointment in criminal cases in exceptional circumstances. The High Court and the Court of Appeal both took the view that because it is the Attorney General who supervises prosecutions, it was by no means ideal for her to make the appointment in those exceptional cases where one is required, although the Court of Appeal considered that this was the only available route pending legislation to provide a suitably funded alternative permitting the appointment of counsel by the court itself. The court drew parallels with the court appointment of counsel to cross-examine rape complainants in cases where defendants represent themselves but are prohibited from cross-examining rape complainants in person.[57] The House of Lords, however, considered that any doubt about the suitability of the Attorney General to make the appointment was misplaced. Giving the opinion of the Appellate Committee, Lord Bingham said:

> It is very well-established that when exercising a range of functions the Attorney General acts not as a minister of the Crown (although he is of course such) and not as the public officer with overall responsibility for the conduct of prosecutions, but as an independent, unpartisan guardian of the public interest in the administration of justice ... It is in that capacity alone that he approves the list of counsel judged suitable to act as special advocates or, now, special counsel, as when, at the invitation of a court, he appoints an amicus curiae.[58]

In *Home Office v Tariq*,[59] the Supreme Court rejected any suggestion that special advocates are not independent because they were appointed by the Attorney General. In this case Mr Tariq was able to make representations as to his choice of special advocate for the closed proceedings that were ordered by the Employment Tribunal in order to determine his claim of unlawful discrimination, and his choice was implemented.[60] The *Open Manual* states that a special advocate does not 'take instructions' either from the Attorney General, SASO or the excluded party, in the traditional sense, but has the discretion to take any decisions that they consider to be in the excluded party's best interest.[61] There was no suggestion on the part of any of the special advocates who were interviewed that the Attorney General's Office had in any way compromised their independence. We have seen that there are now transparent recruitment exercises carried out in order to enlist special advocates on to the special advocate panel, and

56 *R v H; R v C* [2004] UKHL 3, [2004] 2 AC 135.

57 *R v Interlocutory Application under Sections 35 & 36 of the Criminal Procedure and Investigations Act 1996, H & C* [2003] EWCA Crim 2847, [2003] 1 WLR 3006 [33](v). See Youth Justice and Criminal Evidence Act 1999, ss 38(4) and (5).

58 *R v H; R v C* [2004] UKHL 3, [2004] 2 AC 135 [46].

59 *Home Office v Tariq* [2011] UKSC 35, [2012] 1 AC 452.

60 ibid [46]–[47].

61 SASO (n 13) [43].

professional bodies such as the Bar Council are represented in any recruitment exercise. Furthermore, as we have seen, open parties are now asked to choose whom they would like to represent their interests from the special advocate panel.

A matter of greater concern arises where the Attorney General decides *not* to appoint a special advocate or special counsel in a case where the court has made a request for one. The various statutes that provide for the appointment of a special advocate by the Attorney General say merely that the relevant law officer 'may' appoint a person to represent the interests of an appellant.[62] The first edition of the *Open Manual* states that although the legislation is framed in this permissive manner, in practice 'the law officer will invariably agree to appoint a Special Advocate in any case where it is proposed to withhold material'.[63] We have seen indeed that under the SIAC rules, the Secretary of State may not rely upon closed material unless a special advocate has been appointed to represent the interests of the appellant.[64] Where there is no statutory authority for the appointment, however, and the court has requested that a special advocate be appointed, the Attorney General's position appears to be that while she will always give careful consideration to requests for appointment, the Attorney General does not necessarily agree to make an appointment and that it is a matter for her discretion.[65] One of the counsel for the government who was interviewed disclosed that there have been cases where the Attorney General had refused an appointment.[66] In making submissions to the Court in *Murungaru v Secretary of State for the Home Department*[67] counsel on behalf of the Attorney General indicated that among the many factors considered by the Attorney when deciding whether to appoint a special advocate are cost, the increase in administrative burden associated with the introduction of a special advocate into a new jurisdiction, the risk of unnecessary proliferation, the possibility of contamination of special advocates and the limited number of special advocates on the panel. Strangely, there is no reference here to the fundamentally important question that the court has to decide, which is whether it is in the interests of justice to appoint a special advocate. Sedley LJ said that in view of the fact that the Attorney General is not required to comply with the tribunal's request, it is of even greater importance that requests for the appointment of a special advocate should not be made where the Attorney General could legitimately take an opposite view of the need for one, adding that 'the constitutional and forensic misfortune which a refusal on her part would represent needs no elaboration'.[68] There could, however, be a difference of view between the court and the Attorney General as to whether it is in the interests of

62 See SIAC Act 1997, s 6(1).
63 SASO (n 39) [16].
64 See SIAC (Procedure) Rules 2003, r 37(2).
65 JUSTICE (n 53) [403], citing letter from the Attorney General to Justice dated 20 January 2009.
66 GC 39, 19 April 2016.
67 *Murungaru v SSHD* [2008] EWCA Civ 1015 [19].
68 ibid [18].

justice to make an appointment and the question then is whether it is appropriate for the Attorney General's view to prevail in such a situation. If appointed, the special advocate will invariably be drawn into making submissions in the excluded party's interest against the government's side. So when the Attorney General makes a decision not to appoint a special advocate, however impartially she acts in making the decision, there is inevitably going to be a suspicion that, as JUSTICE has put it, the decision is making her a judge, if not in her own cause, at least in that of her fellow government ministers.[69] The court is inevitably going to be seen as making a more impartial decision on this matter than the Attorney General. Whatever the arguments as to who should make the appointment of a special advocate, there would seem to be a strong argument for re-thinking the current position in England and Wales and Northern Ireland on who should decide *whether* an appointment is made in the first place.[70]

It is interesting to note that unlike in the UK where ultimately it is the responsibility of the Attorney General to make the appointment of the special advocate, in Canada and in other countries such as New Zealand and Australia, it is the responsibility of the courts to make the appointment. The security certificate procedure under the Immigration and Refugee Protection Act in Canada, for example, requires the Minster of Justice to establish a list of persons who may act as special advocates and to publish such a list.[71] Designated judges then make the appointment in individual cases from the list after hearing representations from the government and the named person and they are required to give 'particular consideration and weight to the preferences' of the named persons.[72] The New Zealand Law Commission similarly recommends that a reasonably broad panel of designated special advocates be utilised for all appointments.[73] The non-Crown party should then be able to nominate a lawyer from the panel for appointment and having applied to the court, the court would then appoint a special advocate from the panel to represent the non-Crown party's interests. The court would have the power to refuse to appoint the nominated person and appoint another panel instead, but this should only happen in exceptional circumstances and the party's nominee would almost always be appointed.[74]

69 JUSTICE (n 53) [404].

70 In Scotland, it seems that it is the court which makes the appointment when it is determining disclosure applications made by the prosecutor. See Criminal Justice and Licensing (Scotland) Act 2010, s 150(2).

71 IRPA, s 85.

72 ibid, s 83(1)1(b).

73 See New Zealand Law Commission, *The Crown in Court: A review of the Crown Proceedings Act and national security information in proceedings* (NZLC R135, 2015) [9.9]–[9.10].

74 ibid [9.11].

Special advocates' support office

One of the most consistent concerns expressed by special advocates in the JUSTICE survey before the Special Advocates' Support Office (SASO) was created was the lack of administrative as well as technical assistance given to them.[75] The lack of an instructing solicitor was a particular feature that they drew attention to, given that in their normal professional life they had always been used to having a solicitor who would assist in the preparation of the case. This concern was also highlighted in the special advocates' submissions to the HCCAC in 2005.[76] While the Treasury Solicitor formally instructs them, the instructing lawyer employed in the Treasury Solicitor's Department was not security-cleared which meant that she was unable to perform certain functions which she could otherwise have usefully carried out. These included, for example, checking whether documents which the Home Secretary objected to disclosing to the appellant were available from publicly available sources; corresponding with the Home Secretary and SIAC in relation to closed hearings; copying and distributing closed documents; and keeping a record of closed materials, judgments and rulings. The lack of a person able to perform these functions added significantly to the burden imposed on special advocates. As one of the special advocates said in evidence to HCCAC:

> the truth is that Special Advocates are simply operating on their own with no substantive assistance. ... we have no secretariat, we have no solicitor who can see the closed material and we have no expert assistance on which we can call, so it is something of a feeling of being one man and his dog or perhaps two men and their dogs trying to analyse what is invariably voluminous material and often complex material.[77]

Special advocates were not even able to do their own research by checking whether, for example, closed material is in the public domain because they would be in breach of their duties of confidence if they were to put any name of an individual taken from the closed material into an internet search engine. Their only recourse then was to ask the Security Services to do that search for them.[78]

By contrast, both the government and the appellants' lawyers each had full administrative support with access to all the papers relevant to their case, and neither was particularly willing to assist the special advocate, kept at arms' length on the government side and treated with great suspicion by the excluded party's solicitors. As one special advocate in Northern Ireland explained when he

75 Metcalfe (n 14) 36.
76 HCCAC (n 4) Ev 56.
77 ibid Ev 2 (Mr Neil Garnham QC).
78 ibid Ev 6 (Mr Neil Garnham QC).

undertook a case as a special advocate before Northern Ireland's Sentence Review Commissioners (SRC):

> I received no training. There was no SASO in those days. When I began to be a special advocate, there were no rules setting out how the role should be fulfilled (there still aren't). I was rather shocked to find out that my predecessors as special advocates had not seen the accused or excluded party before the hearing and indeed represented them in the hearing without consultation. I think I may have been instrumental in changing this approach as I wanted to see the accused. In my first case I had great difficulty in getting papers sent to me on the history of the accused (eg the original murder conviction). Eventually I got the secretary to the SRC to send them to me. I also sent a letter to the solicitors and got the secretary of the SRC to send a letter to say I wanted to consult with the client but nothing happened. So in my first case I arrived out at the prison with the hearing to commence. I had offered to speak to the prisoner in two letters sent to the solicitor. On the morning of the hearing the solicitor said that I should speak to the panel and say that I wanted some time to speak to the prisoner. I said to the solicitor that I would have been happy to have done this six months ago. We ended up then with the case having to be put back two hours so I could spend the time talking to the prisoner and the legal representative.[79]

In its recommendations to the HCCAC, JUSTICE picked up on the suggestion made by two special advocates in its survey that the problem of lack of assistance could be ameliorated to some extent by the establishment of an independent 'Office of Special Advocates' staffed by security-cleared personnel (some of whom should be legally qualified) responsible for dealing with correspondence, collating relevant documents and carrying out the factual research normally undertaken by solicitors. The government's response to the concerns of special advocates expressed at the meeting with the Attorney General in March 2005 fell short of establishing a fully independent office located separately from government, but it did announce the establishment of a 'Special Advocates' Support Office' located in the Treasury Solicitor's Department which would operate entirely independently of the immigration teams, which act for the Home Secretary, and be staffed by developed-vetted lawyers who would provide a full instructing role for special advocates.[80]

SASO was established in May 2005 and has provided support to special advocates practising in England and Wales and Northern Ireland ever since. The *Open Manual* explains that SASO is located within the Government Legal Department

79 SA1, 3 November 2015.
80 Government Response to the Constitutional Affairs Select Committee into the Operation of the Special Immigration Appeals Commission (SIAC) and the Use of Special Advocates (Cm 6596, 2005) 11.

which acts for most government departments, including the Attorney General, in litigation matters.[81] However, SASO acts independently in supporting special advocates. This means that it has completely separate document-handling, communication, storage and technology facilities and the lawyers who carry out casework in special advocates cases do not carry out any work for any other part of the Government Legal Department. The staffing arrangements are described in the *Open Manual* as follows:

> 38. SASO lawyers are divided into OPEN and CLOSED teams. The SASO OPEN team liaises with the Attorney General's Office and OPEN representatives regarding the selection and nomination of a Special Advocate. It also supports the Special Advocate(s) whilst they remain in OPEN, for example preparing OPEN papers and attending OPEN conferences and hearings.
>
> 39. SASO CLOSED lawyers have security clearance. They have access to the CLOSED material and are therefore able to consider and discuss that with a Special Advocate in CLOSED, and also to attend CLOSED hearings.
>
> 40. As a general rule, to avoid inadvertent disclosure of CLOSED information, only SASO OPEN lawyers will communicate with the excluded party or the OPEN representatives. This prohibition does not apply to the lawyers who represent the Information Owners, who are permitted to communicate with an excluded party and/or their OPEN representatives notwithstanding that they too will have viewed CLOSED material.

Two questions arise from these support arrangements. The first is whether they enable special advocates to operate sufficiently independently of government and the second is whether they actually provide sufficient support to special advocates. The *Open Manual* states that lawyers representing the information owners are also located within the Government Legal Department and that an information barrier and other measures exist to ensure the independence of SASO from them.[82] In *Home Office v Tariq*, it was argued that these arrangements subjected special advocates to a conflict of interest.[83] Reliance was placed on the Solicitor's Code of Conduct which precludes a solicitor from acting without informed consent where there is a conflict of interest, defined as existing, inter alia, where the solicitor or her firm owes separate duties to act in the best interests of two or more clients in relation to the same or related matters, and those duties conflict, or there is a significant risk that they may conflict. The Supreme Court did not accept there was a conflict of interest.[84] The Treasury Solicitor did not have

81 SASO (n 13) [36].
82 ibid [41].
83 *Home Office v Tariq* [2011] UKSC 35, [2012] 1 AC 452 [48].
84 ibid [49].

two clients and was not in breach of the professional code. The special advocate was an independent (security-cleared) member of the Bar or a solicitor-advocate instructed to represent the best interests of, in this case, Mr Tariq, but not professionally engaged by Mr Tariq.

It was further argued that there was not a sufficient 'Chinese wall' between SASO and the remainder of the Government Legal Department, then known as the Treasury Solicitor's Department, to enable SASO to operate independently of government. The Supreme Court rejected this claim also. It considered that the arrangements described in the *Open Manual* and in a further note provided by the Home Office evidenced 'a serious intention to achieve such a separation, and there is no reason to doubt their genuineness or efficacy'.[85] It quoted a passage from Maurice Kay LJ's judgment in the Court of Appeal that although formal instructions originate from SASO, SASO has no input into the special advocates' decisions which are taken only by the relevant independent special advocate. Maurice Kay LJ gave as examples decisions such as whether to appeal a closed adverse judgment or to open part of a closed judgment. The Supreme Court here seemed to be suggesting that even if the separation arrangements could be questioned, which it did not believe they could, special advocates in any case received only formal instructions from SASO. In fact, SASO has made a point of point of stating that it does not give instructions at all.[86] On the question of separation, attention focused on the role of a Grade 6 lawyer who had no casework responsibilities with SASO, but had a line management role in relation to both the SASO team and the Treasury's General Private Law team. This lawyer chaired monthly special advocate meetings at which cases and tactics were discussed, the minutes of which were sent to the Attorney General's Office, and he could brief the Attorney General on open issues only. It was suggested that the contents of any instructions given by Mr Tariq to the special advocate could be shared with parts of the Treasury Solicitor's Department outside the SASO team or even with the Attorney General. In his judgment, however, Lord Mance said that he did not regard this as realistic. The Grade 6 lawyer had no casework responsibilities and would not therefore on the face of it be likely even to know of any instructions given by Mr Tariq. Even if he did know, disclosure to anyone outside the SASO team would involve a serious breach of duty. It was also unlikely that the minutes of the monthly meetings circulated to the Attorney General's office would disclose such instructions and the special advocate would presumably ensure that they did not. Although the lead Grade 6 lawyer now does have caseload responsibilities,[87] disclosure of any instructions in the minutes would presumably also involve a serious breach of duty

The Court contrasted these well-established arrangements in the Treasury Solicitor's Department with the ad hoc separation arrangements established by

85 ibid [51].
86 Email communication from SASO to the author, 27 November 2018.
87 ibid.

the accountants KPMG in *Prince Jefri Bolkiah v KPMG*[88] who had possession of confidential information relating to a former client (Prince Jefri) which might be relevant to instructions which they had accepted from another client (Brunei Investment Agency) to investigate the whereabouts of certain assets suggested to have been used by Prince Jefri for his own benefit. The House of Lords in this case had granted an injunction restraining KPMG from acting for the Brunei Investment Agency, as the Chinese wall which was erected within KPMG to separate the two teams – one which had acted for Prince Jefri and the other for the Agency – contained large rotating memberships of persons accustomed to working with each other.

None of the special advocates spoken to considered that their independence was compromised by SASO. In fact, some special advocates relied on SASO's independence to 'keep them right' and protect their independence. As one put it:

> Everyone has to be very careful to demonstrate they're abiding by the law, by the rules. And SASO play an important role in that. As a special advocate you have to appear not to be too close to the government side because even though you're on the secret side and not on the excluded side, some clients are very paranoid and untrusting and concerned if there's a lot of closeness. So having SASO there is a very useful tool of reassurance and tool of objectivity and independence.[89]

As always, however, it is the perception that matters when it comes to conflicts of interest. One special advocate suggested that it might have been possible to follow JUSTICE's recommendation and hive off SASO completely from government by putting the whole support operation out to private tender. Another special advocate, however, thought this would be unnecessarily expensive. The reality was that in the support which SASO had given special advocates over the years, they had proved their independence from government.

What is the nature of this support? The *Open Manual* states that once appointed, a special advocate may request whatever assistance they require from SASO, much as they would from an instructing solicitor.[90] The support services are listed as follows:

(a) providing an initial briefing, collating the OPEN papers and legal materials;
(b) corresponding with the excluded party, the OPEN representatives and the information owners about case management directions, conferences, evidence, and preparation for hearings;

88 *Prince Jefri Bolkiah v KPMG* [1999] 2 AC 222.
89 SA6, 3 December 2015.
90 SASO (n 13) [42].

(c) attending hearings and corresponding with courts in relation to directions and other procedural matters;
(d) corresponding with information owners and courts regarding communication requests;
(e) preparing CLOSED materials, and filing and serving on various parties;
(f) arranging and hosting meetings for Special Advocates to discuss matters relevant to their work, including developments in the law;
(g) assisting the wider legal and academic community with matters relating to CLOSED litigation (including court working groups, academics, research, and discussions) and lawyers from overseas jurisdictions.[91]

The old manual also makes reference to a few practical matters connected with the delivery and use of closed material.[92] It seems that in the early days special advocates were required to sit in the basement of Thames House (MI5's headquarters) to view closed materials. According to one open counsel, this was considered too inconvenient and it seems that alternative arrangements have now been made that are more convenient, although for some extremely sensitive cases, special advocates may still be required to go there.[93] Special advocates in other jurisdictions complained about the practical arrangements that had been made for them to view closed material. In Canada, for example, special advocates have to go to the Federal Courthouse in Ottawa in order to view closed information. In Northern Ireland, there is a special area in the Stormont Estate where special advocates must go to view the information. One Northern Ireland-based special advocate commented:

> Certainly in Northern Ireland, actually viewing the material can be very inconvenient. You know, there are particular places where you have to go to view it. And any submissions that you do can't be done on your own computer. They have to be done with this special secured computer at the location where you use the material. And all of that just makes the whole process very time-consuming.[94]

There is little doubt that the creation of SASO has transformed the life of special advocates. Special advocates uniformly spoke of the invaluable support SASO had given them in cases. One went so far as to say that part of the reason why he had stuck at the role of being a special advocate over the years was that he found the SASO team so supportive.[95] Obviously there had been some change in

91 ibid.
92 ibid [92].
93 OC4, 15 January 2016.
94 SA2, 4 November 2015.
95 SA4, 25 November 2015.

personnel over the years as some had moved on to other jobs, but they had been consistently very decent to deal with. Another said:

> SASO does a very good job. Its staff are overworked but it's full of committed, decent, intelligent people and they give all the support I need certainly.[96]

A number of special advocates made a distinction between what one called SASO's 'postbox' role and its more substantive role. Each could be very labour-intensive. The postbox role involved ensuring that material was passed and received to the right people:

> A postbox is at a very basic level getting us the material which of course is not as simple as it is in a normal case because a lot of the material gets a security marking. So it can't be emailed or faxed or sent by courier.[97]

Apart from delivering closed material, the other delivery role special advocates mentioned for SASO is dealing with the open representatives and making sure that they are kept informed of what is going on. Some communications, of course, will have to be cleared, but sometimes it is just a question of an update as to what is going on or alerting them to a hearing date that has to be moved. Or it may be that the open representatives want to pass information to the special advocates. One special advocate said that in the early days, the open representatives did not want to involve themselves in what was going on in closed but now there is much more liaising with SASO even before a case begins as to which special advocates are free, who has got the right experience, and throughout the case they will have an involvement in providing instructions.[98]

The 'postbox' role that SASO played has also intensified as special advocates have become involved in more cases. One special advocate drew attention to the recent naturalisation judicial reviews that SIAC was having to deal with as a result of it obtaining jurisdiction in such cases under the Justice and Security Act 2013. These tended to be relatively short cases and SIAC had for the first time sat in two divisions to hear them, dealing in each division perhaps with one review case and one appeal in a week, which might mean dealing with four cases overall in one week. This intensified the role.

The more that SASO had to play a 'fire-fighting' postbox role, however, the less time they had to become involved in the substantive role of advising special advocates on aspects of their case. This advisory role was one that special advocates valued very much. It was particularly useful when special advocates initially

96 SA3, 25 November 2015.
97 SA11, 14 January 2016.
98 ibid.

take on cases. One special advocate said that when he first started, he used SASO for advice a lot:

> I'd be on the phone saying, what should I do now in this situation? How do I respond? What are my limits? They're very good at telling you what your limits are and what you can and can't do.[99]

Another special advocate said that SASO was exceptionally helpful in one case where he was on his own and he had to deal with a planning matter that was new to him.[100] It was the first time that a special advocate had been appointed in a planning case. What was particularly valuable was being able to work things out with SASO in the way that one normally would with a solicitor or somebody else. There were intricate issues involved such as having to appear as the appointed person for five separate institutions and having to consider if a conflict of interest arose. The two lawyers from SASO were 'brilliant in helping out' because if he had been on his own, he would have felt 'very uncomfortable'.

It appears that SASO are particularly good in directing attention to what was done in other cases. One special advocate said that on a number of occasions, he had sent out an email to SASO and other special advocates in very general terms asking whether anyone had had to deal with a particular type of case recently. Sometimes he had to do it verbally because he could not send an email about it.

> SASO may not be able to come back very specifically and say, yes you want this or you want that. But what they're normally able to do is say, well, that popped up in this case, so speak to special advocate X because he'll be on top of it. … I've never been in a position where I have got chapter and verse from SASO, be it now or be it in the old days. But we frequently get summaries of cases emailed to us in open when they come out, saying this is a case for you to know about. And I have certainly in the past tasked them various roles to do, I need you to go and find this, you've got to do this, etc. So for example I've just been instructed in a Jordanian case and I needed them to go and see what was left of the Jordanian papers in two other cases and so they've had to go off and look at that and give me a sort of over-arching view of what's going on there.[101]

This was not to say that SASO played a role like a solicitor in normal proceedings:

> Would I ever get them to draft a witness statement or anything like that? No. But then again, they're not normal proceedings. Certainly if we ever got into a position where we need witnesses, I think they would be involved in that.

99 SA6, 3 December 2015.
100 SA11, 14 January 2016.
101 ibid.

> But I have to say that the practical application of that, I really never foresee a day when it's actually going to happen.[102]

In fact, SASO has pointed out since this interview that there have been at least two occasions when SASO instructed a closed expert and assisted in something akin to a normal solicitor role in terms of finding, contacting and taking a witness statement.[103]

Apart from assisting on aspects of the case, a SASO representative would always be in attendance at hearings and sometimes they would attend some of the purely administrative directions hearings on their own. This could be particularly useful when neither of the two appointed special advocates in a case want to go into closed early but SIAC or the court want a closed hearing. A SASO lawyer could be asked to go into closed so that they can see whether they can deal with the matter themselves or whether it is something that requires the special advocate to go into closed. As soon as the special advocate goes into closed, of course, there is no way back into open:

> So, for example, say the Secretary of State wants to push back the date by which they are due to serve material. The reasons for that may not be in open but they may not affect the case. And so for somebody from SASO to be able to go into closed makes it a lot easier rather than us going into closed and then being stuck in closed.[104]

One concern that many special advocates raised, however, was the limited resources available to SASO who now have to deal with a growing number of cases. SASO was initially comprised of five lawyers and three administrators, with four lawyers and two administrators forming the closed team and the remaining lawyer and administrator forming the open team.[105] The staffing position has not changed much over the years. There are presently five lawyers, four in the closed team and one in the open team, two paralegals (one in open and one in closed) and one administrator who does both open and closed tasks.[106] One special advocate said his experience of SASO was that it was initially well-staffed and well-run, but the pressure of work has meant that it was now not sufficiently staffed for it to provide a reliable service:

> There's too few people in the office and it's gone down to essentially one or two individuals and they've got too much on. And so, when you need things done, there's sometimes a delay in getting things to court. Special advocates have taken to walking each other to and from their chambers with stuff because it's quicker than trying to get somebody to come along and

102 ibid.
103 Email communication from SASO to the author, 12 December 2018.
104 ibid.
105 See *Home Office v Tariq* [2011] UKSC 35 [50].
106 Email communication from SASO to the author, 12 December 2018.

> do the support function. And in terms of preparing bundles of authorities, it's simply quicker to do it in-house and do it oneself than to rely on them. I mean they sit behind you in court and they're useful in terms of being able to get things but you sometimes find the documents have been disclosed to the open representatives or from the open representatives and they don't arrive with us for a period of time. And then suddenly we get everything in one go but it's three days after everyone else has got it.[107]

Another special advocate said that for a number of years now, SASO have not had the same knowledge of cases as they did previously which meant they were of less assistance. It also meant that they had less of a grasp of their role as a whole. He said that SASO had always worked very hard, sometimes exceptionally hard, delivering materials well beyond normal office hours, answering emails well beyond the normal times, but they were under-resourced.

One particular issue of concern raised by special advocates in a number of interviews was the lack of an adequate database of closed judgments. The *Open Manual* makes reference to SASO making open and closed judgments available to special advocates. Special advocates acknowledged that SASO does its best to acquaint them with relevant closed judgments but the lack of a complete set of well-indexed closed judgments, as one can find with open judgments, makes it difficult for special advocates themselves to access relevant case law. The Ministry of Justice Green Paper stated that the Home Office was taking forward work to develop closed headnotes for closed judgments to summarise the broad subject of the judgment and to include keywords for search purposes, but at the time of the interviews this did not seem to have progressed.[108] As one special advocate said, matters such as the closed case database and adequate training were wider government matters which the government was keen to trumpet when the Justice and Security Bill was going through Parliament, but the minute the Bill got through, all these commitments seemed to disappear.[109]

The lack of such a closed database was not only an issue for special advocates. The danger was that over the passage of time, some judgments may get lost from everyone's collective memory. This is reminiscent of the Kafkaesque world where Joseph K discovers that the court's decisions are not published and are not accessible even to judges; and as a consequence, old legal cases are preserved only as legends.[110] Special advocates said that they knew of certain closed judgments but you cannot possibly know them all; likewise, on the Secretary of State's side, the Secretary of State's team may know some but not all. One government counsel confirmed, that contrary to what is sometimes thought, Treasury counsel also do not have access to a comprehensive closed database of judgments.[111] So it was

107 SA7, 3 December 2015.

108 Ministry of Justice, *Justice and Security Green Paper* (Cm 8194, 2011) App F.

109 SA5, 25 November 2015.

110 F Kafka, *The Trial* (Penguin 1953) 171. See A Zuckerman, *Zuckerman's Civil Procedure* (3rd edn Sweet & Maxwell 2013) 933–934.

111 GC 6, 19 April 2016.

perfectly possible that at some point a closed hearing could go wrong because no one was aware of an earlier judgment. Another question that was raised was whether judgments were ever going to be made open after a designated embargo period. Since the interviews took place, a Royal Courts of Justice working group has been set up to examine the management of a closed judgment database. This project is ongoing but there is currently no timeline by which it is expected to be completed.[112]

Finally, SASO can be compared with the much slimmer support operation that exists in Canada for special advocates, known as the Special Advocate Program (SAP). It consists of one senior counsel, one counsel and one administrative assistant and one half-time financial advisor, all of whom work to support the role of special advocates within, but independently of, the Department of Justice.[113] SAP is responsible for the remuneration of special advocates and lobbies to ensure that special advocates get the support they need within courts where closed material is viewed. It holds regular meetings and training exercises.[114] Unlike SASO, however, it seems that SAP has some formal input into policy-making as the senior counsel in the program has a seat in the interdepartmental committee set up to monitor Division 9type cases under IRPA which consists of security services, police, external affairs and the Department of Public Safety – which is the government department that pulls together all these strands. Although this group has a policy remit and there is an opportunity for special advocates' concerns to be reflected, it appears that much of the agenda is driven by the Canadian Security Intelligence Service.

Training

Although special advocates are supported by SASO, they are given very little training when they are first admitted to the special advocate panel. In the early JUSTICE survey, almost all special advocates thought that some kind of training would be a good idea to highlight the practical, ethical and legal problems they were likely face.[115] In response to their concerns following their meeting with the Attorney General in March 2005, the government promised to provide 'a comprehensive training pack, comprising both open and closed material' to special advocates when instructed.[116] None of the special advocates who were interviewed made any mention of this, but newly appointed special advocates do attend a one-day training course facilitated by the Security Service which explains intelligence processes, including how intelligence is assessed (including

112 Email communication from SASO to author, 12 July 2018.
113 Hudson and Alati (n 52) 40.
114 Interview with senior counsel of Special Advocate Program, 8 April 2016 (Mr Keith Wilkins SC).
115 Metcalfe (n 14).
116 HCCAC (n 4), Government Response to Special Advocates' Concerns, Ev 77.

its reliability), how investigations are prioritised, what sort of actions are taken, and why.[117] One special advocate said that this was an 'incredibly good working exercise' in which you were given a number of case studies that evolved throughout the day.[118] Various lecturers came in and informed attendees about the work of the intelligence agencies. This was very useful as most special advocates had no background in security or intelligence matters. Nevertheless, formal training of this kind had its limits:

> It's all very well spending a day learning how intelligence is gathered and what the sensitivities are. It's actually quite difficult in practice to work out what the particular sensitivity of a piece of evidence might be and why it is that national security requires it not to be gisted.[119]

It would seem that special advocates in Canada receive more intensive training when they are first appointed. This consists of three one-week blocks of meetings divided between open and closed sessions and briefings covering several core themes from persons with experience and expertise in Division 9 proceedings, including a designated judge, government counsel and outside counsel, as well as the intelligence agencies.[120]

Special advocates emphasised the importance of continuous training as they eased themselves into the job, even for experienced special advocates. A number emphasised how isolated special advocates can be and how difficult it was to get technical assistance:

> If you think about it from an equality of arms point of view, anybody appearing for the Secretary of State has the ability to sit down with the clients and go, right, explain to me how this works; explain to me how this office is divided, this works, that works; what document should I be looking for, what shouldn't I? So you know everything in a normal open case I would be able to Google or I would be able to speak to somebody else about it.[121]
>
> ... If you are a special advocate, on the other hand, and especially if you are a special advocate working on your own as in some of the recent naturalisation cases, unless somebody from the Special Advocates Support Office can help you, you are literally on your own. It's not like another case where you can come back into chambers and say, 'Look can I bounce this idea off you?' Or, 'Have you heard of something to do with this?' You are really cocooned on your own'.[122]

117 See Ministry of Justice (n 108) [2.25].
118 SA3, 25 November 2015.
119 ibid.
120 Hudson and Alati (n 52).
121 SA11, 14 January 2016.
122 SA8, 7 December 2015.

It is also the case that unlike other advocates who can go and watch how advocacy is practised in open court, special advocates do not get to see how 'special advocacy' is practised in closed proceedings. One advocate said that he had done special advocate work for eight years, but that was enough for him as it was a 'very lonely job'.[123]

The Justice and Security Green Paper recognised that there was a gap in training provision for experienced special advocates who either require refresher modules, re-attendance at the introductory course or specific training on particular issues that arise in CMPs.[124] The government resolved to make available increased training for special advocates, but this does not seem to have occurred. Meanwhile, SASO plays an informal role in assisting in the training of special advocates. Quarterly meetings are convened by SASO for special advocates to share experiences and relevant institutional knowledge on subjects such as disclosure hearings, closed proceedings in the family courts etc. SASO has also produced an 'open manual' and another 'closed manual' to familiarise special advocates with the special advocate function and role. In addition, by 2016–17, SASO was compiling a quarterly newsletter which was sent to all special advocates, sharing updates on cases, including summaries of open decisions and trends. In Canada, SAP also takes the role of continuing education very seriously through an annual, day-long meeting of special advocates aimed at maintaining a sense of community and shared knowledge and by organising knowledge-sharing sessions for all persons appointed as special advocates.[125] Agendas are set each year for the annual meeting and these meetings have included open counsel and special advocates from the UK.

Cooperative learning is now an accepted, and often preferred, instructional procedure at all levels of education and it is well-established that apprentices learn mostly from their peers and their 'communities of practice'.[126] It would seem particularly important that special advocates who are otherwise so isolated in their work get an opportunity to interact with each other on all aspects of their work so that they become better informed and can become socialised into thinking like a special advocate. One step that certainly promotes learning has been for special advocates to work in pairs with a senior and junior counsel involved in each case. According to one special advocate, perhaps the single best way in which special advocates learn 'on the job' is preparing together with a more

123 SA12, 14 January 2016.
124 Ministry of Justice (n 108) [2.26].
125 Hudson and Alati (n 52) 41–42.
126 See D W Johnson, R T Johnson and K Smith, 'The State of Cooperative Learning in Post Secondary and Professional Settings' (2007) 19 *Educational Psychology Review* 19. 'Communities of practice' have been defined as groups of people who 'share a concern, a set of concerns, or a passion about a topic and who deepen their knowledge and expertise by interacting on an ongoing basis'. See E Wenger, R McDermott and W M Snyder, *Cultivating Communities of Practice: A Guide to Managing Knowledge* (Harvard Business School Press 2002) 4.

senior special advocate. In the beginning it is 'terribly useful' to have more than one special advocate involved in the case.[127] Special advocates spoke of the camaraderie between them and how the more experienced assist those who are coming up through the ranks. Over time, a kind of collective professional memory is built up in terms of what has worked and what has not worked and this can be passed on to other advocates. As one special advocate put it:

> I reflect all the time about how I can do it better. If I think something hasn't gone quite as well, I will actively reflect on that. I will actively reflect with junior Special Advocates. ... It's still quite an unusual form of proceeding and there's no embarrassment in saying, 'Right well, I'm going to reflect on what I did. I'll see if I can change anything whether through a user group, through political channels, through my own practice, through discussions among special advocates'. No one thinks, 'Well, that's a terrible thing to do'. I think everyone is really up for that kind of feeding of ideas. So I tend to learn, and you do learn, on the job. There's no doubt about that. But that's in a way not so different to other areas.[128]

In Forcese and Waldman's survey in 2007, there was some concern expressed that the concept of 'tainting' had begun to affect information sharing between special advocates.[129] A view was reportedly being taken that information exchange between special advocates on closed material was inconsistent with the 'need to know' principle whereby even security-cleared individuals should be given access to information only where necessary to discharge their functions, minimising the circle of persons with access to the material. In Canada, special advocates sought permission to correspond with special advocates appointed to other ongoing proceedings under the supervision of SAP and the Federal Court has authorised special advocates to participate in knowledge-sharing sessions organised and supervised by the SAP.[130] All in all, it would seem, however, that there is a more relaxed attitude towards special advocates speaking to each other today and this does not appear to be an issue.

It can be argued that interactive sessions with other advocates not only help special advocates to develop common strategies and techniques but, particularly important for new communities of practice, help to instil common values and ethical standards. Of course, special advocates are members of professional associations which have their own structural frameworks of ethical standards. But as we shall see in the next chapter, special advocacy brings with it certain unique ethical challenges.

127 SA8, 7 December 2015

128 SA4, 25 November 2015.

129 Forcese and Waldman (n 18).

130 Hudson and Alati (n 52) 44, citing *Re Harkat* 2009 FC 59.

6 Ethical issues

Much of the criticism of special advocates in CMPs has centred on the fact that although they are appointed to represent the interests of excluded parties in the closed hearing, this cannot compensate for the inherent unfairness of withholding evidence from a party to proceedings, as it leaves the special advocate unable to take instructions on the closed material.[1] Although the secrecy in which special advocates operate has attracted most attention, it is important to recognise that the appointment of special advocates in itself appears to involve almost as much a break from adversarial tradition as the secret procedures themselves. As in the case of ordinary advocates, special advocates act in the interests of the parties they represent but, as we shall see, they do so in a different capacity from ordinary advocates in that they do not 'act' *for* the parties they represent and do not owe them a duty of care. The effect of this is to sever the normal professional–client relationship whereby counsel are instructed by their clients through solicitors.[2]

The novelty of their role was brought home in the following terms by Lord Bingham in *R v H and C*, the case where the use of special counsel was first authorised in criminal trials:[3]

> a lawyer who cannot take full instructions from his client, nor report to his client, who is not responsible to his client and whose relationship with the client lacks the quality of confidence inherent in any ordinary lawyer-client relationship, is acting in a way hitherto unknown to the legal profession.

Others have gone so far as to argue that the role is no longer one of advocacy at all. In Baroness Kennedy's view:

> to call the [special advocate] an advocate is a denial of what the role of advocacy is all about. The whole purpose of advocacy is that on behalf of your client, you are able to contest the allegation made and to do it acting as – if you

1 See *Al Rawi v The Security Service* [2011] UKSC 34, [2012] 1 AC 531 [36] (Lord Dyson).
2 For the legal basis of the lawyer-client relationship in English law, see A Boon, *The Ethics and Conduct of Lawyers in England and Wales* (3rd edn Hart 2014) 297–300.
3 *R v H; R v C* [2004] UKHL 3, [2004] 2 AC 135 [22].

> like – the spokesperson for that person and to challenge evidence in a way that they would do themselves were they able to and versed in the law. The special advocate has no such possibility. Having had access to the evidence, the special advocate is denied the opportunity of speaking with the person … To call such a lawyer an advocate for the person is a corruption of language as we know and understand it within our system of law.[4]

In this chapter, we consider how different the ethics of 'special' advocacy are from 'ordinary' advocacy and how special advocates have viewed their ethical obligations when they act in this role. To establish a baseline for addressing these issues, we first need to consider the ethics of ordinary legal representation within the adversarial tradition.

The ethics of advocacy in the adversarial tradition

Much ink has been spilt in trying to ascertain how exactly the adversarial tradition should be characterised and how it differs from its antithesis, the so-called 'inquisitorial' tradition.[5] Fundamentally, however, the adversarial tradition involves a mode of proceeding which gives parties to a dispute considerable control over the way in which they wish to present their case rather than handing control of the process over to adjudicators. In his masterful *The Faces of Justice and State Authority*, Damaška sought to uncover the ideological underpinnings of 'adversarial' and 'inquisitorial' modes of proceeding by drawing a contrast between, on the one hand, a commitment to the ideals of personal autonomy and a political ideology of laissez-faire which views the administration of justice as conflict resolution and, on the other hand, an assumption that the state interest or public interest should prevail over private interests which views the administration of justice as policy implementation.[6] More recently, scholars have linked the rise of the adversarial criminal trial with demands to develop the criminal law in a manner that attributes responsibility on the basis of the accused's autonomy and capacity for wrongdoing.[7]

Viewed in this manner, the adversarial tradition entails giving the parties considerable choice over their handling of litigation. Even when criminal proceedings became identified in the modern era with implementing the state's interest in criminal law enforcement, they took on conflict resolving forms throughout the common law world that matched the ideals of liberal ideology by being conceived as a dispute between the government and an autonomous member of civil society. Over time, however, it was recognised that the parties need various facilities

4 HL Deb 15 February 2006, vol 678, col 1224 in the debate in the House of Lords on the Prevention of Terrorism Act 2005 (continuation in force of sections 1 to 9) Order 2006 (renewing control orders).

5 See M R Damaška, 'Evidentiary Barriers to Conviction and Two Models of Criminal Procedure' (1973) 121 *University of Pennsylvania Law Review* 506, 554–578.

6 M R Damaška, *Faces of Justice and State Authority* (Yale UP 1986).

7 See eg N Lacey, *In Search of Criminal Responsibility: Ideas, Interests and Institutions* (OUP 2016), L Farmer, *Making the Criminal Law: Criminalisation and Civil Order* (OUP 2016).

to be made available to them in order that they might advance their case in an effective manner, and foremost of these was access to counsel to advocate on their behalf. The 'standard conception' of the advocate's role within the adversarial system which lays the responsibility on each party to advance its own case then is an obligation to act with partisan zeal on behalf of the client.[8] As Lord Brougham famously put it:

> An advocate, in the discharge of his duty, knows but one person in all the world, and that person is his client. To save that client by all means, and expedients, and at all hazards and costs to other persons, and among them, to himself, is his first and only duty; and in performing this duty he must not regard the alarm, the torments, the destruction which he may bring upon others.[9]

Particularly relevant in the national security context is the statement following that:

> [s]eparating the duty of a patriot from that of an advocate, and casting them, if need be, to the wind, he must go on reckless of the consequences, though it should be his unhappy fate to involve his country in confusion.[10]

Alongside the principle of partiality is the principle of neutrality which requires that advocates act on behalf of any client to whom they are allocated irrespective of any moral considerations about the righteousness of their cause. At the Bar, this is referred to as the 'cab rank' rule.[11] A third principle is sometimes also added to the standard conception – that of non-accountability – which insists that lawyers bear no responsibility for their client's goals or the means used to attain them.[12] Their only accountability is to their client.

The standard conception has been tempered somewhat by the codes of conduct that have been developed to constrain the advocate's performance.[13] The 'cab rank' rule at the English Bar has been described as the 'most famous and distinctive ethical principle of the English Bar'[14] and is still referred to in the Bar Code. This requires that barristers accept instructions received from a professional

8 On the 'standard' conception see A Boon, *The Ethics and Conduct of Lawyers in England and Wales* (3rd edn Hart 2014) 23–25; D Luban, *Lawyers and Justice: An Ethical Study* (Princeton UP 1988) xix–xx; J Herring, *Legal Ethics* (2nd edn OUP 2017) 118–119.

9 2 *Trial of Queen Caroline* 8 (J Nightingale ed. Albion Press) quoted in D Nicolson and J Webb, *Professional Legal Ethics* (OUP 1999) 162 and Boon, ibid 683.

10 ibid.

11 See Bar Standards Board, *Bar Code of Conduct* (2014) r C29.

12 Boon (n 8) 25.

13 See T Smith, 'The "Quiet Revolution" in Criminal Defence: How the Zealous Advocate Slipped in the Shadow' (2013) 20 *International Journal of Evidence & Proof* 111.

14 A Boon and S Nash, 'Special Advocacy: Political Expediency and Legal Roles in Modern Judicial Systems' (2006) 9 *Legal Ethics* 101, 111.

client which are addressed specifically to them irrespective of the identity of the client, the nature of the case, whether the client is paying privately or is publicly funded, and any belief or opinion they may have formed as to the character, reputation, cause, conduct, guilt or innocence of the client.[15] The principle of partisanship has, however, undergone some tempering over time. While the language of the old Code that barristers must 'promote and protect fearlessly and by all proper and lawful means the lay client's best interests' has been retained,[16] the revised Code of 2014 puts first and foremost the duty to the court in the administration of justice.[17] The first chapter of the revised Code is entitled 'You and the Court' and the client does not appear until Chapter 3.[18] The duty to the court overrides any other duty, including the duty to act in the best interests of each client.

It is important to note also that the phrase used to promote partisanship is 'acting in the best interests' of the client.[19] One can compare the preamble to the current ABA Model Code which states that a lawyer, as advocate, 'zealously asserts the client's position under the rules of the adversary system'.[20] It has been suggested that the American model requires loyalty to the client's wishes and not her interests,[21] although recent versions of the Model Code would appear to have moved away from 'a hard line on partisanship'.[22] In practice, while lawyers are required to abide by clients' decisions on the objectives of the representation, they have considerable discretion as to how the case should be conducted, including waiving clients' rights.[23] By contrast, there is no suggestion in the English Bar Code that the advocate is the mouthpiece of the client. Pursuing best interests falls short of an obligation to carry out a client's lawful preferences as it entails no obligation to promote client autonomy. Boon argues that this is a weak version of partisanship and the obligation is consistent with either a participative or paternalistic model of representation.[24] Although the trend in legal practice generally has moved away from paternalism towards participative lawyer–client relationships, in Boon's view the general tone of the Bar Code in defining the relationship between client and advocate casts the advocate as a remote figure reserving a substantial amount of discretion to the barrister.[25] The Code stresses that barristers must not permit their professional client, employer or any other person to limit

15 See Bar Standards Board (n 11).
16 ibid r C15.1.
17 ibid CD1. CD1 is said to 'override any other core duty, if and to the extent the two are inconsistent' (r C1).
18 For commentary see Boon (n 8) 320–21.
19 Bar Standards Board (n 11) CD2.
20 American Bar Association, *Model Code of Professional Conduct 2004.*
21 D Luban, 'The Sources of Legal Ethics' (1984) 48 *Rabels Zeitschift* 262, cited in Boon (n 8) 327.
22 Boon (n 8) 324.
23 See D Sklansky, 'Autonomy and Agency in American Criminal Process' in J Jackson and S Summers (eds), *Obstacles to Fairness in Criminal Proceedings: Individual Rights and Institutional Forms* (Hart 2018) 37.
24 Boon (n 8) 327.
25 ibid 321.

their discretion as to how the interests of the client can best be served.[26] They are personally responsible for their own conduct and professional work:

> You must use your own professional judgment in relation to those matters on which you are instructed and be able to justify your decisions and actions ... notwithstanding the view of your client, professional client, employer or any other person.[27]

The courts have also emphasised that the client does not conduct the case:

> The advocate is not the client's mouthpiece, obliged to conduct the case in accordance with whatever the client, or whenever the advocate is a barrister, the solicitor 'instructs' him. ... [S]ave for well-established principles, like the personal responsibility of the defendant to enter his own plea, and to make his own decision whether to give evidence, and perhaps whether a witness who appears to be able to give relevant admissible evidence favourable to the defendant should or should not be called, the advocate, and the advocate alone remains responsible for the forensic decisions and strategy.[28]

The net result of this is that when lawyers conduct cases on behalf of parties in an adversarial trial, parties lose their procedural autonomy over how the case should be conducted, forcing them, as one commentator has put it, to put their fate in the hands of counsel and hope for the best.[29]

The ethics of special advocacy

Given these constraints on the standard conception, it may be questioned how different the role of the special advocate is from the role of advocates in general. The functions of the special advocate are set out in the rules made under the Special Immigration Appeals Commission Act (SIAC) 1997 as requiring the special advocate to:

> represent the interests of the appellant by –
>
> (a) making submissions to the Commission in any proceedings from which the appellant and his representatives are excluded;

26 Bar Standards Board (n 11) r C15.4.
27 ibid r C20.
28 *R* v *Farooqi* [2013] EWCA Crim 1649 [108].
29 W Wohlers, 'The Role of Counsel in Criminal Proceedings' in Jackson and Summers (n 23) 127, 152. See also M Blake and A Ashworth, 'Ethics and the Criminal Defence Lawyer' (2004) *Legal Ethics* 167, 183. For an historical account of how the accused lost autonomy in the adversarial criminal trial, see L Farmer, 'Criminal Responsibility and the Proof of Guilt' in M D Dubber and L Farmer (eds), *Modern Histories of Crime and Punishment* (Stanford UP 2007) 42, 58.

(b) adducing evidence and cross-examining witnesses at any such proceedings; and
(c) making written submissions to the Commission.[30]

At first glance this does not seem that far removed from the role of an ordinary advocate. Representing 'interests' is, of course, the same terminology used in the Bar Code. However, the role appears different when one examines the relationship between the special advocate and the party whose interests she is there to represent. Although there is scope for determining how exactly the interests of the client are to be assessed, the Bar Code Guidance states quite unequivocally that 'your duty is to your *client*, not to your *professional client* or other *intermediary*'.[31] We have said that in ordinary adversarial litigation the represented party may lose procedural autonomy over the conduct of the case. Ultimately, however, the client retains autonomy or personal responsibility over the litigation and may dismiss counsel and act instead on her own behalf.[32] Where, by contrast, there is a CMP and a special advocate is appointed, the excluded party not only loses control over who should be appointed and how the case should be conducted in the closed proceedings, but loses all responsibility for the case. Section 6(4) of the SIAC Act expressly states that a special advocate shall not be 'responsible to the person whose interests he is appointed to represent'.[33] This severance of the relationship between counsel and client is stated quite unequivocally in SASO's *Open Manual* when it states that the role of a special advocate is different to that of ordinary counsel:

> a Special Advocate is appointed to represent the *interests* of the excluded party, but ... is not accountable to them. As the status of Special Advocate is conferred by appointment, a Special Advocate does not 'take instructions' in the traditional sense, either from the Attorney General, SASO or the excluded party. The Special Advocate thus has the discretion to take any decisions that they consider to be in the excluded party's best interests.[34]

This would appear to put the special advocate in a somewhat different ethical zone from that of other lawyers, who have a client to whom they are accountable. In the last chapter, we saw that special advocates are isolated professionally by virtue of having to work on their own. But the effect of severing the link with the

30 SIAC (Procedure) Rules 2003, r 35. See also CPR, r 76.24 (proceedings under the PTA 2005); r 79.19 (proceedings under the Counter-Terrorism Act 2008 and Pt 1 of the Terrorist Asset-Freezing Etc Act 2010); r 80.20 (TPIMs); r 82.10 (CMPs in civil proceedings).
31 Bar Standards Board (n 11) r C36 (emphasis in original).
32 See N Padfield, 'The Right to Self-Representation in English Criminal Law' (2012–2013) 83 *International Review of Penal Law* 359. In the US, the right to represent oneself has acquired constitutional status. See *US v Faretta* 422 US 806 (1975).
33 See also Prevention of Terrorism Act 2005, sch [7(5)]; Counter-Terrorism Act 2008, s 68(2); TPIMs Act 2011, sch 4 [10(4)]; Justice and Security Act 2013, s 9(4).
34 SASO, *A Guide to The Role of Special Advocates & The Special Advocates' Support Office* (2nd edn Government Legal Department 2019) [43].

client appears to put them at an ethical distance from other lawyers by removing them from any responsibility to the client. In her evidence to the HCCAC back in 2005, Gareth Peirce commented that special advocates have a duty of 'constant soul-searching and indeed morality' which should not be placed upon them any more than it should on the judges who have to operate in SIAC.[35] In the same parliamentary session, Ian Macdonald QC, a senior immigration lawyer who had resigned from acting as a special advocate, explained that he was happy to act as a special advocate in SIAC when it was first established because this was a big improvement on what had happened before in deportation proceedings and had introduced an element of fairness which had previously been lacking. When the jurisdiction under the Anti-Terrorism, Crime and Security Act 2001 was tacked on to SIAC which was purely an immigration court, he stayed on because he thought he might make a difference but there came a point when he had to balance that against 'being some kind of fig-leaf of respectability and legitimacy' to a process which he found odious.[36]

At one level, the dilemma of whether to act in proceedings which fall short of recognised standards of fairness is one that all lawyers may have to face. When lawyers act in their conventional representational role on behalf of clients, however, it is easier for them to defend their role against the challenge that they are providing a fig leaf of respectability to an unfair process. The cab rank rule at the English Bar in particular requires that barristers act on the instructions of their clients irrespective of any views they have about the nature of the proceedings. Sometimes, indeed, lawyers have represented clients even when the procedures involved are abundantly unfair, as, for example, in the case of the habeas corpus and military commission procedures that Guantánamo detainees have been subject to.[37] Here the representational role is justified by the need to safeguard human dignity against government overreaching and abuse, no matter what obstacles are put in its way.[38] But it was not just the principle of representation that motivated the lawyers acting for Guantánamo detainees. They also developed a personal bond with their clients which was stronger than any professional loyalty.[39]

35 HCCAC, *The Operation of the Special Immigration Appeals Commission (SIAC) and the Use of Special Advocates* (2004-05, HC 323-1) Oral evidence, 22 February 2005, Ev 6.

36 ibid, Ev 1. See also I Macdonald, 'Police State?' *Counsel* March 2005, 16.

37 See J Margulies, *Guantanamo and the Abuse of Presidential Power* (Simon & Schuster 2007); D Cole, *Engines of Liberty: The Power of Citizen Activists to Make Constitutional Law* (Basic Books 2016).

38 See D Luban, 'Lawfare and Legal Ethics in Guantánamo' (2008) 60 *Stanford Law Review* 1981, 1986.

39 ibid, 2015, n 204 quoting Wells Dixon. See also Margulies (n 37) 2, commenting that the release of his client, Mamdouh Habib, who had spent six months in a prison outside Cairo and more than two years at Guantánamo, and seeing him re-united with his wife was one of the most gratifying moments of his legal career. For an expression of the gratitude that one Guantánamo detainee felt for the lawyers who had worked tirelessly to secure his freedom, see L Boumediene and M Idir, *Witnesses of the Unseen: Seven Years in Guantanamo* (Redwood Press 2017) 132.

But when the professional–client relationship is severed and the lawyer has no professional or personal bond with the client, lawyers cannot justify their actions purely on the basis of client loyalty. They need to evaluate more objectively whether they are 'doing good' in their role. We have seen that special advocates have been publicly critical of the unfairness of closed procedures. In their written evidence to the HCCAC in 2005, they stated that it should not be thought that, by continuing in their positions as special advocates, they were impliedly warranting the fairness or value of the SIAC appeal process, adding: 'We continue to discharge our functions as special advocates because we believe that there are occasions on which we can advance the interests of appellants by doing so'.[40]

The other special advocate who gave oral evidence in the same session as Ian McDonald, Neil Garnham QC, said that he remained content to serve as a special advocate in relation to detention cases for the simple reason that he took the view that he was more likely to do good by being involved than by not being involved, although he respected the position of others who took a contrary view.[41]

The general position of the special advocates interviewed was that they were more likely to do good than harm in the role that they played. The good that they did was equated with the duty they had to act in the interests of the excluded party and they seemed particularly well motivated in the work that they did, believing that it was a fundamentally important, although very challenging, job. As one special advocate put it:

> I don't particularly enjoy the work, to be absolutely frank. It's very challenging work, you don't get any sort of public recognition of what you're doing. It doesn't pay particularly well compared to commercial work. But it is a fundamentally important job and I take the view for better or worse that it's a job that has to be done and it's worth doing properly. ... The working conditions you operate under with a safe and having to get materials out and having to get somebody to walk you over to court. Sitting very long hours. We call them SIAC hours because SIAC always starts at 10 and finishes at 6. I mean it's not deliberate. And they would sit 10.30 until 4.30 in principle but something always comes up. ... One day, we were sitting until eight on a Friday. It's just punishing. But it is a fundamentally important job. And if these individuals aren't going to get justice otherwise, then I do feel it's incumbent upon me as a representative of the Bar to do my best for them, at least, to make it as fair as possible, consistently within the regime.[42]

A particular question that was put in interview to special advocates was how, apart from justifying operating in apparently unfair closed procedures, they justify their role as an advocate when they do not act for any party. The special advocates

40 HCCAC (n 35), Ev 54-55.
41 ibid Ev 2.
42 SA 7, 3 December 2015.

interviewed tended to reject the idea that being a special advocate took them outside the normal bounds of acting as a barrister. The starting position that most special advocates seemed to adopt was that they are fundamentally bound by the Bar Code subject to any restrictions imposed upon them by statute. Where special advocates operated under a statutory regime, they were required to represent the interests of the excluded party and this imposed a statutory duty to act in their best interests. Where the role was not statutory, they were bound by the Attorney General's instructions to represent the best interests of the excluded person. The effect of these obligations was to impose a professional duty on the special advocate, subject to any duty to the court, to represent the interests of the excluded person and failure to do this would, according to one advocate, mean that they were in breach of their professional duty. So even though a number of statutory provisions have made it clear that they do not owe a legal duty of care to the excluded party, special advocates felt they owed a professional duty to such a person much in the same way as they owe a duty to their client in an ordinary case. Moreover, the nature of the duty – to act in the best interests of the excluded person – was not very different from the obligation in the Bar Code to act in the best interests of the client.

There was less consensus on whether the excluded person was to be regarded as a client. Although in *R v H and C*, Lord Bingham likened the role to acting in a way hitherto unknown to the legal profession, special advocates tended to play down the exceptional nature of the role. Of course, special advocates are appointed by the Attorney General and not by the excluded person, but once appointed, advocates seemed to regard the excluded person as their client and rejected any suggestion that they owed any loyalty to anybody else:

> I feel on a day to day basis that I have a duty to the excluded person. So that would be my motivation … and will trigger the way I think about the case and it would be unthinkable to do something that wasn't in the interest of the person. So in that respect I'm kind of like in a pretty similar relationship to their own counsel.[43]

> I regard the applicant or appellant whatever it might be as the client. So my job is to act in his interests.[44]

> I act specifically in the interest of the excluded party, they remain the client throughout. So everything I do is in the interest of the client. It's just that there are boundaries set on what I can and can't do in their interest.[45]

> I don't see any distinction between my role as a special advocate and my role as counsel for them. There're certain things that are constrained. I cannot consult with them and I cannot tell them what information I have. But I don't have a difficulty with the ethical aspect of it.[46]

43 SA4, 25 November 2015.
44 SA3, 25 November 2015.
45 SA8, 7 December 2015.
46 SA13, 21 January 2016.

> Yes, I think we probably do on occasion refer to them as our clients, although it's a pretty odd sort of client relationship because you don't actually talk to them. But it's akin to a client relationship in that you're allowed to act in their interest.[47]

This last statement is an acknowledgement of the fact that although they may be regarded as clients in so far as the motivation to act in their interests is concerned, the nature of the relationship is very different from that of any ordinary client. The disclosure restrictions placed upon special advocates go much further than in other cases. As one advocate put it, a primary obligation of the Bar is that if you learn something you cannot keep it from your client.[48] For one special advocate, that precluded him from regarding the excluded person as a client:

> I don't perceive myself to have a client as such because that would bring to bear … client duties and I don't perceive myself to have client duties.[49]

Then there is the fact that special advocates cannot speak to the client once the special advocate goes into closed which, as one special advocate said, is unprecedented. At this point, the professional client relationship seems to be stretched almost to breaking point because the client has no ultimate control over the special advocate's conduct of the case. The special advocate has a duty to represent the interests of the 'client', but a divergence may open up between these interests and the instructions that have been given by the 'client'. According to one special advocate, the excluded person is not your client as you have no contractual relationship with him, but you are in a supporting role and you should try to act in accordance with the instructions such as they are.[50] But, according to another special advocate, representing the interests of the client is not necessarily the same thing as putting forward his instructions.[51] Although in ordinary litigation, barristers are required under the Code to exercise their own professional judgment in relation to those matters in which they are instructed, notwithstanding the view of the client, the client does have personal responsibility in relation to fundamental issues such as whether to defend the case or commence an action. Obviously, the lawyer acts in an advisory role in this situation but the decision is ultimately the client's. Because of the nature of the closed proceedings whereby the client does not get to see the case against him, however, a situation can arise, as this special advocate put it, whereby X says he does not wish to defend the proceedings but in the closed proceedings there are flaws which could lead to them being dismissed. The special advocate would then be bound to expose those flaws and make submissions as to their implications.

47 SA5, 25 November 2015.
48 SA3, 25 November 2015.
49 SA7, 3 December 2015.
50 SA14, 5 February 2016.
51 SA9, 7 December 2015.

Other special advocates acknowledged that given the nature of the closed proceedings, they were not bound to act on instructions:

> I'm not bound to follow their instructions nor will anyone be stupid enough to bind me. Because if I think something is a good idea on all the evidence I've seen, I've never once been told, so you know what, whatever, it says on the secret side, you have to do this. I mean no-one … it's an unrealistic way of doing things. So the reality is that I don't think I stand in the same relationship as their own counsel. … I have a decision making role in which I will formulate decisions based on their interests as I judge them to be.[52]

This did not mean that if they were instructed to do something, they would not weigh that very heavily in the balance.

> Generally, if I'm instructed to do something I will think long and hard before I don't do it because I can imagine that if I told somebody to represent my interests, and … I don't know … give them chocolate biscuits and not butterscotch and that person said 'Well, actually, I think butterscotch is in your interest …' It's a very risky thing. But I don't think in practice … it works out like that … I think the cases I've been involved with no one has said to me, 'Right we want to completely restrain you from what you do. This is how it's going to be. You will do x. y, z. If the world falls apart, you'll still do x, y and z'. It isn't really how it would operate.… But if they did say 'whatever happens don't do that', I'd weigh it but my duty is to represent their interests. And that's a clear duty and there's no getting out of it. So if I think that, if I were to take the view, it's theoretically possible that I can take their interest to be the opposite of what they said.[53]

What would seem to be more common is a situation where there are simply no instructions to follow because the excluded party is not able to give instructions based on the closed evidence. This was why one special advocate considered that it would be difficult to say that special advocates owed a duty to the client:

> I think it would be invidious for the client to think somehow that you're acting in a way that you're acting under a duty to them because, basically, how on earth do you know when we're not given instructions? … It would have been an impossible position for a special advocate to be in to say that they have a duty to their client in these kind of cases where we have no idea in some situations what the client wanted. We can only see what may be in their best interest at that point in litigation.[54]

52 SA4, 25 November 2015.
53 ibid.
54 SA6, 3 December 2015.

Another special advocate said that in some cases the open representatives and the appellant may have no view of the evidence: 'You are simply told your naturalisation is being refused and no reasons are given'.[55] In this situation the special advocate has got to be free to represent the appellant's interest as best he can. In some situations, this could mean taking a position which is directly contrary to that taken by the open representative. One example he gave was where a control order is being challenged after previous criminal proceedings in which the appellant had been acquitted. Often when the closed evidence is seen there may be little point in denying the appellant's guilt or indeed the need for a control order which, of course, the open representatives would not do, but in this case an abuse of process point might be made on the ground that the state had held back from the criminal trial information that they then used to substantiate the control order.[56]

One question on which there seemed to be different views was what the special advocate should do when she feels she can no longer represent the interests of the excluded party because there is nothing left for the special advocate to do. Is it appropriate in this situation to simply stay silent or should she withdraw from the case? One or two advocates recognised that a position can be reached where it would not be ethical to continue to represent the excluded party because his interest cannot be advanced:

> I perceive myself to be bound to act in their interests including not acting when necessary. And now, it so happens that I've never felt the need to refrain from active participation in a case. But I respect the views of people who think they will only make matters worse if they cross-examine for example a national security witness. And that is the stance that other people have taken. It's not a stance I've had to take yet. I always felt I could bring to bear something new … [pause] But if the national security case is such that merely asking any question whatsoever gives the witness an opportunity to reinforce an already strong case … then you don't touch it with a barge pole. I've always been able to make submissions and there have been times where I haven't cross-examined in certain areas. But I hope in fact, as it happens, I've always been able to cross-examine.[57]

A further question arises here which is how should a special advocate withdraw from a case. One special advocate said that it was not a question of simply resigning. In his view, you would need to seek the permission from the court to convey the withdrawal to the excluded party. Since the statutes appear to envisage that there must always be a special advocate in a closed procedure, there would have

55 SA11, 14 January 2016.
56 ibid.
57 SA7, 3 December 2015.

to be another appointment and the excluded party would have to be given an opportunity to choose another special advocate from the list.

Others felt, however, that the question whether to participate or not was more a tactical or strategic decision than an ethical one.

> I do think that when I'm acting as a special advocate and I'm having to consider how I represent somebody's best interest, that's more me having to deal with the role properly. But I tend less to look at it from an ethical perspective, thinking 'can I do this, can I do that?' than looking at it … as a tactical strategic matter to assist them to the best extent. … We do what we've always done.[58]

A more difficult ethical problem can arise when an excluded party states that she does not want any involvement in the proceedings. This has happened on occasions. In his appeal against the Secretary of State's certification under section 21 of the Anti-Terrorism, Crime and Security Act 2001 that his presence in the UK was a risk to national security and that he was a terrorist, the notorious radical cleric Abu Qatada indicated that he would not attend the open hearing or participate in the SIAC proceedings in any way because the process deprived him of a fair opportunity to challenge the case against him.[59] The two special advocates appointed in this case decided that it would not be in his interest for them to take any part in the proceedings. As one of the advocates involved in the case put it:

> We had to take a view as to what was in his interests. And in forming that view, it was appropriate to take into account the stance that he had adopted in relation to the proceedings as well as a number of other things which we didn't consider it to be in his interests to articulate to the Commission.[60]

In its decision, SIAC was critical of the special advocates' approach. The appeal was still being pursued and the appellant did not know what was relied on against him in the closed material. In these circumstances, the Commission said that it could not understand how it could not be in his interests for the special advocates, at their discretion, to elicit or identify matters favourable to the appellant and to make submissions to seek to persuade the Commission that the evidence was in fact unreliable or did not justify the assessment made.[61] The Commission went on to observe that the absence of a special advocate made its task even more difficult than it normally was and that the potential unfairness to the appellant was the more apparent, although it went on to say that the evidence in the case was so strong that no special advocates, however brilliant, could have

58 SA11, 14 January 2016.
59 *Othman v SSHD* SIAC SC/15/2002 8 March 2004.
60 SA5, 25 November 2015.
61 *Othman v SSHD* SIAC SC/15/2002 8 March 2004, [9].

persuaded it that reasonable suspicion had not been satisfied. The certification was justified, and the absence of the special advocates had not prejudiced the appellant.[62] The Commission went to such lengths to secure the participation of the special advocates in this case that it contacted the Solicitor General who had appointed the special advocates to seek her help in trying to persuade them to assist the court. The special advocates had misgivings about meeting a member of the government trying to persuade them to take a particular stance in relation to the proceedings:

> Our view was that we had to act in accordance with the Bar Code of Conduct – to act independently – and we could not be seen to be meeting and taking instructions from the very party that was seeking to detain the party in whose interests we were supposed to act.[63]

The case threw up an interesting question as to whether the special advocate owes any duty to the court beyond that which is set out in the Bar Code. As one of the advocates said:

> SIAC felt it was our duty to assist the court essentially. We considered that our duty was fairly clearly to act in the interests of the person who we've been appointed to represent in the closed proceedings.[64]

Following correspondence between the Commission, the special advocates and the Solicitor General about the proper role of the special advocates, the view taken by the Solicitor General was that she would not interfere in any way with the professional judgment of special advocates and would not require them to perform a function which they considered to be contrary to the interests of the appellant. SASO's *Open Manual* states a special advocate may potentially say nothing at all or decline to take part in proceedings.[65]

What is clear, however, is that the special advocates in this case did not feel that they were bound by the stance taken by the appellant not to participate. This was exemplified in another case where the appellant had taken the same stance as Abu Qatada, but in this case the same special advocates did participate and in fact achieved a successful outcome.[66] The position was publicly summed up by one of the advocates involved in both these cases as follows:

> In the first case my leader and I decided to withdraw and in the second case we decided to take part, and that is an illustration of what I believe to be the correct position on this matter which is that Special Advocates have to

62 ibid [10].
63 SA20, 12 April 2016.
64 SA5, 25 November 2015.
65 SASO (n 34) [47].
66 *M v SSHD* SIAC SC/17/2002 8 March 2004.

> take an independent view as to what is in the interests of the appellant in the particular case.[67]

The special advocates spoken to were somewhat divided as to what they would do if an appellant instructed a special advocate not to participate in her case. Their attitude seemed to depend at least in part on the extent to which they considered that they were acting for the appellant as a client. According to one special advocate:

> I have to take instructions from my clients at the end of the day and if I were instructed not to appear, I can't turn up, it seems to me.[68]

Another view, however, was that this went to the difference in the relationship with the person whose interest the special advocate had to represent:

> If a normal client said to you, 'I don't want to be here. I don't want to make any submissions or ask any questions' … provided you were satisfied … [pause] you would be obliged to comply with that. With a special advocate when you're appointed by the Advocate General to represent their interests, I don't think you're bound if they say, 'I don't want to do anything'. … You might be entitled to take the view that I've been appointed to do this job on their behalf and I'm obliged to go and do it.[69]
>
> I don't think I've ever been in that position. But the rules are clear. The special advocate has to be appointed in certain circumstances. If the Secretary of State intends to rely on closed material there needs to be a special advocate. And so, open representatives might if they choose say we're not happy with the way the special advocate's proceeding. But to go so far as to say there should not be a special advocate present … the rules are quite clear.[70]

Another special advocate said that although he had been involved in cases where excluded persons were reluctant to engage, he had never been aware of a case where the person said he should not act on his behalf. If he were faced with such a situation, he said he would probably apply to the court to have the appointment rescinded as he did not think he could rescind the appointment himself. If the court said, 'we want you to act, it would be incredibly tricky' but ultimately,

67 HCCAC (n 35) Ev 5 (Mr Martin Chamberlain). For a fuller explanation, see M Chamberlain, 'Special Advocates and Amici Curiae in National Security Proceedings in the United Kingdom' (2018) 68 *University of Toronto Law Journal* 496, 503–504. See also the views of Neil Garnham, HCCAC (n 35) Ev 4.

68 SA8, 7 December 2015.

69 SA2, 4 November 2015.

70 SA11, 14 January 2016.

he would not want to actively engage against the client's wishes in a closed procedure which the client did not support.[71]

The logic of continuing to represent an excluded person against her wishes, which is what Parliament would seem to envisage in requiring a special advocate to act in the interests of the excluded person when there is closed material, is to take the extreme paternalistic position of assuming that the special advocate can determine the person's best interests better than the person herself. Whether this is true or not, it is a position that deprives the excluded person of her basic autonomy to determine her own interests.[72] When parties lose control over their case, the adversarial ideal of parties controlling their litigation is dealt a severe blow. But the idea of a special advocate acting without the consent of the party whose interests they are supposed to represent also raises questions about whose interests the special advocate is really representing. Conventional advocacy in the adversarial system requires that an advocate acts for some party or, in the case of an amicus, for the court. If special advocates are required to continue to represent the interests of parties who no longer wish to be represented, on whose behalf are they acting? One answer, given that they are appointed by the Attorney General, might be to say that they are really acting on behalf of the government in the public interest to see that justice is served in the closed proceedings.[73] Alternatively, recalling the remonstrations of SIAC when it was deprived of a special advocate in the closed proceedings relating to Abu Qatada, perhaps they are there in an amicus role to assist the court.[74] But neither of these solutions seems to fit with how special advocates see their role. One former special advocate suggested that the role was a 'curious amalgam of the advocate for X and an amicus to the Court'.[75] If special advocates are such a curious amalgam, then this raises questions as to whether their very special position deserves a special ethical Code all of its own.

A new ethical code?

In an article written in 2006 when the special advocate system was expanding but had not yet penetrated into the variety of proceedings in which it can operate today, Boon and Nash observed that while the legal profession had generally given a warm response to the principle of special advocacy, the role could not be coherently accommodated within the Code of Conduct of the Bar. It was suggested that the case for keeping special advocates within the ethical space filled by the conventional professions rests on numerous fictions, in relation to the cab

71 SA7, 3 December 2015.

72 See E Metcalfe, '"Representative but not responsible": the use of Special Advocates in English law' (2004) 1 *Justice Journal* 1, 32–33.

73 Boon and Nash (n 14) 121.

74 Cf Chamberlain (n 67) 503–505.

75 SA9, 7 December 2015.

rank rule, the duties of partisanship and confidentiality owed to clients, and the general duty of independence. Most of these fictions, for example, that a barrister can continue to represent the appellant's best interests when instructions have been withdrawn, appear to bend the conventions of the Bar too far. It was suggested that it would be better to adopt instead a special custom-made regime specially devoted to special advocates.[76]

We have seen that special advocates consider themselves bound by the Bar Code of Conduct and in interviews there was little enthusiasm amongst them for a new professional code marking out the special advocate's particular obligations. As one special advocate put it:

> I've never experienced the need for anything to be set in stone. I didn't see a problem in practice.[77]

This echoes the views of the two special advocates who gave oral evidence to the Joint Committee on Human Rights (JCHR) when it was considering the government's proposal to extend the role of CMPs to civil proceedings. In the words of one:

> The performance of our role does not involve any particular ethical difficulties. ... Our role is clear – to represent the interests of a person who is denied sight of material ... I am not sure that further guidance would assist.[78]

It may be that some of the questions that Boon and Nash raised about the ability of special advocates to perform their duties under the Bar Code are less pressing today. The cab rank rule may well have been compromised when in the early days there was such a small pool of advocates, but as we have seen, there is now a much a larger pool of advocates for excluded parties to choose from. The restrictions on special advocates disclosing closed material to them offends the principle that advocates have a duty to share information with their clients, but the idea of independent counsel giving a confidentiality undertaking not to disclose material to a client is not unknown in certain other aspects of practice at the Bar.[79] As regards the issue of independence, we have seen that special advocates have won the right to withdraw from cases where they consider they can no longer represent the interests of excluded parties. There have been other cases where special advocates have withdrawn their services.[80] In none of these

76 Boon and Nash (n 14) 124.

77 SA3, 25 November 2015.

78 JCHR, *Justice and Security Green Paper* (HC 2012, 1777-i-v) Oral evidence, 31 January 2012, Q 66 (Mr Angus McCullough QC).

79 Counsel for the claimant in *CF v Security Service* [2013] EWHC 3402 [47] cited authority for the use of so-called 'confidentiality rings' in a number of commercial fields.

80 See eg *S v SSHD* SIAC SC/25/203, 27 July 2004, *B v SSHD* SIAC SC/9/2005, 30 July 2008. The special advocate also withdrew in the Northern Irish case of *Re McCafferty to a Remission of Sentences Commissioner* 29 March 2010 (unreported).

cases did the Attorney General seek to have them replaced. The absence of any re-appointment might seem to circumvent the rule that a special advocate must be appointed for the Secretary of State to be able to rely upon closed material, although the rules do not in themselves forbid withdrawal once appointed.

Although all this illustrates the independence of special advocates, questions remain over to whom they are accountable. When an excluded party specifically instructs the special advocate to withdraw from the case, again it would seem to be left for special advocates to make an independent judgement on whether to act notwithstanding such an instruction. This suggests that there are circumstances where special advocates may act without the consent of the persons whose interests they are there to represent. We have also seen that special counsel may be appointed in PII proceedings which the accused has no knowledge of and *a fortiori*, no knowledge of the special counsel having been appointed. The absence of an instructing client makes the advocacy of special advocates 'special' but it is no longer unique. We have seen that counsel are appointed to cross-examine complainants in cases where the accused is representing himself.[81] Such an appointment is made whether the accused consents to it or not. In all these situations, counsel continue to be bound by the professional ethics of the Bar Code and may be considered to be ultimately accountable to their professional body. This raises the question, however, whether the professional bodies should do more to give guidance and indeed protection to special advocates when they exercise their role.

Some of the special advocates interviewed accepted there were certain areas where greater clarity of practice could be provided. One question that arose was whether the communications between the excluded person, the open representative and the special advocate are privileged. It is interesting to note that although the relationship between the special advocate and the excluded party is not that of legal representative and client, legal professional privilege is expressly stated to apply to communications between the party, its legal representative and the special advocate in both the Canadian legislation governing the use of special advocates in immigration proceedings and in Australian legislation governing their use in control order proceedings.[82] No such provision is to be found in the UK legislation. Some special advocates assumed by nature of the de facto client relationship they had with excluded parties that their communications with them were privileged. Others were less clear. One special advocate pointed out that it would be extremely unlikely that the government would ever seek to compel special advocates to disclose information provided to them by excluded parties, as this would discredit the whole special advocate system which is based on the notion that special advocates are giving advice and representing clients.[83] It was

81 Youth Justice and Criminal Evidence 1999, s 38.

82 Immigration and Refugee Protection Act 2001 (Canada), s 85.1(4); National Security Information (Criminal and Civil Proceedings) Act 2004 pt 3A Division 3, Subdivision C s 38PC (2) inserted by Counter-Terrorism Legislation (Amendment Act (No 1) 2016.

83 SA20, 12 April 2016.

therefore academic to question whether in fact information disclosed to them was privileged. According to this special advocate, an issue may arise which is less academic, however, when a special advocate has gone into closed and is seeking permission to communicate certain information to open counsel which is revealed to government counsel and which is then sought to be used by the government against the appellant in open or closed proceedings. The special advocate who raised this issue considered that this would be an abuse of process, because the only reason the government was privy to such information was because it was disclosed for a security vetting purpose and in the process the government was gaining an advantage of seeing information they would not otherwise have seen.

One of the open counsel spoken to considered that there would be value in having some clarity about the status of the information which is disclosed to special advocates by appellants and their counsel because it was often difficult to get appellants to speak to special advocates with any trust.[84] It was difficult enough sometimes to get appellants to speak to their own lawyers, but when a special advocate appears they can become very suspicious. When they ask a question like, 'Can you promise me that this conversation is not subject to interception?', the open counsel cannot promise that it may not be as warrants may be sought to intercept privileged communications.[85] But what they can tell the client is that nothing said in the room will be admissible in evidence before the judge. The security services may know but not the judge. This open counsel said he could say this pretty much with certainty even when the special advocate is present on the assumption that the conversations are privileged, but it is something that it would be good to test.

Even though special advocates treated any information they received as privileged, they felt under the same obligations to the Commission or court as they would in any criminal case:

> So if, for example, the client says, 'Well yes I did actually for example plant a bomb at Heathrow but nonetheless I want to fight my case', if that is essential to the case, you can test the government evidence but you can't advance a positive case that you know is inconsistent with the truth.[86]

A further question is if the excluded person has disclosed inculpatory information that turns out not to be part of the government's case, how far can a special advocate go in following a line of questioning concerning the government's actual information that is somehow distorting in the light of what the special advocate has been told?[87] Are special advocates bound by the same concerns as other advocates not to mislead the court? Or do the *sui generis* functions of special advocates

84 OC6, 5 February 2016.
85 See *Re McE* [2009] UKHL 15, [2009] 1 AC 908.
86 SA3, 25 November 2015.
87 C Forcese and L Waldman, *Seeking Justice in an Unfair Process* (University of Ottawa 2007) 35.

liberate them to some extent from such duties? As we shall see, the special advocate's main function in the closed hearing is to test and probe the government case, not so much advance a positive case, and they are not bound to temper any probing on account of information they have received from the excluded party.

Another situation on which a former special advocate sought clarity was what a special advocate should do when she encounters facts which reveal that, unbeknownst to the excluded party, a civil wrong has been committed, for example, facts which show that the security services have committed a wrong, maybe even a crime.[88] If special advocates are in a de facto client relationship with the excluded party, do they then not owe a duty to protect the excluded party? If it was a criminal matter, one could always refer it to the Crown Prosecution Service but:

> where it is actionable, what do you do? If I'm acting because of their interest, it must be acting in their interest to tell them they've got a civil claim. At the same time, if it is closed material, it cannot be communicated to the open side. It's a hell of a dilemma.[89]

The question as to what special advocates should do in this situation came up in a case where the claimants who were alleged to be members of or associated with the Libyan Islamic Fighting Group (LIFG) had been subjected to control orders and immigration detention pending an attempt to deport them to Colonel Qadhafi's Libyan regime under the 'deportation with assurances' programme. After various challenges to these measures before SIAC and the High Court, information came to light in the course of the fall of the Qadhafi regime in Libya which pointed to UK involvement in human rights violations with the US and Libyan governments, in particular, the rendition to torture of two leaders of the LIFG. The claimants then took proceedings alleging that their detention had been unlawful. Had this information been disclosed, it was claimed, the proceedings in SIAC and the control order proceedings could not have been mounted.[90] The government's response was to apply to strike out the claim on the basis that the action was a *Hunter*-type abuse as the claimants were attempting to mount a collateral challenge to earlier SIAC and High Court judgments.[91] The High Court accepted that the claimants did not know what closed evidence there was before SIAC or the High Court in the earlier proceedings and at the conclusion of the case, the trial judge asked the parties and the special advocates to suggest an answer to the hypothetical question: if in the case of closed proceedings, special advocates were to conclude that closed material may reveal the basis for a private law claim on the part of the appellant, what should they do? The judge recorded that it was common ground that the role and functions of the special advocate

88 SA12, 14 January 2016.
89 ibid.
90 *Kamoka v The Security Service* [2016] EWHC 769 (QB).
91 *Hunter v Chief Constable of the West Midlands Police* [1982] AC 529.

were confined by statute and that although he acts in the interests of the party concerned, he is 'not responsible to the person whose interests he is appointed to represent'.[92] Specified functions were laid down which in effect confined their role to adducing evidence, cross-examining witnesses and making submissions. The judge continued:

> Special Advocates do not represent an excluded party, there is no lawyer/client relationship in the ordinary sense and the attendant professional obligations do not arise. Perhaps most important is the fact that, once seised of the closed evidence, the Special Advocate cannot communicate with the party he or she represents, save to a limited extent with the consent of the other party, and/or the Court or Commission.[93]

Given these limitations on the role of the special advocate, the judge asked how could the excluded party be bound by the actions and decisions of the special advocates in closed proceedings. Although this suggested that an abuse of process in the *Hunter* sense could have no application where closed proceedings apply, in the end the Court did not allow the applicants' claims to proceed because otherwise the courts would be led into a never-ending spiral of litigation. If the claim went ahead, this meant it would also have to be heard in closed proceedings which the claimants would know nothing about and in which they would still be unrepresented in the full sense. If the claimants were dissatisfied with the outcome, could they then simply begin again? The answer had to be no, because that would objectively be a collateral action to a court's ruling. In allowing the claimants' appeal, however, the Court of Appeal ruled that since the special advocates were not the privies or agents of the appellants, there could be no abuse of process with respect to the claims now being made by them, because at the time of the earlier SIAC and control order proceedings in open, the appellants were simply not aware of the cause of action or the points on which they now relied and thus had no opportunity to run that case.[94]

These judgments draw attention to the unfairness in saddling excluded parties with the decisions of special advocates when there is such a vast communication gulf between them after the special advocate is apprised of the closed evidence. The Court of Appeal concluded that there was no basis for criticising the special advocates in this case for not running in closed any of the points in the earlier SIAC or control order proceedings that were now being made even if they had been alive to them.[95] The question remains, however, as to how special advocates should respond when they become aware in closed proceedings of causes of action that excluded parties may run. One way of communicating the grounds

92 *Kamoka v The Security Service* [2016] EWHC 769 (QB) [32].
93 ibid (Irwin J).
94 *Kamoka v The Security Service* [2017] EWCA Civ 1665.
95 ibid [115].

for a possible civil claim to the excluded party might be to say that the special advocate's duty to the court to act with independence in the interests of justice requires her to bring to the court's attention the fact that the closed material may reveal the basis for a private law claim and to request that this is brought to the attention of the excluded party. The same duty might require government counsel not to object to such an application. But such a circuitous route for communicating this information simply emphasises the difference between ordinary representation, where there are constant exchanges between the party and its legal representatives, and the lack of dialogue between a special advocate and an excluded party.

In this chapter, we have seen that special advocates face ethical challenges that are different from the ordinary advocate as a result of severing the professional-client relationship. It has been suggested that in the absence of a client to whom special advocates are accountable, professional bodies to whom advocates are also accountable may need to be more proactive in setting and enforcing standards on how special advocates are to represent the interests of parties. Severing the professional–client relationship means that clients lose control of their case, but it need not place special advocates at such a great ethical distance from ordinary advocates. Both have in common the representation of the interests of a party to litigation and in this respect, they both embody the adversarial tradition of advocacy whereby counsel advocate for parties' interests. When on top of severance of the professional client relationship, special advocates are unable to communicate with the excluded party, however, they are cast personally as well as professionally adrift from that party and must work out on their own what the party's interests are. In the next chapter, we examine how formidable these communication barriers are for special advocates representing the interests of excluded parties and whether they are necessary in order to maintain a balance between national security and due process.

7 Restricting communications

We have seen that a fundamental aspect of the procedures providing for special advocates in the UK is that once the closed material is served upon the special advocate, the special advocate must not communicate any longer with the excluded party or his or her representative unless specifically authorised by the court to do so.[1] In the last chapter, we saw that this rule stretches to breaking point any view that there might or ought to be a professional–client relationship between the special advocate and the excluded party and a duty of care owed by the special advocate to this party. How can one be responsible or answerable to someone one is not able to communicate with? In this chapter, we probe this rule further, looking at what special advocates and others think of it, what practices there are in other jurisdictions and what steps might be taken to relax the rule. But first it must be remembered that the rule only comes into play once the special advocate has sight of the closed material. This prompts the question whether there is much communication between the special advocate and the excluded party up until this point and how important both special advocates and open counsel consider it is to have such communication before special advocates go into closed.

Before going into closed procedures

The rules expressly permit special advocates to communicate with the excluded parties or their representatives at any time before the closed material is served on them.[2] Special advocates accepted that they should meet with the excluded party where this was possible. It was not always possible, because excluded parties may be out of the country and it was difficult to get funding from the Home Office to visit them. According to one special advocate, when they are in the country, they sometimes do not trust the special advocate enough to want to see him anyway but that was very much a question of how well they were advised. Increasingly,

1 SIAC (Procedure) Rules, r 36 (2). See also CPR, r 76.25(2) (proceedings under the PTA 2005); r 79.20(2) (proceedings under the Counter-Terrorism Act 2008 and Pt 1 of the Terrorist Asset-Freezing Etc Act 2010); r 80.21(2) (TPIMs); r 82.11(2) (CMPs in civil proceedings).
2 SIAC (Procedure) Rules 36 (1). See also CPR, r 76.25(1), r 79.20(1), r 80.21(1), r 82.11(1).

it seems that as trust has built up between open representatives and special advocates, people are advised to have a meeting.[3]

Earlier surveys found that special advocates had different views about the utility of meetings with the excluded party.[4] In their evidence to the HCCAC in 2005, special advocates said that communications between the appellant and their representatives before they are shown the closed material were unlikely to be much use to special advocates since they do not know the nature of the closed case the appellant had to meet.[5] But perhaps with the benefit of greater experience, all special advocates in this survey considered there was value in such meetings, even if they only served to establish rapport with the excluded person and the open representatives:

> I would like to think that they would have confidence in me stepping into the barrister's shoes when they leave the room. So in the same way with one of my own clients, when I meet them it is a forum or an opportunity for confidence building, I do that in the same way with the excluded person … It's obviously nerve racking for anyone to go through a court system, go through litigation. It's quite a scary thing. So I think it's the right thing to do to try and give them some confidence that I'm independent, that I understand the difficulties that they're facing, perhaps a very difficult personal situation or they're faced with expulsion, whatever it might be; just to say, I understand and please do continue to send me instructions because they can always send something to me. … So it is for confidence building really and possibly their own lawyers could do nearly as much but that's not quite the point.[6]

> I always like to consult with the excluded person and the open lawyers. Because I always like the client to feel as I'm very much part of their team and on their side and doing my best for them and I think it helps if you meet them with the open lawyers, particularly if you know the open lawyers for them to introduce you and explain your role. Whereas if you just show up on your own without their own lawyers, I think sometimes the person whom you're representing will be a bit confused in what exactly your role is, maybe a bit suspicious if they haven't themselves appointed you.[7]

> I think it's always helpful to meet the excluded person at least in part because it helps to dispel what might otherwise be a fairly profound suspicion of the system and to explain the role and for them to see that, although they don't

3 SA3, 25 November 2015.

4 See eg C Forcese and L Waldman, *Seeking Justice in an Unfair Process* (University of Ottawa 2007) 34.

5 HCCAC, *The Operation of the Special Immigration Appeals Commission (SIAC) and the Use of Special Advocates* (2004-05, HC 323-1) Ev 55 [9].

6 SA4, 25 November 2015.

7 SA2, 4 November 2015.

see it in the proceedings, there is a real person acting for them and trying to promote their interests in the closed procedures.[8]

One advocate said he thought the meeting was a good opportunity to give general guidance to the appellants on the sort of approach they may want to adopt in the substantive claim and their own advisers will have their own views.[9] The special advocate, of course, cannot say anything specific about the closed evidence because they will not have seen it at this stage, but in general the appellant had a choice as to whether to engage fully or play their cards close to their chest.

The other main purpose in meeting the excluded party was to receive relevant information and instructions where possible about how to proceed in the closed hearing:

> Before I go into closed I try to get as much information as I can. Because I really want to get the feel for how they want to run the case, what instructions they've really got, what they think about their chances, the way they ought to approach the evidence that they've been given, and also what else I might usefully probe for when I get into closed.[10]
>
> I need to understand where they're coming from with the open material. I mean it's not a guessing game as to what's in the closed material because we really don't know. But I think I need to understand the open material from their perspective and also to formulate a strategy for the case. And they may have instructions that they're giving to their own lawyers which I'll be given and I have got to make sure I understand. Exactly the same way that with a normal client you say, 'Do you know what? I've seen that document you've given me. But what exactly does it mean?' And I can't quite understand how it fits in with the witness statement or something like that. … Perhaps their own barristers could do that and send us a note or something like that. But I just quite like to do it myself just so I know that going forward I'm not going to be like, 'Oh my goodness, I have not got the foggiest idea what you're really saying'.[11]

It seemed that in the early days, appellants and their open representatives often refused to engage with the special advocate even before she went into closed. In their evidence to the HCCAC, the special advocates speculated that this was perhaps in part a reflection of the lack of confidence in the *unilaterally* appointed security-cleared lawyer.[12] We have seen that parties now have a say in whom they wish to appoint as a special advocate. How candid excluded parties were

8 SA5, 25 November 2015.
9 ibid.
10 SA3, 25 November 2015.
11 SA4, 25 November 2015.
12 HCCAC (n 5) Ev 55 [9] (emphasis in original).

with their special advocates seems to depend very much on each individual case. According to one special advocate, some clients remain very guarded and they didn't really understand who special advocates were. In other cases, they seemed to accept that this was the system, and this was the best they were going to get and they wanted to use the special advocate to their full advantage. According to one open counsel, before a client saw a special advocate, you had to do a 'sales campaign':

> And you say, let me explain how this works. This person is on your side. To which the response is yeah, approved by the government to be on your side. And security cleared by government.[13]

According to this counsel, rapport was not easy to build up when the client had a single meeting for a couple of hours with the special advocate who then disappears. There could be further consultations, but often there was not that much to ask because all there was to go on was a one page security statement.

There was general agreement that the relationship between open counsel and special advocates had evolved enormously over the last ten years:

> I would like to think that we have a pretty good relationship with counsel and solicitors for the open representatives which has grown up. I think that's partially individual. I think it's partially the way the system has moved on and that we are here. But partially a realisation that not talking to us doesn't actually help their clients. But certainly, the difference over the last 10 years when I started is huge.[14]
>
> There was a lot of non-engagement for a while but what then happened was actually, people saw that there was a benefit from the closed procedure and it wasn't simply a rubber stamp. And so, more recently, there's been much higher levels of active involvement pre going into closed.[15]

The natural suspicion that open counsel and solicitors have for closed hearings and the special advocate is understandable. As Gareth Pierce explained in her evidence to the HCCAC in 2005:

> What our fundamental job is as defence solicitors is to investigate and to know the persons we are representing and his back teeth, to know everything about what makes him tick and to look for evidence that establishes his case. In this situation, we do not even know what he is accused of. We do not know the basis, we cannot respond and we cannot investigate.[16]

13 OC6, 5 February 2016.
14 SA11, 14 January 2016.
15 SA7, 3 December 2015.
16 HCCAC (n 5) Ev 6.

According to one open counsel, no matter how diligent a special advocate may be in assisting the defence, no counsel representing a client can be happy with a situation where she is excluded from hearing evidence against her client and is unable to make representations on it.[17] A former special advocate took the view that special advocates can never be on the same side as the open representatives because, unlike instructing lawyers, instructions are not binding on special advocates:

> When you see the special advocates, you tell them what legal strategy you're intending to adopt. And sometimes, you'll have as you're permitted to have one-way communications then about things you want them to do. And they will listen and doubtless they will give this close attention. I doubt they won't do what you don't want them to do unless there's some good reasons. But they can do what they like. And you can't bind them by instructions because you're not their client. You can expressly demand that they do something. And they can decide in closed not to do it. You can expressly demand that they don't do something, and they can do it. So, you know, neither will be steps that will lightly be taken. But both are open to them, on the grounds that they have to form their own objective view about what it is they think is in the best interest of the client. It's almost like a court of protection jurisdiction at the end of the day.[18]

Over the years, however, open representatives in England and Wales have learned to live with special advocates. There is a very big difference between being an instructed lawyer and acting in someone's interest. But the relationship has developed. According to one open counsel, one reason for this was that over time, closed procedures had become more normal:

> To be honest, it's become the norm …, this is one criticism of course of the process that it becomes a normal process. And what is on the face of it a massive departure from a fair hearing and all of the core principles of due process becomes a new norm. And that's true in the sense that once you're in the process, you can't argue about it, you can't complain in any meaningful sense because Parliament has legislated, the courts have upheld it, Europe has upheld it. It is therefore regarded as the least worst way of dealing with a particular issue.[19]

Another open counsel said that ten years ago in the early days of control orders and SIAC, there was no purpose whatsoever in talking to a special advocate or

17 OC3, 6 November 2015.

18 SA12, 14 January 2016. The Court of Protection has jurisdiction to make decisions on behalf of a person who lacks capacity to make decisions on their own behalf. See N Munro, 'Taking Wishes and Feelings Seriously: the Views of People Lacking Capacity in Court of Protection Decision-Making' (2014) 36 *Journal of Social Welfare & Family Law* 59.

19 OC5, 2 February 2016.

having your client meet the special advocate because it was considered that you were dignifying an inherently unfair procedure.[20] That was still very strongly the view of most claimant lawyers, but the decision of the House of Lords in *AF*[21] marked a significant change in how special advocates cooperate with open lawyers. It was now accepted that special advocates can do something valuable in certain cases because there is a baseline minimum amount of disclosure that has to be given in open, so that at least there is some detail on each of the allegations sufficient to allow the client an opportunity to rebut them. This counsel said that in these cases there are basically two approaches that can be taken. The first kind of case is where the client says that 'the allegations are all rubbish, he is not a terrorist and is not planning attacks in the UK' and he wants to defend this case. He may admit that he has lots of friends who are Islamist and some of them are 'dodgy'. In this kind of case, disclosure and engagement with the special advocate are really valuable. It was:

> good to put your client in with the special advocate so that the special advocate can ask them every question they can think of and try to get some detail out so that the client can give some useful instructions.

This could work to good effect because in many cases there might be strong evidence on some allegations and considerably weaker evidence on others, often more serious allegations. If special advocates are able to tease out the fact that there is not much lying behind some of the allegations, they may be dropped or the court may not accept them.

But there was another kind of case which was where the client does not say very much to their open advocates because they may recognise that 'they have been up to no good in the past' and they may recognise that the government is likely to have very damaging closed material about their conduct. According to this open counsel, in these cases there is not much contact with the special advocate because there is not very much to say to them in terms of useful instructions. Of course, it could be difficult to get to the point of knowing which kind of case is which, whether there should be engagement or where it may be better to offer no challenge to the national security case:

> Just as in the criminal trial, criminal defence clients don't tell you everything the first time you meet. … They give you a bit and then what happens is that you talk to them about the evidence and they give you a bit more. … and part of the job of the open advocate is to try and encourage your client to do something sensible which can include not challenging the national security case and basing the challenge upon the restrictions placed by, say, a TPIM. That's where the special advocate can be useful as well. And they can tell

20 OC6, 5 February 2016.
21 *SSHD v AF* [2009] UKHL 28, [2010] 2 AC 269. See Chapter 3.

> someone, 'You don't have to tell me. Go away and think about it but if your phone was tapped and all of these calls with all these people were intercepted and everything you said was written down and was going to be in front of the judge and all the websites you looked at, go and think if there's a load of stuff which the judge is going to see which will paint you in a terrible light, the judge is going to confirm your TPIM'. And sometimes, they'll come back and they say that they do not want to challenge the national security case.[22]

One special advocate likened the process to 'shadow-boxing', as you do not know what is in the closed material:

> One strategy is to get them to provide ... every detail they can remember of their lives, who they've met, friends at school and at every stage thereafter, and political beliefs, religious beliefs, the rest of it in the hope that along the way, something is of use to the special advocates once the special advocates have seen the closed material.[23]

According to one open counsel, the challenge for both open counsel and the special advocate working together is to get over the hump of the inability to give instructions:

> So you don't know what the case is. You've got to try and speculate what the case may be. Obvious things you know. Where have you travelled? Well, if you've been to any country of interest, you have to explain why you've been there. So if they're going to say, you went to Jordan or Syria or whatever on certain dates. A competent claimant lawyer is going to be asking their clients to explain their movements and whatever. Then, if they've been to Afghanistan or Spain or whatever, to explain why. And you don't know if that's going to form part of the case against you. Is that going to be the standard allegation that you attended a terrorist training camp in Afghanistan? That used to be all the rage in the 2000s. Is that allegation going to be current? If so, did you go to Afghanistan? If you did, what did you do? Were you there for charity work? Whatever. So, you've got to anticipate the case made against you and equip the special advocate as best you can with material to meet them.[24]

It was accepted that some of the problems have been alleviated by the improved gists that are now given in many cases. So, for example, allegations about going to terrorist training camps used to be made all the time in closed, but now because of the change in requirements in gisting after *AF*, those types

22 OC6, 5 February 2016.
23 SA5, 25 November 2015.
24 OC5, 2 February 2016.

of allegations tend to be in open. But even with the gist, it could be frustrating not having access to all the relevant information. One special advocate considered that consultations with excluded persons could be frustrating:

> You're dealing with a gist. And very often the client will say, 'I have absolutely no idea where that's coming from. I don't know who's giving you that information, it's wrong. But I cannot tell you anything more than that'. And you end up asking them questions like, 'Can you make any kind of guess as to who might've said this about you? Or can you think of anything that you might've said or done which would be misconstrued?' And it's all a very artificial exercise. So it can sometimes be quite frustrating because you cannot ask them straight questions about evidence. They can't give you straight answers about what is alleged against them if they don't really know where it's coming from.[25]

One counsel who had acted as a special advocate said it helped to have knowledge about how a security case is going to be constructed, what elements it is going to have and what type of issues are likely to arise. This could mean going through well-worn topics anticipating what kind of case it is going to be, which may entail the client setting out their financial affairs, getting a full list of their associations and whether any friends or family might be of interest to the security services. In which case, why are they still friends with them?

> Why do I still associate with them? Well he's my brother, you know. He's married to my sister. I think he's a bit of a jerk. I think he's a bit of a lunatic. But nevertheless I see him on family occasions. These are the 10 times I've seen him recently. One was my daughter's marriage, one was this, one was that one.[26]

It was sometimes possible to agree tactics and strategy on what the special advocate should do if something comes to light in the closed material. Much would depend on how much was disclosed in open. According to one special advocate who had been doing naturalisation cases recently, the amount of information that was given in any category of case could vary.

> So in some cases the open decision letter will say something like: you've not met the requirement of good character because of your association with Islamic extremism. That would be a particularly useful sort of letter. Some of them just say: you've not met the requirements of good character and it would not be in the interest of national security to give you any further reasons. ... And you can't come up with much of a strategy in those

25 SA2, 4 November 2015.
26 SA12, 14 January 2016.

> circumstances, so you spend your time in open saying to the client, 'Right. Talk to me about any organisation you've been a member of. Can you think of anybody you know or where you've travelled to?' … You try and find all sorts of things, and in some cases the things you talk about turn out to be relevant to the issue. In other circumstances, you go into closed, and you go, 'OK, none of us talked about anything like that at all'. And I will never know whether that's because the individual was lying to me or because they didn't know either. So there's only so much of a strategy you can identify, really. In a complex case, there might be circumstances in which you could ask for instructions on a specific point, subject to approval that we talked about in that sense. But mostly no, you just have to use your own judgement.[27]

According to one former special advocate, it was important for open counsel to understand the pressures and difficulties of the special advocate position, to be sympathetic to it and to organise yourself in such a way as to maximise the chances of the special advocate being able to do what they do well. This meant talking through the issues in the case very clearly with the special advocate before they go into 'purdah', explaining your tactics with them and to build up some kind of trust and agreement as to how they are likely to deal with issues. You could talk through some of the dilemmas in advance and try to build up a bit of a decision tree – if this, then that; if this, then that – 'so that you try as much as you can to tilt at the potential windmills'.[28]

One open counsel gave an example of the kind of hypothetical that could be gone through in a case where former agents who claimed to have been working as informants for the British Army in Afghanistan, providing information about the Taliban, were now bringing judicial review proceedings against the Ministry of Defence (MoD) claiming that since the British withdrawal at the end of 2014, their lives have been threatened by the Taliban and they have not been properly protected. In such a case, 'what you would do is you would meet with the special advocate and try to imagine what the closed material will be':

> So in this case there are various possibilities as to why the MoD might have refused to accept a duty of care. It's not we suspect that they deny that these men operated as agents because the evidence that they were being handled by the British Army over a number of years in Afghanistan was overwhelmingly strong and clear and therefore we couldn't really believe that it was a denial. And so the question was whether or not, for example, we speculated that they were double agents, that they were all in fact working mainly for the Taliban. And the view was that they worked for the British Army in a way to get information off the British. And therefore the claim now that they were in trouble was a cynical attempt just to get some money because their supply of money had run out, so that was one possibility. And so it could just

27 SA8, 7 December 2015.
28 SA12, 14 January 2016.

> be a factual issue and what we would do then would be prepare a briefing paper for the special advocates which would anticipate all the kind of ways of undermining our clients' account. And to do that in a way that would enable special advocates to press for more and more disclosure because that's the role of the special advocate – to press to disclose material into open so that the open advocates can have a better understanding of what the case is. And so the idea was to put the special advocate in the best position to argue for greater disclosure on the basis that he has an answer to some of the points made against him.[29]

Special advocates confirmed that there would now be conferences with the open representatives before going into closed where there would be discussions about how the case should be run. In order to maintain as much communication between the open representatives and the special advocate as possible, it could be useful to try to keep one of the special advocates in open for as long as possible while the other goes into closed early. But the special advocate who has gone into closed may not communicate with her leader or junior who remains in open.[30] A lot would depend on the circumstances of the case:

> It is strategy because a lot would depend on what you're actually expecting to get from the open representatives. What is your reason for staying in open? Because there is probably no reason to go into closed until you receive the first tranche of material from the Secretary of State. Because, you know you might as well wait until they give you something proper before you go into closed unless you're already tainted. On the other hand, once you've got that first tranche of material and you're starting to complete the rule 38 process in respect of it, you've got to ask yourself: is there any good reason for not being in closed? And it might be that there are still issues happening in open because it may be that there's proceedings going on overseas, and so one of you will stay in open; the other will go into closed. And it could be that what will happen is I will go into closed. I will draft the submission to the hearing, but my leader will then come in a couple of days before the hearing so he is included for the hearing. On some occasions I will deal with the closed hearing on my own so that the leader can stay in open as long as possible. … Normally, the junior special advocate will go into closed first unless there's good reason not to.[31]

This special advocate said that you can even have a situation where a special advocate had to be replaced because the open representatives wanted to have a chance to discuss fresh evidence that had come into play with a new special advocate.

29 OC5, 2 February 2016.

30 SASO, *A Guide to The Role of Special Advocates & the Special Advocates' Support Office* (2nd edn Government Legal Department 2019) [64].

31 SA11, 14 January 2016.

The lead special advocate remained in closed. It was then possible to have a conference and then for the new special advocate to go into closed and discuss what the open representatives had said with the lead special advocate.

A number of special advocates and open counsel also stressed the importance of keeping communications going between the open representatives and the special advocates once the latter have gone into closed. While there was a bar on special advocates communicating with open representatives, once they have gone into closed, one-way communication from the open representatives to the special advocates was still possible and from the special advocate's point of view very helpful:

> After we have sight of the closed material, all we can do is acknowledge receipt of documents but what I try and do with the open representatives now is tell them how I would value their input even once I've gone into closed, simply being kept in the loop on matters of strategy, disclosures etc and any specific concerns or requests they have. I say, 'Look, send them all to me'. I will receive them and say 'Thank you, received'.[32]

Whereas in the past, according to one special advocate, once the special advocate went into closed, they would be lucky to get any communication, now it seems that open counsel are more forthcoming. According to one open counsel:

> Now, after the special advocate has gone into closed you can still have one-way communications on a privileged basis and I try and do that as much as possible to try to explain to the special advocate what's going on … I will often send the special advocate a note saying, 'Dear special advocate, I'm aware you can't respond to this apart from confirming receipt but you should know that our current tactical position is X, Y and Z. We are pushing these points very hard, we're not pushing these points so hard and this is what we're focusing on'. And they'll say, 'Thank you very much. Very helpful'.[33]

One special advocate said that in a recent case he had been receiving briefing notes from the open representatives once he had gone into closed which were really helpful because they told him the strategic positions they were taking, the steer they were taking, the legal submissions they were proposing to make or not to make and where they wanted him to dovetail with what they were doing, 'and that was brilliant'. It helped that he knew the open representatives, he used to be in chambers with the lead counsel and what they had done prior to him going into closed was that they had agreed that he would be kept briefed as much as possible on the position open counsel were taking.[34]

32 SA7, 3 December 2015.
33 OC6, 5 February 2016.
34 SA7, 3 December 2015.

To conclude this section, it would seem that there has been a growing acceptance on the part of open counsel and special advocates that there is considerable value in working together to agree strategy before the special advocate goes into closed and for communications to continue once he or she has gone into closed. Part of this acceptance is due to the normalisation of the special advocate system. Over time, a high degree of trust has developed between certain open counsel and special advocates as open counsel realise that each has an important role to play in furthering the interests of their clients. This provides an interesting explanation of how an exceptional measure like the special advocate system becomes increasingly accepted as the norm. We have seen that human rights law has played an important part in legitimising the special advocate system. We might view this as external validation. Here we see another factor at work, what we might call internal validation. It has been suggested that those representing clients in closed systems play their own part in legitimising the closed proceedings system.[35] As open counsel have begun to work with special advocates to further the interests of their clients, they have themselves lent a certain legitimacy to the special advocate system. This places open counsel in similar dilemmas to those that we saw in the last chapter that special advocates face. Unlike special advocates, however, open counsel have a responsibility to their clients to do what is best for them and this would seem to provide a strong pointer for them to continue to engage with the special advocate system. The irony is that the more closely open counsel work with special advocates, the more what is acknowledged to be an unfair system becomes accepted.

The non-communication rule

While much creativity has gone into trying to maintain one-way communications from open counsel to special advocates once the latter have gone into closed, one-way communications cannot be expanded easily into two-way communications because of the rule prohibiting special advocates from communicating with the excluded party or their representatives once they have gone into closed without the permission of the court or tribunal, which can only be given after the government has had a chance to respond to the request. Special advocates have gone on record to explain how these restrictions on communication limit the effectiveness of their function to represent the interests of the excluded party. In evidence before the Joint Committee on Human Rights (JCHR) in March 2007, one prominent special advocate put it this way:

> [Y]ou may have no idea what the real case is until you have gone closed, and therefore there has been nothing provided to you by way of either prior statement, or prior meeting or conference with the person concerned, and

35 A Boon and S Nash, 'Special Advocacy: Political Expediency and Legal Roles in Modern Judicial Systems' (2006) 9 *Legal Ethics* 101, 120.

> it is only after you have gone closed that you want to talk about say country A in 2003 or what a person was doing in city B or something of that sort, which may at least be directing the mind to the kind of relevant material that you might need. That is extremely frustrating and counter-intuitive to the basic way that lawyers are used to doing their job. It used to be the basic rule, of course, of cross-examination that you should not ask a question you do not know the answer to but, of course, you never know what even the question is you would have wanted to ask until it is too late.[36]

Later on in his evidence, the special advocate said it would help if special advocates under a more relaxed regime were able to keep contact with people who wanted to communicate:

> Sometimes you know that the person whose interests you are representing probably has little interest in communicating material that you can use, but that is not always the case, and indeed, there are cases where people are prepared to spend many hours talking and are very anxious to help you do your job on their behalf if they could be given some steer as to what it would be useful for them to do. Often it is difficult to know whether it is worthwhile for a person to get audits of bank accounts or businesses or whether that is a complete waste of time or money, or whether it would be a useful task, … to communicate, for example, yes, the Commission would be assisted if you explain about X business or X bank account … [That] would make the process a little bit more real.[37]

In numerous responses to parliamentary committees and consultation exercises, special advocates have complained about these restrictions on their ability to communicate with excluded parties.[38] The rule has nevertheless remained strict despite calls by parliamentary committees for it to be relaxed.[39] It seems that one exception originally related to employment tribunals where the regime once permitted communications between the special advocates and the open representatives after the former received the closed evidence save in relation to the

36 JCHR, *Counter-Terrorism and Human Rights: 28 days, intercept and post-charge questioning*, 19th Report of Session (2006-07, HL 157, HC 394) Ev 14, Q44 (Mr Nick Blake QC).

37 ibid.

38 See eg Special Advocates' Submission to Lord Carlisle, Independent Reviewer of Terrorism Legislation 3 December 2009 reported in JCHR, *Counter-Terrorism Policy and Human Rights (Sixteenth Report): Annual Renewal of Control Orders Legislation 2010*, 9th Report of Session (2009-10, HL 64, HC 395) Ev 60-61. Angus McCullough, giving evidence to the Committee said that the lack of communication remains a 'profound concern' of special advocates, ibid Ev 9 Q 47. See also *Response to Green Paper Consultation from Special Advocates* (2011) [29].

39 See HCCAC (n 5) [86], JCHR (n 36) [205], JCHR, *Counter-Terrorism and Human Rights (Eighth Report): Counter-Terrorism Bill*, 9th Report of Session 2007–08, [67]–[69] and JCHR (n 38) [72].

substance of the closed material.[40] In its Green Paper on the Justice and Security Bill, the government said that it would address this anomaly by bringing these rules into line with those in other courts and tribunals, and this has since been done.[41] In its response to the Green Paper, the special advocates commented that it was significant that in a forum where there may be closed material that is at least as sensitive as that depicted in other statutory CMPs, it had not been thought necessary to impose the absolute bar on direct communications that characterise every other statutory CMP in England and Wales.[42]

Another situation where there was at one time a more relaxed regime is in relation to communications between special counsel and open counsel. One counsel who used to act as special counsel said that in a case shortly after *R v H and C* was decided, his instructions on appointment were not limited by a non-communications rule.[43] This counsel said that he had made submissions to the effect that there should be no blanket rule prohibiting communications between special counsel and counsel in criminal proceedings, as the role of special counsel in these proceedings is limited to making representations on specific issues such as PII or anonymity orders and special counsel are unlikely to want to have the kind of extensive contact with open counsel that special advocates might wish when they exercise a more substantive role. It appears, nonetheless, that those who are appointed to be special counsel in criminal proceedings are now subject to such a rule.[44]

One question which the JCHR put to the Home Office Minister some time ago was why if special advocates are prepared to be trusted to have access to closed material, they are not trusted to decide what questions they can ask the excluded person, after having seen the closed material, without revealing anything which may be damaging to national security.[45] The Minister responded that it was not a question of trust but of placing undue burdens on the special advocates in terms of the balance between their interests to their clients and serious slips detrimental to public security and national security threats.[46] There needed to be a clear line drawn between what can be open material in the public domain and what must remain closed. Once we

40 Employment Tribunals (Constitution and Rules of Procedure) Regulations 2004 (SI 2004/1861), sch 2, r 8(4). For interpretation see *Rahman v Metropolitan Police* ET Case Nos 220288/07 & 3200438/07.

41 Ministry of Justice, *Justice and Security Green Paper* (Cm 8194, 2011) [2.38]. See Employment Tribunals (Constitution and Rules of Procedure) Regulations 2013 (SI 2013/1237), sch 2, r 4(6)–(8).

42 *Response to Green Paper Consultation from Special Advocates* (2011) [29](ii).

43 SA21, 23 May 2016.

44 AGO2, 14 July 2016 at the Attorney General's Office. See also Criminal Justice and Licencing (Scotland) Act 2010, s 152(3) which states that 'special counsel … must not communicate with the accused or the accused's representative (if any) about the relevant application or appeal except (a) with the permission of the court, and where permission is given, in accordance with such conditions as the court may impose'.

45 JCHR (n 36) [204].

46 ibid Ev 29, Q 128 (Mr Tony McNulty MP).

are in the realm of closed material, the ability of special advocates to converse with individuals having seen the closed material would put inordinate pressures on the special advocates, not because they would intentionally disclose it in the interests of their client (they are bound as part of their role not to disclose closed information), but in terms of the balance between doing their job in the interests of their 'clients' and not inadvertently letting information slip out that might compromise national security.[47] Successive governments have been adamant that the special advocate cannot possibly know what communications might in fact reveal to the excluded party who an agent is or what the nature of the intelligence-gathering process is.[48] As the Green Paper on Justice and Security put it, a special advocate may believe that they are able to construct communication in such a way that would not risk damage to the public interest, but the answer to which would, nonetheless, aid the special advocate's ability to represent the interests of the individual.[49]

> However, without detailed knowledge of the investigation, or other linked investigations, the special advocate could inadvertently disclose sensitive information, for example the identity of an agent or details of related ongoing investigations. In order to know whether the proposed communication could be damaging to national security, those familiar with the day-to-day operation of that (and connected) investigation(s) must be able to review any proposed communication.[50]

Not surprisingly perhaps, the government counsel interviewed in this research supported the need for a non-communication rule. According to one, it rather defied the logic of having special advocates at all if they were to be allowed to speak to open lawyers after seeing the closed material:

> The very reasons there are special advocates is that they are supposed to step in when the party himself and his lawyers are unable to participate. So it seems somewhat tendentious to think that the special advocate should be able to join in being with the open people when the only reasons they're there at all is because the open people are excluded.[51]

Another considered that if there is going to be a system of having closed evidence, there needs to be a rule against unauthorised communication:

> Unauthorised communication will be unworkable. If the government knew that what they disclosed could be disclosed without their control, then they

47 ibid Ev 28, Q 122.
48 HCCAC (n 5) Ev 35, Q 244 (Lord Goldsmith).
49 Ministry of Justice (n 41) [2.30].
50 ibid.
51 GC5, 14 April 2016.

> are effectively inhibited from disclosing anything. It's never going to happen. Because you've got to remember the people you are talking about disclosure to are the very people who wish to have this information. ... If there's no control what is to stop the crucial piece of information which effectively identifies the source, or effectively tells that a particular circle has been penetrated even if it doesn't identify the source. And the very fact of that particular network being penetrated by means of electronic interception or human intelligence source or some other means, that in itself can be devastating. And if there is not control over that, nor would it be possible to make use of what we call liaison material ie CIA or foreign shared material. Because you have to get their consent, clearance before you can use it. But if you can't say to them, 'Under no circumstances will this be communicated beyond the court or the special advocate. If we're made to disclose it, we will simply withdraw it'. If you can't say that, it will never be capable of use.[52]

This lawyer reiterated that it was not a question of trusting the special advocate. Special advocates are simply not in the position to know what is going to do damage in that way. They might be able to know sometimes, or some of the time. Often indeed, the security services themselves do not know what is the one piece of information which if you gave it to an appellant would allow them to put two and two together and say, 'Ah the only reason they could know this is because of X or Y'. And often they don't know what that is:

> Because you know, they might have told X, Y and Z to half the world. But they might have told A, B and C to only one person. But you don't know which is X, Y, Z and which is A, B, C.[53]

A constant thrust of government counsel's argument, then, was that special advocates will never see the whole picture and that the communications rule is a comfort for security services who know that when material is disclosed to special advocates, it will never leak out. Even if a judge were to order disclosure, there is still the option for the government to withdraw the material and not rely on it rather than have it disclosed.

Authorised communications

It seems that, at least in the early days, attempts by special advocates to seek permission to communicate with the excluded party after they had seen the closed material were very rare. The nine special advocates who gave written evidence to the HCCAC in 2004 made it clear that there was in fact no contact between the

52 GC4, 12 April 2016.
53 ibid.

special advocate and the appellants' chosen representatives after special advocates became privy to closed material:

> Although SIAC itself has power under r 36(4) to give directions authorising communication in a particular case, this power is in practice almost never used, not least because any request for a direction authorising communication must be notified to the Secretary of State. So, the special advocate can communicate with the appellant's lawyers only if the precise form of the communication has been approved by his opponent in the proceedings. Such a requirement precludes communication even on matters of pure legal strategy (ie matters unrelated to the particular factual sensitivities of a case).[54]

In subsequent proceedings before the JCHR, special advocates expanded on the reasons why the power to seek permission for communications is rarely used.[55] Two explanations have been given. First, there is the point that permission would rarely be granted if the purpose of the communication was to discuss anything to do with the closed case. According to one special advocate, if the communication had anything to do with the substantive closed case:

> the anxieties of those who are supplying the information and the nature of the information is that any form of communication after you go closed would inadvertently or otherwise – I think inadvertently is probably the principal cause of concern – alert the person whose interests you are representing to something about the case.[56]

The other explanation is the anxiety that special advocates themselves have about giving away 'to the opposing party the parts of the closed evidence in relation to which the controlled person does not have an explanation'. As one special advocate explained:

> [W]e cannot raise a point except by going through the very person who is going to be making submissions against us. So just to take a completely hypothetical example, you have a case where the appellant's open evidence is entirely silent about some activity which the appellant may know is vaguely implicated in the case but you know as special advocate that it is central to the case, so you want to ask the appellant in private or you would want to ask the appellant in private if you could, 'You need to give us more details of activity that you were involved in'. Let us suppose that in response to that question the answer is that there are no further details; it is a gift of a submission to your opponent, who can then say to the tribunal, 'There are no

54 HCCAC (n 5) Ev 15, [10].
55 JCHR (n 36) [201].
56 ibid Ev 14 Q 44 (Mr Nick Blake QC).

> details given by the appellant about this important issue'. It is exactly the sort of question which one would want to ask in private, precisely because one does not know the answer to the question, and the requirement to go not only to the Security Service or to some appropriate agency who can tell you whether what you are about to ask is going to endanger national security but to the actual person who is appearing against you in the case that you are in is really a very strong constraint on using this power.[57]

In evidence the following year to the JCHR, another prominent special advocate made the point that giving notice to the Secretary of State of the questions that the special advocate would like to pose to the appellant 'is entirely counter-intuitive to any lawyer, that you disclose your case to the other side before you even get permission to ask the question'.[58]

By contrast, one government counsel who was interviewed for this research did not think it unreasonable for there to be a vetting process and he was impatient with the notion that the special advocate would be giving away their strategy by complying with it.[59] He considered that the proceedings were different from ordinary civil proceedings, as each side had a duty to put its cards on the table. On the government side, a full exculpatory review has to be completed on the basis of cards on the table. He said that what each side should be doing is putting their cards on the table and saying, 'Look, this is effectively everything that helps you', and in his view, the special advocate best assists the court when they take the same attitude. Even if the special advocate were to reveal tactics in the course of the vetting process, the government cannot change tactics in the light of learning what the strategy is going to be.

In their research on special advocates in 2007, Forcese and Waldman reported that some special advocates had occasionally sought (and received) permission to communicate in writing.[60] The information imparted in these letters was reportedly of an unproblematic sort related to procedural matters, but was sometimes more substantive. One example was a communication by a special advocate that grounds for appeal existed in a case. It would seem, however, that the communications did not seek information from the excluded person.

> The questions asked – passed through the tribunal and security services – could well spark the interest of the security services, in a manner prejudicial to the named person. A subsequent failure of the special advocate in the proceeding to then rely on whatever answer was provided by the named person would also attract the attention of the security services.[61]

57 ibid Ev 15 (Mr Martin Chamberlain).
58 JCHR (n 39) Ev 6 Q 23 (Mr Neil Garnham QC).
59 GC4, 12 April 2016.
60 Forcese and Waldman (n 4).
61 ibid 36–37.

The government Green Paper on the Justice and Security Bill acknowledged that in practice special advocates had only rarely sought permission from the court to communicate with the individuals whose interests they are representing after service of the closed material and acknowledged that one reason for this is that such communication, once requested of the Secretary of State, would reveal litigation and other tactics and strategy and consequently benefit the Government side.[62] One innovation that the Green Paper considered might enhance the willingness of special advocates to make use of existing procedures in communicating with the excluded individual after the service of closed material was to erect a properly functioning 'Chinese wall' between government counsel and those clearing the proposed communication. The arrangement could be further strengthened by a protocol which would confirm that within the Agencies, the minimum number of people necessary to carry out the security check would be involved. It would seem that some such mechanism has now been put in place. The *Open Manual* states that an agreed process has been put in place between SASO and government lawyers acting for the information owners to ensure that communications which attract legal professional privilege are transmitted by administrative staff and are not seen by the lawyers acting on behalf of the information owner in the case.[63]

Apart from the concern about revealing strategy to government lawyers, the special advocates in their response to the Green Paper explained the rarity of communications between special advocates and open representatives on the ground that anything that could permissibly be communicated between them could just as easily be gisted by means of disclosure, rendering the requirement to communicate through the Court redundant.[64] An example was given of an issue that might come up in the closed material relating to an individual's overseas travel in 2006. Rather than formulating a communication to be made through the Court ('Please give an account of your overseas travel in 2006'), it would be routine to address this in the disclosure process by way of a gist ('The Appellant's overseas travel in 2006 is of relevance to the case against him', or something to that effect). If such a gist could not be given because of the asserted sensitivity of the information even at that level of generality (which the special advocates said was routinely encountered), then there would be no possibility of framing an equivalent question to be communicated through the court and the government Agency.

In interviews with special advocates, a rather mixed picture was given of the degree to which communications are sought to be made through the court or otherwise to the appellant and his representatives after the closed material has been viewed. A distinction was made between what were called 'procedural' communications and 'substantive' communications about the case. According to one experienced special advocate, special advocates have become a bit more conscious

62 Ministry of Justice (n 41) [2.29].
63 SASO (n 30) [67].
64 *Response to Green Paper Consultation from Special Advocates* (2011) [28] n 17.

over the years than they used to be of the need to keep the open representatives informed as to what was going on procedurally.[65] He referred to a recent Practice Note for proceedings before SIAC which states that throughout the proceedings the Secretary of State and the special advocates have a duty to inform the appellant's/claimant's representatives of the nature and purpose of any closed steps in the proceedings (including written submissions, oral hearings, rulings and decisions) in so far as this is possible consistently with rule 4(1) prohibiting the disclosure of any information contrary to the public interest).[66] In particular, at the end of any closed hearing and following any closed ruling or decision, the Secretary of State and special advocates shall consider, and if possible agree, what may be said to the open representatives by the Commission in relation to that hearing, ruling or decision.

In practice, it appears that after every closed hearing, the special advocate now drafts a proposed note setting out what happened in the most general terms, what the next steps are and what appellants and their lawyers should expect going forward.[67] One special advocate confirmed that he would try to let the open representatives know as much as he could say about what he was doing:

> since you can anticipate if you're being excluded, not only thinking what on earth, you know, is someone really looking after me? And what's really going on? How frustrating it is that I don't know what they're saying against me or how they're answering my claim.[68]

What is less clear is how often requests are made for communications which go to the substance of the case. The SIAC Practice Note states that rule 36, which on one reading would seem to require that every request for communication must go through SIAC, does not require authorisation or direction from SIAC where the Secretary of State does not object to the authorised communication. According to one special advocate, picking up the point made in the Green Paper consultation, communications in relation to anything that relates to the substance of the closed material are not of much practical use because anything you can formulate in a communication, you can and probably more appropriately should have disclosed by way of a gist:

> So rather than seeking to communicate whether you were in the country on a particular date which it would be useful to know, the same effect can be achieved by agreeing or getting the court to rule that a gist should be given that the Secretary of State considers that what you were doing between 2012 and 2014 abroad is significant. And this is may be all the Secretary of

65 SA5, 25 November 2015.
66 *Practice Note for Proceedings before SIAC*, 30 April 2014 [20].
67 SA5, 25 November 2015.
68 SA6, 3 December 2015.

> State can agree to be given, rather than it was May 2006 in Afghanistan or whatever.[69]

Another special advocate said that you are always trying to get more into open which might give you further instructions, but he could not recall if he had ever had a case where he had asked to get permission to go back and receive further instructions:

> If you don't succeed getting more information within the open, it seems to me that any such application is probably doomed to failure because inevitably you'll be wanting to convey something from the closed that's likely to be something that the security service would object to because you're giving something away.[70]

At the same time, according to other special advocate interviewees, it is not uncommon for special advocates to want to communicate on some points of substance relating to the case. One situation is where the special advocate wants to communicate certain points of law that he or she thinks should be made in open or wants to inquire as to how to deal with a point of law. Points of law were easier to communicate about, as there was less risk of implicitly disclosing strategy to the other side. In one example, a special advocate said there was an EU point which he was not sure whether he should run as this would require a reference to the European Court of Justice which might delay matters.[71] So he sought instructions as to whether he should run the point. In fact, the individual wanted a quick appeal and did not want to get bogged down in a reference procedure. So the open representatives came back and said, 'Please don't run the EU point'. This was a concrete example of where the special advocate can get permission from the court to make a communication.

Another special advocate said that it was always very important to hear as much about what the open case is. Situations can arise where one wants to hear more open argument or submissions about a point, and one has to somehow convey that 'because you want as much from them as possible to know where they see the answer'.[72]

Another situation that arises quite commonly, according to one special advocate, is when further material comes to light, for example when material moves from closed into open, and there are specific things that you want to get some information on.[73] In this situation, it is not at all uncommon for something to be formulated that might be put to the client in writing. This advocate said that

69 SA5, 25 November 2015.
70 SA2, 4 November 2015.
71 SA7, 3 December 2015.
72 SA6, 3 December 2015.
73 SA8, 7 December 2015.

these communications are always done in writing. He could not envisage circumstances in which oral discussion would be permitted.

According to one open counsel, the proposed note that is drafted by special advocates after each closed session provides an opportunity to get as much information back to the open lawyers as possible.[74] If the government objects to the note, the special advocates can write a letter to open counsel for government lawyers to approve, stating that they have prepared a communication for the open lawyers which they consider is entirely anodyne in open but which the government lawyers have vetoed and they may wish to make an application to see a copy. Often the government would not refuse this. Generally speaking, it was fair to say that there was now lot more communication than there used to be.

One government counsel reflected on the fact that there was quite a variance in the degree to which some special advocates make applications to communicate with open representatives.[75] In his view, such communications could turn out to be very helpful to the open representatives. Applications were often deployed, for example, to communicate to the open representatives an absence of evidence on a certain point. So special advocates might communicate that there is no evidence in closed to support proposition X, Y or Z. There could sometimes be an objection that a communication of this kind could disclose a particular vulnerability in intelligence coverage, but often it was pitched at a more general level and 'could be very helpful':

> It tells the open advocate that if you were going to attack that point, you have got sight of all the relevant material. So you're not going to be bitten behind a closed curtain, you're not wasting your breath. You can absolutely go for that.[76]

Mixed views were expressed on the extent to which the Chinese walls advocated in the Green Paper were being implemented on the ground. One special advocate explained that there were two ways of seeking clearance for communications.[77] One was by going straight to the government team on the other side. If there is any possible privilege connected to the communication, an alternative procedure is followed whereby a separate Home Office security team vets the application. He gave the example of an appeal he wanted to lodge against a declaration for a CMP that had been granted in a judicial review case. He wanted to appeal but the open representatives did not. In his view, the open representatives really should appeal before anything else happened, so he communicated this through the more complicated Chinese walls procedure.

74 OC6, 5 February 2016.
75 GC4, 12 April 2016.
76 ibid.
77 SA3, 25 November 2015.

Another special advocate, however, took a more cautious approach towards seeking clearance for communications that go to substantive issues. He gave the example of a case where the special advocate is asked a question by the open representatives on how to conduct the litigation, in particular whether they should carry on or appeal the decision made by the judge. It might be possible to answer the question decisively, but depending on the context, it might be not be easy to give a clear answer. He acknowledged that there is supposedly a Chinese wall so that a separate section of the government's legal team, as opposed to those conducting the litigation in the case, will review the request for communication, but it could still be sensitive:

> You're telling the other side what you're thinking and what you're going to do, whether you're going to appeal something or not going to appeal and what you think in terms of the merit or the merits in appealing something. And there is a reluctance. Even though there is a Chinese wall there and I am not aware of any underhand behaviour in the 20 years I've been doing this … there's still a reluctance, no lawyer gives up privileged information. 'My advice to you is that you should do the following'. That's classic LPP [legal professional privilege] even though we're not in a lawyer-client relationship, strictly speaking.[78]

Another special advocate highlighted the artificiality of the Chinese walls concept:

> First of all, it's a sealed envelope. I'm passing this to you. Can you pass this to the other person in your team without looking? And when the response comes back, it will come back in a sealed envelope to us.[79]

One government lawyer explained that his experience of the way the Chinese wall works is that government lawyers very often get copied into a request by the special advocates, but they do not get to play any part in advising the government whether to comply with it:

> It's not a question whether it would be a good or a bad idea if you comply with it as if it were some sort of litigation tactic. There's only one basis to object, and that is: 'will that damage security to communicate that?' And I'm not in a position to judge that. Only the security services. Sometimes, I guess you could provide the context more fully, explain the context in which the question is asked. So you may raise a point saying this question arises because of this context. But the answer as to whether that's going to do any harm is something only they would know.[80]

78 SA14, 5 February 2016.
79 SA11, 14 January 2016.
80 GC4, 12 April 2016.

This comment illuminates the scepticism of some special advocates about the way the Chinese wall operates, as it illustrates how difficult it is in reality to prevent communications between the Security Services and government lawyers. It certainly highlights a certain imbalance in the manner in which communications are regulated between the parties. Special advocates are under statutory restrictions not to communicate at all with the excluded party or his or her legal representative after they have seen closed material. Meanwhile, it would seem that there are no restrictions on government counsel and the Security Services communicating with each other after a Chinese wall is erected between them regarding clearance requests that may reveal arguably privileged material.

Keeping the non-communication rule?

There remains the question of what special advocates think about the non-communication rule, after years of having to live with it in practice. In their response to the Green Paper on the Justice and Security Bill, special advocates recognised that communication in relation to the substance of any closed material is likely to create difficulties and may often be impossible. Nevertheless, they questioned whether the absolute bar on all direct communication was truly necessary.[81] One former special advocate has gone on record, however, to say that a relaxation of the rule would not make much of a difference in practice. Special advocates would still be precluded from revealing any of the closed case and this presumably includes asking any question from which part of the closed case could be inferred.[82] As one special advocate who was amenable to the idea of relaxation put it to the JCHR:

> the difficult problem is how far you could engage in a conversation which directs someone's mind to a topic or an area without crossing the line that would give something away which might endanger the public interest or public security.[83]

One special advocate who was interviewed in this study considered that, at the end of the day, it all comes down to disclosure. Unless you are able to discuss the allegations against the excluded party, being able to communicate with him is not really going to assist his representation:

> Let's say there are 10 allegations and he has only one of them disclosed. You can sit in the room with him and he can say, 'That one kilo of cocaine that's found in the boot of my car, my brother-in-law put it there because he's a drug

81 *Response to Green Paper Consultation from Special Advocates* (2011) [29].
82 M Chamberlain, 'Special Advocates and Procedural Fairness in Closed Proceedings' (2009) 28 *Civil Justice Quarterly* 314, 322.
83 JCHR (n 36) Q 44, Ev 14 (Mr Nick Blake QC).

> dealer and I was stupid enough to say to him, "On this one occasion, I'll look after them", because I didn't want him to be murdered and so I let him do so'. But let's say there are nine other allegations that he doesn't know about. You can talk about the one allegation he knows about – the cocaine in the boot in his car – until the cows come home but when there are other allegations of significance or multiple allegations … communication is only valuable when you've got something to talk about. If you make disclosure of the other nine allegations, you don't need to sit in the room with the person. His lawyers will be perfectly capable of providing you with an answer to them saying. 'Allegation one, this is our response. Allegation 2 …' and so on. You don't need to have a face to face meeting. But when there are 10 allegations and he only knows the one allegation, you can have a theoretical discussion and say, 'Well, what if the allegation is that you produced the one kilo of cocaine that was in the boot of your car, that you've got a factory in your loft? What would you say to that?' And you could have an endless discussion with any number of possibilities, any number of theories and it would be without direction … very, very unfocused, hypothetical, speculative, but no use in reality.[84]

A few special advocates made the point that government counsel in contrast to special advocates are not precluded from speaking to open counsel. It has also been noted that a special advocate is not in a position that is any different from that of an intelligence officer questioning a suspect or a witness when the former has secret information that he or she wishes to verify whilst at the same time trying to avoid involuntary disclosures.[85] The skills obtained in years of work as a barrister might be thought to adequately equip the special advocate to steer around the problem of involuntary disclosure.[86] One open counsel said that there could be significant inadvertent disclosure by government lawyers:

> You can't talk to the special advocates, so the special advocates are not going to make any inadvertent disclosure. Whereas you can talk to the government. And it's amazing how much they will let slip, usually due to incompetence, with a bit of gentle interrogation. And the number of government lawyers who just sit there with a bright red bundle that says 'top secret, for your eyes only' on their desk with an index page open in front and you kind of go, 'That's interesting'. Or they just tell you something they didn't mean to. Special advocates are not trusted to speak even about procedural things directly to open advocates once they've got into closed but the government lawyers are. Apparently, government lawyers are more trustworthy but no less human.[87]

84 SA14, 5 February 2016.
85 Forcese and Waldman (n 4) 37.
86 ibid 37.
87 OC6, 5 February 2016.

The fact that government counsel can sometimes inadvertently reveal closed material to open counsel is not an argument for relaxing the rules for special advocates. One government counsel admitted that there was a real danger that they could reveal something in closed inadvertently.[88] He said that before cross-examining a witness in open, he would rehearse the cross-examination with his clients (the intelligence services) to prevent him adverting to anything in closed; and it was amazing how many times his clients would object to a line of questioning. One special advocate considered that experienced special advocates could conduct meetings with open counsel without giving anything away, but that the existing noncommunication rule was a protection for special advocates who were in a different position to government lawyers:

> It's there to protect you from inadvertently discussing something which has the effect of … could have all kinds of repercussions. It's there so you're not put in a difficult position. And yes, technically the government lawyers are sighted on the closed material, they do have conversations with the open lawyers and make oral submissions openly in open court but your relationship is different. … You're seeking information, you're asking questions about specific matters and your interest in a particular area may reveal that that area is of importance in the case and your lack of interest in an aspect of the individual's life may suggest that that's not a very important issue in this case.[89]

This advocate considered that maintaining the prohibition was the safer course:

> And in the end there is something to be said about protecting the public interest where if you assume for a moment that the individuals that are subjected to these measures are dangerous terrorists, if you assume that that is the case as opposed to assuming that the person is just literally some innocent person standing at the bus stop who's been rounded up. Think of the damage that might be caused if you inadvertently give up something that leads that person to a right or a wrong conclusion and could have some really serious repercussions. … Now, I don't work on the basis that the individuals are guilty as charged or are dangerous individuals but if you do … this is the government's argument. If you work on that basis, then … as opposed to someone with half a brain you know who just enters the scene quite innocently to whom it will go over their head anyway, there is a good reason and unless you can advance things very significantly by having these meetings post having seen the secret material, then why not just sort of take the cautious approach?[90]

88 GC7, 24 April 2016.
89 SA14, 5 February 2016.
90 ibid.

While one group of special advocates accepted the need for the non-communication rule, there were occasions, as we have seen, when it was important to communicate matters of substance to open counsel and there was a view that it should be possible to relax the rule requiring that all applications for communication go through government lawyers. According to one special advocate, a 'real bugbear is our inability to send communications to the open representatives without them being seen by the Secretary of State'.[91] In his view, it should be possible for such applications to go through a judge, maybe even a retired judge or a panel of judges with an intelligence background:

> But what can't be happening even if it's notionally through a Chinese wall is that it is going via the Secretary of State's team.[92]

One former special advocate said that in his experience he had only once managed to circumvent the rule that all communications should be vetted by the government and it was in an unusual extra-statutory civil case before the Justice and Security Act was enacted where closed proceedings were consented to by the claimant.[93] The special advocate had wanted to communicate to the open representatives his view that the facts revealed the existence of a civil cause of action. He gave the judge and the Secretary of State an undertaking as to the nature of the communication that he wanted to disclose. The judge then agreed to the communication being made without being shown to the Secretary of State, because the special advocate did not want to reveal a legal view that was adverse to the Secretary of State. Another special advocate said that judges had sometimes been helpful in facilitating contact between special advocates and open counsel and limiting the extent to which the state representatives know about it, but he did not expand or give specific examples.[94]

Canadian experience

We have seen that the non-communication rule is rigidly adhered to in the UK. In their collective response to the Green Paper consultation, however, special advocates submitted that an absolute prohibition on direct communication is not a feature of procedures used to deal with closed evidence anywhere else in the world. They drew a contrast with Canada where special advocates are permitted to communicate with open representatives, save in relation to communications involving the substance of closed material, which have to be sanctioned by

91 SA11, 14 January 2016.
92 ibid.
93 SA12, 14 January 2016.
94 SA9, 7 December 2015.

the court but do not necessarily require the approval of the government.[95] This is not an entirely accurate summary of Canadian law and practice. The Senate Committee reporting on Canadian terrorism law in the aftermath of the decision of the Canadian Supreme Court in *Charkaoui v Canada*[96] that the procedures employed in the security certificate system violated section 7 of the Canadian Charter of Rights and Freedoms strongly recommended that the special advocates should be able to meet with the excluded person after accessing secret evidence.[97] But the legislation providing for special advocates ultimately seems to require judicial authorisation for any communication regarding the proceedings between the special advocate and the excluded person or a third party, as in the UK.[98] It is correct to say, however, that there is one difference in practice. Although there is no express provision in Canadian law that would allow special advocates to seek permission from the presiding judge on an ex parte basis to consult the excluded person or her lawyers, it appears that practice has evolved to enable special advocates to minimise the risk of revealing their litigation strategy by making submissions to the designated judge in the absence of the government lawyers or even to seek leave to present a request to communicate to a different judge.[99]

95 *Response to Green Paper Consultation from Special Advocates* (2011), [29](i). See also the reference to the Canadian position in JCHR (n 38) [74]–[76].

96 *Charkaoui v Canada (Citizenship and Immigration)* 2007 SCC 9, [2007] 1 SCR 350.

97 See Senate Special Committee on the Anti-terrorism Act, *Fundamental Justice in Extraordinary Times* (2007) 36 cited in Forcese and Waldman (n 4) 38.

98 See Immigration and Refugee Protection Act 2001, s 85.4 as amended stating that 'after the information or other evidence is received by the special advocate, the special advocate may during the remainder of the proceedings communicate with another person about the proceedings only with the judge's authorisation and subject to any conditions that the judge considers appropriate'. See also s 85.5(b) which states that 'with the exception of communications authorised by a judge, no person shall (a) disclose information or other evidence that has been disclosed to them under section 85.4 and is treated as confidential by the judge presiding at the proceedings; or (b) communicate with another person about the content of any part of a proceeding under any of sections 78 to section 82 and 82.2 that is heard in the absence of the public and of the permanent resident or foreign national and the counsel'. It has been suggested that this latter provision provides a more tailored restriction on the basis that it seeks to restrain the special advocate with respect to confidential information and information heard in the absence of the public and the affected party (see K Roach, 'Charkaoui and Bill-C3: Some Implications for Anti-Terrorism Policy and Dialogue between Courts and Legislatures' (2008) 42 *Supreme Court Law Review* 281, 318). But the Federal Court of Appeals and the Supreme Court seem to have taken the view that *any* communications by a special advocate to the named person after receiving the confidential information must be authorised by the judge. See *Harkat v Canada* Fed CA 2012 FCA 122 [114] and *Canada (Citizenship and Immigration) v Harkat* 2014 SCC 37, [2014] 2 SCR 33 [68].

99 See *Re Almrei* 2008 FC 1216, [2009] 3 FCR 497 [65]. See D Cole and S I Vladeck, 'Navigating the Shoals of Secrecy: A Comparative Analysis of the Use of Secret Evidence and "Cleared Counsel" in the United States, the United Kingdom and Canada' in L Lazarus, C McCrudden and N Bowles (eds), *Reasoning Rights: Comparative Judicial Engagement* (Hart 2013) 161, 167; G Hudson and D Alati, 'Behind Closed Doors: Secret Law and the Special Advocate System in Canada' (2018) 44 *Queen's Law Journal* 1, 52–56.

The Supreme Court in *Harkat v Canada* stated that the broad discretion conferred by the Act upon judges to authorise communications pre-empts the unfairness that might otherwise result from restricted access.[100] According to the Court, the restrictions were designed to avert the '*serious* risks of disclosure of information or evidence whose disclosure would be injurious to national security or to the safety of any person'.[101] The Court continued:

> While the IRPA scheme requires the judge to minimise risks of inadvertent disclosure of information, the judge must also give special advocates significant latitude. The special advocates are competent and security-cleared lawyers, who take their professional and statutory obligations seriously. They have the ability to distinguish between the public and confidential aspects of their case. The judge should take a liberal approach in authorising communications and only refuse authorisation where the Minister has demonstrated, on a balance of probabilities, a real – as opposed to a speculative – risk of injurious disclosure. As much as possible, the special advocates should be allowed to investigate the case and develop their strategy by communicating with the named person, the named person's public counsel, and third parties who may bring relevant insights and information.[102]

The Canadian experience suggests that it is possible to enable special advocates to communicate more meaningfully with open parties under a more relaxed authorisation scheme. A recent study of Canadian practice, however, found that the ease with which a special advocate may secure authorisations depends very much on the designated judge and this depends on trust-building and familiarity between the special advocate and the judge and between the government, the Canadian Security Intelligence Service and the judge.[103] It seems that special advocates are still reluctant to make applications on the ground that it may prejudice the excluded person by enabling the judge to infer something inculpatory about them. The answer to this would be to enable communication requests to be made to a judge other than the designated judge who is hearing the case, but this does not seem to have occurred in practice.

Following the Canadian experience, the idea of making ex parte applications to the judge has been recommended by the JCHR in the UK and suggested by special advocates in their submissions to the Independent Reviewer on Terrorism Legislation.[104] It has been proposed that the application might be made to a High Court judge with experience of national security matters, but not the one who

100 *Canada (Citizenship and Immigration) v Harkat* 2014 SCC 37, [2014] 2 SCR 33.
101 ibid [70] (emphasis added).
102 ibid.
103 Hudson and Alati (n 99) 54–55.
104 See JCHR (n 39) [69] and Special Advocates' Submission to Lord Carlisle, Independent Reviewer of Terrorism Legislation reported in JCHR (n 38) 63.

is hearing the case.[105] If the judge considered that the proposed communication gave rise to any possible issue of national security, then it could be directed that the Secretary of State be put on notice of the communication, if the special advocate still wished to pursue it, so as to enable any objection to be considered.[106] In this regard, it is interesting to note that in its final report on *Crown Proceedings and National Security Information* recommending the selective use of special advocates where national security information is involved in civil and criminal proceedings and in appeals and judicial review of administrative decisions, the New Zealand Law Commission favours an approach under which the court oversees any communications between the special advocate and the excluded party or their lawyer after the special advocate has been provided with access to the national security information and that 'court oversight' is preferable to any requirement that the Crown be notified of communications.[107]

105 JCHR (n 39) Ev 6, Q 23 (Mr Neil Garnham QC).
106 *Response to Green Paper Consultation from Special Advocates* (2011) [31].
107 New Zealand Law Commission, *The Crown in Court: A review of the Crown Proceedings Act and national security information in proceedings* (NZLC R135, 2015) [9.23].

8 Disclosure

The last chapter considered the constraints that are imposed upon special advocates in terms of their communications with parties and legal representatives excluded from the closed procedures. We saw how these constraints can make life frustrating for special advocates who have to represent the interests of these parties in closed procedures. Before we turn to look at this 'representational' role in more detail, however, we need to examine the other important function that special advocates have in relation to disclosure. Special advocates have consistently said that arguing for greater disclosure is one of the key functions that they perform when they are served with the closed material, apart from representing the excluded person in the closed proceedings.[1] As one practitioner put it, many special advocates felt their most important function was on the 'disclosure front' which meant:

> what, if anything, can go from closed to open, and also, what is not before the Commission [SIAC] as a whole which ought to be by way of further investigations, collateral investigations, exculpatory material and things which tend to undermine the hypothesis of the case which is being presented against the person whose interests you represent.[2]

As this statement suggests, the term 'disclosure' has been used to cover two distinct processes.[3] First of all, it relates to what can be disclosed to the appellant regarding the material that the Secretary of State's case relies on. According to rule 4(1) of the Special Immigration Appeals Commission (SIAC) (Procedure) Rules 2003, when:

> exercising its functions, the Commission shall secure that information is not disclosed contrary to the interests of national security, the international

1 C Forcese and L Waldman, *Seeking Justice in an Unfair Process* (University of Ottawa 2007) 42.
2 JCHR, *Counter-Terrorism and Human Rights: 28 days, intercept and post-charge questioning*, 19th Report of Session (2006-07, HL 157, HC 394) Ev 10, Q 34 (Mr Nick Blake QC).
3 See *Y and Othman v SSHD* SC/36/2005, SC/15/2005, 12 July 2006 [3].

relations of the UK, the detection and prevention of crime, or in any other circumstances where disclosure is likely to harm the public interest.[4]

It is to be noted that there is no balancing test required here. If the disclosure of the information is likely to harm the public interest, it must not be disclosed. One can compare this with PII applications where the judge is required to balance competing public interests: the public interest in non-disclosure against the public interest in disclosure.[5] We have seen, however, that in certain cases where *A* or *AF*-type disclosure applies, the case may not be allowed to proceed unless some minimal threshold of disclosure has been reached which is specific enough to allow the appellant to give effective instructions to the special advocate.

Apart from what can and must be disclosed to appellants regarding the case against them, 'disclosure' also has a second sense relating to the production by the Secretary of State, whether to the appellant or to the special advocate, of material on which the Secretary of State does not intend to rely but which the appellant or the special advocate considers ought to be made available, whether by way of documents, or answers to questions, following, if necessary, the making of inquiries of other domestic or foreign officials.[6] We shall see that there are now rules that require the Secretary of State to file exculpatory material with SIAC as well as a statement of the evidence on which she relies in opposition to the appeal.

Essentially there are, correspondingly, two sorts of disclosure jobs for special advocates. As one special advocate put it in interview,[7] the first was to make sure that counsel got into the litigation everything that could usefully link back to conferences with open counsel. Then secondly, there is the question of how much of this material can be disclosed to the open representatives. Within SIAC, submissions on both types of disclosure are known as Rule 38 submissions.[8] The SASO *Open Manual* describes these as submissions on what, if any, of the closed material should become open and requests to the information owner for further information or documents to be provided in closed (or indeed in open).[9]

4 Cf CPR r 76.2(2) (proceedings under the PTA 2005); r 79.2(2) (proceedings under the Counter-Terrorism Act 2008 and Pt 1 of the Terrorist Asset-Freezing Etc Act 2010; r 80.2(2) (TPIMs); r 82.2(2) (CMPs in civil proceedings).

5 See *R v Chief Constable of the West Midlands Police, ex p Wiley* [1995] 1 AC 274.

6 *Y and Othman v SSHD* SIAC SC/36/2005, SC/15/2005, 12 July 2006 [4].

7 SA6, 3 December 2015.

8 SIAC (Procedure) Rules 2003, r 38. Cf CPR, r 76.29 (proceedings under the PTA 2005); r 79.26 (proceedings under the Counter-Terrorism Act 2008 and Pt 1 of the Terrorist Asset-Freezing Etc Act 2010); r 80.25 (TPIMs); r. 82.14 (CMPs in civil proceedings).

9 SASO, *A Guide to the Role of Special Advocates & The Special Advocates' Support Office* (2nd edn Government Legal Department 2019) [75]–[76].

Disclosure to the special advocate

Special advocates remarked upon the initially daunting experience of receiving closed material. As one interviewee who used to practise as a special advocate put it:

> The material you tend to get is often very raw. It could be very raw. It could be a covering letter with just a series of documents behind it, and often very little attempt to explain what the potential, let's say exculpatory significance of the document is. … It's very dense. Who's on the copy list? What are the references to the other reports? What's the significance of this, that and the other? Who are these people who are being cross-referred? What are these events? Etc etc.[10]

The special advocate is then expected within a short period of time to perform the two disclosure functions simultaneously:

> When the materials are served on you, what you will invariably do is you'll make a set of submissions about what should go into open and what should go into closed … So you could say, this document can be redacted and disclosed in this form or a gist saying this can be disclosed and so and so forth. So you'll have a path of negotiation in relation to that. But equally, you'll be saying, 'I haven't seen documents of this category. Or this document refers to that document, or these other documents. I need to see this additional material'. And, very often, what will happen is you'll have a fight about that. And then, lo and behold, the material will arrive two days before the hearing.[11]

A constant complaint of special advocates over the years has been late disclosure.[12] In 2010, one special advocate provided the Joint Committee on Human Rights (JCHR) with a Note from the special advocates in a control order case which set out a chronology of the Secretary of State's disregard of the Court's directions and claimed that the efficacy of the disclosure hearing had been 'seriously compromised' as a result.[13] Another special advocate giving evidence to the Committee said that 'in almost every case a very substantial volume of disclosure, sometimes very important disclosure, arrives on the Friday before a Monday hearing or a couple of days before' and this prevented special advocates performing their disclosure functions effectively.[14] Sometimes the additional material came as

10 SA12, 14 January 2016.
11 ibid.
12 Forcese and Waldman (n 1) 42.
13 Special Advocate's Open Note in *SSHD v AN*, PTA/42/2009, dated 20 Oct 2009 in JCHR, *Counter-Terrorism Policy and Human Rights (Sixteenth Report): Annual Renewal of Control Orders Legislation 2010*, Ninth Report of Session (2009-10, HL 64, HC 395) Ev 64–66.
14 JCHR, ibid, Ev 15, Q 96 (Ms Helen Mountfield).

a result of late review, but in other cases documents disclosed late were available many weeks or months before. The logistical difficulties for special advocates were exacerbated by their being unable to take material home. If material arrives on a Friday before a Monday hearing, that was extremely problematic. Another special advocate in his evidence asserted that every single special advocate had experience of this problem. There were two inevitable consequences:

> The first is that this material is incredibly dense, it is incredibly difficult to parse, and parse it you have to do word by word often, unpicking the various synonyms or codes used in this documentation. It takes a long time to read and you read it without the benefit of someone to help you with it because you do not have a client, or do not have an intelligence expert to tell you what this document means or does not mean or what its implications are for other documents. You do not read it in isolation, you have to read it with the documents it has to be read with or refers back to. To do that job properly takes time and you cannot do it if you are dumped with the material the day before court. The second point is that late disclosure inevitably means that the thing which is lost is the disclosure process, and it is the disclosure process which is one of the two most important jobs that a special advocate does, namely ensuring that insofar as it can be the material in question is put in open, or a gist is provided for it or some form of follow-up occurs. That process always goes out the window when you get late disclosure.[15]

For their part, government counsel in interviews explained how their disclosure duties could lead to late disclosure revealing a tension between thorough and expeditious exculpatory review. Given their ongoing disclosure duty, sometimes the best time to do a review was close to the hearing so as to ensure that nothing new that was relevant to the case had come to light.[16] Another government counsel explained that under the rules they were expected to do two exculpatory reviews, one which is carried out at the beginning before the statement of evidence is served and another when the appellant has responded.[17] The second is dependent on the appellants responding. Another explained that occasionally there could be a new development in the case which had not been foreseen which would require further review. For example, in a safety on return case, the situation can change on the ground following political developments in the country to which the appellant is to be deported..

The government Green Paper on Justice and Security in 2011 rejected the allegation that there was a systemic problem of late service of closed material by the Secretary of State. It was the courts who were responsible for setting the timetable for service of material and it was open to a judge to adjourn the proceedings if any real prejudice has been caused to the individual represented by the

15 ibid, Ev 16, Q 99 (Mr Thomas de la Mare).
16 GC7, 28 April 2016.
17 GC6, 19 April 2016.

special advocate.[18] As one special advocate put it in her evidence to the JCHR, however, there was no effective sanction owing to the nature of the material being disclosed:

> What can the court do? In private proceedings they might say, 'We will not allow that late evidence to be used' but they cannot do that here because it is evidence about national security. You cannot say, 'we will decide a national security case based on only half the evidence'. There is no cost sanction, it is money moving from one part of the Treasury Solicitors to another. If you really need an adjournment, I guess you would seek it, but the [applicant] does not really want this to go on for still longer than it already has, given the delays which are inherent in the system.[19]

Another former special advocate explained the dilemma that confronted the special advocate in such a situation:

> Your problem as a special advocate is you're the ham in the middle of the sandwich, with no control as to what condiments are spread on you, effectively. And what always happens is the appellant wants everything done immediately. Because obviously they don't like being in immigration detention or the threat of losing nationality or whatever it may be. The urgency is a real imperative for them. The Secretary of State's rarely in a position to gainsay that. And after all, he or she has the luxury of having got their case together, perhaps over a considerable body of time, anyway. And then, a huge amount of things have to be done in a very short period of time. And as special advocates, you always get hit with vast amounts of material late, often a day or two before hearing. It's incredibly difficult.[20]

There was a broad consensus, however, that the problem of late disclosure had now eased, at least in SIAC cases, as a result of a Practice Note issued by the Commission in 2014.[21] The Note emphasises the need for directions which make proposals for timely disclosure. The latest Practice Note requires that schedules must contain sufficient detail and precision to be useful.[22] If issues are not identified in the Schedule, the Commission may decline to permit their later introduction. One special advocate considered that the Practice Note was valuable as it exhorted everybody to perform their functions on time:

> And for us, that's proved pretty valuable because if we get things late, the multi-tasking involved is very difficult. We have to read it, think about whether there are any disclosure issues, go through the issues of process, at the same

18 Ministry of Justice, *Justice and Security Green Paper* (Cm 8924, 2011) App F [5].
19 JCHR (n 13) Ev 16, Q 99 (Ms Helen Mountfield).
20 SA12, 14 January 2016.
21 *Practice Note for Proceedings before SIAC*, 30 April 2014 [1(5)].
22 *Practice Note for Proceedings before SIAC*, 7 December 2015 [5].

> time as drafting our scheduled argument or writing the cross-examination or sitting in court, whatever it may be. So the thing about it is that if you're a party, you at least know roughly what your own side is going to produce and you have the other side's bundle which you have to cope with. But for us, it's quite often the sort of last minute rush, we'll be given lots of things by both the parties and that means it's pretty intensive. So the SIAC practice note which says all the parties have got to work through these cases methodically and give notice to everybody about what they're doing is very good. And I'd say that has made a marked improvement over the past three years.[23]

Another special advocate agreed that the Practice Note was a positive development, intended as a palliative against the strong tendency in government for 'dumping stuff' late on special advocates.[24]

Disclosure of closed material

Another area of procedural evolution concerns the standards relating to exculpatory disclosure enabling at least special advocates, if not the open representatives, to obtain disclosure of material that does more than rely on the Secretary of State's case. Although the SIAC rules originally made no reference to exculpatory material, in a letter to the House of Commons Constitutional Affairs Committee (HCCAC), dated 9 March 2005, the Attorney General stressed that the Secretary of State was under a public law duty to act fairly in the proceedings and sought to assure the Committee that there were procedures in place for dealing with material on which the Secretary of State does not propose to rely:

> This provides for all unused material concerning the appellant to be checked by the Secretary of State's counsel to see whether it includes exculpatory material. Any such material is disclosed to the special advocate in the first instance. There follows further consideration by the special advocate and SIAC as to whether any of the exculpatory material should be made open and disclosed to the appellant. Even where unused material remains completely closed, SIAC will be aware of the position and can ultimately decide on the fairness of the proceedings.[25]

Since then, special exculpatory disclosure duties have been written into the rules of certain closed procedures. After the HCCAC raised concerns about disclosure during the passage of the Prevention of Terrorism Act 2005, an amendment was made to the rules governing control orders requiring the Secretary of State to 'provide the court with all the material available to him and which is

23 SA4, 25 November 2015.
24 SA12, 14 January 2016.
25 HCCAC, *The Operation of the Special Immigration Appeals Commission (SIAC) and the Use of Special Advocates* (HC 2004-05, 323-1) 3 April 2005, Ev 79 (Lord Goldsmith QC).

relevant to the matters under consideration'.[26] This duty was inserted into the Civil Procedure Rules along with a duty to make a reasonable search of relevant material.[27] Changes were also made to the SIAC Rules requiring the Secretary of State who is opposing an appeal to file with the Commission any 'exculpatory material of which he is aware' together with a statement of the evidence on which he relies in opposition to the appeal, and where the appellant serves a statement of evidence in support of his appeal the Secretary of State must make a 'reasonable search for exculpatory material'.[28]

'Exculpatory material' has been taken to mean 'material which may undermine the SSHD's [Secretary of State for the Home Department's] own case or assist the appellant',[29] or, as it is put in the SIAC Practice Note, 'any material which adversely affects the case for the SSHD or would lend support to the position of the appellant/claimant'.[30] In arguments before SIAC, it was contended that the test should be broader, more akin to the approach taken in criminal procedure, and encompass providing material which had a real as opposed to a fanciful prospect of generating a line of inquiry in relation to an issue already in the case, or which related to any issue which disclosure might possibly raise. But SIAC rejected the necessity for such a broader test, considering that the test which reflected the approach of the Civil Procedure Rules was perfectly adequate to require the Secretary of State to provide what was relevant and of assistance to the appellants and the Commission.[31] Taking the appellants' suggested test at its broadest would mean that the examination of documents could be endless, with so many documents having drafts, comments, cross-references etc, and with so many different aspects of the state's functions engaged.[32] These were not criminal proceedings, and there could be no real cut-off to the search by reference to material issues, because appellants do not usually raise issues in any specific way.

The SIAC rules imposing a duty on the Secretary of State to search for exculpatory material in appeals do not apply in judicial review cases where the court is asked to make a ruling on whether a decision was rational and based on relevant considerations rather than making findings of primary fact to determine whether the decision was actually correct. But government counsel have a general duty in judicial review cases to maintain high standards of candour and make full and fair disclosure of relevant material.[33] The SIAC rules require the Secretary of State to file a statement of the evidence on which he or she relies in opposing the

26 See Prevention of Terrorism Act 2005, sch 1 [4.3].
27 CPR rr 76.27, 76.30. See also r 79.23 (proceedings under the Counter-Terrorism Act 2008 and Pt 1 of the Terrorist Asset-Freezing Etc Act 2010); r 80.23 (TPIMs).
28 SIAC (Procedure)(Amendment) Rules) 2007, rr 10(1), 10A (2).
29 *AS & DD (Libya) v SSHD* SIAC SC/42/2005, SC/50/2005, 27 April 2007 [416].
30 *Practice Note for Proceedings before SIAC*, 7 December 2015 [9].
31 *AS & DD (Libya) v SSHD* SC/42/2005, SC/50/2005, 27 April 2007 [420].
32 ibid [421].
33 *R (Quark Fishing Ltd) v Secretary of State for Foreign & Commonwealth Affairs* [2002] EWCA Civ 1409 [50].

application and material relevant to the issues.[34] In view of the difficulty of challenging in full the reasons for a decision partly based on closed material, SIAC has interpreted this to mean not merely serving on SIAC and the special advocates the summary prepared for the official or the Secretary of State who took the decision, plus any other documents not before the summary writer that were taken into account by the official, but disclosure of such material as was used by the summary writer or author of the assessment to justify the conclusion reached.[35] A more inclusive approach was considered necessary in order that SIAC could make a proper determination of the proceedings as required under rule 4(3) of the rules.

The implication of this is that special advocates may see a lot more information than ordinary counsel would see if there were no closed procedures or special advocates. SIAC has made the point that if an immigration case involving information that would damage national security or international relations were heard by an ordinary immigration appeal tribunal instead of SIAC, the competing issues would be dealt with differently.[36] A balance would have to be struck between the public interest being protected and the interest of the appellant and any disclosure would be subject to PII. That balance is not struck in SIAC. Instead, a wide range of materials is produced without any balancing between public and individual interests because its production is restricted to the special advocate where disclosure would be damaging. Some of that material might be disclosed pursuant to a PII balancing test in an ordinary court, but other material would never see the light of day in anyone's hands. The contrast was thus made between the SIAC procedures of full production and restricted disclosure and the ordinary court procedures of partial production and unrestricted disclosure of that partial production.[37] The consequence, as one government counsel put it, is that in an ordinary asylum case there may be a file somewhere in GCHQ which might suggest that a certain individual would be very much at risk if he were to return to a country.[38] In a nonSIAC case, that material will never surface, will never be looked for, will never be discovered and will never be served. The balance shifts in SIAC because that material should be found, it should be searched for, it should be identified and it should be disclosed to a special advocate and it may prove decisive in the case.

34 SIAC (Procedures) Rules 2003, r 10B(1).

35 *Ignaoua v SSHD* SIAC SN/6/2013, *AHK v SSHD* SIAC SN/2-5/2014 upheld in *SSHD v SIAC* [2015] EWHC 681 (Admin).

36 See *Y and Othman v SSHD* SIAC SC/36/2005, SC/15/2005, 12 July 2006, [50]. See also *RB (Algeria) v SSHD* [2009] UKHL 10, [2010] 2 AC 110 [103].

37 ibid.

38 GC4, 12 April 2016.

Exculpatory review

In his letter to the HCCAC, the Attorney General acknowledged that as in all proceedings (not just those before SIAC), the process of disclosure inevitably relies on the integrity and professionalism of those operating it.[39] He quoted from a decision of SIAC in which SIAC did not consider that, notwithstanding occasional complaints and concerns about disclosure of material to special advocates,[40] there had been any unfair withholding of material, although it said it could not know for sure.[41] The system was operated honestly so far as it could tell and it was not persuaded from anything which emerged that there had been a failure to appreciate significant material which would help an appellant, albeit that the respondent was not best placed to judge how particular material might be used by an advocate.

Although the HCCAC was encouraged by the fact that exculpatory disclosure was being written into the rules governing closed procedures in control order cases, it picked up on the point made by SIAC that the Home Secretary's counsel would not necessarily approach the evidence in the same way as a defence lawyer would, seeking to identify linkages that could prove exculpatory.[42] Furthermore, those doing the detailed assessments of closed material would often be intelligence officers who were not trained to assess evidence with exculpation in mind, but rather as part of an intelligence assessment process. The difficulty exposed by the HCCAC, therefore, was that 'the special advocate is not given the opportunity to consider all the material held by the Home Secretary to decide whether it is potentially exculpatory'.[43]

In his review of anti-terrorism law in 2004, the Independent Reviewer on Terrorism, Lord Carlisle, concluded that there had been 'meticulous attention to the importance of disclosure in an appropriate way of material adverse to the Secretary of State's case or otherwise of assistance to the appellant'.[44] For their part, not surprisingly perhaps, government counsel who were interviewed said that they took their disclosure duties very seriously. Some emphasis was placed on the fact that, unlike ordinary civil litigation, where disclosure would be done by a solicitor, in these proceedings counsel has the final word. According to one counsel, it was performed by junior counsel on an independent basis, and this was a strength:

> My perspective is that, as an independent counsel, you have a duty to the court. Fairness of the procedure as a whole is underpinned by duties like that

39 HCCAC (n 25).
40 See eg *Abu Qatada v SSHD* SIAC SC/15/2007, 26 February 2007 [528].
41 *Ajouaou and A, B, C and D v SSHD*, SC/1/2002/, SC/6/2002, SC/7/2002, SC/9/2002, SC/10/2002, 29 October 2003 [281].
42 HCCAC (n 25) [92].
43 ibid [61].
44 A Carlisle, *Anti-Terrorism, Crime and Security Act 2001 Part IV Section 28 Review* (Home Office 2004) [86].

> being properly discharged. I would not participate in hearings if I didn't feel they were fair. And you have to be quite robust with clients sometimes. Obviously, I've never had a difficulty that they always acknowledged that in the final analysis if counsel says such and such must be disclosed, it must be disclosed. Sometimes, they will argue why certain documents are not exculpatory. They need not be disclosed or need only be disclosed in parts or whatever it is. And that's fine. You have those discussions. And sometimes, they can be very, very helpful. But the final analysis is if something has been in the possession of the public body concerned which undermines its case or supports the appellant's case then, that goes in.[45]

This interviewee added that the exercise could often bring out new information:

> A lot of the searching is done electronically, since the files are now housed electronically rather than creating big stacks of paper. A lot of thought goes into what the search terms should be. ... They're independently reviewed by counsel. Further search terms can be added. And then that produces a vast array of material. And counsel has to sit down and spend days, sometimes weeks, going through it all. The material it produces can be, and it has been, decisive against the Secretary of State.[46]

Ideally, the exculpatory review should be done after appellants have responded to the case against them:

> Because what you're looking for is not only anything which undermines a positive association made by the Secretary of State. You're also looking for material which will positively support the defence. Sometimes they just fail to produce any indication of what their defence is. They're silent. In which case you just have to say, 'Right, well, the time has come we have to proceed'. But you know normally at an early stage, the Commission or the tribunal or court, or whatever it is, set down a timetable and the directions for when various stages must be completed. And if they're not observed, you'll go back and say, 'Well look. We're going to begin the exculpatory review at this stage, unless we hear from you'. And that's their decision. But assuming they've advanced the case, stating, 'You know this is what I've been doing. It's nothing nefarious. But it's for religious or charitable reasons only that I've been attending these places. It's nothing to do with any extremist activity, or whatever'. You're looking for material which supports that. You're looking, for example, for source reports ... in which the source has commented, you know. 'Yes, he attends, he's a religious man. He attends the mosque'. Anything which could help.[47]

45 GC4, 12 April 2016.
46 ibid.
47 ibid.

Another government counsel said he was not keen on the term ‘exculpatory’.[48] In his view, the key question was whether the material was relevant and if it is relevant, it is disclosed. As in ordinary litigation, there are always bits of evidence that are damning, bits that are incriminating and bits which may not be, but he could not think of a single case where there was something unambiguously exculpatory in the sense that you could say, ‘Whoops, we misidentified him. It was in fact somebody with a similar name but completely different’. In his view, the same approach towards disclosure in closed procedures was adopted in civil litigation where you are only going to disclose relevant material. It was really immaterial whether the rules required an exculpatory review, because in all cases you had to disclose the material on which you rely, the material which is adverse to your case, and the material that supports the other party’s case.

In contrast with this view, however, another government counsel suggested that knowing the nature of the procedures to be closed made the exculpatory review all the more intense than in an ordinary case. As he put it:

> Our training as lawyers I think makes us very wary of getting into territory whereby you’re putting forward information that is negative to an individual, when that individual doesn’t really get to see it or certainly doesn’t get maybe more than a gist of it. There’s a discomforture about that. So you want to make sure you’re really pushing and interrogating as far as you can [for exculpatory material].[49]

Special advocates by and large considered that government counsel discharged their duties fairly. One said that counsel were meticulous about the exculpatory review and the witnesses they put up, in his experience, were ‘terrific, straightforward, and very well versed – if they don’t know the answer to something, they will go away overnight and get it’.[50] There seemed to be quite a high level of trust and engagement between government counsel and special advocates on disclosure issues. According to one government counsel:

> In general, the working relationship that I’ve had with special advocates has usually been very cooperative. You don’t always get that, but you can usually have very frank discussions. There’s usually a high degree of trust. And, who knows, we ought not to overgeneralise, but that has been my experience pretty much overwhelmingly. I mean, there have been exceptions where you get someone who’s more interested in just throwing up obstacles and objections to everything because they judge, no doubt, that that’s the best prospect of assisting their client’s interest. Simply just to try and set up some sort of procedural argument, there’s been a procedural failing. And concentrate on that. But generally, that’s not ultimately going to avail an appellant.

48 GC5, 14 April 2016.
49 GC1, 4 November 2015.
50 SA3, 25 November 2015.

> Generally, they're more interested in going to the substance of the issue. And when you have that mindset, you can have pretty productive conversations. And you can say that this is what we've got, this is where we've drawn the line. This is the system. This is the answer to your question.[51]

This counsel added that closed procedures made for franker discussions:

> although obviously it's disadvantageous to an appellant in many respects, not being able to see the evidence and so forth, one significant quirk of the system is when as a counsel for the Secretary of State you're talking to a special advocate, you could be more frank than you normally would be to your opposing counsel. Because you know that you can say things which will not go back to the ultimate client. And actually that assists in the degree to which you can be frank. Obviously you can be a lot more frank than if I knew that everything I say they felt duty bound to pass back to their client. Technically they could say, 'Oh mm … that's very interesting. I'm going to make an application to pass that on'. But generally speaking, the sorts of things you're talking about are not going to fall into that category, because you're talking about security risk attached to something. You're talking about some highly classified material. You can be very open about it.[52]

Seeking more closed material

The extent to which special advocates sought further information varied from case to case and sometimes from special advocate to special advocate. One government counsel said that sometimes the demands were very case-specific and in other cases the special advocate took a strong principled view that he ought to see X, Y and Z. Another offered the illustration that special advocates often pick up a document and there might be a cross-reference to a previous document:

> And they say, 'Can we see HB3159?' And then you would review it and you would either say, 'Yeah, here it is'. Or 'It's completely irrelevant because it was actually dealing with X and only Y is material'.[53]

Special advocates confirmed that the degree to which they sought further information varies, just as in the ordinary disclosure process. The difference, as one special advocate put it, was that it was one step removed from the individual:

> Sometimes, documents might come with redactions. I'll come back and say, 'Why has this been redacted? I was supposed to see everything'. And then they give me a reason for it, I'll grab the evidence of whatever it may be.

51 GC4, 12 April 2016.
52 ibid.
53 ibid.

> So you see, even with the closed process there is a dialogue to be had. … To make sure that I've got everything I need. That in some respects comes with experience. The more cases you do, the more you can spot possibly what you need.[54]

Some advocates, however, were wary about asking for certain closed information when they were unclear what impact it could have on the appellant. As one special advocate explained, special advocates do not get to roam freely over the material and engage in investigatory research to find out answers to questions. That was inherent in the absence of a client-facing function. So any factual queries have to be resolved through the disclosure process, asking the Secretary of State for material and if their request is declined, taking it to the court.

> The difficulty really is if you unearth something that is actually unhelpful. If you're not in a closed system, you could work out whether or not having unearthed it, you deploy it or whether you're obliged to deploy it. Both the claimant and the defendant have a duty of candour to the court. … But if you unearth something that is not immediately massively relevant, that isn't helpful, and looks bad and the other side would almost certainly want to deploy it, you have a decision-making process then to work out whether or not you're obliged to disclose it to the other side. … Of course, if you do that in closed, I mean unearth something that makes the case even worse, you're not complying with your duties to act in the best interest, you've just dug the hole a bit deeper. So it's quite a difficult process … It's always case specific. It's always contextual and you have to look and see what are the pros and cons … how crucial is it that I know the answer to this?[55]

Another explained that there may be issues that arise that seem to require more information in closed. He pointed to a contrast between the role of SIAC and that of the special advocate. Under rule 4(3) of the SIAC rules, the Commission must satisfy itself that the material available to it enables it properly to determine proceedings and this may sometimes require more information. But the special advocate may be inhibited from asking for it because he has to act in the best interest of the 'client' either advancing her case if she is appealing, or defending her case if she is made the subject of a preventive measure:

> You're not in control of the material, someone else is. … In a criminal case, when you ask for disclosure, you're generally speaking, you're asking for something very specific. 'Can I have a police officer's notebook?' Or 'Can I have a tape recording from the 999 call made by this witness?' And sometimes you know exactly what it's going to say, sometimes you've got a pretty

54 SA8, 7 December 2015.
55 SA7, 3 December 2015.

> good idea. It's pretty rare to ask for something that you have no idea what it's going to contain and similarly, in these proceedings, if you know something … what's contained in the document, great. If you have a good idea, great. But if you don't have any clue, you just have to think carefully about whether to invite the government to serve more evidence which may be a gamble.[56]

One solution to this problem would be to hand over entire files of closed information relating to the excluded party to special advocates to search through for themselves. When this idea was put to one government counsel, he said that to present all your files to the special advocate would go far beyond anything which exists in ordinary civil litigation. It seems, however, that until recently this has been what happened in Canada in relation to information relating to the individual subject to the security certificate regime. In Canada, as in the UK, duties of candour and good faith apply when parties rely upon evidence in ex parte proceedings. The party relying upon the presentation of ex parte evidence must conduct a thorough review of the information in its possession and make representations based on all of the information, including that which is unfavourable to its case.[57] In addition, section 85.4 of the Immigration Refugee Protection Act 2001 (IRPA) requires that the Minister of Citizenship and Immigration provide the special advocate not only with a copy of undisclosed information relevant to the case on which a certificate is based but also with any additional relevant information that is in the Minister's possession but is outside the scope of the certificate. Beyond this, analogous to the disclosure regime governing criminal cases, the Canadian Supreme Court in *Charkaoui II v Canada*[58] required the Minister to file with the court and deliver to the special advocate any and all of the information in the possession of the Security Service concerning the named person. The Court also held that a long-standing policy of the intelligence service that required the destruction of raw intelligence violated the Canadian Security Intelligence Service Act and the Charter.

This framework placed the special advocate on the same footing as government lawyers regarding the government's evidence, allowing the special advocate to make her own assessment of what evidence might be helpful to the affected party and to make arguments based on any contradictions in the government's files.[59] More recently, however, the Canadian Government would seem to have resiled from giving special advocates full access to the intelligence file. In an

56 SA14, 5 February 2016.

57 *Ruby v Canada (Solicitor General)* 2002 SCC 75, [2002] 4 SCR 3.

58 See *Charkaoui v Canada (Citizenship and Immigration)* 2008 SCC 38, [2008] 2 SCR 326, [62].

59 D Cole and S L Vladeck, 'Navigating the Shoals of Secrecy: A Comparative Analysis of the Use of Secret Evidence and "Cleared Counsel" in the United States, the United Kingdom and Canada' in L Lazarus, C McCrudden and N Bowles (eds), *Reasoning Rights: Comparative Judicial Engagement* (Hart 2014) 161, 174.

amendment to IRPA under the Anti-Terrorism Act 2015, the Minister now only needs to disclose information and other evidence 'that is relevant to the ground of inadmissibility stated in the certificate and on which the certificate is based'.[60] The effect of this is that the Minister only has to disclose information that the Minister considers relevant. In order to avoid disclosing to the special advocate highly sensitive information, the Minister can apply for an exemption where the information 'does not enable the named person to be reasonably informed of the case made by the minister'.[61] Special advocates objected strongly to the government unilaterally deciding what is relevant. They pointed to a case which dated back to the more restricted test which applied before *Charkaoui* where the government, applying its criteria of relevance, did not disclose any of the secret information that the special advocates later received in accordance with court orders, which was then used to convince the judge that the government's secret evidence was untenable.[62] When interviewed in this research, the special advocate involved in that case elaborated on the value of being given the entire case file. By trawling through the information that was disclosed to him, he was able to come across inconsistent statements made by CSIS sources. It was, of course, extremely burdensome to comb through what was a lot of irrelevant information. It was the equivalent of 'hunting for a needle in a haystack'. Nevertheless, in this case, he was able to find the needle and it had affected the outcome of the case. This interviewee concluded 'If I am given the choice between slogging through the stuff, I'd rather that than have someone else doing the selection'.[63]

There is, of course, a further difficulty. Even if special advocates were given all the information relating to the excluded person, they would still be inhibited in their use of it by being unable to obtain full instructions from the individual concerned regarding the case against them. This limitation highlights the importance of getting as much information as possible into the open process so that excluded persons can give instructions on it. We now move on to consider this part of the disclosure process.

Disclosing more information into open

All special advocates interviewed in this study emphasised the importance of trying to get as much closed material into open as possible without damaging the public interest. According to one advocate, one of the most important jobs and sometimes *the* most important job is trying to persuade the other side or the

60 IRPA, s 77(2).

61 ibid, s 83(1).

62 *Re Almrei* 2009 FC 1263. See *Submission of the Special Advocates to the Standing Committee on Public Safety and National Security Re: Bill C-51* (on file with author). See also C Forcese and K Roach, *False Security – The Radicalization of Canadian Anti-Terrorism* (Irwin 2015) 68–69.

63 SA16, 8 March 2016.

tribunal to open up more information to the excluded individual.[64] As another put it:

> the role you play at the outset in obtaining disclosure is very important, the more they get, the better they'll be able to defend the case or advance their case – I mean the ideal scenario is for them to do all the work.[65]

In this sense, it could be said that the role of the special advocates is to make themselves redundant. Cases varied in the degree to which there was material in open: in some cases, there could be a great deal of material; in other cases, much less. This depended on the particular circumstances of the case, including any legal requirements imposed on the government regarding disclosure. For many special advocates, however, the baseline of what was already in open was beside the point. As one put it, 'the starting point … is that every document which is relevant to the issues, whether it helps either party, or hinders either party, is disclosable unless somebody gives me a good reason why it cannot be disclosed'.[66]

One senior special advocate said that he thought it very important that the process of disclosure to open counsel was handled by an experienced advocate. Even though, as a silk, he could delegate this task to a junior, this interviewee became very involved in the process. In his view, whatever the nature of the case put, the Secretary of State is obliged to make good the public interest objection to withholding the evidence: 'even though it may not make much difference to the case on either side, if we can think of a way of getting it into open, we will need to do that':

> I don't know whether that is just considered pedantry by the open representatives. But it seems to me that my duty is to open as much as possible. And it may not be of much use to anybody but I'm not the one to pre-judge that really. … Obviously these things may not be going to the centre of the case. But as a matter of principle, it's my duty to get it out there in the interest of open justice because I'm not in the best position to judge the relevance or weight that the court might give it. That's for the parties to make submissions on. So just put it all out there.[67]

As described by one special advocate, the government first of all produces the closed evidence and special advocates then produce a schedule of submissions indicating that which they say should be made open, either because they say it can be made open without any risk to the public interest, or because as a result of the decision in *AF*,[68] it is required to be made open.[69] The Secretary of State then responds

64 SA8, 7 December 2015.
65 SA14, 5 February 2016.
66 SA8, 7 December 2015.
67 SA4, 25 November 2015.
68 *SSHD v AF* [2009] UKHL 28, [2010] 2 AC 269.
69 JCHR (n 13) Ev 11, Q 55 (Mr Angus McCullough).

'by way of a schedule, point by point, document by document ... and then a meeting takes place between the special advocates and counsel instructed on behalf of the Government'.[70] Government counsel then tend to go away and take instructions from those concerned and come back and tell the special advocates what information they can have voluntarily and what will have to be argued for before a judge.[71]

The JCHR considered that in relation to control orders, the Secretary of State took a 'precautionary' approach to treating material as being closed rather than open, even if there is only the slightest possibility that what is going to be disclosed will damage national security.[72] Special advocates have given examples of the tendency to be over-zealous in protecting national security. One mentioned a situation where the security services were attempting to keep in closed a particular assertion that had been in the Buckingham Palace section of *The Times* not very long before.[73] Another said that the security services perhaps naturally tend to be institutionally cautious, and 'if you start with that caution in-built, then there will be a tendency to maximise the extent to which you will want to restrict what is disclosed'.[74] He thought there was more information that could be disclosed, taking proper account of the risks involved and the individuals concerned.

> Sometimes my impression is that the abilities, intelligence-gathering capabilities, interests, sophistication of the opponent you are putatively keeping the information from is exaggerated; one is modelling for a Cold War scenario rather than the type of intelligence problem that we currently face.[75]

When the open and closed evidence is served, it comes with an open schedule of reasons why some of the evidence is closed. But this is usually cast in very general terms such as 'national security requires intelligence-gathering techniques to be kept closed' or sometimes 'lives will be in danger'. Sometimes a closed schedule might give more detailed reasons why things are in closed. But special advocates have said that without access to any independent expert evidence, they find it very difficult to gainsay what is, in the end, a judgement on risk assessment made by experts in their field.[76] As one advocate put it:

> In terms of challenging the government's argument that disclosure would damage national security, we are not in a position to do it because we do not have access to expertise and because that is, I think invariably, dealt with on class basis; disclosure of the fact that a particular kind of intercept is possible

70 ibid.
71 ibid.
72 JCHR (n 2) [196].
73 JCHR, *Counter-Terrorism Policy and Human Rights (Eighth Report): Counter-Terrorism Bill*, Ninth Report of Session (2007-08, HL 50, HC 199) Ev 7, Q28 (Mr Neil Garnham QC).
74 JCHR (n 13) Ev 11-12, Q 57 (Mr Thomas De La Mare).
75 ibid, Ev 11, Q 54 (Mr Thomas De La Mare).
76 See eg M. Chamberlain, 'Special Advocates and Procedural Fairness in Closed Proceedings' (2009) 28 *Civil Justice Quarterly* 314, 320.

> may damage the public interest. There is not a question of what is or is not damaging in this particular case and therefore it is not something you are in a strong position to rebut.[77]

In the end, if there is no agreement, the issues will go to court, but special advocates have suggested that the courts tend to defer to what the security services say. Chamberlain has said that where an allegation is known only from a closed source such as intercept or agent reporting and the objection is that disclosure could compromise the source, this objection is almost always upheld by the court.[78] Another special advocate said that in debates which go on as to whether more should be disclosed, special advocates usually come out on the wrong side.[79]

In interviews, special advocates acknowledged the difficulties they face when a deferential approach is taken by the court. As one interviewee put it:

> Where the government has said there is a danger to national security or to a relevant interest if we disclosed X, the court is going to struggle to second guess that and say, 'We don't think there's a danger to national security if we disclose X'.[80]

But some interviewees considered that they could make headway even when it was claimed that disclosure would lead to a danger to national security. One special advocate maintained that, while there was no point disagreeing with the Home Office for the sake of it, 'you had to have a go'. His view was that SIAC at least, with its expert judicial and professional panel, will provide 'an objective third pair of eyes'.[81] Another conceded that in a vetting, SIAC or employment type of case, you cannot do much about documents where there is clearly a national security interest in keeping them closed, no matter how important they might be for the excluded individual.

> But there are usually documents about which there's at least room for debate as to whether it's necessary to keep them in closed. I've been in SIAC … done about four cases in the last month actually. All about precisely that. And the argument is always about whether it can be safely taken out of closed and put into open … There are some pretty experienced tribunals out there, particularly SIAC I think. It's more difficult in the employment tribunal where the employment judges have to use their general judicial experience and common sense. And obviously, a statement from government saying that national security would be prejudiced, that's difficult. But you can analyse why and to a greater or lesser extent, depending on cases, they are prepared

77 JCHR (n 13) Ev 7, Q 46 (Ms Helen Mountfield).
78 Chamberlain (n 76) 320.
79 JCHR (n 13) Ev 11, Q 54 (Mr Angus McCullough).
80 SA7, 3 December 2015.
81 SA4, 25 November 2015.

> to be sensible about it. The usual routine would be, I put in my request, I get some responses. ... One I did last week, I probably made 20 requests. I don't know, maybe six or seven of them, they said, 'Yes. Fair enough. Okay'. And another three or four, they gave me an explanation and I said, 'Fair enough. I won't push that any further'. And then we went to the tribunal and argued over the balance of 7 or 8. And we had very experienced panel members on SIAC and they'll often test the Secretary of State.[82]

Government lawyers also said in interview that they had no experience of a tribunal or Commissioner simply rubber-stamping the Secretary of State's position. One said that where objection is taken by the special advocate, they 'look at it pretty closely and ask some pretty searching questions'.[83] Obviously, the more experienced the tribunal, if they see points that have been decided before, the more they can resolve things quicker, one way or another. When a new broom of commissioners comes in, there could be quite a few battles. But he added that in SIAC, there is always one member on the panel with considerable security and intelligence experience and this meant you had to be very careful what you said.

Given the inherent difficulties in challenging national security claims that certain documents cannot be disclosed, there are broadly speaking two kinds of submissions that may be made relating to the opening up of closed information. First, special advocates may urge that the actual information in question should be opened up because it has already been put in the public domain in another context.[84] This can involve an extensive search by counsel of internet sources. If parts of the closed material have been found to have been opened in, for example, other litigation, then according to one special advocate, there was an argument for opening it up now.[85] He cited one case where the High Court ruled that material in parts of an earlier closed judgment should be opened up in the light of subsequent litigation where more elements of a witness statement relating to allegations that a prisoner had been subjected to serious mistreatment following transfer to Afghan authorities were disclosed than had been disclosed in the original case to the claimant and her legal representatives.[86] This advocate mentioned that he was currently involved in litigation where the appellant was challenging an exclusion decision that had previously been the subject of Italian criminal proceedings. In order to work out what could be in open and what should be in closed, his team needed to have as much information as possible about what had been disclosed in the Italian proceedings because there was no secret material in those proceedings.

82 SA8, 7 December 2015.
83 GC4, 12 April 2016.
84 JCHR (n 13) Ev 9, Q 46 (Mr Thomas de la Mare).
85 SA6, 3 December 2015.
86 *R (Evans) v SSHD* [2013] EWHC 3068 (Admin).

Special advocates have in the past made submissions about the difficulties in undertaking these searches. In their evidence to the HCCAC, special advocates said that they try to keep a 'weather eye' on materials released in other jurisdictions, but there were very substantial constraints on their ability to do so, owing to:

(i) the security strictures under which they must work;
(ii) limitations in their knowledge as to relevant foreign proceedings or disclosures; and
(iii) constrained resources.

Keeping track of such material was an especially large job given the extent of potentially significant relevant information available as a result of shared (but subsequently disclosed) intelligence, in a potentially significant range of languages.[87]

In oral evidence before the JCHR, one special advocate subsequently gave a particularly telling example of a control order case where there was a document in closed that seemed to be highly sensitive, from a very senior Al Qaeda suspect to another very senior dangerous individual, mentioning someone else's name:

> That was a closed document until a Security Service witness, who was giving evidence about it, explained that this document had been published by the Iraqi government on the internet a year previously and therefore it should never have been closed but of course, since it was published in Arabic and not many of us are Arabic linguists and able to do the research, none of us could make this point until we heard that. Once that point was made, the document became open and it became quite an important opportunity for the appellant to deal with some observations on it. That was an example of not having the language skills and internet skills to research that job. Much of our work on disclosure is seeing whether there is an open source for materials and that is still a time-consuming and difficult task.[88]

In the same evidence session, another special advocate said that it would be helpful where there are two sources for the same information, one of which is in the public domain, if the Secretary of State would rely on the open source. She said that in one case, she had spent a few hours carrying out internet research and found an open source for a particular fact. She got quite excited about it and thought it would assist. But the next day she received papers in another case where that same document had been disclosed as part of the Secretary of State's case:

> One wonders in that case whether the left arm quite knew what the right arm was doing. If open sources are not put into the Secretary of State's evidence

87 HCCAC (n 25) Evidence submitted by a number of Special Advocates, Ev 56.
88 JCHR (n 2) Ev 13, Q 43 (Mr Nick Blake QC).

> at an early stage, we have to unearth them through the disclosure procedure which causes delay in getting them to the appellant and thus may cause prejudice in preparing their case.[89]

The other kind of submission made by special advocates to obtain more open disclosure requests the 'gisting' of the allegation in question. This has been described as trying to 'divorce the substance of the allegation from the supposedly sensitive material that surrounds it'. Special advocates have indicated that this is often the most fruitful approach to adopt. As one put it, the prospects of persuading the Commission or court to put into open a closed document are 'vanishingly small', but sometimes one can get somewhere if one can suggest a gist that gets the burden across without disclosing where it comes from.[90] Another said, however, that the danger with a gist was that while it may provide more information, it may result in an allegation of such vagueness as to merely compound the frustration of those sitting outside the process, leaving them none the wiser.[91] It seems that there can be quite an intense period of negotiation, trying to reach an agreement on what is mutually acceptable to both sides, who represent different interests. As one government counsel put it, a process of negotiation is gone through with the special advocate about the extent of gisting or whether it is really necessary for a piece of information to be in closed and whether it could not be moved over to open.[92] How that negotiation plays out can depend on how much leverage each side is able to exert.

A/AF-*type disclosure*

Until greater government disclosure was required in ECHR Article 6 cases and in cases with an EU component, special advocates felt they had very little leverage over the framing of the gist. Sometimes there could be no gist at all in relation to core allegations against the excluded individual, with the government claiming that any disclosure at all about the allegation could damage national security. The result, according to one special advocate, was that even a core allegation might remain hidden and could not be dealt with by any form of disclosure. In these cases, the special advocate had to more or less fly blind.[93]

As we have seen, the ECtHR's decision *A v UK*[94] and the House of Lords decision in *AF*, now demands there is a need for a minimal level of disclosure in certain kinds of cases governed by Article 5(4) or Article 6, even when this could damage the public interest. One special advocate saw this in terms of a hard-won

89 ibid (Ms Judith Farbey).
90 JCHR (n 73) Ev 7, Q 25 (Mr Neil Garnham QC).
91 ibid, Ev 9, Q 46 (Mr Thomas de la Mare).
92 GC1, 4 November 2015.
93 SA3, 25 November 2015.
94 *A v UK* (2009) 49 EHRR 29.

battle fought over many years to establish the principle that, at least in Article 6 cases, the position whereby national security trumps disclosure should be recalibrated to the extent that if the government considers it cannot disclose the minimal necessary to meet the *AF* test, it has to withdraw the allegation, whatever the cost to national security.[95] It was precisely this reversal that one government counsel lamented, because it set an artificial minimum about what needs to be disclosed above the necessary balancing of interests that should take place.[96] In his view, the common law was perfectly capable of deciding cases fairly in individual cases and there was no need for another rule in Article 6 cases. Judges had to make a judgement which balances security with fairness. A threshold test arguably skews the nature of that balancing test, which involves giving as much disclosure as is compatible with the public interest. The effect, as one open counsel admitted, was that it could be difficult for the government to win Article 6 cases where a core element of disclosure must be satisfied. The damage to national security or other interests that this may entail may prevent the Secretary of State pursuing the case.[97] A judge who has sat in SIAC also expressed the view that *AF* was not helpful in terms of getting to the core of the issue, which was whether someone represented a risk to national security.[98] *AF* had a chilling effect on the government, in the sense that it could prevent it putting forward its best national security case against the excluded person.

A number of special advocates have complained, however, that the government was slow in practice to embrace the implications of *AF*.[99] In her evidence to the JCHR in 2010, one special advocate said that the Home Office took quite a minimalist view, giving headline allegations only: 'You are involved in terrorist fund-raising' to take a hypothetical example, whereas if you looked at the ECtHR ruling in *A v UK*, the court gave the example that if you are going to say somebody has undertaken terrorist training, you need to tell them when and where. That, however, was not the level of detail that was given at that time.[100] Another special advocate giving evidence at the same time said that the basic approach of the government was to rely on everything without taking into account *AF* and then leave it to the courts to tell them what they are allowed to rely upon as a result of *AF*.[101] He added that, at that time, the court's approach was still bedding down and no universal approach had yet emerged. There was a strand of judicial thinking which applied an 'iterative' approach whereby a bit of disclosure is given to a controlled person, the idea being that that may be enough for them to respond effectively and give instructions to their own lawyers and the special advocates, and if it turns out that it is not, then to give a bit more. Apart from

95 SA14, 5 February 2016.
96 GC5, 14 April 2016.
97 OC5, 2 February 2016.
98 J3, 15 March 2016.
99 See *Response to Green Paper Consultation from Special Advocates* (2011) [17].
100 JCHR (n 13) Ev 7, Q 35 (Ms Helen Mountfield).
101 ibid Ev 8, Q 44 (Mr Angus McCullough).

the practical difficulty that this meant having to deal with disclosure issues right up to the time of the substantive hearing, it was in principle unfair to require the excluded party to respond to part of the case before letting him know all the disclosable information. One open counsel pointed to another problem with this iterative approach, which he claimed still occurred. By delaying full implementation of the *AF* test, special advocates might be deprived of instructions from the excluded party, as they would have already gone into closed.[102]

Another problem has been in predicting how the *AF* test would be applied. Combining the phrases used in *AF* and subsequent cases, there now appears to be agreement on the required general approach that the test relates to the disclosure of *allegations*, not of *evidence*, but that the threshold is a relatively high one: 'where detail matters, as it often will, detail must be met by detail'.[103] There must be a 'real opportunity for rebuttal',[104] and disclosure must be sufficient to enable sufficient instructions 'not merely to deny, but actually to refute (in so far as that was possible) "the essential allegations" relied on'.[105] It would seem that the test is whether there is enough specificity to enable the excluded party to provide sufficient instructions to the special advocate in the closed proceedings, which means that it can only be applied by relating the gisted allegation to the closed material as a whole. The difficulty lies in applying the test and the phrases associated with it to specific cases.

This difficulty is borne out by situations where there has been disagreement between the courts on exactly how much specificity is required to meet the test. In one case before the Parole Commissioners for Northern Ireland, a life sentence prisoner had been recalled to prison on the basis of allegations that he had been engaged in activities relating to the Continuity IRA (CIRA), a dissident Republican proscribed organisation. The allegations that were considered sufficiently specific by the Commissioners to meet the test were that the prisoner had been involved with a CIRA member in recruitment activities and procuring weaponry up until the time of his revocation, that he had met members of the CIRA, one of whom was named, at a filling station in the Republic of Ireland on the evening of a named date, and that after the meeting, he had made his way to the home of another CIRA member. On a judicial review of the Commissioners' decision, the High Court considered that the first allegation did not reveal any 'factual nexus' to allow it to be refuted other than by bare denial and while some factual nexus was provided in relation to the other allegations, the information contained in the allegations did not provide a link to any specific CIRA activities.[106] In allowing the Secretary of State's appeal, however, the Court of Appeal considered that the allegations were sufficiently specific in the circumstances,

102 OC6, 5 February 2016.
103 *SSHD v AF* [2009] UKHL 28, [2010] 2 AC 269 [87] (Lord Hope).
104 ibid [96] (Lord Scott).
105 *Bank Mellat v HM Treasury* [2010] EWCA Civ 483 [6] (Lord Neuberger MR).
106 *Re Corey* [2012] NIQB 56, [69]-[70] (Treacy J) [2012] NICA 57.

placing particular emphasis on the response of the detainee and the ability of the special advocate to refute the allegations consistently with the instructions given to him.[107]

> By way of example if it were alleged that the detainee was part of a criminal gang which engaged in some criminal activity at a particular location on a particular day the response may be that the detainee was not there. In those circumstances it may not be necessary to expand on the allegation. The special advocate may well have effective instructions. If, however, the response is that the detainee was there when the criminal activity was committed but did not know what was going to happen and did not participate it may be necessary, for instance, to determine whether the detainee should be provided with the allegation that he was present at a meeting where the criminal activity was planned.[108]

Another example of a difference of opinion on the application of the *AF* test is to be found in decisions of the Administrative Court and the Court of Appeal relating to the *Bank Mellat* litigation.[109] The Bank was challenging a financial restriction order which had the effect of exiling it and all Iranian banks from the financial markets. In the course of a closed judgment subsequently opened up, the Administrative Court agreed with government counsel that the essence of the allegations lay in the fact that the Iranian banking system as a whole was engaged in supporting the Iranian nuclear programme through a variety of methods in which they were duped or persuaded or coerced to go along with it. It was therefore not significant whether any particular bank was engaged in such collusion. In the course of a closed judgment also subsequently opened up, however, the Court of Appeal considered that what the judge had said about the essential case being allegations about the Iranian banking system as a whole missed the point that the allegations gained their force through other material that was not gisted. What the judge said about the adequacy of the open gist would have been acceptable if all that was required was to disclose enough to enable the bank to *deny* the case, but was inadequate in circumstances where the bank must be told enough to *refute* that case.[110] The case was remitted to the Administrative Court for the issue of disclosure to be reconsidered. In holding that some material may be withheld but other material must be disclosed, the Court made a distinction between undisclosed material which is the sole or decisive basis of a particular allegation

107 *Re Corey* [2012] NICA 57.
108 ibid [26] (Morgan LCJ).
109 Cf *Bank Mellat v HM Treasury* [2014] EWHC 3631 (Ouseley J); [2015] EWCA Civ 1052 (Richards LJ).
110 [2015] EWCA Civ 1052 (emphasis in original). Open version of the closed judgment.

and undisclosed material which is a further example of an allegation in respect of which other material has been disclosed.[111]

Looking back on how practice has evolved since *AF* was decided, a number of special advocates interviewed in this study considered that, although there could be considerable argument still about what exactly the *AF* test requires in individual cases, the test had made a contribution to enhancing disclosure. According to one special advocate, it was difficult to get documents opened up in the course of the disclosure process until *AF*. Now one gets much greater particularity in relation to the allegations that are being made in the first instance, with the result that the individual knows in broad outline what the case is.[112] Furthermore, it gave them much greater leverage in terms of arguing for greater disclosure. This was not simply because *AF* set a baseline which could be argued about; it was also because the courts themselves were more confident in applying a test which was concerned with due process, something much more within a court's competence, than determining whether disclosure would damage national security. One special advocate gave the example of a pure immigration case not governed by *AF* and with no EU component in which a serious core allegation was not revealed.[113] As a result of a Court of Appeal ruling, the client was let back into the country for a further appeal. Having returned, he applied for bail and now, because his liberty was at stake, the client ended up getting the gist of the material he was not entitled to before.

Special advocates and government counsel both referred to the protracted negotiation that could go on in *AF* cases. As one government counsel described it, the gisting process is now itself a key issue in cases where Article 6 requires it under *AF*.[114] The special advocate will come up with certain requests and counsel instructed by the government will go back to the client and ask:

> Could we do a gist that looks like this? Is there an open document that we can use such as a newspaper report? If the gist proposed would be damaging, we explain why on paper. We then meet with the special advocates and all the time the question for us is can this be gisted into the public domain?[115]

This interviewee explained that his key obligation was to his client, but one is always looking at the same time to what the judge might say, all the time testing whether the arguments are good, and whether a better gist could be formulated.

Another government counsel said that the iterative disclosure process can become very protracted in *AF* cases. Echoing the judgment of the Northern Ireland Court of Appeal mentioned above, the degree of disclosure required can

111 *Bank Mellat v HM Treasury* [2017] EWHC 2931 (Admin).
112 SA7, 3 December 2015.
113 SA3, 25 November 2015.
114 GC7, 28 April 2016.
115 ibid.

vary according to what the excluded person discloses in terms of a defence. As this interviewee explained:

> There can be circumstances in which we have to go back and say, 'Actually, we need a bit more here in the light of the way the appellant's case has developed'. It's now clear that more has to be disclosed. I mean that should not happen too much. In principle, it should be clear from the outset what the appellant's case is and therefore how much detail is actually relevant.[116]

Such remarks suggest that the excluded party in *AF* cases is given an opportunity to engage with the allegations in a manner that is quite different from a case where core allegations are never presented to her. Where a party does respond in a detailed way, other than by a complete denial, 'detail must be met by detail'. Special advocates considered that it was impossible to generalise whether the *AF* test does enough to enable the excluded person to meet the case against her. One said that in certain cases there may be a fairly simple core allegation so that the gist is enough for the client to give very detailed instructions.[117] In other cases, there may be a whole range of allegations over an extended period of time based upon a series of sources and information intended to build a multi-faceted picture. In these cases, there is no centrepiece to the evidence; the evidence is based on a variety of different strands woven together to form a 'mosaic':

> This is all compressed into a series of allegations which don't really give a proper reflection of what you then see in the closed evidence because there's a whole range of material. This may be files and files which are condensed into a statement of four or five pages. Obviously, the more specific it can be the better. Suppose it is an allegation that you're procuring arms over a particular period of time. And then someone had a meeting or something like that. ... The more detail you can get with that, the better. If you can get a date disclosed, then they might be able to say, 'No well actually I was on holiday or I was in America'. If you can get a location disclosed they might be able to say, 'Well, no, I can prove that I was in a different location on that day'. So it is all about getting as much detail as possible which enables you to get more detailed instructions. ... But details are the very things that the security service very often don't want disclosed. And they will say, 'All we have to do is to give the gist'. And the gist is not evidence.[118]

Most special advocates admitted that, whether the case was governed by *AF* or not, they usually managed to get some more information opened up. But just how much and how useful it was varied from case to case. One described a

116 GC4, 12 April 2016.
117 SA2, 4 November 2015.
118 ibid.

common argument, where 'the government just says that what we are asking for is evidence, not grounds, and we say no':

> And there's quite a bit of to-ing and fro-ing going on, but it works in the sense that ultimately you keep going on with it. It's a grinding process. I mean, it takes months. There's an awful lot of detail but you can argue backwards and forwards over a word for weeks. Most of it is done in correspondence and in my experience maybe 5% or 10% of the argument actually ends up getting aired in front of SIAC. But you can predict, we're pretty good at saying, 'Okay this is one we're going to fight on'. And I'd have thought that when we go and argue for a piece of disclosure, we've got it in 90–95% of cases. And the great advantage of these cases was that there was a bench mark to go on.[119]

Other special advocates were not quite so optimistic. One interviewee, for example, considered that even in *AF* cases you rarely get much opened up that was previously in closed.[120] The best one could hope for is to reach a stage where the tribunal indicates that fairness requires a further gist to be given and the government, when put to its election, withdraws the allegation. This could be termed a success, but there was still the problem that, by that stage, the tribunal will have seen the allegation, and although judges are supposed to be imbued with a superhuman quality enabling them to put material out of their minds, the damage may have been done. Another difficulty when allegations were withdrawn was that this may not be known by the excluded party, so there is often not much to show for all the work. In an extreme case the order is revoked, but otherwise this legal skirmishing merely adds to the party's delay and frustration.

This last reflection is an indication, once again, of the isolated position that special advocates are in. As we have seen, some open counsel seemed to have an appreciation of the work special advocates do and they can see the fruits of their labour when more information comes into open. But equally in other cases when nothing more is opened up, there is no indication as to whether this is because special advocates have been rebuffed in their disclosure requests or whether in fact they have managed to get entire allegations withdrawn from the case. When it comes to the representation function that special advocates discharge in the closed procedure, which is the topic of the next chapter, their work is even more hidden from view and shrouded in secrecy.

119 SA3, 25 November 2015.
120 SA2, 4 November 2015.

9 Substantive representation

The special advocate's representation function has been described as representing the appellant's interests in relation to that part of the hearing held in camera. It entails making the best case possible from all the available evidence – both open and closed – but without informed instructions from the appellant.[1] It will be recalled that the SIAC rules from which many of the rules regarding special advocates in other proceedings derive state that the functions of a special advocate are to represent the interests of the appellant by

(a) making submissions to the Commission at any hearings from which the appellant and his representatives are excluded;
(b) adducing and cross-examining witnesses at any such hearings; and
(c) making written submissions to the Commission.[2]

These functions appear to confine the special advocate's representation duties largely to the closed hearing, but the reference to written submissions suggests that special advocates can make such submissions to the Commission at any time. This raises the question as to what role, if any, the special advocate might play at the open hearing. We will examine this question first before going on to consider the role at the closed hearing.

The open hearing

SASO's *Open Manual* states that special advocates will attend the open hearing, although they will not usually contribute substantively.[3] The manual goes on to

1 House of Commons Constitutional Affairs Committee (HCCAC), *The Operation of the Special Immigration Appeals Commission (SIAC) and the Use of Special Advocates* (HC 2004-05, 323-1) 3 April 2005 [58].
2 SIAC (Procedure) Rules 2003, r 35. See also CPR, r 76.24 (proceedings under the PTA 2005); r 79.19 (proceedings under the Counter-Terrorism Act 2008 and Pt 1 of the Terrorist Asset-Freezing Etc Act 2010; r 80.20 (TPIMs); r 82.10 (CMPs in civil proceedings).
3 SASO, *A Guide to the Role of Special Advocates & the Special Advocates' Support Office* (2nd edn Government Legal Department 2019) [84].

say that it is helpful for them to see how the excluded party puts his case as they can be guided on possible cross-examination topics from the lines of questioning pursued by the excluded party's counsel.[4] Open representatives are usually happy for special advocates to attend. One special advocate recalled a case where it was proposed to deport the appellant to Algeria and the appellant wanted to call a witness who could give evidence which was relevant to safety on return, but who required a guarantee of confidentiality that his evidence would not be passed on to the Algerian authorities before he gave evidence, fearing reprisals in Algeria if there were any such disclosure.[5] In this case, the open representatives wanted to submit that SIAC was empowered to make an order to this effect in the absence of both the Secretary of State's counsel and the special advocate. The Supreme Court ultimately decided that it was open to SIAC to make a non-disclosure order where it was in the interests of justice to do so.[6] This was the only case the special advocate could recall where the special advocate was not able to be present along with the open representatives and the appellant. It was a quite limited exception.

For their part, the open representatives interviewed in this study highlighted the limitations on them in terms of putting a 'case' to the Commission or a court. Speaking in the context of challenging control orders, one open solicitor giving evidence to the Joint Committee on Human Rights (JCHR) said that 'the evidence we get justifying the control order is very limited, and for us to take instructions from the client to address the assertions is very difficult, and for that client to respond in any meaningful way'.[7] He continued:

> In essence his evidence is given in a vacuum because he does not know quite a lot of the case that is being alleged against him. Equally the client will be suspicious of how any information he gives may be used, and clearly if you are trying to challenge an allegation against you the allegation needs to be made to you. That is not, as I say, rocket science, and it obviously builds the frustration for the clients and is frustrating for representatives such as ourselves trying to represent the client with limited information.[8]

In interview, one open counsel speaking in the context of TPIMs elaborated on the difficulty for the open advocates:

> I originally thought these cases were like icebergs, that you had a sense of what the real allegations were and the real issues were. That you could see the top of the iceberg, it's a tip and there's a lot underneath it. But you have

4 ibid.
5 SA11, 14 January 2016.
6 *W (Algeria) (FC) v SSHD* [2012] UKSC 8, [2012] 2 AC 115.
7 JCHR, *Counter-Terrorism Policy and Human Rights (Sixteenth Report): Annual Renewal of Control Orders Legislation 2010*, Ninth Report of Session (2009-10, HL 64, HC 395) Ev 2, Q 5 (Mr McLoughlin).
8 ibid.

> an idea at least where the iceberg is and then you should stay a very long way away from that … But the truth is, in these cases, there are many icebergs and a number of them are beneath the waterline. And the closed case … is often of a completely different nature to the open case. And you have absolutely no idea that that's what your client was accused of.[9]

This interviewee was consequently very concerned that the client would 'drop themselves in it' by saying something that was unhelpful. That was why people on TPIMs were virtually never put up to give evidence. This counsel would say to judges that his client would like to give evidence, but had been strongly advised not to do so because, even with the benefit of *AF* disclosure, government counsel will ask questions which seem entirely innocent but which are designed to create an inconsistency with some of the closed material which will then not be put to his client for comment:

> So you ask them something about, you know, what have you been doing for the last couple of months? And if you don't mention something which is in the closed, then it will be said that you're being inconsistent, but your client will never have the opportunity to respond or to explain. And that's the standard tactic in the rare occasions when people have been put up to give evidence. And it's so dangerous because most people don't remember what they were doing three months ago. And it's very tedious and unfair even for someone who is entirely innocent but for someone who may have had some slightly suspicious contacts with some slightly suspicious people, it's invariably devastating to their case.[10]

Most of the procedural rules governing CMPs do not specifically preclude special advocates from making submissions or asking questions of witnesses in open proceedings.[11] But they were generally content to allow open counsel to make all the running that they could in the open proceedings and not to interfere. As one put it, the excluded party will have two open barristers, and they are doing the job they have been instructed to do, so it was not for the special advocate to interfere with that.[12] The excluded party has the right for his counsel to be the authoritative voice in the open session and not for somebody that is not instructed by him to start weighing in. There was also the danger that the special advocate could inadvertently disclose something to the open lawyers or the client that they shouldn't.

9 OC6, 5 February 2016.

10 ibid.

11 Cf however CPR, r 82.12 (5) (governing CMPs in civil proceedings) which states that a special advocate is entitled to adduce evidence and to cross-examine a witness only during a hearing or part of a hearing from which the specially represented party and the specially represented party's legal representatives are excluded.

12 SA4, 25 November 2015.

> So I think you should really just sit there and you should make sure that the lines of argument or submission you're making in closed are consistent with what the open lawyers are saying in open.[13]

Having said that, there were occasions when special advocates considered they could play a positive role. As one put it:

> We can't have any formal role or active part in the open proceedings. That said, every now and again, if there's a point of law ... and it's obvious that the parties have missed some obvious legal point, I wouldn't feel inhibited from piping up and saying we may want to look at this case or that statutory provision just to save the court's time from chasing down what may ultimately be a hare and a waste of everyone's time. But that's not really pursuant to our role as special advocates. And if we did anything substantive, I'm sure the Secretary of State would squeal in protest because they would be concerned that we would be revealing sensitive aspects of the closed case.[14]

In one case, a special advocate said he and his junior put in a skeleton argument on the law on an application for a closed hearing under section 6 of the Justice and Security Act 2013 because he was concerned that the open representatives did not understand the law in the way it should be understood.[15] He said the government side got very upset about it as the government would always object if special advocates were seen to 'invade' the open space. Another special advocate said that he had known a situation where it was plain that the open advocates had misunderstood what was being alleged, and the special advocate was able to obtain permission to make a statement in open court which clarified the position.[16] Another situation where it might be tempting to try to intervene was when the open representatives miss a point in questioning an open witness. Of course, the open representatives might be deliberately not asking the question. A special advocate recalled one case where the open representatives missed asking a question of a probation officer relating to the level of support which the prisoner's family had given the prisoner when he was released on licence. He asked the question instead and then outside court, the open representative came up and said, 'Thank you very much, I should have asked that'. Now some counsel might have said, 'You made me look bad' but the special advocate said he asked the question in such a way as to avoid any implicit criticism.[17]

It could sometimes be frustrating to watch open proceedings and feel unable to participate. One special advocate gave the example of a security vetting case

13 SA2, 4 November 2015.
14 SA5, 25 November 2015.
15 SA3, 25 November 2015.
16 SA9, 7 December 2015.
17 SA21, 8 July 2016.

where the claimant was representing himself. The special advocate had spent a lot of time constructing a case on the closed information only for the case to be damaged by the claimant's ineptitude. Having seen the closed information he could not communicate with the litigant and he could not intervene in the open proceedings.[18] The same thing could happen in represented cases where the open representatives do their best to run a case which seems on the information they have to be helpful but in fact is actively damaging in the light of the closed material. But as we have seen open counsel were wary of mounting much of a case to contradict the allegations. If there is enough precision in the allegations to enable a witness to come forward to contradict them in open, then that may be done, as one special advocate recalled;[19] but even that could be fraught with danger. If, for example, it is alleged that the excluded party assaulted a named individual for not paying debts which were allegedly owed to him as part of his drug dealing operations, the defence might consider locating the individual to see if he were willing to contradict the allegation in open evidence. Open counsel might be able to find out if the individual has a relevant criminal record before deciding whether to call him. But what she will not know is whether there are intelligence reports which might serve to corroborate rather than undermine the allegations.

Challenging the case in closed

A number of special advocates insisted in interview that the fact that the closed proceedings took place behind closed doors did not make them any less inclined to challenge the case against the excluded person. They considered that they still acted in an adversarial role:

> I think it's possible to try within the role to minimise the difference between ordinary barristering and this. So that will mean no cutting corners, no cosying up to the other side too much. ... You might think, 'Oh no one's watching and I can do what I like'. I don't have any truck with that. I try throughout to open up the whole process to maintain the adversarial elements.[20]

One special advocate explained that the context can be very different from ordinary courts, and there was a sense in which you had to attune your advocacy to the particular tribunal in hand. He said there was perhaps a greater emphasis on developing a relationship of trust with the tribunal, which could be very experienced in national security matters. You had to be particularly persuasive in a way that came across as credible and responsible and you needed to have a certain gravitas; you could not 'go in with hobnail boots'.[21] This counsel also said

18 SA8, 7 December 2015.
19 SA21, 8 July 2016.
20 SA4, 25 November 2015.
21 SA8, 7 December 2015.

that the scope for challenging witnesses was more limited in a special advocate context:

> The difficulty you have I suppose is traditionally, you say, you never ask a question you don't already know the answer to. That being the normal context. You have so many fewer answers in this context.[22]

But in terms of the role, that is asking questions or making submissions, this counsel considered that the process of advocacy was the same as in an ordinary case. It was just rendered less effective because you did not have the same instructions.

Another special advocate agreed that the essential nature of the advocacy remained unchanged. Obviously, the context is different in closed proceedings and you have to tailor the case accordingly, just as you wouldn't cross-examine a doctor in the same way as you would cross-examine a police officer:

> But do I feel it's a million miles away from what we do in our day job? No. The experience is important so you pick up how you should be doing it ... You are dealing with experts. But I don't see that necessarily being a different skill set to how I would do things elsewhere.[23]

There are, broadly speaking, two ways in which any counsel can challenge the case against their client. They can specifically rebut it by exculpatory evidence of their own on the basis of instructions, or they can serve to undermine it by trying to discredit the reliability of the state's evidence in its own terms. The absence of full disclosure of the case against the excluded party means that the first means of challenge is necessarily limited. Where there was not even a gist of the allegations provided to the excluded party and everything is in closed, as can still happen, then as special advocates explained in a joint submission to the House of Commons Constitutional Affairs Committee (HCCAC) some time ago:

> The special advocates have no means of pursuing or deploying evidence in reply. If they put forward a positive case in response to the closed allegations, that positive case is inevitably based on conjecture. They have no way of knowing whether it is the case that the appellant himself would wish to advance. The inability to take instructions on the closed material fundamentally limits the extent to which the Special Advocates can play any meaningful part in any appeal.[24]

Where, on the other hand, what is in closed is simply a more detailed version of what is in open, then there may be some instructions to go on. But as one

22 ibid.
23 SA11, 14 January 2016.
24 HCCAC (n 1) Ev 55 [10].

special advocate put it, you are never going to be in the same position as somebody who is directly instructed, adding:

> I've not done a single case where I haven't sort of felt that it's like having a bit of plaster over a broken arm. Sticking a plaster over a broken arm is not a proper solution.[25]

Another special advocate said that even where the allegations are put to the client and some instructions can be taken:

> the key feature that is missing is input from the client. You can conduct a cross-examination of a witness but you don't have your client sitting behind you to say he's telling the truth or he's lying or he's made a mistake or that's inconsistent or look at page 500 and compare it with page 45. Clients make a huge difference in a case. I defended in a murder trial in the summer just gone in a case that always looked unanswerable but the input of the client resulted in him being found not guilty in a case which on the face of it had no answer but he actually answered it and really did answer the case. I mean a great example. Yes, so you have the right to cross-examine, you have the right to make submissions but you don't have the right to have the central person in the case sitting there, instructing you on the allegations and the detail and the evidence. So that's the difference.[26]

This advocate further elaborated on the difference:

> In the criminal context you see it time and time again. The defendant will be adamant about something, absolutely adamant, 'This is what happened'. By the time you get nine-tenths of the way through [examining] the client, the penny drops to everyone that he's actually telling the truth. That one thing. He might be a murderer, he might be guilty of murder but that one thing … he was right about. He didn't bring the knife to the scene, the victim brought the knife. And the victim pulled the knife on him. He may still be guilty of murder but on something that is quite an important issue, he's always been telling the truth about it. And now, if you exclude him from the proceedings, you will never see that side, the benefit of his input, his ability to call witnesses, his ability to say, 'He bought that knife from that hardware store. Check the CCTV camera and you will see him walking in, buying it. And check his Visa debit card and you will see that he paid £5.00 for it'. And with that input, the picture is different or may be different. So it's pretty significant and it's pretty fundamental. It's like having a Ferrari with no engine in it. You've got a Ferrari, bright red paint work, beautiful curves, Italian

25 SA6, 3 December 2015.
26 SA14, 5 February 2016.

> styling but no engine in the back. So yeah, you've got a lawyer, you've got cross-examination, you've got submissions, the right to appeal on a point of law, someone to counter the government lawyers but you don't have the client there.[27]

Another special advocate explained how the absence of the client made the cross-examination of the security experts very difficult. The client will provide a statement but in closed this is traversed by detail able to be given by the security analyst. In a criminal case you will have a back-stop, a witness or the defendant, able to put a counter case. But in the closed proceeding all you have is a very sterile one-off account of the client which cannot be developed by going back to the client and saying, 'They say this, what do you say?'[28]

In the absence of specific instructions, special advocates were left to test the case by cross-examination and submissions by trying to identify any respects in which the allegations were unsupported by the evidence relied upon and to check the evidence for inconsistencies.[29] In a published article, Chamberlain argues that special advocates can perform a useful contribution even without instructions or assistance from the excluded person.[30] They can identify assessments contained in the witness statements that can be shown to be unreliable from the material attached to the statement; they can point to inconsistencies internal to that material; they can make submissions on the 'exculpatory' material produced to them; and they can compare the closed case with the publicly available material. But where, as happens in the vast majority of cases, most of the assessments made by the government are consistent with the material filed in support of them and are not undermined by any exculpatory material, special advocates have no practical way of displacing the assessment without evidence of their own.

Special advocates also had to be careful not to make matters worse. One open counsel said that special advocates told him that they could hamper the appellant's case by cross-examining security service witnesses, particularly on factual matters:

> So the kind of cross-examination you can do is, you can test the quality of an assessment. You can deal with an issue that doesn't involve the individual about some extraneous piece of evidence or the quality of the evidence or where it is sourced from. They can test whether or not evidence was in fact obtained by torture and then get it excluded. And they can get more disclosure. But they are very reluctant to cross-examine on the substance of the fact because they just worry that they're like a bull in a china shop.[31]

27 ibid.
28 SA10, 14 January 2016.
29 HCCAC (n 1) Ev 55 [10].
30 M Chamberlain, 'Special Advocates and Procedural Fairness in Closed Proceedings' (2009) 28 *Civil Justice Quarterly* 314, 323–324.
31 OC6, 5 February 2016.

One special advocate described his task as very document-dependent:

> It depends on one's own careful reading and assessment of the documents which may enable you to show that an assessment that the Secretary of State has made has been based on a misunderstanding or a misinterpretation of the underlying material. … Or points that are inconsistent elsewhere in the evidence that may not have been properly taken into account or are irreconcilable with the assessment made.[32]

It was possible to examine whether the various sources corroborated each other or whether there were inconsistencies between them. The difficulty for special advocates, however, was that the security services witnesses were often very experienced and came to hearings very well prepared. One special advocate explained how this kind of cross-examination could be quite futile.

> You've cross-examined somebody for half a day or a day and of course you will find holes. That's the process. But if there are holes which are simply a lack of their actual reading or a lack of something in the file, they can fill it overnight. … But you've nothing up your sleeve. All you can do is test by reference to all the materials which they know you've got and of course great cross-examinations come from the thing in your pocket that you lead six questions towards.[33]

One government counsel sympathised with the special advocate's predicament.

> Unless there are inherent contradictions in the information, how do they get behind it? They can put forward X's case and what X has said about the gist but that will already have been done probably by open counsel. So the special advocate doesn't have any greater insight as to what X might say about the full information because clearly he hasn't been able to go to X with that full information. But it's still quite an important role to test the evidence and at times I've been impressed by what the special advocates have been able to do in terms of finding out inconsistencies. They can make all kinds of points about the grading of information etc. But in large measure I think their real role is in terms of the submissions they make to the decision making body. I'm not sure I could say I've ever seen any kind of killer-blow in cross-examining.[34]

One factor that made the closed procedure quite different from normal cross-examination of witnesses was that the witness who is speaking for the security

32 SA5, 25 November 2015.
33 SA3, 25 November 2015.
34 GC1, 4 November 2015.

services is not the person on the ground, so the underlying intelligence may be second, third or fourth-hand hearsay and it may not be possible to identify the primary source. One advocate interviewee gave an illustration of the difficulty that this created for the special advocate:

> So, for example, you have an excluded person who is supposed to have attended a training camp in Afghanistan or Yemen and he says he never did that. But there is only so often you can say, 'I never did that'. The difficulty is that you cannot challenge them about the conversation the witness is supposed to have had with the excluded person when they were in Afghanistan. All you can say is that it never happened. You'll not be able to cross-examine the witness about whether or not they were ever in Afghanistan or Yemen to be able to give the information about that meeting or that conversation because the material you've got in closed is simply a closed statement which might or might not be a reliable statement.[35]

The difficulty of being unable to get to the sources of the intelligence was mentioned by a number of special advocates.

> The other frustration in SIAC is that by and large the witness you get is not the first hand witness. He or she will be a desk officer who has spent six weeks preparing the case and will be completely immersed in it. But when you ask, 'What was the agent handler's impression of the agent?' or whatever, the best they could do is say, 'We'll have to go and ask him'. And when you say, 'I want to cross-examine the handler', everybody says, 'No. You can't'.[36]

One counsel who used to act as a special advocate elaborated on this difficulty. He explained that 'when you get the open allegations, you have a pretty good idea that in closed you will get intelligence information about individuals and this will come from a number of sources'. It may come from police sources who have been watching them, or it is going to come from some sort of electronic eavesdropping or it is going to come from an individual. With regard to the latter possibility, this interviewee would always ask the client before going into closed whether he can think of anybody who would have an axe to grind against him. And the client say, 'Yes, Fred Smith'. 'Oh why is that?' 'Because I had an affair with his wife and he would really want to see me hurt'.

> So my intention would be when I get into the closed material hearing to say, 'Were any of the people who gave you this information Fred Smith?' … That's the type of thing I'm asking about to see if I can get anything at all. The difficulty is when I get into the closed hearing, you're given the closed

35 SA6, 3 December 2015.
36 SA3, 25 November 2015.

> material which gives you four pieces of fact or six pieces and I say to the person who appears with it, 'Well can you tell me who gave you that information?' 'How did that information come about?' And they say, 'We're not going to tell you'.[37]

This former special advocate explained that, eventually, he withdrew from the whole process because it left him with no opportunity properly or even 'semi-effectively' to represent the individual. There was no point in him consulting with the excluded party and going into a closed hearing and being given information about which he could say nothing constructive. The other reason this interviewee gave for standing down as a special advocate was that he was unable to get any information about the covert human intelligence source (CHIS) on whose evidence the case might turn.

> I want to know, for example, is he paid? Is he paid by piece of information or by year? Is the CHIS, does he have a drink problem? Does he have a psychiatric problem? Generally speaking, is this information reliable that he uses? I ask a series of questions about the individual that would be a very useful thing for the commissioners to listen to. But they won't give me any of that information. ... Because if somebody you don't actually see says that the client was seen on the corner of the street with two dissident IRA men that closed material may keep the chap in jail. But if you knew that the person who gave that information had a mental health problem, was a confirmed alcoholic or had always hated this man because of some childhood argument and was being paid for every piece of information, that might make a difference to a commissioner looking at that piece of information.[38]

The special advocate said he did not necessarily want the CHIS sitting there under cross-examination but what he did want to know is whether there were issues that would allow the advocate to cast some doubt on the veracity or reliability of the source.

> But when somebody just says, 'I'm sorry, I can't go beyond the fact that he was seen with Jo Bloggs and Fred Smith', I might as well send my dog along to do as much good as I can, because I can't [do any].[39]

This advocate was at a loss to see how such a procedure could be compatible with Article 6 of the ECHR. In his view, the whole point of having a closed material process is to allow the information that cannot be open to be tested forensically.

37 SA13, 21 January 2016.
38 ibid.
39 ibid.

But if all the special advocate gets is that there was a sighting on such and such a date and nothing more, then he cannot represent the individual effectively.

Other special advocates seemed to obtain more information about key sources. A judge with huge SIAC experience said that in SIAC special advocates got a lot of information in terms of the background of the CHIS and the checks that had been done on them.[40] One special advocate said that if they asked the witness to go and get more information about the CHIS, they would do so.[41] But according to another former special advocate, the difficulty was that you were relying entirely on the security service view.

> And how do they form it? Well they form it over the source's activity in another case. But does what he has done in another case corroborate what he says in this case? Is that something relevant? See, it's very tricky. Because almost generally, when you present evidence in court, you don't present evidence on the basis of, 'Here's my witness and I assess him to be credible'. It's up to the court to decide upon the credibility of the witness. But of course the source is never going to be produced, as they have to be in a criminal context and cross-examined, so it's hearsay.[42]

Another special advocate pointed out that all the intelligence information is graded by the security services and it was very hard, in his experience, to challenge the grading:

> So you might well find that some stuff which is very damaging towards the person whose interest you are representing is graded as being very reliable. And it's very hard to second-guess that judgment that it is reliable. Particularly because the CHIS assessments that you get are pretty limited as well. So, you can ask some questions around it, but very often the security service will just fall back on saying, 'Listen. That's our assessment. We've looked at it carefully, we've graded it. We think it's reliable'. And it can be hard to go behind that. The flip side of that is that occasionally you will get extra exculpatory material. And the security service will say, if I'm being cynical, the security service will say unsurprisingly that the exculpatory stuff is not very reliable in their view because it doesn't tie in with other things or they'll have reasons why that's from a particular source who doesn't give particularly high-grade intelligence or they're perhaps not terribly close to the subject or it's only one isolated piece of information rather than a frequent flow of information. So you'll find the stuff which is damaging, they say is reliable,

40 J2, 29 February 2016.
41 SA3, 25 November 2015.
42 SA12, 14 January 2016.

> the stuff which is perhaps helpful, they say it's not reliable. And it can be very difficult to go behind that assessment.[43]

This advocate went on to say that he had experience in one or two cases where the client has said that he thinks he knows who it is that has been making the allegations and they are someone who has a grudge against him and they are telling the security services this maliciously to get him in trouble. If the tribunal accepted this explanation, that would be a very helpful way of undermining the intelligence which had been received. But in this special advocate's experience it was very difficult to get anywhere with a point like that because, to establish it, you would need to know if the person who is providing the information is the person who the client says has a grudge against him. But the one thing the security services will never do is to give any indication of the identity of a CHIS. So if the client says, 'I think that person is A and they have an animus against me', the security services will never confirm or deny whether the CHIS is indeed A or is in fact B or C or D.

These responses all point to a stark contrast between closed proceedings and ordinary civil and criminal cases. In an ordinary case, as one commissioner observed, a huge amount of attention is devoted through the rules of evidence to ensuring that evidence is robust enough to be considered by the court and the investigator's job is to gather evidence that is going to be brought before a court.[44] In closed proceedings by contrast you never know the full context in which the reports that are given to you were made and you are only going to get the absolute minimum of information because the intelligence services operate on a 'need to know' basis. It would seem that in Canada it was possible until recently for judges to allow special advocates to interview and cross-examine human sources in a closed hearing. Under section 85.2(c) of the Immigration Refugee Protection Act 2001 special advocates may exercise, with the judge's authorisation, any powers that are necessary to protect the interests of the named person. In *Canada v Harkat*[45] the Canadian Supreme Court refused to extend police informer privilege to Canadian Security Intelligence Service (CSIS) human sources but added that the discretion to permit special advocates to interview human sources should be exercised as a last resort. The record before it established that a generalised practice of calling CSIS human sources before a court, even if only in closed hearings, may have a chilling effect on potential sources and hinder CSIS's ability to recruit new sources. Disclosure to the special advocate of the human source files and other relevant information regarding the sources will suffice in most cases to protect the interests of the named person. The Court held that the case before it was not one of those rare cases in which it was necessary to interview and cross-examine the CSIS human sources. The special advocate had

43 SA2, 4 November 2015.
44 J6, 9 August 2017.
45 *Canada (Citizenship and Immigration) v Harkat* 2014 SCC 37, [2014] 2 SCR 33.

been able to undermine the credibility of one of the human sources, leading the judge to rely on information originating from this source only when corroborated. Recent legislation now guarantees that any human source or informer who has been promised confidentiality by CSIS can veto any subsequent disclosure that might identify them.[46]

Calling witnesses

One of the difficulties identified by special advocates in challenging the evidence of security service witnesses was that they were often treated as experts whose expertise was difficult to impugn. Security service personnel came to court having done their homework and were impressive witnesses. One special advocate spent many hours of preparation going through the material to try to find inconsistencies to put to the security witnesses and they still very often had answers for everything.[47] The security services were used to acting under conditions of uncertainty and they were therefore very careful in their assessments and what they said was often very plausible. Another special advocate said that these witnesses played a dual role at the hearing – they were treated as an expert but they were also able to act as an advocate.[48] First of all, they would pin-point amid all the intelligence data evidence establishing that the excluded party is, say, associated with certain individuals and when you say that there is nothing there to connect him with crime, they would then act as an expert by interpreting the intelligence to explain how it constituted a code for something which shows involvement based on other intelligence in other cases. The 'expert' quality of security service evidence was attested to by special advocates in their evidence to the HCCAC. When they said that when faced with (for example) a coded conversation which is said to bear a particular meaning or a question about the reliability of a source, SIAC treated the assessment of the security service witness as a judge in civil proceedings would treat the evidence of a doctor or surveyor or engineer giving expert evidence. However, unlike ordinary civil litigation, special advocates have no opportunity to call expert witness evidence in reply.[49]

A constant complaint on the part of special advocates has been their lack of access to independent expertise and evidence. In their evidence to the HCCAC, they explained that some of the closed evidence which special advocates had to deal with would, in ordinary civil litigation, be referred to independent experts such as those with particular knowledge of the political situation in a particular country or region or, in some cases, scientific or technical experts.[50] But special

46 See C-44 (2015) and CSIS Act 1985, s 18.1; for discussion, see C Forcese and K Roach, *False Security* (Irwin Law 2015) 301–305.

47 SA20, 12 April 2016.

48 SA10, 14 January 2016.

49 HCCAC (n 1) Ev 58, [29].

50 ibid Ev 57, [18].

advocates have no access to any such experts and instead have to rely on experts provided by the Secretary of State. Until 2007 closed procedures did not even permit special advocates to adduce evidence. The rules were changed to allow special advocates to adduce evidence in SIAC and the Proscribed Organisation Appeals Commission (POAC) and later, in 2009, in control order and asset freezing proceedings.[51] One special advocate explained that the impetus for this change came from proceedings in the House of Lords cases of *MB*[52] and later *AF*[53] where the Law Lords asked the special advocates why they could not call witnesses.[54] In *MB* Baroness Hale commented that '[a]lthough not expressly provided for in CPR r 76.24, the special advocate should be able to call or have called witnesses to rebut the closed material'.[55]

The reality, however, is that this hardly ever seems to happen. The main practical difficulties were pointed out in an open note submitted by special advocate Angus McCullough to the House of Lords in *SSHD v OO (Jordan)*

(i) if the expert (or other witness) were to give evidence in a closed hearing about closed matters, he or she would need to have been subject to developed vetting (DV). The cost, delay and issues of funding for DV clearance render this impractical.
(ii) The identification and instruction of a suitable witness poses further profound – and thus far – insuperable – difficulties.[56]

These difficulties appear insurmountable to this day. In the context of discussing the difficulty of challenging an assertion by the Secretary of State that a particular disclosure would harm national security, one special advocate giving evidence to the JCHR raised the possibility of identifying an expert who has been in the Security Service or one of the intelligence services but has recently retired and who could satisfy the requirements of being suitably qualified and sufficiently independent.[57] However, this option seemed to be ruled out in the government's Justice and Security Green Paper where it was said that it would not be appropriate for serving or former employees of the Agencies to take on such a role.[58] The Green Paper went on to say that if the special advocate identified another

51 See now SIAC (Procedure) Rules 2003, r 44 (5A); POAC (Procedure) Rules 2007, r 25(6). See also CPR, r 76.26 (5A) (proceedings under the Prevention of Terrorism Act 2005); r 79.22(4A)(proceedings under the Counter-Terrorism Act 2008 and Pt 1 of the Terrorist Asset-Freezing Etc Act 2010); r 80.22(6)(proceedings under Terrorist Prevention and Investigation); r 82.12 (CMPs in civil proceedings).
52 *SSHD v MB* [2007] UKHL 46, [2008] 1 AC 440.
53 *SSHD v AF* [2009] UKHL 28, [2010] 2 AC 269.
54 SA7, 3 December 2015.
55 *SSHD v MB* [2007] UKHL 46, [2008] 1 AC 440 [66].
56 *Special Advocate's Note* [6] reproduced in JCHR (n 7) Written Evidence, 58–59.
57 JCHR, *Counter-Terrorism Policy and Human Rights: 28 days, intercept and post-charge questioning* (2006-07, HL 157, HC 394) 30 July 2007, Ev 19-20, Q 78 (Mr Andy Nicol QC).
58 Ministry of Justice, *Justice and Security Green Paper* (Cm 8194, 2011) App F [4].

suitable witness, either the witness would have to be subject to security vetting or the questions would need to be posed in an open hearing following notification being given to the Secretary of State.[59]

One special advocate interviewed in this study considered it practically impossible to call an expert witness:

> The problem is firstly, to have any weight with the court, they're going to have to be somebody who almost certainly has a history of national security. And most of those people will not go and give evidence for the appellants even if they're retired. But secondly, of course, if they do so, the problem is, will they be allowed to look at the closed [material].[60]

It does seem, however, that expert witnesses are occasionally called by special advocates. The Independent Reviewer of Terrorism Legislation has referred to two cases in which evidence has been called in response to evidence submitted in CMPs.[61] One former special advocate said he had been involved in a case where the open representative identified an expert who was already developed-vetted and the government permitted the expert to have the closed material once he had made an open report.[62] This interviewee thought that the expert must also have been under an undertaking not to communicate any closed material. What he was unsure about was whether the expert was barred from communicating with the open representatives in the same manner as special advocates. We have seen that SASO has instructed witnesses to appear in closed on two occasions, but has commented that the government side is obviously very reluctant to allow extra people to read the closed material.[63] SASO did not fund the expert as it has no budget, and the expert's fees were invoiced to the government side in the same way that special advocates' fees are.

One special advocate said that the government has never really cooperated with special advocate requests to identify individuals as potential expert witnesses.[64] Another said that, even if a suitable individual could be identified, the constraints on such an expert would make it unlikely he or she would wish to give evidence in closed proceedings.

> Now, say you're an expert at Chatham House or in a normal university, etc, and we want you to give evidence. We're going to need to let you see the closed material. Once you've seen the closed material, you may be considerably hampered in then how you're allowed to continue talking about various other matters you've seen closed material about. Because, of course, having

59 ibid.
60 SA11, 14 January 2016.
61 D. Anderson and C. Walker, *Deportation with Assurances* (Cm 9462, 2017) [3.65].
62 SA19, 12 April 2016.
63 Email communication from SASO to the author, 12 December 2018. See Chapter 5.
64 For similar difficulties in Canada, see G Hudson and D Anati, 'Behind Closed Doors: Secret Law and the Special Advocate System in Canada' (2018) 44 *Queen's Law Journal* 1, 57.

done a case I don't need to continue talking about it because I've moved on to the next case. But if you're an expert on Algeria or anything else, the security in Algeria, once you've seen the closed material, that is clearly going to affect your view on it.[65]

This special advocate said that there were times when special advocates would have liked to put questions to one or two open experts and he thought it had been tried on several occasions, but these efforts had floundered for various reasons. It was possible, of course, for special advocates to ask experts called for the government questions, but the difficulty is that the questions are asked in full knowledge of opposing counsel and the Commission, revealing counsel's strategy. Sometimes, what they wanted to ask an expert may be as important as the detail itself.

Affecting the outcome

The degree to which it is possible for special advocates to affect the outcome of cases depends, in part, on the threshold test that must be met by the special advocate to defeat the government case. From early on, special advocates have drawn attention to the difficulties they face in challenging cases where the government has only a very low legal and evidential threshold to meet. One special advocate commented in evidence before the JCHR that what goes on in closed sessions is not a process whereby, as in a civil or criminal trial, you put forward your best evidence to prove a proposition on all the available evidence. Instead, it is a process whereby selected highlights of a plausible hypothesis are put forward. Responding to that is challenging. At the end of the day, the tribunal is ultimately not saying, 'We prefer X over Y'. It is saying, 'Is there a reasonable case?'[66] As well as highlighting the selective nature of the evidence relied on, this comment also alludes to the flexible standard of proof employed, which can vary according to the context of the case. Judicial review cases, for example, are much harder to challenge on the facts than appeals on the merits. Even in full appeal cases, the evidential threshold is much lower than that in criminal cases where the standard of proof is proof on which the trier of fact feels 'sure' or is satisfied beyond reasonable doubt.

In their evidence to the HCCAC, special advocates highlighted the threshold of reasonable suspicion governing the Secretary of State's decision to detain persons suspected of being involved in acts of international terrorism under the Anti-Terrorist, Crime and Security Act 2001 as being especially difficult to challenge:

Special Advocate: Do you accept that document A, though consistent with the sinister explanation you attribute to it, is equally consistent with another completely innocent explanation?
Witness: Yes.
Special Advocate: So, the sinister explanation is no more than conjecture?

65 SA 11, 14 January 2016.
66 JCHR (n 57) Ev 19 Q 75 (Mr Nick Blake QC).

Witness: No. Document A has to be considered alongside documents B, C, D and E. When viewed as a whole, on a global approach, the sinister explanation is plausible.

Special Advocate: But you have already admitted that documents B, C, D and E are in exactly the same category: each of them is equally consistent with an innocent explanation and with a sinister one.

Witness: Yes, but when viewed together they justify the assessment that the sinister explanation is plausible and form the basis of a reasonable suspicion.[67]

Over the years, it would seem that the courts have come to apply a greater intensity of review over issues of national security. It has been argued that since the House of Lords ruling in *SSHD v Rehman*,[68] where it was considered that the scope for judicial intervention over matters of national security was limited, the lower courts have engaged in more robust and intense judicial scrutiny of ministerial decisions concerning national security.[69] This has particularly extended to national security assessments that relate to events as opposed to decisions that relate to suspected future activity, as well as past decisions that depend on evidence as opposed to pure assessments of risk. Thus, even though the threshold of reasonable grounds for suspicion that someone has been involved in terrorism-related activity in control order cases is low, the Court of Appeal has ruled that whether there are reasonable grounds for suspicion is an objective standard. A court cannot review such a decision without deciding itself whether the facts relied upon amount to reasonable grounds.[70]

SIAC has also been quite bold in setting out its principles for scrutinising the decisions of the Secretary of State to deport or exclude persons on grounds of national security. First of all, it has refused to adopt the 'self-denying ordinance', as it has been described,[71] proposed by Lord Hoffmann in *Rehman* that the Home Secretary is in a superior position in assessing matters of national security because she 'has the advantage of a wide range of advice from people with day-to-day involvement in security matters which the Commission, despite its specialist membership, cannot match'.[72] SIAC has taken the view that it

> has accumulated considerable experience in determining what individuals, assessed to have undertaken activities inimical to the national security of the UK, have in fact done and in assessing the future threat which they may or may not pose to it. Great weight is always given to the assessment of the Secretary of State or, more particularly, of her security advisers; but the

67 HCCAC (n 1) Ev 58 [27].
68 [2001] UKHL 47, [2003] 1 AC 153.
69 See A Tomkins, 'National Security and the Role of the Court: A Changed Landscape?' (2010) LQR 543.
70 *SSHD v MB* [2006] EWCA Civ 1140.
71 See *Zatuliveter v SSHD* SIAC SC/103/2010, 29 November 2011 [8].
72 [2001] UKHL 47, [2003] 1 AC 153 [57].

> Commission has not felt inhibited from differing from their assessment if persuaded that it is wrong ... The principal issues on national security are invariably: what has an appellant done? And what inference can be drawn from his past actions and current capacity and beliefs about the threat, if any, which he poses to national security.[73]

SIAC went on to emphasise that these are matters of individualised assessment, which it is particularly well-placed to make, and indeed its procedures almost certainly ensure that the case of an individual appellant is subjected to greater scrutiny than could be given to it by the Secretary of State.[74] All this did not, of course, mean that the ministerial and security service assessments will not be respected, especially on issues relating to future risk.[75] SIAC has said that the security services are perfectly entitled to make the assessments they make and to take action on the basis of information from a reputable source and that it would be quite impossible to investigate on every occasion to see whether that piece of information is indeed supported. But the courts had in addition a responsibility to ensure that such assessments were accurate where they impact on persons who may lose their liberty for an unspecified period.[76]

Second, SIAC has considered that its task is ultimately evaluative. The circumstances which give rise to a decision to deport or exclude for reasons of national security are many and varied, as is the evidence, information and intelligence upon which the evaluation is made.[77] This means that a degree of flexibility of approach may be required. It has accepted the ruling in *Rehman* that it is an error of law to hold that the decision of the Secretary of State has to be justified by individual facts proved to a high degree of probability. But it has tried as a starting point to make findings of past fact on the balance of probabilities. This has been its general approach, without excluding the possibility of circumstances in which a decision to deport or exclude would be upheld even where no such finding adverse to the appellant could be made.[78]

More recently, SIAC has been given jurisdiction to review the Secretary of State's decision to refuse to grant naturalisation or to exclude non-European Economic Area (EEA) nationals from the UK. Although SIAC has considered that such reviews should be conducted as a judicial review and not as an appeal on the facts, in all cases the factual basis for the judgement of the Secretary of State should be scrutinised very carefully, 'anxiously', by the Commission, since the facts cannot be tested as they would be in conventional judicial review proceedings by either the claimant or the special advocates, who may not be able to

73 *Al Jedda v SSHD* SIAC SC/66/2008, 7 April 2009 [8].
74 ibid.
75 ibid [9]–[10].
76 See eg *M v SSHD* SIAC SC/17/2002, 8 March 2004 [11].
77 *Zatuliveter v SSHD* SIAC SC/103/2010, 29 November 2011 [6].
78 ibid.

get instructions in response to the closed material.[79] Once the facts and inferences from fact have been reviewed and the factual or evidential conclusions reached by the Secretary of State are found to be reasonable, the Commission should then review the judgements made by the Secretary of State based on that factual picture. This view has been endorsed by the Divisional Court, which has said that it is not sufficient to apply the principles familiar in other areas of judicial review where the claimant can challenge in full the reasons advanced for the decision.[80]

Despite these more demanding standards of scrutiny applied by SIAC, the special advocates interviewed in this study were very guarded about their own ability to affect the outcome of cases. Some suggested that they had made a difference to the outcome but such cases were 'few and far between'.[81] One special advocate referred to one case where he took a closed point on appeal. There was no reported decision, but he won the appeal and the Secretary of State withdrew. In that case, the open representatives had no idea about the appeal because it was in closed and the ruling was closed as well. It was a victory he could never discuss except with other special advocates. But other than this:

> There are times when you think, 'my goodness, what on earth are we doing here?' because the national security case is compelling and the individual doesn't play ball and doesn't give an account of what he or she's been doing. And there's really not an awful lot you can do for them. … You pick away at the edges. You do what you can. I mean, you can't make ludicrous submissions or submissions that don't have a basis but you recognise the difficulty and try to suggest ways round it while acknowledging that it's pushing a very large ball up a very big hill.[82]

One notable success referred to by a number of special advocates occurred in *M v SSHD*,[83] where the statutory threshold of mere reasonable suspicion that the appellant was a terrorist pursuant to the Anti-Terrorism, Crime and Security Act 2001 was all that needed to be shown. SIAC indeed said that its concern was only to decide whether reasonable suspicion was established, notwithstanding that there may be an innocent explanation for individual pieces of evidence. The Secretary of State had issued certificates on the ground that the appellant was a member of a group of Mujahideen engaged in active support for various international terrorist groups, including networks associated with Usama Bin Laden. The appellant admitted that he was a supporter of the Libyan Islamic Fighting Group (LIFG) and the respondent accepted that LIFG as a group did not pose a current

79 *AHK* SIAC SN/2-5/2014, 18 July 2014 [30], [32]. See also *Ignaoua v SSHD* SIAC SN/6/2015, 28 July 2015.
80 See *Ignaoua v SSHD* [2015] EWHC 681 (Admin) [28]–[29].
81 SA12, 14 January 2016.
82 SA7, 3 December 2015.
83 *M v SSHD* SC/17/2002, 8 Mar 2004.

threat to national security. The case against the appellant was that some members of the LIFG supported and had links with Al Qaeda and the appellant was one of these. But according to SIAC, the special advocate carried out a detailed and most effective cross-examination of the witness called on behalf of the respondent and he was able to illustrate to the satisfaction of SIAC that the assertions made in the statements provided by the respondent were not supported by the evidence. In particular, SIAC was satisfied that the special advocate's submission that there was a 'consistent exaggeration of the extent to which the documentary evidence relied on to support the links alleged between the appellant and Al Qaeda linked extremists was correct'.[84]

In dismissing the Home Secretary's application for permission to appeal against the judgment, the Court of Appeal said that the case had demonstrated that, while the procedures which SIAC had to adopt are not ideal, it was possible by using special advocates to ensure that those detained can achieve justice and it was wrong to undervalue the SIAC appeal process.[85] In their evidence to the HCCAC, however, special advocates stated that they did not consider that the existence of one case in which the detainee's appeal was allowed demonstrated, as a general proposition, that the use of special advocates made it possible to ensure that those detained could achieve justice.[86]

Since *M*, there have been further cases where special advocates have been successful in challenging the security services' assessment of the evidence. But one notable feature has been that the appellant appeared to engage quite consistently in the process so far as he or she could. One particularly striking example of this was in *Zatuliveter v SSHD*[87] where the appellant took, according to one open counsel,[88] the unusual step of actually giving evidence to challenge the Secretary of State's decision to make a deportation order against her on the ground that she was a Russian spy and that her presence was not conducive to the public good for reasons of national security. When the Secretary of State served an open statement setting out reasons why certain bail conditions should be put in place, the appellant filed a detailed statement setting out her history and her response to the Security Service's assessment that she posed a threat to national security which ran to 257 paragraphs and 95 pages and had 267 pages of exhibits. In the course of the disclosure process, the appellant filed 6 further statements, 26 statements by witnesses of fact and at the hearing she gave evidence, as did two witnesses for the Secretary of State and an expert witness. The 'constructive' approach taken by the appellant enabled SIAC to make findings of fact on the balance of probability on 'critical questions' and upon this basis they were able to reach a confident

84 ibid [10].
85 *M v SSHD* [2004] EWCA Civ 324 [34].
86 HCCAC (n 1) Ev 54 [7].
87 *Zatuliveter v SSHD*, SC/103/2010, 29 November 2011.
88 OC6, 5 February 2016.

conclusion that the appellant was not a Russian spy.[89] It would seem that her open assertions were tested against the open and closed evidence. The Commission stated that support for the conclusion was to be found in the closed judgment as well as in the open reasons. It would seem that material conclusions were drawn from the closed evidence relating to the Security Service's assessments of the appellant's relationships with various men in influential positions who would have access to sensitive information. The special advocates instructed in the case would seem to have played a central role in challenging these assessments.

Conversely, sometimes the appellant does not engage with the process at all. In *Zatuliveter*, SIAC accepted that it was not impossible to envisage circumstances in which a decision, say, to deport or exclude could be made, even if the factual basis for the reporting could not be established on the balance of probabilities.[90] It gave the example of a decision to exclude a possible assassin based only on information provided by a friendly state. In such a case, a decision adverse to the appellant would be more likely to be made if he did not participate constructively in the appeal. But we have seen that open counsel can be very reluctant to advise their clients to answer allegations, especially where the appellant may have no idea what the case is about. One special advocate commented that SIAC has found it difficult to grasp why an appellant should not make a clean breast before the Commission of his history and background. This interviewee had conducted a couple of cases where essentially the appellant had been given nothing in open about the core problem.

> The difficulty then is persuading the tribunal there may be perfectly good reasons why it has not occurred to the appellant to raise an answer to the problem. He knows he's in trouble but he does not know what the tribunal knows. And there may be all sorts of reasons. For a start, like hypothetically, let's say that there is an informant in the closed material who says X, Y and Z. Now X, Y and Z may be utterly false because the informant may be very malevolently inclined. In an immigration case you're not going to inform the appellant of the content of that information let alone who's giving it. So it's impossible for him to know that there may be somebody who's simply lying about him.[91]

One judge with considerable SIAC experience, however, said that he was very careful about drawing inferences from closed material in the absence of the party who could say what happened.[92] Judges were therefore constantly having to speculate about whether there is an innocent explanation for the closed material.

Special advocates indicated that it was the inability to take instructions from the excluded party that made their role very different from that of an ordinary advocate. But one judge suggested that this actually gave them the freedom to act in the

89 *Zatuliveter v SSHD*, SC/103/2010, 29 Nov 2011, [6]–[7].
90 ibid [6].
91 SA3, 25 November 2015.
92 J2, 29 February 2016.

best interests of the excluded party.[93] Not being bound by instructions when they see the closed material gives them the freedom to challenge the case to the hilt, and this was professionally liberating. One special advocate admitted that the absence of instructions did mean they had a certain licence to do what was in the objectively best interests of the client. The starting point was to equate the excluded party's interests with getting the decision challenged, overturned or varied:

> So if it's a control order, for example, there are quite a few cases where realistically, you're never going to get the control order removed because of the relatively low threshold of there being a national security risk that is engaged. So in most cases, I tend to think, well, actually, what's actually realistically in his interest? If I go all out to say, well you shouldn't have this at all, then that's going to fall flat. So you say, well, you probe the national security case but then you try and get the restrictions lifted that are imposed on the individual, alleviate things to make life as tolerable as it might be. ... It's just the 'art of the possible' advocacy in many ways. If you stand up and make a ridiculous submission that won't find any favour whatsoever, it just damages your credibility. So you have to focus on what is the best achievable outcome for this individual.[94]

One special advocate working in Canada also considered that it can be advantageous not having to talk to clients:

> It's a great game for me because I don't actually have to talk to the clients, to tell you the truth. Yeah, it's much more, you know, you're able to exercise your judgment unfettered, in that way. Clients can be difficult, not all clients are, but some are, and some come up with crazy ideas which you should advance. And there's always this tension between your exercise of your judgment and what the client thinks is the best thing to do. So in this instance, I don't have any of those concerns. So I don't have to navigate that.[95]

One counsel working at the Special Tribunal for Lebanon, who had experience of representing defendants in absentia and was required to act without instructions, said that acting in the absence of the defendant was a double-edged sword. It was a huge obstacle in some respects, the principal obstacle being ignorance of the client's version of events is.

> You don't know what they take issue with. You can never ask your client, 'Well, what about this phone call?' This record suggests that you were in location X at time Y. 'What do you say about this?' We can't do that. So it's very difficult to defend somebody if you don't know what they say about the

93 ibid.
94 SA7, 3 December 2015.
95 SA18, 12 March 2016.

evidence. ... The flipside to that is that when your task is to challenge evidence, to test the evidence, you as the lawyer, are able to decide for yourself what defence to run, you know how to test the evidence. And you use your best judgment to decide how to go about that.[96]

He said all defence lawyers had been in the position where they have been given the wrong sort of defence to run or they have been given the wrong kind of instructions. It was professionally improper to tell your client, 'This is not the right defence', whereas when you are not bound by the wrong defence, you can choose the right strategy as you see it.

Special advocates explained that there were some cases where it was easier to make headway than others. It could be much easier, for example, to challenge safety on return cases than cases than where there were allegations against the appellant.

> Most of the case is in open anyway of course. If you're thinking about sending somebody either to Jordan or Ethiopia then by and large the conditions there are going to be well known. If it's deportation with assurances, the assurances have to be sufficiently transparent to be persuasive anyway. So again there's an awful lot of stuff in open. The difficult cases are those where they're saying, 'Here's the intelligence stuff focusing on this person here'.[97]

Another special advocate involved in a case where a deportation order was quashed on the basis of a risk to return said that these cases were distinctive because the open representatives could make detailed submissions on general country conditions:

> Where we brought value to bear was being able to tie that into some of the material that the open representatives didn't see. We definitely added value, and for my money, I think [the special advocate] who was leading me in that case, won the case for the individual.[98]

A similar distinction was drawn by another special advocate, between cases against the appellant built on intercepting or sources and cases where the issue that has to be dealt with in closed pivots around confidentiality in dealings between states.[99]

Government counsel were quicker than special advocates to say that special advocates had made a real difference in affecting the outcome of cases. One counsel considered that special advocates made a massive difference to what would otherwise be an ex parte hearing, with only the government present. If the

96 SA22, 21 July 2016.
97 SA3, 25 November 2015.
98 SA7, 3 December 2015.
99 SA12, 14 January 2016.

alternative is closed hearings where effectively the government is the only person in there, 'I'd rather have a special advocate'.[100] Another, however, acknowledged that there were reasons why special advocates did not succeed in many cases.[101] First of all, as we have seen, the threshold for showing reasonable suspicion or belief that an individual is involved in terrorist-related activity is not a high one. In a criminal case, all that the defendant must do is raise a reasonable doubt about guilt, whereas in SIAC cases, to resist all the allegations counsel must negate the reasonable suspicion of terrorism involvement, which is a very different proposition. Second, it had to be borne in mind that the government gets to hand pick its cases and will only go forward on the basis of the strongest. In a criminal case, by contrast, prosecutors must go forward on the basis of only a realistic prospect of conviction, unless the public interest precludes prosecution.

That said, all government counsel insisted that there were cases where special advocates had made a real difference to the outcome. According to one:

> I think that can be said with some confidence. I'm not sure that there are any cases where it's actually said in the judgment that it's only because of the special advocates that [the court] made this finding. But I'm confident that there are cases where that has been the case.[102]

Another counsel pointed to instances where the Secretary of State's case was not strong and where the special advocates had been effective in pointing this out to the court.[103] For example, the appellant may have been a risk to national security in the past but was no longer so. This had enabled a number of control orders to be quashed, revoked, modified or not renewed. In *R (SSHD) v Bullivant*,[104] the High Court ruled that, while in the past there had been reasonable grounds to suspect Bullivant of involvement in terrorism-related activity (he had been associating with people who were trying to leave the UK for Syria), such grounds had evaporated by the time of his hearing and so the control order could no longer be lawfully maintained. Specifically, the people Bullivant had been associating with who had also been subject to control orders had absconded and, despite the Security Service's assessment to the contrary, Bullivant had shown no desire to leave the UK for terrorist purposes.

In another case, *SSHD v GG*,[105] the High Court ruled that while it was reasonable to view the control order imposed on the controlee as necessary in 2005, by the time of his hearing there was no evidence that in the intervening period

100 GC 5, 14 April 2016.
101 GC6, 19 April 2016.
102 GC5, 14 April 2016.
103 GC4, 12 April 2016.
104 *R (SSHD) v Bullivant* [2008] EWHC 337 (Admin).
105 *SSHD v GG* [2009] EWHC 142 (Admin).

he had attempted to pursue any terrorist related activity.[106] There have also been cases in SIAC where it accepted the Security Service case as to what the appellant had done in the past, but did not consider him to be a continuing risk. In *T v SSHD*,[107] for example, the appellant who was challenging a decision not to revoke his deportation order prepared a statement in which he admitted attending a training camp in Afghanistan and associating with Abu Doha and his group when he came to the UK, but that he had since married and devoted himself to his family. The Security Service assessment was that his passivity since release on SIAC bail was due to the stringency of his bail conditions and not due to any change of heart. But SIAC's assessment was that his conduct and circumstances suggested that he had put any thought of fighting, or of assisting those who might wish to fight, for an Islamist cause behind him, so there were no longer any convincing grounds to believe that he now posed a risk to national security.

The outcome of SIAC appeals

To get a sense of how often special advocates have been successful in cases where they have been involved, the database of open SIAC judgments was examined. The database, which can be viewed on the SIAC website, records the outcome of decisions in which judgments were issued from the present day back to 29 October 2003, which was when the first substantive appeals against detention under Part 4 of the Anti-Terrorism, Crime and Security Act 2001 were heard. We have seen that in the three cases that SIAC heard before this date, the appeals were allowed. The database is split between outcomes prior to 2007 and outcomes after this date. SIAC did not keep up a database from 2003 to 2006 and it cannot be certain that all judgments between 2003 and 2006 have been entered on to it.[108] The database is nevertheless able to give a fairly comprehensive picture of the types of cases SIAC has decided since 2003 and their outcomes. It records a total of 152 rulings involving special advocates between 29 October 2003 and the end of 2017. This total excludes certain cases, involving, for example, applications for bail or preliminary issues of law, which were entirely heard in open court and did not involve special advocates at all. Of the 152 rulings, a total of 107 involved substantive appeals, such as appeals against being certified as a suspected international terrorist under section 21 of the 2001 Act (prior to its repeal) and appeals against deportation orders, refusal of entry to the UK and deprivation of citizenship. Also included are rulings in respect of judicial reviews of the Secretary of State's decision to refuse to grant naturalisation or to exclude non-EEA nationals from the UK which came under SIAC's jurisdiction as a result of the Justice and Security Act 2013. SIAC judgments on applications for bail

106 See also *SSHD v AV* [2009] EWHC 902 (Admin), *SSHD v Al Saadi* [2009] EWHC 3390 (Admin).

107 *T v SSHD* SIAC SC/31/2005, 22 March 2010.

108 Email correspondence from the SIAC and POAC Office to the author, 4 January 2018.

were also included where persons were detained under the 2001 Act or under immigration powers and special advocates were involved.

Table 9.1 shows that out of the total number of 107 substantive appeals, reviews or bail applications, 21 were successful outcomes for the appellants or applicants concerned and 86 were unsuccessful. This is a headline success rate of 19.6%. It should be noted that some rulings involved multiple appellants or applicants where only certain appellants or applicants were successful. Mixed rulings of this kind are indicated by brackets. This success rate seems higher than what had been indicated by the special advocates, open counsel and government counsel interviewed in this study. However, as can be seen from the table, successful outcomes cluster in certain types of cases. If we drill down into the types of cases where appellants or applicants were most successful, the numbers in certain categories were too small to draw any meaningful comparisons. However, we can see significant variations in success rates as between bail applications where the success rate was 38.1% and appeals against certifications of terrorism under the 2001 Act which were only successful in 5.5% of cases. As might be predicted, there was also a difference in success rates as between fullscale appeals and judicial reviews with the difference between deportation appeals (where there was a 25.8% success rate) and naturalisation reviews (where the success rate was 11.1%) being most pronounced. Interviewees suggested that it was harder for appellants to be successful where the central issue concerned whether an appellant was a threat to national security than where the issue was one of safety on return. This was borne out to some extent by the fact that appellant successes in deportation cases tended to relate to safety on return (four cases) more than national security threats (two cases) with successful appeals on both issues occurring twice. It is also noticeable that in a number of deportation appeals (12 out of 33 cases) the risk to national security was not disputed by the appellant and the appeals were argued on the basis of safety on return.

Table 9.1 Outcome of substantive appeals or reviews in SIAC cases (2003–17)

Type of case	*Successful*	*Unsuccessful*	*% success*
Appeals against certification under ATCSA 2001	1	17	5.5
Appeals against deportation	8 (2 mixed)	23	25.8
Appeals against refusal of entry	1	8	11.1
Appeals against deprivation of citizenship	0	6	0
Claims to asylum	0	2	0
Reviews of refusal to grant naturalisation	2	16	11.1
Reviews of exclusion of non-EEA nationals from UK	1	1	50
Bail applications	8 (2 mixed)	13	38.1
Total	21	86	19.6

One must be cautious in trying to translate these case outcomes into special advocate successes, as final dispositions do not in themselves indicate whether the outcomes were based on open or closed evidence. Although we had no access to the closed judgments which would enable a more accurate assessment to be made of special advocates' contribution to case outcomes, the extent to which the outcome of the case turned on open or closed evidence could be inferred from open judgments. From a perusal of each ruling, we assessed the degree to which the decision was based on open or closed evidence according to the following six categories: decisions based entirely on open evidence; decisions based substantially on open evidence; decisions based on a mix of open and closed evidence; decisions based substantially on closed evidence; decisions based entirely on closed evidence; and finally, decisions where it was impossible to make such an assessment. We found that we were unable to make an assessment in only 10 of the 107 cases considered, 7 of which were bail applications where it was not clear in the judgment what weight was being placed on the open or closed evidence. Amalgamating the categories of 'entirely open' and 'substantially open' evidence and 'entirely closed' and 'substantially closed' evidence and referring to these compendiously as 'open' or 'closed', Table 9.2 illustrates whether the outcome of the decisions in the different types of cases was based on 'open' evidence, 'closed' evidence, or a mixture of both. As the issues in deportation cases generally divided into whether the appellant was a threat to national security and whether it was safe for the appellant to be returned, an assessment was made in each case as to whether these issues were determined on the basis of open or closed evidence, although in a number of cases both issues were argued.

Table 9.2 Outcomes of substantive SIAC appeals or reviews based on open, closed or mixed evidence (2003–17)

Type of case	*Successful outcome*			*Unsuccessful outcome*		
	Open	*Mixed*	*Closed*	*Open*	*Mixed*	*Closed*
Appeals against certification under ATCSA 2001			1	7		7
Appeals against deportation	2	2	1	10	4	3
National security:	4		1	9		3
Safety on return:						
Appeals against refusal of entry				1		7
Appeals against deprivation of citizenship				3		3
Claims to asylum						2
Reviews of refusal to grant naturalisation	1		1	1	1	14
Reviews of exclusion of non-EEA nationals from UK			1			1
Bail applications	3		2	3	1	5
Total	10	2	7	36	6	45

It can be seen that 12 out of the 19 (63%) successful outcomes for appellants or applicants were based on open evidence or a mixture of both open and closed evidence, which suggests that it would be wrong to categorise SIAC as a completely closed court. Given that special advocates are very reluctant to engage with open evidence, one can infer from this that open advocates play a significant role in SIAC and have scored successes, particularly, it would seem, on issues relating to safety on return and bail. Having said this, it can equally be said that quite a high proportion of successful outcomes for appellants or applicants (9 out of 19 (47%)) were based on closed or on a mix of open and closed evidence, suggesting that special advocates played a significant role in these cases.

Of course, it cannot be said that the outcome in any of these cases was due entirely to the advocacy of either the open advocates or the special advocates. It will be recalled that SIAC is a specialist court with the 'lay' member sitting on it usually someone who has a background in secret intelligence. The proceedings can be quite inquisitorial. As one special advocate put it:

> It is an expert tribunal. It makes clear what its views are. It will interrupt a cross-examination. The submissions tend to be a debate, which I love. I think that's as it should be. The closed sessions are very interesting because they're very much, 'Right. What do you say about this evidence? Can you support the open case on this?'[109]

There is perhaps a danger with an expert tribunal that the panel members will make up their own minds about cases without paying much attention to what special advocates say. One open counsel in *Zatuliveter* (a case discussed above) applied unsuccessfully to get one of the panel members, Sir Stephen Lander, a former head of MI5, to recuse himself on the ground that he was biased.[110] In its judgment, SIAC said that this was the first pure counter-intelligence, as opposed to counter-terrorism, case that SIAC had had to consider and it was important to have someone of Sir Stephen's background in assessing intelligence on the panel. SIAC noted that the special advocate in this case had plenty of experience of SIAC counter-terrorism cases, but he disclaimed any knowledge of counter-intelligence cases. The open counsel in the case said in interview that it was clear in hindsight that Sir Stephen was decisive in helping the appellant to refute the arguments of MI5.[111]

Zatuliveter was an unusual case. It would seem that SIAC does value the contribution that special advocates make in acting as a counter-weight to the Secretary of State's case. Several open judgments have acknowledged the assistance given

109 SA3, 25 November 2015.
110 See *Z v SSHD* SIAC SC/103/2010, 29 September 2011.
111 OC5, 2 February 2016.

to the Commission by special advocates, as well as by open advocates.[112] It is true that some of the sentiments expressed can be characterised as no more than the customary politeness that courts often extend to counsel. But when the contribution that special advocates make to the outcome of cases was probed with SIAC judges and others who had sat in closed cases, they were unanimously of the view that special advocates played a vital role in closed proceedings.

Judges and commissioners considered that special advocates undoubtedly added value to closed proceedings, first, in terms of the disclosure role they played and, second, in probing the closed material. Comments included:

> The panel provide a measure of protection to appellants but it was not their role to examine witnesses robustly.[113]
>
> I've been struck by how very conscientious [special advocates] are. ... What they're good at, as any good advocate would be, is interrogating and testing the evidence they've got.[114]

One judge said that there were two important roles that special advocates brought to closed proceedings. First, they were able to examine all the files in great detail, which was not something judges had the time to do. As he put it, 'Someone has to do the leg work and this work is done by the special advocate'.[115] Second, over time they were able to build up some knowledge about how the security services operate and in consequence appellants and claimants got a much better service than they would ever get with open advocates. This judge said he had seen cases in which the special advocate had demolished the Security Service's case. But even in cases where the special advocate has not been able to make much headway, their very presence instilled a measure of rigour into the process, with the security service witnesses knowing that their case will be probed by another voice. In his view, special advocates were not just an additional safeguard; they were an essential safeguard. With experience, they can get to know how the security services operate over time, and then if there is some weakness in the case, they will expose it.

To round off this discussion, there was a clear contrast in the interviews between the views of special advocates and those of other professionals with experience of closed procedures on how effective special advocates can be in their role. Chamberlain refers to one explanation for this, occasionally mooted by the government, that special advocates have tended to act as cheer-leaders for those whose interests they represent, even when expressing public views about the

112 See eg *MK v SSHD* SIAC SC/1/2002, 24 May 2005 [4], commenting that the special advocate raised a number of aspects on risk to national security in a 'helpful cross-examination' in closed session.
113 J1, 21 January 2016.
114 J6, 9 August 2017.
115 J3, 15 March 2016.

system.[116] One interviewee suggested that special advocates underplay their role because they rely for work from open counsel and solicitors who are distrustful of the system.[117] But as Chamberlain points out, special advocates responsible for the main critiques of CMPs do at least as much work for the UK government as they do for solicitors who represent terrorist suspects. By contrast, it might be suggested that judges and government counsel who work in closed procedures are minded to *overplay* the special advocate's role, because they may be anxious to promote a greater legitimacy for the system than it deserves. Leaving aside these motives for giving greater or lesser credence to special advocates' effectiveness in their role, Chamberlain has suggested that the adversarial stance that special advocates take in closed procedures may genuinely lull judges – and, it may be added, government counsel – into thinking that the procedures are more adversarial than in fact they truly are, when in reality special advocates may be hampered significantly in what they can do by the inability to take instructions from the excluded party.[118] Conversely, however, it may be suggested that special advocates are acutely aware of this limitation on their role and this may lull them into thinking that they are less effective in representing the excluded party's interests as a whole than in fact they are. Just how compatible the special advocate's role is with the adversarial system is something that we consider in the final chapter, Chapter 11.

Giving reasons for decisions

There is a well-established common law principle that parties have a right to know the reasons for decisions. Where CMPs have been involved, it is common for there to be entirely separate open and closed judgments, preventing the parties knowing the full reasons why the tribunal or court came to its conclusion. We have seen that pre-publication drafts are served, first of all, on the Secretary of State and the special advocates, but not the open parties, to enable the government to argue that certain material in the open judgment ought not to be disclosed in the public interest and for the special advocate to respond to such arguments.[119] We have also seen that the SIAC rules provide an opportunity for the special advocate to apply to amend both the open and the closed judgment on the grounds that the closed judgment contains material the disclosure of which would not be contrary to the public interest.[120]

116 M Chamberlain, 'Special Advocates and Amici Curiae in National Security Proceedings in the United Kingdom' (2018) 68 *University of Toronto Law Journal* 496, 507.

117 J2, 29 February 2016.

118 Chamberlain (n 116) 507.

119 See SIAC (Procedure) Rules 2003, r 48. See also CPR, r 76.33 (proceedings under the PTA 2005); r 79.29 (proceedings under the Counter-Terrorism Act 2008 and Pt 1 of the Terrorist Asset-Freezing Etc Act 2010; r 80.29 (TPIMs); r 82.17 (CMPs in civil proceedings).

120 See SIAC (Procedure) Rules 2003, r 47(5).

The representations that special advocates make on amending the open and closed judgments may be seen as an extension of the special advocate's disclosure role. But another way of characterising this activity is as an expression of 'transparency', ensuring that the reasons for the tribunal's decision are as fully stated in public as possible. This was not an aspect of their role that was emphasised much by special advocates, however, and it has been somewhat neglected in discussion about the special advocate's role. According to one special advocate:

> It is part of the duty to scrutinise the open decision in order to make submissions about whether more could be disclosed. This may result in additional disclosure of the closed reasons but usually no more than a few phrases.[121]

A parole commissioner interviewed in this study recalled a case where the panel had taken quite an active stance in responding to objections from the Secretary of State about what was in the open decision it had drafted.[122] One of the issues that arose was the degree to which there could be disclosure of the contents of any arguments made in closed hearings as opposed to the content of closed material. There was quite a bit of back and forth between the panel and the Secretary of State on the content of the open decision before the decision was issued to the open party. However, the special advocate played little part in the process.[123]

From one point of view, it might be considered less pressing to ensure that open decisions are as full and complete as possible than to ensure that there is as much disclosure of the evidence as possible to the open parties before the hearing. It is vital that as much relevant evidence is disclosed to the parties in order that it can be tested and challenged by the parties concerned. Where a decision is issued, on the other hand, there is no further testing of the evidence required. But it is arguably just as important for parties to know as much as possible about the grounds for decisions, especially where the decision goes against them, so that they can consider any possibilities of appeal. Of course, it is possible for special advocates who have seen the closed reasons to be given permission to contact the excluded party and advise an appeal or indeed to consider launching an appeal in closed themselves. But there is something Kafkaesque about an appeal being mounted on behalf of a party who knows nothing about the grounds of the appeal and may be given no reasons why it is allowed or dismissed.

Besides being able to appeal adverse decisions, it is important as a matter of fairness for parties to know the reasons for decisions which are made in their favour. Many of the open parties who have brought appeals or applications that are heard in closed procedures have already been subjected to detention at the hands of the state, or experienced restrictions on their liberty, on the use of their assets or property, or on their family life or, in relation to immigration

121 SA9, 7 December 2015.
122 J6, 9 August 2017.
123 ibid.

decisions, through being deprived of citizenship or of a right to remain in the country. Knowing the full reasons why these restrictions or deprivations were not considered justified by the tribunal can help give appellants a sense of closure to any injustice that has been perpetrated, as well as opening up possibilities for compensation.

Beyond this, there is also the important issue of maximising confidence, so far as possible, in closed procedures and the courts and tribunals that have to administer them. While the representational role considered in this chapter necessarily involves special advocates acting behind closed doors in secret, when special advocates promote greater transparency they are helping to open matters up to the scrutiny of appellants and the public as much as possible. The ECtHR has ruled that for the requirement of a fair trial to be satisfied for the purpose of Article 6, the accused, and indeed the public, must be able to understand the verdict that has been given, adding that 'this is a vital safeguard against arbitrariness'.[124] This chimes with the idea that the rule of law can only be achieved through open justice which lets in the light and allows the public to scrutinise the workings of the law.[125] We have seen that access to open judgments, for example, on the SIAC database, helps to gain an understanding of the way in which its open procedures operate and how outcomes are reached, as well as providing some indication of the reasons for these outcomes in so far as they are contained in open judgments. Given widespread concerns about the secrecy of closed procedures in SIAC and other courts and tribunals, it arguably behoves these tribunals to ensure that there is as much transparency as possible. On one view, the closed procedures in these courts are inevitably compromised by a lack of transparency, but special advocates can play an important role in minimising the deficit.

There is limited guidance indicating how special advocates should fulfil their transparency role in relation to closed judgments. We have seen that the Supreme Court has said that judges should say as much as they can in the open judgment about the closed material they have relied upon.[126] But special advocates also need to be encouraged to ensure that open judgments are as transparent as possible. As we have mentioned, the SIAC rules (although noticeably not the rules governing other closed procedures) permit special advocates to argue for greater disclosure of closed determinations where it would not be contrary to the public interest. If special advocates are to play a meaningful role in ensuring that open judgments are as transparent as possible, it is clearly important that there is a consistency of practice across all courts and tribunals where closed judgments may be issued. This requires that special advocates are given access not only to draft open judgments, but also at the same time to draft closed judgments so that they may not only respond to government objections to the open content but may

124 *Taxquet v Belgium* (2012) 54 EHRR 26 [90].

125 See *R (Guardian News and Media Ltd) v City of Westminster Magistrates* [2012] EWCA Civ 420 [1].

126 *Bank Mellat v HM Treasury* (No 1) [2013] UKSC 38, [2014] AC 700 [69].

also make applications themselves for opening up aspects of closed judgments.[127] The public interest arguably needs to be recalibrated not only to ensure that any closed information that may put lives at risk or compromise national security is not disclosed, but also to ensure that judgments are as open as they can be in the interests of the administration of justice. This suggests a role for special advocates akin to their function in PII applications, taking on the broader mantle of acting in the interests of the administration of justice. Before drawing any conclusions about the future role of special advocates more generally, however, we need to consider whether there are other, and possibly better, ways in which the functions that special advocates have performed could be discharged.

127 A SIAC Practice Note issued on 5 October 2016 seems to make reference to this when it states that with effect from 5 October 2016 the 'practice will be that draft CLOSED judgments are sent to the special advocate at the same time as the draft OPEN judgments are sent for security checking' ([26]).

10 Alternatives to special advocates

While the special advocate system has developed a presence in a range of different common law systems and has been adopted in certain Scandinavian systems such as Denmark, it is not the only technique that can be employed, in ECtHR terms, to accommodate legitimate security concerns about the nature and sources of intelligence information and yet accord the individual a substantial measure of procedural fairness. We have seen that the Canadian Supreme Court in *Charkaoui v Canada*[1] considered that there were a number of other less intrusive alternatives to the security certificate system that Canada had chosen to use to exclude non-citizens and it did not simply refer exclusively to the special advocate system that had been adopted in the UK, although this was the system that Canada decided to adopt.[2] It will be recalled that the Court singled out three important disadvantages faced by special advocates – the inability to take instructions from the appellant once they have seen the confidential information; the lack of resources of an ordinary legal team; and the fact that they have no power to call witnesses.

In previous chapters, we have seen that these have been only very partially ameliorated. *A* or *AF*-type disclosure gives the appellant some notion of the case against him and may enable him to give effective instructions to the special advocate, although we have seen this test only applies in certain types of cases affecting 'objectively high level rights', and special advocates are still inhibited in both the UK and Canada from seeking authorisation for communications once they have seen the closed information. The Special Advocates' Support Office (SASO) in the UK and the Special Advocate Program (SAP) in Canada have provided important logistical support to special advocates and have facilitated better communication between special advocates, but this does not compare with the kind of support that they would get from an instructing solicitor in an ordinary case. The rules now enable special advocates to call witnesses, but in practice this happens very rarely because of the difficulty in accessing independent security-cleared experts. Given these continuing difficulties, in this chapter we consider alternative models to the special advocate system to see whether they may offer a more

1 *Charkaoui v Canada (Citizenship and Immigration)* 2007 SCC 9, [2007] 1 SCR 350.
2 See Chapter 4.

effective way of balancing the need to protect the disclosure of sensitive information and the need to treat individuals fairly.

Other less intrusive alternatives

Apart from the special advocate system, the Canadian Supreme Court referred to four other alternatives which impaired the rights of non-citizens less than the existing security certificate system that left it up to judges alone to ensure the fairness of the procedures. Not surprisingly, perhaps, it devoted quite a lot of space to the previous system for issuing security certificates to permanent residents in Canada. As we have seen, this involved the use of security-cleared counsel within the Security Intelligence Review Committee (SIRC) which investigated the grounds for non-citizens being excluded before any security certificate could be issued. According to the Supreme Court, the role that the independent security-cleared SIRC counsel played in cross-examining witnesses for the Canadian Security Intelligence Service (CSIS) and in negotiating with CSIS the contents of the summary to be provided to the excluded person illustrated 'how special counsel can provide not only an effective substitute for informed participation, but can also bolster actual informed participation by the affected person'.[3]

The Court went on to refer more briefly to other less intrusive alternatives. One was the procedure under section 38 of the Canada Evidence Act 1985 whereby the government may seek non-disclosure orders from judges of the Federal Court in civil, criminal and administrative proceedings, analogous to PII applications made in the UK, on the basis that the harm of disclosure to national security, national defence or international relations outweighs the public interest in disclosure. As with PII applications, the judge performs a balancing test and is not required to order non-disclosure if she considers that disclosure would be injurious to national security but that the public interest in disclosure outweighs the public interest in non-disclosure, although the Attorney General has the power to issue a certificate overriding the court's decision.[4] Furthermore, unlike the security certificate procedures in immigration cases, the Act makes no provision for the use of information that has not been disclosed.

This procedure does not require the use of security-cleared counsel per se, but one special advocate informed me that judges are increasingly using their discretion to appoint a security-cleared amicus drawn from the pool of special advocates in Canada.[5] Although the terms of appointment vary from case to case, they may be given a specific role to counteract government counsel arguing for non-disclosure by submitting arguments for disclosure in the interests of an

3 ibid [74].
4 Canada Evidence Act 1985, s 38.13.
5 SA15, 8 March 2016.

excluded person.[6] It was exactly this role that the Supreme Court in *Charkaoui* referred to when it mentioned another example of the use of special counsel in Canada, namely their use in the specific context of the Arar Commission, which was a multi-million dollar inquiry in Canada into the actions of Canadian officials in relation to the rendition and torture of a Syrian-born Canadian citizen.[7] The court referred to independent security-cleared legal counsel with a background in security and intelligence, acting in an amicus role on confidentiality applications which had to be determined by the Inquiry, again in the manner of PII applications.[8] Roach, however, has noted that the Court neglected to mention the more important place of security-cleared Commission counsel who, like SIRC counsel, were given a wide-ranging role to demand greater disclosure from the government, to call relevant witnesses, to communicate with excluded parties and to test in camera evidence by means of cross-examination when necessary.[9]

The final example mentioned by the Supreme Court of a less intrusive solution was the procedure adopted in the Air India trial on the bombings of Air India Flight 182 in which 329 people died, whereby the Crown and the defence came to an agreement under which defence counsel obtained consent from their clients to review material that the Crown was withholding on the basis of relevance, national security privilege and litigation privilege, on an undertaking not to disclose the material to anyone, including the client.[10] Counsel would then negotiate with the Crown and the Canadian Intelligence Service (CSIS) as to which documents were of real importance to the defence such that the public interest in disclosure would outweigh any competing public interest in non-disclosure. It appears that defence counsel did not need any security clearance in this trial but as Roach mentions,[11] there are other examples in both the US and Australia whereby disclosure is sometimes made to an affected person's lawyer on condition that the lawyer obtains a security clearance.

If we return to the spectrum referred to by the New Zealand Law Commission in its Issues Paper on proceedings involving national security information between open adversarial proceedings at one extreme and closed inquisitorial proceedings at the other,[12] it is possible to extrapolate from the alternatives mentioned by the Canadian Supreme Court three different models of security-cleared counsel

6 ibid. See also G Hudson and D Alati, 'Behind Closed Doors: Secret Law and the Special Advocate System in Canada' (2018) 44 *Queen's Law Journal* 1, 67.

7 Commission of Inquiry into the Actions of Canadian Officials in Relation to Maher Arar, *Report of the Events Relating to Maher Arar: Analysis and Recommendations* (2006).

8 *Charkaoui v Canada (Citizenship and Immigration)* 2007 SCC 9, [2007] 1 SCR 350 [79].

9 K Roach, 'Charkaoui and Bill C-3: Some Implications for Anti-Terrorism Policy and Dialogue between Courts and Legislatures' (2008) 42 *Supreme Court Law Review* (2d) 281, 300–301.

10 *Charkaoui v Canada (Citizenship and Immigration)* 2007 SCC 9, [2007] 1 SCR 350 [78]. See *R v Malik* [2005] BCJ No 521 (QL), 2005 BCSC 350.

11 Roach (n 9) 297.

12 New Zealand Law Commission, *National Security Information in Proceedings* (NZLC IP38, 2015) [6.41]. See Chapter 1.

which lie between these extremes, as can be seen in Table 10.1 below. The first model may be classified as 'own counsel undertaking confidentiality' where, as in the Air India case, an excluded party's own counsel is allowed into closed proceedings on an undertaking not to disclose closed information. The second 'special advocate' model, which lies in the middle of the spectrum, enables a special counsel to be appointed to represent the interests of the excluded party in a closed procedure, but who has no professional ties towards such a party nor any duties to the court over and above those owed by ordinary counsel. The third model consists of counsel who are appointed to assist the inquiry, tribunal or court, either as amicus counsel in a specific task such as in hearings under section 38 of the Canada Evidence Act on whether to order disclosure or nondisclosure of evidence, or as in the case of SIRC counsel or Commission counsel in the Arar Commission, with providing a more wide-ranging adversarial counter-point to government counsel who is representing the interests of the state. The 'own-counsel' model has been situated closer to the adversarial end of the spectrum because as the excluded party's own counsel, she can be expected to know the most about the case and may be considered more effective in acting in the excluded party's interests than someone who is further removed. The inquiry/tribunal/court/amicus counsel model by contrast is situated closer to the inquisitorial end of the spectrum because such counsel are less attached to the excluded party and furthering the interests of the excluded party and are closely aligned to the court, with the ultimate responsibility of assisting the court. As we look at the pros and cons of these models in greater detail, however, we will see that they do not merely represent choices in terms of the weight to be given to the values of procedural fairness on the one hand, and protection of national security on the other. They each need to be considered in terms of other factors such as what the proceedings themselves are designed to achieve and different perceptions as to how adversarial values are best represented in different legal cultures. This suggests that no one model is likely to be appropriate across the full range of proceedings where sensitive information is engaged.

Own counsel undertaking confidentiality model

This model, which is sometimes equated with the use of 'confidentiality rings', essentially involves independent counsel representing the affected person

Table 10.1 Different models of security-cleared counsel for handling sensitive information

Open or in camera adversarial proceedings	Own counsel undertaking confidentiality	Special Advocates	Inquiry/ tribunal/court/amicus counsel	Closed inquisitorial proceedings
Natural justice	<<--		--->>	Protection of security

being furnished with sensitive information on an undertaking of confidentiality. The New Zealand Law Commission considered that this model had both 'the advantage and disadvantage of being a unique and largely un-trialled (in Commonwealth jurisdictions) system'.[13] The Commission considered that it is difficult to reconcile this model with the normal understanding that lawyers will share all information with their clients so that they will be able to receive proper instructions. As it said:

> It will be difficult for lawyers to build an effective case if they cannot communicate with their clients and discuss the significance of security information. This risks distorting the traditional view of a lawyer/client relationship.[14]

However, the Commission went on to acknowledge that when this model is compared with the special advocate model there were potential advantages. Although lawyers who give a confidentiality undertaking cannot communicate the content of any closed information, unlike special advocates they remain able to keep in contact with their clients after seeing the closed information. A further advantage is that the excluded person's own advocate is the person most familiar with the case and most likely to be able to place the information within the broader context of the narrative of the case.[15]

The idea of independent counsel giving confidentiality undertakings is not as unknown in the Commonwealth world as the Law Commission suggested. Mention has already been made of the Air India case in Canada, and Code and Roach have reported that since then there is a considerable body of case law, as well as practical experience, in Canada suggesting that limited disclosure to counsel on an undertaking of confidentiality is a useful way to resolve disputes over potentially privileged information.[16] By contrast, the practice is discouraged in criminal cases in England and Wales. The Attorney General's Guidelines on Disclosure state that '[t]here is no basis in law or practice for disclosure on a "counsel to counsel" basis',[17] although in the parole context, the England and Wales Parole Board rules make provision for information or reports to be withheld from the prisoner and served instead on the prisoner's representative if the

13 ibid [6.55].

14 ibid [6.56].

15 ibid [6.83], citing K Roach, 'Secret Evidence and its Alternatives' in A Masferrer (ed), *Post 9/11 and the State of Permanent Legal Emergency* (Springer 2012) 187, 197. See also the comment of Moses LJ in *R (Mohammed Serdar) v SSHD* [2012] EWHC 3454 (Admin) [20] that open counsel are in a far better position to understand the nature and needs of their client's case than a special advocate.

16 M Code and K Roach, 'The Role of the Independent Lawyer and Security Certificates' (2000) 52 *Criminal Law Quarterly* 85, 109.

17 See *Attorney-General's Guidelines on Disclosure* [46]. See also *R v Davis* [1993] 1 WLR 613, *R v Botmeh* [2002] 1 WLR 531 and J Jackson and S Summers, *The Internationalisation of Criminal Evidence: Beyond the Common Law and Civil Law Traditions* (CUP 2012) 322–323.

representative is a barrister or solicitor or other person deemed suitable by the Board.[18] The practice is also not unknown in other contexts.[19] There is authority for the use of confidentiality rings in competition cases, intellectual property cases and procurement cases.[20] In *Al Rawi v Security Service*,[21] Lord Clarke referred to the use of confidentiality undertakings when setting out the considerations to be taken into account in permitting disclosure of material as part of the PII process. In a later case concerned with a judicial review challenge to the lawfulness of the transfer of detainees in Afghanistan to the Afghan authorities, Moses LJ considered that there was no principle which prohibits a court considering whether to uphold or reject a claim for PII from ordering that, whilst the claim should not be upheld, nonetheless the documents or material should only be disclosed to those identified within a confidentiality ring on terms to be specified in an undertaking agreed by the parties.[22] If the client is to be excluded, it is clear that the lawyers must consent to receiving the material on that basis. Moses LJ proceeded on the assumption that there was no distinction between the principles applying to judicial review claims and civil claims, but there remains some doubt as to whether this approach can be adopted in criminal cases.[23]

This case has been described as the 'high water mark' for confidentiality rings,[24] but even here, it was accepted that any decision by the judge as whether to allow this depends very much on the facts of the case and on whether, in his or her view, confidentiality can be maintained. In the instant case, the client was imprisoned in Afghanistan, there was no possibility of counsel communicating with him and the client was unlikely to have anything useful to add to the context of the documents.[25] It would seem that any idea of open counsel receiving information on a confidential basis in SIAC cases has been ruled out. In one case, the suggestion that closed material could be disclosed to a legal representative, given appropriate undertakings and the consent of the appellant not to seek sight of the documents or to be present at parts of the hearing when a particular matter

18 Parole Board Rules 2016, r 8(6). See *R (Paul Rowe) v Parole Board* [2012] EWHC 1272.

19 R Pattenden, *The Law of Professional-Client Confidentiality: Regulating the Disclosure of Confidential Personal Information* (OUP 2003) [17.02].

20 See the authorities cited in *CF v The Security Service* [2013] EWHC 3402 (QB) [47].

21 *Al Rawi v Security Service* [2011] UKSC 34, [2012] 1 AC 531 [145]. See also *R v Chief Constable of West Midlands ex p Wiley* [1995] 1 AC 274, 307. Cf *Sommerville v Scottish Ministers* [2007] 1 WLR 2734 [153]–[153] per Lord Rodger, [203]–[204] per Lord Mance.

22 *R (Serdar Mohammed) v SSSD* [2012] EWHC 3454 (Admin) [27].

23 See *R v Davis* [1993] 1 WLR 613, 617. Cf *Archbold: Criminal Pleading, Evidence and Practice* (Sweet & Maxwell 2019) Ch 12:107 preferring the approach in *Davis* with *Blackstone's Criminal Practice* (OUP 2019) D 9.61 considering that Moses LJ's reasoning in *Mohammed* can be applied to criminal cases. In *R v Duffy* [2015] NICC 13 [29], Colton J preferred Archbold's view.

24 *R v Duffy* [2015] NICC 13 [29].

25 *R (Serdar Mohammed) v SSSD* [2012] EWHC 3454 (Admin) [21].

was discussed, was considered so problematical that the Commission could not conceive of any instance in which it would be proper to allow such a practice.[26]

The Commission referred to three objections. The first was that there would be an obvious risk of inadvertent disclosure by the legal representative in discussions with other representatives or clients, or to others. This mirrors the objection that has been made to special advocates communicating with the excluded party and open counsel after seeing the closed material. SIAC went on to elaborate on this objection as follows:

> It is self-evident that the more who have the material, the greater the risk of inadvertent disclosure. The difficulties in managing the separation between open and closed material in terms of questions of witnesses, discussions with advocates in submissions, indeed judgment writing including technical support and publication, would all be greatly increased. All this increases the risk of accidental disclosure. … If cross-examination is proceeding on a topic which involves a restricted open document or point, it would have to stop while people left the court; the point would be potentially highlighted and inferentially it could be revealed widely. It might give rise to very strong questions from a client to his representative as to why a point had not been pressed, leading to inadvertent disclosure. The answer to a judicial question raised in open submission might make avoidance of reference to such material very difficult, and asking questions in open is already inhibited enough by knowledge of the closed material. … The ability to remember which different system applied to which material during a hearing would make for errors on all sides.[27]

The Commission seemed fortified in its view of the risks of inadvertent disclosure by the fact that this practice had been adopted by it in the early case of *Rehman v SSHD* and this, according to government counsel, had not prevented repeated open disclosure of restricted material by the open advocate.

The second objection was that if the information became public, there would be inevitably a risk that suspicion would fall on the innocent, whether the open advocate, special advocate, the Secretary of State's representative or the Commission and its staff.[28] The fewer who had access to the restricted information, the less that risk would materialise. The third objection was that it would involve the Commission being asked to take a view on the willingness and ability of an advocate or representative, barrister or solicitor, to abide by the terms of his undertaking.[29] This would put the Commission in the invidious position of potentially distinguishing between representatives, or even representatives from

26 *BB v SSHD* SIAC SC/39/2005, 14 November 2006 [31].
27 ibid [32].
28 ibid [33].
29 ibid [34].

the same firm or chambers, on what might be impression or closed objection, or of having to raise such matters with a representative which could give an impression of bias.

The Court of Appeal upheld SIAC's refusal to countenance any role for undertakings by open counsel not to disclose closed material.[30] In the present context, such an arrangement would undermine the careful division between counsel appearing in the open proceedings and the special advocates. Counsel would be put in the impossible position of being asked to play, part-time, the role of the special advocate, but without the protection, and formal position, that the special advocates play. In a later judgment, Ouseley J who had chaired the panel in the SIAC case repeated these objections in a case involving a judicial review, as he considered they were equally applicable outside the SIAC context, adding in parenthesis that he had experience of inadvertent disclosure in a criminal case where in camera material was referred to in one court by leading defence counsel, wholly inadvertently, on two occasions.[31] He also raised the particular objection that a confidentiality ring in national security cases would bypass the protections against the disclosure of protected material as this material can only be disclosed to those who have the highest level of security vetting.[32]

One of the two special advocates who gave oral evidence to the JCHR's review of the government's Justice and Security Green Paper pointed out that a confidentiality ring whereby the lawyer but not the client has access to information was better than total nondisclosure.[33] The other considered that a confidentiality ring was better than the special advocate process, because at least it meant that the lawyer who is directly representing the interests of the defendant has access to the defendant:[34]

> That person will have a much closer relationship with the person he is representing and will be setting the overall strategy of the case. Although they will not be able to communicate the information that is confidential, they will still be able to allow it to influence the overall approach they take to the case.

In interviews, however, special advocates and government counsel adverted both to the principled objection to confidentiality rings – that it impairs the lawyer–client relationship – and to the practical difficulties there would be in implementing such a scheme:

> When you know something about your client or something that is relevant to the case and you can't talk to them about it, I think that inhibits the

30 *MT (Algeria) v SSHD* [2007] EWCA Civ 808.
31 *AHK v SSHD* [2013] EWHC 1426 (Admin) [23].
32 ibid [28].
33 JCHR, *Justice and Security Green Paper* (HC 2012, 1777-i-v) Oral evidence, 31 January 2012 Q 52 (Mr Angus McCullough QC).
34 ibid (Mr Jeremy Johnson QC).

> lawyer-client relationship. But there's also a risk that accidentally you stray or cross the line. I don't see that as being a really workable solution.[35]

> There are a number of difficulties. The first is that very many members of the bar would not feel comfortable in holding information they couldn't give to a client and I have seen that. Another is that you could not police the tainting process whereby an advocate doing one case hears of closed information which bars you from being instructed in another case. ... Also I think in terms of public perception, the public might think that someone acting for some clients could not be trusted and I think that would be the wrong perception. There would have to be security clearance and some firms might get security clearance and others might not.[36]

The latter reference to the need for security clearance deals with the objection that otherwise open counsel would get to see protected material that counsel for the government and special advocates only see on the basis of being developed vetted. This raises issues, however, about the desirability of having a list of security-cleared representatives whom parties would have to choose from in order to be represented in any proceedings that might require a CMP. Of course, under the special advocate system, excluded parties must choose from the list of security-cleared special advocates, but with this difference that under an own-lawyer security-cleared system, that lawyer would be their representative in both open and closed proceedings. As this special advocate hinted, it could well be the case that only certain types of lawyers would be willing and able to get on such a list, with the result that parties' choice of advocate would be skewed in a manner which is worse than under the special advocate system where at least parties can choose whom they wish to represent them in the open proceedings.

These issues have been raised in the context of the security clearance scheme that operates under the National Security Information (Civil and Criminal Proceedings) Act 2004 in Australia.[37] Under the scheme, if the defendant's legal representative receives notice that an issue of disclosure of information that is prejudicial to national security is likely to arise, the representative must apply for security clearance before having sight of the material. Members of the legal profession have argued that this threatens the independence of the legal profession by potentially allowing the executive arm of the government to effectively 'vet' and limit the class of lawyers who are able to act in cases involving national security.[38] The requirement for security clearance has also been said to have a highly

35 GC1, 4 November 2015.

36 SA3, 25 November 2015.

37 See National Security Information (Criminal and Civil Proceedings) Act 2004, ss 39 and 39A.

38 Law Council of Australia, *Inquiry into the operation of the National Security (Criminal and Civil Proceedings) Act 2004* (2013) [156]. See also A Lynch and G Williams, *What Price Security: Taking Stock of Australia's Anti-Terror Laws* (UNSW Press 2006) 83–84.

intrusive impact on the professional and private lives of legal representatives, with the result that practitioners have refused to undergo such a process.[39] This in turn potentially restricts a person's right to a legal representative of her choosing by limiting the pool of lawyers who are permitted to act in cases involving national security information.[40] It has been argued that if the security clearance process is not repealed, the provisions should at least be amended to enable the court to play a greater role in determining whether a defendant's legal representative requires a security clearance before accessing information and in reviewing a decision to refuse a legal representative security clearance. The difficulty with handing over decisions like this completely to the courts, however, is that they themselves are then put, as SIAC has said, in the invidious position of determining who within the independent legal profession should, and who should not, be trusted with security clearance.

The US own-lawyer security-cleared counsel system

In terms of workability, one of the best developed systems of confidentiality undertakings is to be found in the United States where lawyers are required not to disclose classified information. In criminal proceedings, the regulation of classified information in federal criminal trials is governed by the Classified Information Procedures Act 1980 (CIPA) which requires the court to issue an order to protect against the disclosure of any classified information disclosed by the United States to any defendant in any federal criminal case.[41] CIPA was originally directed at the problem of so-called 'graymail', where government officials who were being prosecuted threatened to disclose classified information in the course of the trial, and it does not on its face refer to the courts requiring defence lawyers to obtain security clearance as a condition of obtaining access to classified information. However, the courts have interpreted CIPA to give them this power and it has since been used to enable security-cleared defence counsel in federal terrorism prosecutions to gain access to classified information.[42]

39 ibid [157].
40 ibid [158].
41 18 USC App III, s 3.
42 See A Chandran, 'The Classified Information Procedures Act in the Age of Terrorism: Remodeling CIPA in an Offence-Specific Manner' (2015) 64 *Duke Law Journal* 1412; L K Donohue, 'Terrorism Trials in Article III Courts' (2015) 38 *Harvard Journal of Law & Public Policy* 105, 132. 'Classified information' is defined as 'any information or material that has been determined by the United States Government pursuant to an executive order, statute, or regulation, to require protection against unauthorised disclosure for reasons of national security'. See 18 USC §1(a).

CIPA does not change the discovery rules that operate in all federal criminal cases under rule 16 of the Federal Rules of Criminal Procedure.[43] The defence still have a right to see exculpatory information in accordance with *Brady v Maryland*.[44] But, as one federal prosecutor confided,[45] the reality is that in practice CIPA has an inhibiting effect on disclosure. Classified information can only be disclosed on the basis of a 'need to know' the information, which is a determination made exclusively by the government, not the courts. This prosecutor said that there was considerable anxiety within the intelligence community about any classified information being disclosed even to federal judges who automatically have security clearances. Rather like a PII application which is made ex parte, section 4 of CIPA permits the government to make a request ex parte for permission to withhold certain classified discovery and the judge then has the burden of deciding whether this is favourable to the defence and must be produced either in raw form or in the form of a substitution which provides the defence with the substance of the information.[46] According to one security-cleared counsel,[47] a practice has developed, although it is not provided for in the statute, whereby the defence at this point may request their own ex parte audience with the judge in order to apprise the court of certain projected defences. Although the defence are at a disadvantage in not knowing what the government's arguments for withholding the material are,[48] the judge is put in the position of mediating between the two sides on what information can be given to the defence and this can result in more disclosure to the defence.[49]

Protective orders

Before providing the defence with any discoverable material, the government will move for a protective order pursuant to section 3 of CIPA to ensure that classified information will not be disclosed. These orders usually require defence counsel to obtain security clearance at the appropriate level of classification, sign a memorandum of understanding agreeing to the terms of the order, agree to review or discuss classified evidence only in a secure area of review (known as a Secure Compartmented Information Facility (SCIF)) and refrain from discussing the

43 Chandran ibid 1417.
44 *Brady v Maryland* 373 US 83 (1963). See J Dratel, 'Section 4 of the Classified Information Procedures Act: The Growing Threat to the Adversary Process' (2007) 53 *Wayne Law Review* 1041, 1044.
45 FP2, 12 July 2017.
46 J Dratel, 'The Unique Challenges in Defending a Terrorism Prosecution' (2017) 43 *Litigation* 28.
47 SCC4, 4 May 2016.
48 Dratel (n 46) 1059–1060.
49 SCC4, 4 May 2016.

classified information with anyone, including the defendant himself.[50] Defence counsel will then review the classified information that is disclosed and identify that which is useful for the defence at trial and then move under section 5 of the CIPA, in non-public proceedings, to use it at the eventual trial.[51] The court can never compel the government to disclose classified information, but if the court agrees that the evidence is favourable to the defence, the government is then compelled to choose between either declassifying the material, offering substitutions that provide the defence with the substance of the information, or suffering sanctions which may involve dismissing the charges altogether, dismissing specified counts of the indictment or preventing the government using certain evidence.

The same system of disclosing classified information to counsel on condition that they obtain security clearance and sign protective orders has also prevailed in cases involving Guantánamo Bay detainees. Ever since 2004 when alien detainees won the right to a court review of their detentions,[52] which was reaffirmed as a constitutional right in 2008,[53] lawyers acting for detainees have been able to get access to classified information which they cannot share with their clients.[54] The same cleared counsel system is also used for the military and civilian lawyers who defend detainees charged with committing acts of international terrorism under the Military Commissions Act of 2006, later replaced by the Obama administration with the Military Commissions Act of 2009. The classified information disclosure provisions of the 2009 Act are substantially similar in form and substance to CIPA.[55] But protective orders have been quite extensive, going to the lengths of not disclosing the detainees' own statements to the detainee and not even being able to use any information obtained from a detainee as anything said by the detainee is presumptively classified information.[56]

50 Chandran (n 42) 1418. The memorandum of understanding typically requires the defence attorney to agree never to divulge, publish, or reveal either by word, conduct or any other means, such classified documents and information unless specially authorised to do so by an authorised representative of the US Government, or as expressly authorised by the court pursuant to CIPA. See Donohue (n 42) n 135.

51 Dratel (n 46).

52 See *Rasul v Bush* 542 US 466 (2004).

53 See *Boumediene v Bush* 553 US 723 (2008).

54 D Cole and S Vladeck, 'Navigating the Shoals of Secrecy: A Comparative Analysis of the Use of Secret Evidence and "Cleared Counsel" in the United States, the United Kingdom and Canada' in L Lazarus, C McCrudden and N Bowles (eds), *Reasoning Rights: Comparative Judicial Engagement* (Hart 2014).

55 Cf Military Commissions Act of 2009, 10 USC § 949. See G Rona and R Wala, 'In Defense of Federal Criminal Courts for Terrorism Cases in the United States' in F Ní Aoláin and O Gross (eds), *Guantánamo and Beyond: Exceptional Courts and Military Commissions in Comparative Perspective* (CUP 2013) 137, 151 n 34. Cf C W Bevan, 'Military Commissions and the Conundrum of Classified Evidence: A Semi-Panglossian Solution' (2013) 37 *Southern Illinois University Law Journal* 643, 663–672.

56 See eg *In re Guantanamo Bay Detainee Litigation*, Misc no 08-0442 issued by Judge Thomas F. Hogan, 11 September 2008. Protective Order and Procedures for Counsel Access to Detainees at the United States Naval Base in Guantanamo Bay, Cuba. 11 September 2008.

These restrictions can create formidable obstacles for counsel trying to defend their clients. As one counsel put it:

> We had an issue, for example, that was litigated in the Guantánamo cases where a lot of the intelligence reports that were being used to justify the detention would have been the detainee's statements. Many of the documents were the detainee's own statements. Detainee told investigator this, detainee told so and so, detainee admitted this. There was a real question, well if those documents are classified, how am I supposed to talk to my client and ask him, did you make that statement? If you made the statement, why did you make it? Were they hanging you upside down by your toes? So that was litigated and eventually that was resolved with a judicial order that said you could take the individual detainee's statements out of the report and ask the detainee about them. Did you say this? What were the circumstances?[57]

Another counsel pointed to the absurd lengths to which these restrictions could go when counsel are conversing with a detainee who is their client:

> You had this situation early on when he would say something to us and then we couldn't even say it back to him. Hypothetically, it's absurd, it's like he says, 'Oh I'm feeling sick to my stomach today', and I cannot say back to him. 'So you're feeling sick to your stomach today'. Because that would be me getting top secret information from him and then releasing it back to someone who doesn't have security clearance.[58]

Apart from the protective orders which set out very detailed rules on access to classified information, there are also very detailed procedures regulating counsel's access to detainees at the naval base in Guantánamo Bay.[59] The restrictive conditions governing access pose problems for lawyers trying to establish a rapport with their clients, which have been compounded over the years by various tactics that have been used by the interrogators and others to sow mistrust between the lawyers and their client and to undermine the lawyer–client relationship.[60] The military lawyers who represent detainees in the military commission face additional difficulties in establishing rapport with their clients, including, according to one civilian lawyer who had represented clients in the military commissions, the very fact that they have to wear a uniform.[61] But there is no rule that

57 SCC2, 3 May 2016.
58 SCC6, 13 July 2017.
59 ibid.
60 See D Luban, 'Lawfare and Legal Ethics in Guantánamo' (2008) 60 *Stanford Law Review* 1981.
61 SCC6, 13 July 2017. For challenges facing military lawyers representing detainees in Guantánamo Bay see M Ivey, 'Challenges Presented to Military Lawyers Representing Detainees

prevents lawyers who have been security-cleared from communicating with their clients after they have seen classified information. One lawyer who had considerable experience of Guantánamo litigation said that he interfaced with clients at Guantánamo all the time and he would have read 'hundreds and hundreds of pages of classified documents'.[62] In his view, being able to take meaningful instructions from and to collaborate with the client whilst having the classified material was quite a 'powerful advantage'. He drew a contrast with the UK and Canadian special advocate system on the basis that US security-cleared counsel could go back to their client after seeing classified information.

Of course, there are risks for lawyers in having the ability to communicate with their clients when they have had access to classified information. The penalties for any unauthorised disclosure can be severe, resulting in the termination of access to classified information and possible charges of contempt of court and criminal prosecution.[63] As one lawyer put it:

> We can go back to our clients but there is a risk for us. You know, you go back to your client and you tell your client the wrong thing, you get in a lot of trouble. ... It's a tremendous burden. I mean you have to be very careful about what you say and what you do, and a lot of times there's just information that you can't share with your client.[64]

One lawyer said the whole process of reading documents which are confined to the SCIF was very burdensome.[65] On the one hand, he would try to remember what he had seen because this would inform how he would look at everything else, but at the same time he had to keep it segregated so that he did not reveal anything. Another lawyer drew a comparison with prosecutors who do not have the same level of segregation in their head all the time between classified and non-classified information and will often let something slip out. According to him:

> The small group of us [defence lawyers] who operate in this genre know very well that we're the ones who are going to get in trouble if we let anything get out.[66]

in the War on Terrorism' (2010) 66 *NYU Survey of American Law* 211. See also F Ní Aoláin, 'Lawyers, Military Commissions and the Rule of Law in Democratic States' in C King and G Lennon (eds), *Counter-Terrorism, Constitutionalism and Miscarriages of Justice* (Hart 2018).

62 SCC1, 18 March 2016.

63 Protective Order (n 56) [51].

64 SCC2, 3 May 2016.

65 SCC4, 4 May 2016.

66 ibid.

Support mechanisms

To help offset these risks, a number of support mechanisms are available to help support and protect security-cleared counsel in both federal criminal cases and in Guantánamo Bay litigation. First of all, they may go to the judge ex parte to sanction or approve any communications they wish to make. According to one lawyer, a judge will not necessarily give a ruling but will sometimes tell you what you can and cannot do.[67] Alternatively, they can seek advice from Court Security Officers who are technically Department of Justice employees, but who operate as impartial officers on behalf of the court in cases where classified materials are present to help lawyers on a range of logistical as well as technical issues.[68] Each protective order which must be signed by the lawyer agreeing to its terms will designate a Court Security Officer (CSO) for the 'purpose of providing security arrangements necessary to protect against unauthorised disclosure of any classified documents or information to be made available in connection with these cases'.[69] The orders go on to state that the petitioners' counsel 'shall seek guidance from the CSO with regard to appropriate storage, handling, transmittal, and use of classified documents or information'.[70] One important protective mechanism for cleared lawyers is that the CSO shall not:

> reveal to any person the content of any conversations he or she hears by or among petitioners' counsel, nor reveal the nature of documents being reviewed by them or the work generated by them, except as necessary to report violations of this Protective Order to the Court or to carry out their duties pursuant to this Protective Order.[71]

In addition, 'the presence of the CSO or CSO designee shall not be construed to waive, limit, or otherwise render inapplicable the attorney-client privilege or work product protections'.[72] So as one lawyer said:

> I can go to my court security officer and say, 'Look, I'm dealing with this issue. I don't know what to do'. They're not going to tell me how to handle my client but they're going to help me with classified information questions. 'Can I do this? Can I do that? Would it be okay if I did this?' And when they say you can do something, you are protected because everything is subject to government consent. So if the government says yes, you can ask your client this, that gives you a lot of protection. … And they're very valuable. We're very glad to have them … there's not a week that goes by that I don't

67 SCC2, 3 May 2016.
68 Dratel (n 46).
69 See eg Protective Order (n 56) [15].
70 ibid.
71 ibid [27].
72 ibid.

> speak to them about something. Some of it's more trivial than others but they're also the people who manage our clearances. They are a sort of sword and shield.[73]

It seems that the CSOs are also responsible for protecting lawyers from any unwarranted government intrusion into the SCIF, which is the secure area to which counsel have access where all classified information and all documents prepared by counsel containing classified information must be stored including notes, memoranda or pleadings intended for filing with the court. One counsel has related how in one of his cases, a government agent appeared at the defence's SCIF demanding entry and the return of classified material which had been provided inadvertently.[74] The intervention of the CSO was vital in impressing upon the government the sanctity of the SCIF as a privileged defence location into which the government could not intrude.

Although we have seen that there is much scepticism in the UK about the viability of lawyers within confidentiality rings being able to refrain from unauthorised disclosure, the combination of tough sanctions and the support of the CSO would seem to have been remarkably successful in preventing unauthorised disclosure. One lawyer said that in over a decade of experience now with literally hundreds of security-cleared habeas corpus counsel representing Guantánamo detainees, he was not aware of any instance where the US government had accused cleared counsel of passing classified information to detainees.[75] Another lawyer, speaking in the context of federal criminal cases where there have been hundreds of cases involving classified information, said that to his knowledge there was not one documented case of a defence attorney divulging classified information.[76]

Another protection for security-cleared lawyers in the Guantánamo Bay context is the access that they have to what is called the Department of Defence (DoD) privilege team who work for the DoD but are also walled off from the DoD and work for the court. This team decides what is classified and what is not and whether anything may be released to the detainee. As it was put by one lawyer:

> So if I get a new stack of intelligence documents that are classified by various agencies, I want to know if this particular statement in this document is classified or not. Can I use this particular statement that's in here, this bigger classified document? Can I pull this one statement out and use this … I would give it to them. I would pull it out and I would say, I want to use this one statement, you can see that it doesn't look like it's classified. They will review it and when they stamp something as unclassified, I can do whatever the hell I want with it.[77]

73 SCC2, 3 May 2016.
74 Dratel (n 46).
75 SCC1, 18 March 2016.
76 SCC4, 4 May 2016.
77 SCC2, 3 May 2016.

Another lawyer said you would often try to get a summary of points to put to the client:

> The real challenge is figuring out what were the key points in the classified factual return and then trying to get those in front of your clients in a way that they can respond together. So rather than go up to the client and say, 'Hey do you know if there's somebody who would have said that you were in Iran in 1999?', you would run a line through the privilege team and make sure you'd be able to say it.[78]

The privilege team is also used when the lawyer wants to use information that she has obtained from her client but which is presumptively classified. As it was put:

> When I go and meet with my client, everything that comes out of their mouth is classified. My client writes me a letter from Guantánamo, presumptively classified, OK? My client writes me a letter and hypothetically says the sky is blue and my favourite food is pizza. Presumptively classified. That is obviously no way to represent a client. You can't do anything with what the client tells you. So what you can do is you can take that information to the privilege team and say, 'Will you review this and tell me whether it's classified, actually classified or not?' They will review it and they will mark it. Again they are the censor. If they say, it's unclassified, you can do whatever you want with it.[79]

On occasion, it seems that the privilege team have to go back to the agencies but before they do this, they will go back to the detainee's lawyer to ask for permission. By agreeing to this, privilege is not waived because the person at the agency who will look at it will herself be walled off from the others on the government's side. If the lawyer is not satisfied with the classification review, she can litigate ex parte against the privilege team, without the government's side being present at the hearing. The judge cannot order something to be declassified, but other remedies may be available and it appears that things tend to work through cooperation most of the time without seeking rulings. As one lawyer put it:

> I would say 75 per cent the process works smoothly. Particularly now after doing this for many, many years, it runs very smoothly. Every once in a while, you run up against issues where maybe they classify something as ridiculous. 'My client likes pizza'. And if that happens, you have the ability to go to court, where the privilege team will have their own lawyers who are walled off and they argue for the privilege team and the judge issues a ruling.[80]

78 SCC3, 4 May 2016.
79 SCC2, 3 May 2016.
80 ibid.

Although there are strict rules governing the disclosure of classified documents, two other advantages stressed by lawyers apart from continuing face-to-face contact with clients were that they are allowed to conduct their own investigations from the classified documents and that they are presumptively permitted to share classified information with other cleared counsel. As one put it:

> We can get cleared interpreters, we can have cleared investigators to go out and investigate. They're subject to all the same rules but they can go out. And we investigate cases. We can even do it ourselves. So I could read a classified intelligence report that says so-and-so was seen with so-and-so doing this and I might not be able to talk to my client about this but I can certainly go out and investigate that myself as long as I do not disclose the information.[81]

The lawyers essentially work in teams, often three or four lawyers in a case, all of whom have access to the classified information and furthermore they can presumptively work with teams of lawyers working in other cases, although such a presumption does not apply to 'top secret' or 'secret compartmentalised information' in cases involving so-called high value detainees.[82] So to take a fictitious example given by one lawyer,[83] if there are 30 detainees who are alleged to be bodyguards of Osama Bin Laden, counsel for all 30 detainees might get permission to share and compare information, and because all the detainees were captured together, and they have a similar profile, with similar witnesses against them, this can be particularly helpful. The CSO might help to get this permission from the judge. The judge cannot force the government to agree to this, but if they do not agree, there are other remedies. If, for example, the government do not want counsel to share information on a witness, then every allegation by that witness may be ordered to be stricken from the record.

Cultural perceptions

There would appear to be certain advantages for detainees in the 'own-lawyer' cleared counsel model over the special advocate model. According to Cole and Vladeck, it is the inability of UK and Canadian special advocates to consult with the client and the client's lawyer that is perhaps the single biggest obstacle to mounting an effective defence in these jurisdictions.[84] At the same time, we have seen how wary intelligence services are about classified information being disclosed even to security-cleared judges and it must be asked whether an own-lawyer security-cleared model involving direct contact with the client creates an inbuilt disincentive on the part of the intelligence community to share intelligence, as

81 ibid.
82 Cole and Vladeck (n 54) 165–166.
83 SCC2, 3 May 2016.
84 Cole and Vladeck (n 54) 172.

compared with the special advocate model where there can be no communication with parties once they have seen the closed information.

In the end, however, much of the preference for one model over the other would seem to come down to different cultural perceptions as to which model does the least damage to adversarial principles. There is a consensus that the use of secret evidence which is not disclosed to the parties erodes the adversarial principle that the parties have access to all the evidence in the case. On the one hand, however, disclosure to the party's own lawyer which is held back from the party may be considered to allow for greater participation and engagement with the case than the special advocate system, as it is the party's own lawyer who is more familiar with the case and can use the secret evidence to better effect than a lawyer who is totally removed from that party once she sees the secret evidence. On the other hand, putting up barriers between a party and her own lawyer in terms of what can be discussed between them impairs the confidential relationship between lawyer and client in a manner that a special advocate who is not in a professional client relationship does not do. It has been suggested that a pragmatic client who has confidence in her counsel will readily agree to her counsel getting disclosure of information and only when the client does not agree should the appointment of a special advocate be contemplated.[85] In reality, counsel is not the agent for the client and he or she must make a number of decisions independently of the client in the course of the proceedings when deciding matters such as which questions to ask, which witnesses to call and which points of fact and law to argue. Conducting in camera proceedings independently of the client and with the consent of the client is arguably little different from other areas where counsel must exercise independent judgment.

The difficulty is that many clients, especially in terrorist cases, are not pragmatic and may not be willing or able to act in their best interests. As one lawyer who had worked as a defence attorney in federal terrorist cases for many years admitted, trust is a big problem where half of the defendants in these cases are foreign nationals:

> You know, a lot of these guys are not criminals in the sense that they don't have experience of the criminal justice system like most of my clients. So they're like, 'You're appointed by the court, I don't hire you, I don't choose you. You are paid by the government to represent me and then you have this other relationship with the government that I don't have where you share information that you can't share with me. What kind of advocate are you?'[86]

This lawyer went on to say that trust was very important in presenting a case, because if you are spending time fighting with a client about what to do and

85 Code and Roach (n 16) 110.

86 SCC4, 4 May 2016. See also J L Dratel, 'Ethical Issues in Defending a Terrorism Case: Stuck in the Middle' (2003) 2 *Cardozo Public Law, Policy & Ethics Journal* 65, 68–69.

having to justify every decision to the client, this is a distraction which does not help in defending the case.

A further difficulty with this model arises when the defendant or detainee chooses to represent herself or refuses to have anything to do with her own legal representative. It has become the practice in federal terrorist cases when defendants insist on representing themselves for 'standby' counsel to be appointed to review the classified material in the absence of the defendant once counsel has secured the necessary security clearance.[87] In one case where the defendant challenged his exclusion from reviewing the classified information, the federal district court where he was tried ruled that his Fifth and Sixth Amendment rights were adequately protected by standby counsel.[88] It has been argued indeed that a failure to provide counsel of any sort who could see classified materials would almost certainly result in a lack of fairness to the defendant in the course of the trial.[89] In the military commissions, counsel must be appointed for detainees even when they do not wish to have one.[90] This creates ethical difficulties for counsel whose duty as defence counsel is to act as the defendant's representative. One counsel who had represented defendants in the military commissions explained the difficulties that arose in one case:

> This guy did not want to have anything to do with an American military lawyer. And so at his trial he refused to put on a defence and ordered the lawyer who agreed. ... We can debate whether the lawyer did the right thing but he had ordered his lawyer not to say anything during the trial, and so essentially he had to stay silent on the entire trial. So he was unsurprisingly convicted.[91]

We have seen that a similar situation has arisen in the special advocate system, but the ethical challenges here are arguably not so acute as there seems to be a consensus that the special advocate who is not a representative of the excluded party may intervene against the wishes of the party so long as it is considered in the interests of the party to do so.

There is the added problem that we have seen that the requirement of security clearance inevitably skews the pool of lawyers from whom clients may choose and many lawyers will not choose to go through what is a very intrusive process. One security-cleared lawyer in the US who had been given top security clearance gave a stark picture of what lawyers have to go through:

> Generally the FBI does a background investigation, they interview your family, your friends, your acquaintances, your lovers, your everything over a

87 Donohue (n 42) 139. For discussion of the role of 'standby' counsel, see A B Poulin, 'The Role of Stand By Counsel in Criminal Cases: In the Twilight Zone of the Criminal Justice System' (2000) 75 *New York University Law Review* 676.

88 See *US v Moussaoui* No. CRIM.01-455-A, 2002 WL 1311741 (E.D. Va. June 17, 2002), *US v Abdulmutallab* 739 F 3d 891 (6th Cir 2014).

89 Donohue (n 42) 139.

90 10 USC §948k (2012).

91 SCC6, 13 July 2017.

> period of time. Generally it's ten years. They look at drug use, they look at financial insolvency, they look at foreign contacts. Anything that would in their mind make you susceptible to blackmail or exploitation. … And then there are requirements. If I leave the US, I have to report where I'm going, when I'm going to be back, what I'm going to be doing. … If I want to write an article, a news article, or a law review article about a topic that's related to my work, I have to get it reviewed. And that can be a burden. … But what's most concerning for us is that notwithstanding our clearances and notwithstanding all of the procedures that we follow, the very near certainty that we ourselves are being surveilled, right? … We operate under the assumption that we are subject to surveillance and that annoys me. I have no doubt that all of my emails and phone calls are surveilled and that I find intolerable.[92]

It is not surprising that some lawyers do not wish to be subjected to such a process, and this in turn leads to the prospect of certain clients being disadvantaged by the fact that their own lawyer is not security-cleared, as against others whose lawyer is security-cleared. There is a further complication in systems such as the UK where clients tend to be represented by both solicitors and barristers, with the result that solicitors who instruct barristers would also have to be security-cleared. The special advocate model has the advantage of treating all defendants the same, in the sense that they may all choose a special advocate from the list to represent them in closed proceedings while having their own lawyer in the open proceedings.

In the end, the New Zealand Law Commission opted for the special advocate model having taken into account concerns raised by the New Zealand Law Society and the New Zealand Bar Association that the 'own counsel' undertaking model cut across the lawyer–client relationship.[93] If this represents the Commonwealth perspective, however, it is not the American perspective, which is more accepting of the need for defendants to be represented by their own lawyers, even if appointed for them, whatever the compromises involved, than having a special advocate foisted on them. One commentator has said that most attorneys would rather have access to the information to defend the case and grapple with non-disclosure in lieu of not having the information, although she conceded that some defence lawyers would not choose to have access to classified information because of the inherent conflict this creates within the lawyer–client relationship.[94] In her view, however, it is important to uphold the constitutional adversarial system that relies upon the tripartite system of judge, prosecutor and defence lawyer, with the defence lawyer playing a full part in all aspects of justice.[95]

92 SCC2, 3 May 2016.

93 New Zealand Law Commission, *The Crown in Court: A Review of the Crown Proceedings Act and National Security Information in Proceedings* (NZLC R135, 2015) Appendix 3.

94 E C Yaroshefsky, 'The Slow Erosion of the Adversary System: Article III Courts, FISA, CIPA and Ethical Dilemmas' (2006) 5 *Cardozo Public Law, Policy and Ethics Journal* 203, 217.

95 ibid 230.

Among US interviewees, there was some scepticism as to whether a special advocate model could ever be regarded within the US as free from the taint of government interference. If such a model was going to work in any meaningful sense, the special advocate would have to be philosophically directed towards the client even if they technically did not represent the client. As one lawyer put it:

> And it sounds like in the UK, you have within the barrister bar of people who have become special advocates, a defence orientation that keeps them as close as they can to acting in the interest of the affected party. Because if that didn't exist, you could see how it can become basically another arm of government. … And I suppose from the US [perspective] there would be a little bit of suspicion there culturally that it may operate in that way. … We'd be very, very worried about the appointment power held by the Attorney General. Why is the prosecutor appointing a special advocate to act in the interests of the defence?[96]

Another lawyer said:

> At the core of attorney ethics in the United States is client-centred representation, right? So like your first obligation is representation to your client and I think the US would be very, very itchy about some sort of special advocate system that you have in the UK because you're not really acting in that relationship. The traditional view we have of the lawyer is you have to be the agent of someone, and we get round that by sometimes having an amicus but then the representation is to the court and not to the client.[97]

This reference to an amicus system leads us on to consider another model that differs from the special advocate system.

Inquiry/tribunal/court/amicus counsel model

We have seen that in *Charkaoui*, the Canadian Supreme Court pointed to examples in Canada where independent security-cleared counsel have been appointed by more inquisitorial or quasi-inquisitorial bodies to assist them in their inquiries by acting as a kind of 'devil's advocate' against government counsel arguing for the non-disclosure of evidence or taking on the role of challenging government witnesses. Although the role that these counsel play is somewhat akin to that of special advocates, there are a number of respects in which the role is different. First of all, as counsel acting on behalf of the inquiry or court, they may be in a stronger position than special advocates to demand that the government disclose more relevant information to them. Second, they have been able to communicate

96 SCC5, 28 June 2017.
97 SCC6, 13 July 2017.

with excluded parties after they have access to secret information and before questioning the government witnesses. Third, however, although they can be asked by the inquiry to explore all lines of inquiry including the perspective of those who cannot participate in the process, they do not act specifically in the interests of the excluded party and, unless this is ordered by the court, communications between them and the excluded party or his or her own counsel are not privileged.

If we move away from the Canadian examples referred to by the Supreme Court, such as the role of SIRC counsel and counsel in the Arar Commission, we can see other examples of this model operating in other jurisdictions. It is interesting to note, for example, that various suggestions were made to make the Foreign Intelligence Surveillance Court (FISC) in the US more transparent and adversarial in the light of leaked revelations by Edward Snowden, a former contractor for the National Security Agency, that the court had approved largescale collections of telephone records of American citizens on an ongoing basis. FISC was created in 1978 in response to concerns about the abuse of electronic surveillance, but applications to the court concerning foreign surveillance were made in secret and ex parte; its orders and judicial opinions were secret as well, and it has increasingly been given powers to approve programmes involving what is called 'bulk collection' rather than individual surveillance requests.[98]

Amid concerns that the Court was simply rubber-stamping government applications and not taking account of positions other than those of the government, a number of proposals were made to make it more adversarial. These ranged from creating an independent 'Special Advocate' office within the executive or judicial branch of government which would advocate in support of legal interpretations that would protect individual privacy and civil liberties to more modest proposals that a panel of 'special advocates' outside government be appointed who could be brought into cases involving novel and significant issues by the FISC judges and would make legal arguments addressing privacy, civil rights and civil liberties interests.[99] It is interesting that the term 'special advocate' was deployed, not because it was suggested that the special advocate would act in the exclusive interests of an excluded party (the need for secrecy meant that the targets of surveillance had no locus standi before the Court) but in order, it would seem, to advocate for privacy and civil liberties interests.

In the end, Congress legislated in favour of an even more watered-down version of these proposals which envisaged the court appointing a security-cleared 'amicus' from an approved list who would not have any independent litigation powers and would not act as a party, but would be appointed by the court to assist it in the consideration of any application for an order or review that, in

98 W C Banks, 'Exceptional Courts in Counterterrorism: Lessons from the Foreign Intelligence Surveillance Act (FISA)' in Ní Aoláin and Gross (n 55).

99 See B Cook, 'The New FISA Court Amicus Should be able to Ignore its Congressionally Imposed Duty' (2016) 66 *American University Law Review* 539.

the opinion of the court, 'presents a novel or significant interpretation of the law'.[100] The designation of the term 'amicus' suggests that the role is one of simply providing the court with helpful arguments. But, rather analogous to the amicus appointments made by the Federal Court in Canada which are designed to assist the Court by presenting disclosure arguments in the interests of the defence in hearings under section 38 of the Canada Evidence Act, it seems that the amici appointed by FISC are given a specific role of providing to the court 'legal arguments that advance the protection of individual privacy and civil liberties', although they also have a role to provide the court with 'legal arguments or information regarding any other area relevant to the issue presented to the court'.[101] The legislation is couched in prescriptive terms *requiring* an appointment to be made where the Court is presented with a novel or significant interpretation of the law 'unless the court issues a finding that such appointment is not appropriate'.[102] In addition, the Court is also given the power to appoint an individual or organisation to serve as an amicus, including to provide technical expertise, in other instances which it deems appropriate or upon motion to permit an individual or organisation leave to file an amicus brief.[103] It does not seem that the court has made extensive use of these powers to date.[104] However, the provisions provide the potential for the court to take account of the views and positions outside government.

Examples of an inquiry, tribunal or amicus counsel given a specific brief to act as a devil's advocate can be found in certain UK procedures. First of all, it appears that on occasion, courts themselves have appointed counsel to act on their behalf in relation to PII matters. In *CM v SSHD*,[105] for example, the President of Upper Tribunals of the Immigration and Asylum Chamber rejected a request made by counsel for a special advocate to be appointed to represent the interests of the appellant before determining the outstanding issues of disclosure. The case concerned an adjudication on a claim for PII made by the Foreign Secretary in respect of material relating to an evaluation of political circumstances in Zimbabwe of potential relevance to the assessment of risk of return for those claiming asylum in the UK. The material did not relate to the appellant personally and the Tribunal President did not think it necessary to appoint a special advocate, but he did take the unusual step of asking the Attorney General to appoint an advocate to assist the Tribunal with respect to the resolution of the PII process

100 USA Freedom Act 2015 50 USC § 1803(i)(2)(A).
101 ibid §1803(i)(4).
102 ibid §1803 (i)(2)(A).
103 ibid §1803(i)(B).
104 In 2015 and 2016, there were only five instances when an amicus was appointed, none under the requirement to appoint where the court is presented with a novel and significant interpretation of the law. See Administrative Office of the US Courts, *Report of the Director on the Activities of the FIS Court* (2015) and (2016). See https://fas.org/irp/agency/doj/fisa/2015rept-aousc.pdf and https://fas.org/irp/agency/doj/fisa/2016rept-aousc.pdf.
105 *CM v SSHD* [2013] UKUT 59.

and to determine whether any material should be disclosed to the appellant. The decision seemed dictated largely by the volume of material to be processed over the Long Vacation and the need to prevent the Tribunal delaying in its final determination. But the process had the effect of ensuring that further material was supplied to the appellants before the start date of the appeals.

Another example is the role that counsel to the Tribunal have played before the Investigatory Powers Tribunal (IPT) whose function is to decide complaints of unlawful intrusion by public bodies, including the intelligence services. Although the Act establishing the Tribunal and the rules made thereunder originally made no mention of a counsel to the Tribunal,[106] the Tribunal's report for 2011–15 referred to the Tribunal having to sit in closed private hearings with the assistance of counsel to the Tribunal in order to consider points of law or other matters raised by the complainants.[107] One former special advocate who had acted in this capacity said that he had appeared in a couple of cases where the issues were entirely open but the Tribunal considered it would help the proceedings to have counsel to the Tribunal appointed.[108] The role that counsel to the Tribunal can play in proceedings was highlighted in one of the Tribunal's high profile cases where Liberty, Privacy International and other human rights and privacy interests groups claimed that regulations covering access by GCHQ to emails and phone records intercepted by the United States National Security Agency breached Articles 8 and 10 of the ECHR.[109] One of the issues raised was whether a special advocate should be appointed to represent the interests of claimants in the closed hearings. The Tribunal asked counsel to the Tribunal to make written submissions and these distinguished between the role of the special advocate and counsel to the Tribunal:[110]

> 15.1 A Special Advocate is appointed (normally, but not necessarily, pursuant to statute) to represent the interests of a party at hearings from which that party is excluded. A Special Advocate is required to be partisan. He or she makes submissions (if any) as he considers will advance the interests of the excluded party. If the Special Advocate reaches the view that it would not advance the interests of the excluded party to make submissions at all (as has happened in a few cases), then the proper course is to decline to make submissions at all, even though this leaves the Tribunal without assistance.
>
> 15.2 Counsel to the Tribunal performs a different function, akin to that of amicus curiae. His or her function is to assist the Tribunal in whatever way the Tribunal directs. Sometimes (eg in relation to issues on which all parties

106 See Regulation of Investigatory Powers Act 2000 Pt IV, and Investigatory Powers Tribunal Rules 2000.
107 *Investigatory Powers Tribunal Report 2011-2015* (2016) [2.8].
108 SA19, 12 April 2016.
109 *Liberty v GCHQ* [2014] UKIPTrib 13/77-H, [2015] HRLR 2.
110 ibid [8].

> are represented), the Tribunal will not specify from what perspective submissions are to be made. In these circumstances, counsel will make submissions according to his or her own analysis of the relevant factual issues, seeking to give particular emphasis to points not fully developed by the parties. At other times (in particular where one or more interests are not represented), the Tribunal may invite counsel to make submissions from a particular perspective (normally the perspective of the party or parties whose interests are not otherwise represented).

The role of counsel to the Tribunal was thus in principle distinct from that of a special advocate. The function of the former was to assist the Tribunal by performing such functions as she is directed by the Tribunal to perform and the precise roles may vary depending on the circumstances. Counsel to the Tribunal went on to conclude that in the present circumstances, there was a broad measure of agreement between the claimants and the respondents that counsel to the Tribunal could best assist the Tribunal by performing the following roles:[111]

> (i) identifying documents, parts of documents or gists that ought properly to be disclosed; (ii) making such submissions to the Tribunal in favour of disclosure as are in the interests of the Claimants and open justice; and (iii) ensuring that all the relevant arguments on the facts and the law are put before the Tribunal. In relation to (iii), the Tribunal will expect its counsel to make submissions from the perspective of the Claimants' interests (since the Respondents will be able to make their own submissions). If the Tribunal decides to receive closed oral evidence from one or more of the Respondent's witnesses, it may also direct its counsel to cross-examine them. In practice, the roles performed by counsel to the Tribunal at this stage of the current proceedings will be similar to those performed by a special advocate in closed material proceedings.

The IPT accepted that this was the correct analysis and approach and the government has enacted rules formalising the role of the counsel to the Tribunal along these lines.[112] The rules empower the Tribunal to appoint counsel to assist the Tribunal where the complainant is not legally represented; the respondent objects to the disclosure of documents or information to the complainant; the Tribunal intends to hold a hearing (in whole or in part) in the absence of the complainant; or in any other circumstance in which the Tribunal considers it appropriate to do so.[113] The rules go on to state that the Tribunal may request counsel to perform any of the functions outlined above in the submissions of counsel to the Tribunal and to perform any other function that would assist the

111 ibid [10] citing Counsel's written submission to the IPT [19.2].

112 See Investigatory Powers Tribunal Rules 2018, r 12.

113 ibid r 12(1).

Tribunal.[114] This formalisation of the role of counsel to the Tribunal makes it clear that counsel's role is to assist the Tribunal, akin to that of an amicus curiae, but in an interesting twist which would seem to bring the role somewhat closer to a special advocate, acting in the interests of the complainant, the rules require counsel to identify any arguable error of law in relation to any decision or determination made by the Tribunal consequent on a hearing held in the absence of the complainant and to notify the Tribunal of this, whereupon the Tribunal must disclose to the complainant the arguable error of law.[115]

This brings into focus the similarities and differences between the role of counsel to the Tribunal and a special advocate. Calls were made for David Anderson, the Independent Reviewer on Terrorism, to recommend in his report on investigatory powers that the IPT should have available to it special advocates to represent the interest of affected persons. However, Anderson decided not to make a recommendation on this. He concluded that there was an argument that the nature of IPT cases reduced the need for an advocate to be able to take instructions on behalf of the claimant and there was also a strong belief in some quarters that counsel to the Tribunal was capable of having more influence in IPT procedures than would be attainable by a special advocate.[116]

A counsel who had acted as counsel to the Tribunal drew a number of contrasts between the role of such counsel and that of special advocates. There was no bar on counsel to the Tribunal communicating with open representatives and equally he could speak to the Tribunal and raise points with them without the government knowing, as any counsel to an inquiry can do. This meant that they had more clout over the government than a special advocate would have in terms of getting access to information.

> If I'm asking for information, or for them to provide clarification, the government may say well, essentially, this is being asked on behalf of the tribunal. And if we're not going to provide it now, the tribunal are going to ask for it. If there is a closed hearing, then this is something that's going to be pushed in closed cross-examination.[117]

This leads on to the question whether a more inquisitorial-type inquiry with inquiry counsel appointed might be able to achieve more in terms of getting access to information than an adversarial process involving special advocates. One government counsel drew attention to the role of the parliamentary Intelligence Security Committee in conducting investigations, which is a more paper-based

114 ibid r 12(2).
115 ibid r 12(3)(4).
116 D Anderson, *A Question of Trust: Report of the Investigatory Powers Review* (2015) [14.108].
117 SA19, 12 April 2016.

process but can be quite effective in ferreting out information by means of dialogue with the agencies.[118] As he put it, however:

> The difficulty is that to be really effective you want to be able to get the desk officers and the investigators from the field or whatever, get them in and just talk to them. And that's very difficult because it takes them away from their real work. And there are issues about how forthcoming they will feel like being and how nervous they will feel about the process.[119]

But this counsel said that when an inquiry goes completely into closed, there can be a different feeling about the willingness of people to speak openly. He gave the example of the Rosemary Nelson inquiry in Northern Ireland which was established to investigate the circumstances surrounding the murder of a solicitor in Northern Ireland after allegations were made of collusion between British security forces and paramilitaries in her murder.[120] He said he had heard that once the intelligence officers

> felt they were in a kind of safe space, the quality of the information they gave was much better. But if you were to add that on to an adversarial process, they may feel that if I say something there's going to be an attempt to pull it over into open and there will be a reluctance there.[121]

The difficulty, of course, with more inquisitorial closed procedures, is that although they may be more effective in getting to the truth of certain issues, they move away from any idea of open parties having their interests represented.

The different models re-appraised

This chapter has considered different kinds of security-cleared models that have been employed in various jurisdictions. At the beginning of the chapter, we invoked the New Zealand Law Commission's spectrum for handling sensitive information in legal processes which ranged, at one extreme, from completely open adversarial processes of justice to completely closed inquisitorial processes at the other extreme. We suggested that the various security-cleared counsel models that had been employed could be fitted into this spectrum, with the 'own-counsel' undertaking confidentiality model at the more adversarial end of the spectrum, the amicus/inquiry/court counsel model more at the inquisitorial end and the special advocate model lying in the middle. This characterisation aligns due process or natural justice with adversarial processes of justice and concern for

118 GC3, 29 February 2016.
119 ibid.
120 *The Rosemary Nelson Inquiry Report* (HC 2011, 947).
121 ibid.

security with processes of inquisitorial justice, suggesting that the policy choices determining whether to adopt a more adversarial or inquisitorial process with either, respectively, an 'own-counsel' or inquiry model of security-cleared counsel depends simply on how much weight we wish to give to due process or to national security.

Having considered in more depth a number of different security-cleared advocate models situated in different types of legal proceedings, this appears to be a somewhat over-simplistic approach. Rather than simply reflecting a choice being made as to the weight to be given to due process or national security, the type of security-cleared model used, if any, may depend on a number of factors, such as what the proceedings are ultimately designed to achieve, the interests at stake and which type fits best within the procedural legal culture of the system as a whole. We can return at this point to Damaška's distinction between policy-implementing and conflict-resolving processes that we mentioned in Chapter 6. The former processes are associated with an activist state which structures legal proceedings so as to permit a search for the best policy response to a particular event, while the latter are associated with a reactivist state which structures legal proceedings around a conflict between two parties. Inevitably, as Damaška said, the former type of proceedings cognate to what is conventionally termed 'inquisitorial' or 'non-adversarial' proceedings while the latter cognate to 'adversarial' proceedings, although he was reluctant to use such terms because they can carry misleading connotations.[122]

We have seen that there was a view expressed in the *Al Rawi* litigation, though not one shared by all the judges, that in proceedings where the judge is called upon to sit as an 'arbiter' between claimants – as in that case where a claim for damages was made against a number of state agencies – there was such a fundamental principle at stake that the parties should see and hear all the evidence that is seen and heard by the court that it was not for the courts to override it by ordering a CMP without parliamentary authority.[123] Different considerations, however, may apply to cases where the proceedings not only concern the interests of the parties to the litigation but also have a significant effect on a third party, or where a wider public interest is engaged, such as where the case directly impinges on the interests of a child, or where there is an overriding public interest to protect the public as in parole proceedings. SIAC proceedings may also be put into this category, as SIAC is a specialist court invested with a public interest duty not to disclose information that may harm the public interest in its implementation of immigration policy, with the result that it is required to import procedures that are less adversarial than more conventional civil and criminal proceedings.

This is not to say that in proceedings classified as a 'lis inter partes', there may not be other considerations than those to do purely with the parties involved

122 M R Damaška, *The Faces of Justice and State Authority* (Yale UP 1986) 87.

123 Chapter 3. See *Al Rawi v The Security Service* [2010] EWCA Civ 482, [2011] UKSC 34, [2012] 1 AC 531.

which may dictate something other than a purely adversarial approach. PII claims sometimes necessitating ex parte applications are now accepted in both civil proceedings and criminal proceedings. In rejecting the view that a court can *never* adopt a CMP (subject to appropriate safeguards) in a claim in tort for damages, Lord Clarke in *Al Rawi* considered that the boundaries between, for example, private law claims and judicial review actions are often blurred.[124] The question in *Al Rawi* was what to do when the public interest was already engaged by the minister using a public interest immunity certificate. Parliament has, of course, since legislated to permit CMPs in civil proceedings like *Al Rawi*. Once the principle of CMPs in these types of civil proceedings is conceded, the question then becomes what type of security-cleared counsel should be deployed to act in the interests of the claimant in what is fundamentally still a private law action. In order to comport as closely with the equality of arms necessitated by a conflict-resolving process, it may be thought that civil claimants ought to be able to have their interests represented in closed procedures by a security-cleared counsel of their own choice with whom they are able to communicate and instruct even after such a counsel sees the closed material. Conversely, it may be thought that in procedures which have at their core the need to implement public policy, the interests of excluded parties can be adequately represented by an amicus, court or inquiry counsel who can ensure that the perspective of such parties is brought to bear upon the trial, without, however, necessitating such parties having to be represented by a separate security-cleared lawyer. The more central a party's interest is to the proceedings as a whole, the more such a party can claim the need for a security-cleared lawyer with the exclusive function of representing that party's interest in any closed procedure that is deemed necessary.

Rather than viewing the choice of security-cleared advocate along a spectrum which is singularly concerned with what weight to give to due process or the protection of security, we may adapt Table 10.1 above by separating out the types of procedures involved from the competing value preferences of natural justice and protection of security, so as to create two axes reflecting on a horizontal level different types of proceedings (from 'adversarial' at one end to 'inquisitorial' at the other) and on a vertical level the value preferences attached to natural justice at one end and protection of security at another. The different models of security-cleared counsel then fall into four boxes as seen below in Figure 10.1.

A purely functional approach which takes account of what proceedings are designed to achieve might suggest that only two models of security-cleared counsel are necessary – one acting exclusively for the client, appropriate for more adversarial proceedings, and the other acting for the court, but with a mandate to represent the excluded parties' interest or perspective in more inquisitorial-type proceedings. This view would seem to leave little room for the special advocate model. But in fact it may be that this model offers ways in which due process and national security concerns can be accommodated within the overall

124 *Al Rawi v The Security Service* [2011] UKSC 34, [2012] 1 AC 531 [170].

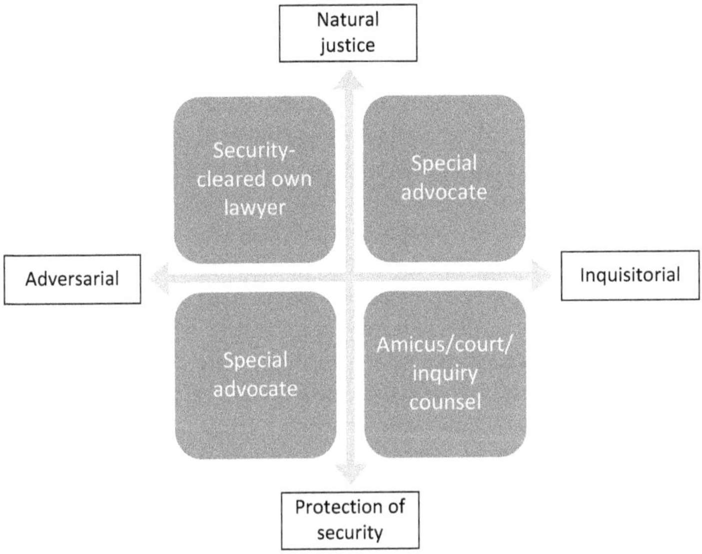

Figure 10.1 Appropriateness of different models of security-cleared lawyer.

purpose of what the proceedings are designed to achieve. The advantage of the special advocate model to those in adversarial-type proceedings who are suspicious about the capacity of the system to protect information leaking out from security-cleared lawyers to their clients (in a system which values the confidential relationship between lawyer and client) is that it professes to represent the interests of excluded parties in closed procedures without depriving them of their own lawyers to represent them in the open proceedings. Of course, from another perspective, it is the very ability of a special advocate to represent the interests of such a party that is called into question when she is removed from the professional-client relationship. It may be argued that instead of this model, the excluded party should be provided with a security-cleared lawyer who is able to remain in communication with her after the lawyer views the closed material. This may require large resources being put into protecting security by providing the lawyer with a network of support such as access to court-appointed officers who can advise the lawyer on what can be communicated to their client. Conversely, to those who are suspicious in inquisitorial-type proceedings about the capacity of the system to give counsel to the inquiry the freedom and flexibility to represent the interests of excluded parties and give them any meaningful due process, the special advocate model offers at least an actor who is fully committed to representing their interests. From another perspective, however, it is the very concern in such proceedings that a special advocate *will* instil an adversarial element into the proceedings that may tilt the choice of advocate to put the excluded party's point of view in favour of an amicus or counsel to the inquiry models so as to encourage the intelligence services to be more forthcoming about disclosing what may be essential for an inquiry dedicated to finding the truth.

The special advocate model may also offer advantages in accommodating certain cultural factors which have to be taken into account in shaping choices as to what procedures to adopt and what type of actors to deploy in legal proceedings. We have seen that such a model may fit better into certain common law systems than others. A view was expressed that the special advocate system would be hard to transplant on to American soil. It would seem that there is a strong agency culture within the legal profession there whereby legal professionals identify strongly with their clients and develop enduring links with them, whether as prosecutors on behalf of the government or as defence lawyers on behalf of criminal defendants. This makes it difficult to conceive of a special advocate appointed by the government who is truly able to act solely in the interests of defendants. If in the US system, agency becomes impossible because a party is unaware of the proceedings – as in the FISC, for example – then it is better to have the court appoint an advocate to act in their interests, as can now happen. Similarly, we have seen the court can appoint a 'standby' counsel in criminal cases to represent the interests of defendants who refuse to be represented by counsel.

Within the UK, by contrast, the cab rank principle which has endured within the Bar makes it possible for barristers to represent very different clients from case to case. A certain distance from the client becomes inevitable in such a system. It is possible to see how the special advocate system has been able to develop in this climate. The special advocate appointed by the Attorney General but chosen from a list by the excluded party to represent their interests in the case is not so very different from the way in which she might be chosen from other lists to represent clients in other cases. The special advocate may be tainted and unable to engage with certain other clients, thus fettering the advocate in a manner that seems to infringe the cab rank principle.[125] But the special advocate is still able to act as an ordinary advocate in other cases. The service provided in each case is advocacy in the party's interest and once the case is over, the advocate may go on to represent a completely different client in another case.

We may conclude by suggesting that it is possible to mark out a role for each model of security-cleared counsel to play in representing the interests of excluded parties in closed procedures. But there is no necessarily correct model to be employed in each type of proceeding, as the choice of model will involve a judgement, not only as to where the proceedings are situated and how the interests of natural justice and national security are to be accommodated along the two axes but also which will fit best within the wider legal professional culture in which the model is situated and how effectively each model will operate within this culture. There remains the question, however, whether *any* model can ever be truly

125 A Boon and S Nash, 'Special Advocacy: Political Expediency and Legal Roles in Modern Judicial Systems' (2006) 9 *Legal Ethics* 101, 112.

justified, as each involves derogating from fundamental tenets of the adversarial tradition, not only, as we have seen, from the principles of open and natural justice but also from the principles of party autonomy and confidentiality between lawyer and client. In the final chapter, we return to this issue as we consider the future of special advocacy.

11 The future of special advocates

Although we looked at other models of security-cleared counsel in the last chapter, we have seen that special advocates have now become an increasingly recognised part of the legal landscape in a number of jurisdictions. In England and Wales, it was considered at first that they would only be used in the very exceptional context of providing persons who had been subject to deportation orders on national security grounds with some means of challenging such decisions in the courts. They can now be deployed across a range of administrative, civil and criminal proceedings and they have been exported beyond the shores of the UK to other common law jurisdictions including Canada, New Zealand and Hong Kong, as well as to Scandinavian jurisdictions. New Zealand is the latest country which is actively considering whether their use should be extended, as in the UK, beyond appeals in immigration cases to criminal and civil proceedings as well.

While they may not yet have much of a public profile, a sure sign of a heightened awareness of them in the public consciousness is to be seen in the fact that they are creeping into fiction as well as real life. In an apparent reference to the then-impending Justice and Security Act 2013 permitting closed procedures in civil cases, one of the protagonists in John le Carré's 2013 novel *A Delicate Truth* who risks being exposed as one of the architects of a botched counter-terror operation is advised that, should he elect to bring a suit against the government which would be naturally his 'good right … then the resultant hearing would be conducted by a hand-picked group of approved lawyers, some of whom do their best to speak *for* you'. But '*you* the *claimant* would be banished from the court while the government presented its case to the judge without the inconvenience of a direct challenge by you or your representatives …'.[1]

As we saw in Chapter 1, the rise of special advocates can be attributed to the need to find a mechanism that can protect parties' rights to a fair trial against the background of the growing use of intelligence in courts and the consequent need to protect sources from the risks that would arise from routine disclosure. The attraction of special advocates to governments is that, if they are judged to meet international human rights fair trial standards, their use in closed procedures can

1 J le Carré, *A Delicate Truth* (Viking 2013) 295 (emphasis in original).

operate to allow sensitive information to be put before a court that would otherwise be excluded.[2] By and large, we have seen that they have been endorsed by the ECtHR as a sufficient counterbalancing mechanism to compensate excluded parties for the lack of full disclosure of the allegations and evidence against them, so long as an irreducible core minimum of disclosure is provided in certain cases.

This innovation has not, however, ended the controversy. It was universally acknowledged by all the experienced professionals interviewed in this research that special advocates did a very difficult and challenging job as well as they could and that they were completely dedicated to acting in the interests of excluded parties. There remains deep unease, however, not least amongst special advocates themselves, about the legitimacy of their use. This raises a set of normative questions, quite apart from whether the use of special advocates satisfies human rights norms. The first of these is whether there is something fundamentally objectionable in principle about the use of special advocates which goes against the common law adversarial tradition. We have seen that in *Al Rawi v Security Service*,[3] a majority of the members of the Supreme Court refused to consider that the courts had an inherent jurisdiction to authorise closed procedures with special advocates in a common law civil claim, because they felt that such procedures undermined key tenets of justice which the courts had spent centuries defending. This raises the question whether the use of special advocates per se goes against long-established traditions of adversarial justice. The strength of a great tradition is that it can adapt to innovation and in the context of the common law which has been so open to practical considerations, it has been said that unpredictability is one of its few predictable features.[4] It was interesting to observe in the course of this research that there was something of a contrast between the cautious attitude of senior judges in the higher courts towards the use of special advocates in CMPs and the more positive attitude of judges on the ground with direct experience of working with them within closed procedures which appear quite inimical to adversarial justice.

Assuming that the use of special advocates is not considered wholly unacceptable, a second question then emerges: in what circumstances may they be employed? Here we come to the different types of cases in which special advocate procedures have been deployed. We have seen that special advocates can operate in many different contexts across administrative, criminal and civil processes. Is there a line then that can be drawn between when they should and should not be used?

Finally, if we accept that there are legitimate uses of special advocates and if they are to become an enduring institution in our justice system, we need to consider how special advocate systems could be improved, drawing on what

2 See New Zealand Law Commission, *The Crown in Court: A review of the Crown Proceedings Act and national security information in proceedings* (NZLC R135, 2015) [9.1].
3 *Al-Rawi v The Security Service* [2011] UKSC 34, [2012] 1 AC 531.
4 *Al-Rawi v The Security Service* [2010] EWCA Civ 482 [69] (Lord Neuberger MR).

special advocates have said previously on the record and in this research and from comparative experience elsewhere. We have seen that best practice is a concept that needs to be handled with care, as there may be different cultural expectations of what is best practice within different jurisdictions. However, there may be achievable improvements which might lend greater legitimacy to what is still a fledgling institution.

Special advocates and the adversarial tradition

The question of justifying special advocates has tended to focus on whether they provide enough compensation for the use of closed procedures that strike at the heart of the core adversarial values of open and natural justice. But special advocates may subvert the notion of adversarial justice even more directly. Adversarial procedure, for some, is not just a mode of litigation but is fundamentally linked to notions such as dignity and the rule of law, in terms of giving individuals an opportunity to participate in proceedings to which they are subject.[5] Fundamentally, the adversarial tradition involves a mode of proceeding which gives parties to a dispute considerable control over the way in which they wish to present their case, rather than handing control of the process over to adjudicators. While the introduction of professional lawyers has arguably reduced the procedural autonomy of parties,[6] adversarialism remains dedicated to the notion that parties must be able to make key autonomous choices over how to participate in the proceedings. In the criminal context particularly, this is why the presence of the accused is so essential and why the adversarial tradition looks askance at the notion which is accepted in continental jurisdictions and in certain international criminal proceedings (for example, in the Special Tribunal for Lebanon) of any trial or proceedings taking place in absentia.[7] But it is not just the presence of the defendant that is required; she must also be competent to make the key decisions required of an active participant. Without a competent accused, the trial cannot proceed at all. Hence the need to determine, if there is doubt, whether an accused is fit to plead in the first place before a trial can take place. If an accused is deemed unfit to plead in England and Wales a hearing, not a trial, will take place to determine whether 'he did the act or made the omission charged against him as the offence', but not, as in a trial, whether he is guilty.[8] In such a hearing, counsel is appointed by the court rather like a special counsel 'to put the case for

5 See eg J Waldron, 'How Law Protects Dignity' (2012) 71 CLJ 200.

6 See Chapter 6. See also L Farmer, 'Criminal Responsibility and the Proof of Guilt' in M Dubber and L Farmer (eds), *Modern Histories of Crime and Punishment* (Stanford University Press 2007) 42, 58.

7 Note though that the right to be present at one's trial can be waived by the accused. See *R v Hayward; R v Jones; R v Purvis* [2001] QB 862.

8 Criminal Procedure (Insanity) Act 1964 s 4A(2) inserted by the Criminal Procedure (Insanity and Unfitness to Plead) Act 1991. Cf *R v H* [2003] UKHL 1, [2003] 1 WLR 411 where the House of Lords held that proceedings under s 4 which determine whether a defendant is unfit

the defence', but it can be argued that the proceedings no longer qualify as an adversarial criminal trial because it is not a process in which the defendant is called to answer the charges against him.[9]

With the notion of an autonomous party able to make key decisions tied so centrally to the adversarial trial, the idea that special counsel might be appointed during the trial to represent the interests of the accused without owing any responsibility to her would seem quite inimical to the adversarial tradition. It is true that counsel chosen by the accused or appointed to represent the accused can be given the authority to make many decisions on behalf of the accused that may be key to the outcome of the proceedings. But counsel here is acting, at least in theory, on the authority of the accused who can dismiss her at any point and decide to appoint a different counsel or represent himself instead. The United States Supreme Court in *US v Faretta* famously recognised that the accused has a constitutional right to represent himself, holding that:[10]

> The language and spirit of the Sixth Amendment contemplate that counsel, like the other defense tools guaranteed by the Sixth Amendment, shall be an aid to a willing defendant – not an organ of the state interposed between an unwilling defendant and his right to defend himself personally. To thrust counsel upon the accused, against his considered wish, thus violates the logic of the Amendment.

There is, however, an alternative narrative which does not tie the adversarial tradition so closely to the need to preserve the defendant's autonomous decision-making throughout the trial. This narrative does not challenge the importance of values such as autonomy per se but argues that within the institutional context of the state taking action against the individual and depriving her of basic political rights, it is meaningless to speak of the individual possessing the kind of autonomy that she otherwise would or ought to enjoy.[11] As philosophers such as Raz have argued, autonomy requires more than being mentally competent; it requires independence and the ability to choose among an adequate range of valuable options in order to enjoy the 'good life'.[12] These conditions do not so clearly pertain in judicial proceedings where individuals are being prosecuted or are challenging state actions that have been taken against them. In these circumstances, institutional safeguards are required to counterbalance the full might of the state which bears down on them.

---

to plead and under s 4A do not involve the 'determination of a charge' within the meaning of art 6 ECHR.

9 See A Duff, L Farmer, S Marshall and V Tadros, *The Trial on Trial (3): Towards a Normative Theory of the Criminal Trial* (Hart 2007) 132.

10 *US v Faretta* 422 US 806, 820 (1975).

11 R E Toone, 'The Incoherence of Defendant Autonomy' (2005) 83 *North Carolina Law Review* 621, 650.

12 J Raz, *The Morality of Freedom* (OUP 1986) 154, 378.

It was the majority's acknowledgement in *Faretta* that protecting the defendant's right to self-representation could lead to the dangers of unjust convictions that motivated Blackmun J's dissent. He could not agree to such 'a drastic curtailment of the interest of the State in seeing that justice is done in a real and objective sense'.[13] One way of promoting this interest is to require that an accused's best possible case should be presented to the court. This involves more than simply aligning adversariality with the party's wishes. Although due regard may be given to these wishes, in order for the best possible case to be presented, the accused needs to be assisted by counsel whose role is elevated beyond simply being a mouthpiece for the party to encapsulate a duty to take advantage of all the tools that are available to present the best case. The duty to act in the best interests of the client, which is a core duty enshrined in the Bar Code of Conduct,[14] would seem to entail exercising professional judgement to put forward a defence even when the client does not wish the defence to be raised.[15]

A second feature of modern adversarial proceedings also reduces the procedural autonomy of the parties to the dispute. Increasing recognition has been given to the interests of other parties. Once litigation is viewed less as a dispute between two adversaries and more as a process that has to cater for a range of different interests, then adversariality has to adapt to providing institutional safeguards for enabling parties' interests to be represented without losing sight of other interests that must accommodated. An example in the criminal trial process has been the growing realisation of the need to give weight to the interests of complainants in sex cases and certain other cases as well. Parliament has circumscribed the accused's autonomy by taking away her right to cross-examine complainants personally.[16] The principle of fair or humane treatment does not apply uniquely to the defendant, but must apply to other citizens involved in the proceedings against the defendant.[17] However, in recognition of the paramount need to ensure that the interests of the defence are protected so as to safeguard against a wrongful conviction, adversariality has been preserved in the trial by enabling the court to appoint counsel to cross-examine the complainant. An appointed counsel is not responsible personally to the defendant and may be imposed over the objection of the defendant.[18]

Special advocates or counsel coming in to represent the interests of parties who are unable for whatever reason to represent their own interests is a fairly recent innovation that it seems the adversarial tradition is having to embrace. In the case

13 *US v Faretta* 422 US 806, 851 (1975).

14 Code of Conduct, CD2, r C15.

15 The Code of Conduct, r C20 states that a barrister must use his own professional judgment notwithstanding the views of the lay client.

16 See Youth Justice and Criminal Evidence Act 1999, ss 35–37.

17 See A Zuckerman and P Roberts, *Criminal Evidence* (2nd edn OUP 2010) 21–22, I Dennis, 'The Right to Confront Witnesses: Meanings, Myths and Human Rights' [2010] *Criminal Law Review* 255, 260.

18 Youth Justice and Criminal Evidence Act 1999, s 38(5).

of an incompetent accused who is unfit to plead, the Law Commission has proposed that hearings to determine whether the accused person did the act charged against him should be reconstituted as an 'alternative finding procedure', involving consideration of actus reus and mens rea elements of the relevant offence, as well as defences.[19] Such a procedure appears to resemble a criminal trial in all but name, with a counsel representing the interests of the accused who is unable to represent herself. If the concept of a special counsel cannot be opposed simply on the grounds that it undermines the principle of party autonomy, then this takes us back to the question of when, if ever, their use in closed procedures may be justified.

Justifying the use of special advocates

The paradigm of a fair, adversarial legal hearing of a dispute has been said to be one which enables the court or tribunal to deal with the case justly in a context in which, so far as is practicable, the parties to the dispute are on an equal footing.[20] Several distinctive features would seem to be core to the paradigm. First of all, dealing with a case justly requires in a case involving the state that the court is independent enough to make rulings that do not defer unduly to the executive. Secondly, the parties must be afforded substantial participation in the proceedings, which includes at the very least knowledge of the case against them. Thirdly, in order to provide assurance that justice is being done, the paradigm requires transparency not only to the parties but also to the public, mandating some public awareness of what is going on.

Closed procedures that exclude one of the parties and the public strike irretrievably at the heart of this paradigm. A court or tribunal sitting even with independent judicial members in closed procedures where a party to the dispute and the public is not present is likely to be substantially impeded in doing justice in terms of reaching a correct result because there will be inadequate testing of partisan arguments and evidence. Even if such a court or tribunal were able to reach the correct result, the failure to involve a party fully in the proceedings offends the dignitarian value that parties ought to be able to participate in proceedings that affect their interest.[21] Moreover, even if the parties are allowed to participate in the proceedings, the failure to hold proceedings in an open forum confronts a deep ideological preference underpinning the adversarial paradigm which is suspicious of justice being conducted behind closed doors, especially when the executive is one of the parties to the proceedings. In the words of one commentator,

19 Law Commission, *Unfitness to Plead Volume 1: Report* (Law Com No 364, 2016).

20 D Bonner, *Executive Measures, Terrorism and National Security* (Ashgate 2007) 37, 276. Note that both the Civil Rules of Procedure (CPR) and the Criminal Rules of Procedure (Crim PR) state that the overriding objective is to deal with cases 'justly' (CPR 1; Crim PR 1.1(1)). In the case of the CPR, this includes 'ensuring that the parties are on an equal footing'. In the case of the Crim PR, it includes 'dealing with the prosecution and defence fairly'.

21 See A Zuckerman, *Zuckerman's Civil Procedure* (3rd edn Sweet & Maxwell 2013) 944.

a closed procedure 'robs court decisions of their ability to command public confidence'.[22]

If the reality of much modern litigation, however, is that it is not so much a dispute between two parties (lis inter partes) and more a process which has to accommodate a number of different interests at stake, then this can sometimes justify information being held back from a party. In the last chapter, Chapter 10, we saw that there is a variety of different civil proceedings that cannot be described as a 'lis inter partes'. Chapter 3 distinguished between the use of special advocates in certain types of proceedings where it has already been accepted that a party could not be present and their use in closed procedures where rights to be present were being eroded. In considering the types of proceedings where special advocates may be justified, it is convenient to distinguish between criminal proceedings, proceedings involving judicial scrutiny of executive measures, and conventional civil proceedings.

Criminal proceedings

Criminal proceedings are sometimes characterised as the archetypical dispute between the state and the individual requiring proceedings to be as transparent as possible. But even here, as we have seen, there are occasions when the public, and sometimes also the accused, has been excluded. As prosecutors have been required to disclose more information to the defence in criminal proceedings, other interests such as the need to secure the safety of informants and potential witnesses have generated PII applications that exempt prosecutors from having to make full disclosure. When special counsel are appointed to represent the interests of the defence in PII hearings which defendants and their counsel cannot attend, it is hard to argue that they pose a significant threat to the modern adversarial trial, especially since their role is limited to arguing for greater disclosure to the defence of 'unused material' rather than taking over the running of the case from the defendant and regular counsel.[23] It is true that the question of disclosure and substantive issues in the trial can sometimes become blurred, as in entrapment cases where a special counsel might be invited to assess an arguable case for entrapment based on material undisclosed to the defence. If there is, the judge can order disclosure of the material so that the issue can then be fully litigated. If, on the other hand, there is no potentially useful material bearing on whether an individual was improperly encouraged or enticed into committing a crime, there would be no purpose in revealing it.[24] The key point, however is that in

22 ibid 946.

23 See *R v Austin* [2013] EWCA Crim 1028, where in an abuse of process case, it was argued on appeal that the trial judge should have appointed a special counsel to deal with disclosure issues but not to deal with the substantive issue of abuse of process itself, as it was wrong for any substantive issue in criminal proceedings to be decided on the basis of information which is not communicated to the defendant.

24 SA14, 5 February 2016.

these circumstances the presence of special counsel actually *enhances* adversariality by enabling defence interests to be represented. We have seen that the use of security-cleared counsel is common in terrorist prosecutions in the US because of the amount of classified information generated by investigations. In its final report, the New Zealand Law Commission recommended that a special advocate be used in a pre-trial hearing on the question of non-disclosure of national security information.[25] Although such counsel are a rare phenomenon in UK prosecutions, where PII applications are made for a large amount of closed material, the judge might benefit from having representations made on behalf of the defence indicating its relevance to the defence case.

There may be other instances where special counsel could help advance the interests of the defence in criminal prosecutions. One scenario in England and Wales is where anonymity orders are sought by the prosecution for certain witnesses and it is necessary to test whether the criteria for making the order are made out.[26] Here the role of special counsel is not simply to argue for greater disclosure of information potentially bearing on witness reliability, but also to make submissions on the merits of making an order in the first place. One special advocate revealed in interview that he had acted as defence counsel for a 13 year old accused in a murder case where the prosecution relied on a number of anonymous witnesses.[27] Five or six young witnesses from an estate in East London were to give evidence anonymously and he applied to the judge for the appointment of special counsel to determine, first of all, whether an anonymity order should be made and, secondly, to what extent there should be disclosure of misconduct and other material relevant to the account they were going to give. According to this interviewee, a great deal of information that would not otherwise have been disclosed was revealed about these witnesses in a redacted and anonymised form, and the accused was ultimately acquitted of murder in that case.

Arguments can be made for greater use of special counsel in cases involving extensions of detention under the Terrorism Act 2000.[28] This raises the question whether special counsel could be deployed in other situations where ex parte applications are made for certain kinds of pre-trial measures such as search warrants or surveillance warrants. There is already a practice whereby independent counsel instructed by the police are appointed to be present during the execution of a search warrant in cases where there may be legally privileged material outside the scope of the warrant.[29] Although independent counsel are instructed by the police, they are in effect acting in the interests of those subject to such warrants. Although not appointed by the Attorney General as special counsel, they

25 New Zealand Law Commission (n 2) [8.21]–[8.26].

26 See Coroners and Justice Act 2009, s 86 and *Guidelines on the Prosecutor's Role in Applications for Witness Anonymity Orders: Criminal Evidence (Witness Anonymity) Act* D.

27 SA14, 5 February 2016.

28 See Chapter 3.

29 See *R (A and B) v Central Criminal Court and Chief Constable of West Midlands Police* [2017] EWHC 70 (Admin).

effectively act in a parallel fashion.[30] In Chapter 4, we observed that independent counsel have been appointed by the ICC to play a similar kind of role. We also saw that in certain Australian states, Public Interest Monitors have been appointed to introduce an element of adversariality into ex parte police applications for search warrants and surveillance warrants. The monitor is tasked with appearing at any application for a surveillance warrant or covert search warrant to test the validity of the application. For that purpose, the monitor questions applicants, examines or cross-examines any witness and makes submissions on the appropriateness of granting the application. The New Zealand Law Commission has recommended that where the disclosure of grounds for a search or surveillance warrant may prejudice national security, the person subject to the warrant should be able to challenge it through a special advocate.[31] In Denmark and Sweden, security-vetted 'privacy' advocates are appointed in certain cases to represent the interest of parties targeted by surveillance measures.[32] These are all examples of situations where adversariality is enhanced by the appointment of an independent counsel to represent designated interests. It is an open question which mode of security-cleared counsel is more appropriate in ex parte applications of this kind – a special advocate, a court appointed advocate or a public interest monitor. These are not adversarial proceedings per se and the role here is more one of assisting the court in testing the grounds for the measure than one of representing the interests of a party to the proceedings. As we noted in Chapter 10, the Investigatory Powers Tribunal has adopted this model rather than a special advocate mechanism.

Judicial scrutiny of executive measures

We have seen that special advocates have been increasingly used in CMPs where individuals challenge executive measures taken against them. In the UK, a large number of these proceedings have involved immigration measures that are heard in SIAC, which was originally established to give individuals an effective judicial remedy against such measures. In addition, the High Court has heard challenges on issues that can range in seriousness from the revocation of an individual's passport to the use of control orders and TPIMs placing severe restrictions on an individual's freedom. These proceedings are not purely adversarial in the conventional sense of being 'lis inter partes' proceedings. They have to balance a 'triangulation' of interests, protecting the public, protecting the excluded party and protecting the disclosure of information that may harm the public interest. But it can be argued that those who are deprived of fundamental rights as a result of the coercive measures of the state must have the opportunity to challenge such measures in a judicial process which conforms to the core adversarial features we

30 *R (Faisaltex Ltd) v Crown Court at Preston* [2008] EWHC 2832 (Admin) [82]–[83].
31 New Zealand Law Commission (n 2), [8.14]–[8.19].
32 See L B Langsted, P Garde and V Greve, *Criminal Law in Denmark* (3rd edn Djoef Publishing 2011) 156.

identified earlier.[33] In their comparative study of security-cleared counsel who operate in closed procedures where individuals' liberty is at stake, Vladeck and Cole found that, despite improvements, all systems shared common problems that made their implementation 'inescapably flawed'.[34]

First of all, Vladeck and Cole pointed to the difficulty cleared counsel have in challenging executive assessments that disclosure would harm national security. Their very presence may have the perverse effect of lending legitimacy to a system that relies heavily on undisclosed evidence and reduces the pressure to declassify.[35] There seems to have been a trend in the UK towards lower courts being less deferential to executive assessments, especially where tribunals like SIAC include members with national security expertise. But such tribunals are also dependent on special advocates having the time and resources to do the 'leg work', first of all, in satisfying themselves that they have access to all the relevant closed material and then making arguments for more open disclosure. We noted different practices operating between Canada and the UK in terms of disclosing closed material to special advocates. In Canada, special advocates have been able to gain access to the full intelligence file. In the UK, it is left to government counsel to undertake an exculpatory review. In principle, there appears to be an adversarial deficit in excluding special advocates from such reviews, as they may be able to determine better than government counsel what material is exculpatory from the point of view of the interests of the party they are representing. There is, of course, the national security interest that sensitive material should only be disclosed on a 'need to know' basis, and extending the role of exculpatory review to special advocates would widen the circle of those privy to such material. But if special advocates are security-vetted to the same level as government counsel, does the principle of equality of arms not dictate that they should be given all the closed information that government counsel see?

Special advocates themselves have not called for their responsibilities to be extended in this way. A further difficulty would be whether they have the time and resources to undertake such reviews. Special advocates do not have the benefit of solicitors to instruct them. But it would appear that the exculpatory review is one that government counsel conduct themselves as part of their role as independent counsel. Why then could special advocates not be given such a role as well by having access to whatever intelligence has been given to government counsel on the Secretary of State's side? At present, special advocates have to take it on trust that the Secretary of State has done a proper exculpatory review. Whilst none of the special advocates interviewed in this study impugned the ethical integrity of

33 See D Barak-Erez and M C Waxman, 'Secret Evidence and the Due Process of Terrorist Detentions' (2009) 48 *Columbia Journal of Transnational Law* 3, 37.

34 D Cole and S L Vladeck, 'Navigating the Shoals of Secrecy: A Comparative Analysis of the Use of Secret Evidence and 'Cleared Counsel' in the United States, the United Kingdom and Canada' in L Lazarus, C McCrudden and N Bowles (eds), *Reasoning Rights; Comparative Judicial Engagement* (OUP 2014) 161, 174.

35 ibid 175.

government counsel in any way, this does not address the need to ensure that there is an opportunity for as much adversarial testing of the evidence as is possible. Another matter is whether there could be greater equality of arms in terms of giving special advocates some direct assistance from national security experts.[36] As more experts with experience of closed procedures retire, a pool of experts is potentially becoming available comprising individuals who could theoretically provide assistance to special advocates as experts, provided they were willing to keep up their security clearance. The government's position has been that it is inappropriate for ex-intelligence officials to act as expert witnesses on behalf of the excluded party, but it seems to be quite content for such officials to sit as judicial members on the SIAC panel.[37]

The second problem identified by Cole and Vladeck was that it remained to be seen how far the gisting requirement imposed by the ECtHR, mandating some core minimum disclosure to individuals affected by closed procedures, could compensate for the denial of the right to be given notice of incriminating evidence.[38] The denial of such a right has fairness costs for the individual and the lack of adversarial testing that this entails could undermine the accuracy of the outcome. The question here, as the Canadian Supreme Court recognised in *Canada v Harkat*,[39] is whether special advocates with the gist provided are able to perform as a 'substantial substitute' for personal participation by the individual and his counsel. Much depends on the nature of the particular challenge to executive action. As one special advocate put it, 'you can't approach matters in a kind of monochrome fashion'.[40] In his view, it was highly problematic to say that a substantial measure of procedural justice can be achieved in closed procedures when a TPIM or a control order or detention pending deportation has been imposed on an individual. But even then:

> There may be differences in degree because some parts of the case may be based upon effectively closed, sensitive information but objective evidence in relation to which a special advocate may be just as well placed to comment as an open lawyer. So it's not a subject requiring client instructions to the same degree. And therefore the gap between that and the kind of tactics that will be employed if there was full disclosure may not be so great.[41]

The classic example suggested by this interviewee was where the central issue in an immigration deportation case concerns the question of safety of return. Unless

36 See the written submission of Lord Carlisle to HCCAC, *The Operation of the Special Immigration Appeals Commission (SIAC) and the Use of Special Advocates* (HC 2004-05, 323-1) Ev 39.

37 I owe this point to Sebastian Walker.

38 Cole and Vladeck (n 34) 175.

39 *Canada (Citizenship and Immigration) v Harkat* 2014 SCC 37, [2014] 2 SCR 33, [47].

40 SA12, 14 January 2016.

41 ibid.

there is a risk to a particular individual's safety on return, many of the issues can be dealt with 'pretty generically' without reference to specific individuals.

But when, by contrast, the issues do concern actions allegedly taken by the individual concerned, the lack of full disclosure can be a real problem. Many immigration cases do not require any core minimum of disclosure at all. Even when a core minimum of disclosure is required, there are, as we have seen, difficulties of interpretation as to what such a core minimum comprises, and there remain further obstacles barring special advocates from communicating effectively with the excluded individual. Special advocates do seem to be quite successful in getting more material gisted after the first gist, but the problem at this stage is that the special advocate will have gone into closed and can no longer consult directly with the excluded party and his counsel as she might have been able to do initially. The excluded party can, of course, continue to give instructions to the special advocate through his counsel, but there is no opportunity for vital two-way communication unless permission is granted by the government side. If the whole purpose of the gist is to enable the excluded party to convey adequate instructions to the special advocate as well as to their own counsel, then the rule prohibiting communications clearly limits the manner in which the special advocate can be instructed. Comparative experience provides some guidance here. In Canada, the special advocate can make an ex parte application to the judge to communicate with the affected party without the government being made aware of the nature of the communications. The New Zealand Law Commission has recommended that the court should oversee such communications without the government being notified of them. A further innovation to prevent the judge in the case inferring something prejudicial against the affected party from the nature of the communications would be to permit the special advocate to make the application to a different judge. There is some precedent for involving other judges in disclosure decisions. In Northern Ireland, for example, disclosure judges are appointed when PII applications are made in non-jury criminal cases so as to avoid prejudicial information being seen by the trial judge.[42] A more radical suggestion would be to allow special advocates direct access to intelligence officers, as cleared lawyers have in the US, who could advise them on a privileged basis on what can and what cannot be communicated to the excluded party and their counsel. In the end, the question whether or not the threshold of 'substantial substitution' is reached would seem to require a very fact-specific judgement to be made in each individual case, turning on the amount of closed information, the extent to which it can be gisted and whether the special advocate can receive effective instructions from the excluded party.

A third feature of closed procedures that cleared counsel are unable to ameliorate, according to Cole and Vladeck, is the notion that justice should be open

42 J Jackson, 'Many Years On in Northern Ireland: the Diplock Legacy' (2009) 60 *Northern Ireland Legal Quarterly* 213, 226.

and transparent.[43] This lack of openness has two undesirable effects. First of all, however effective a special advocate may be in closed procedures, the public will often have very limited, if any, access to the crucial determinative facts and issues in a case, with the result that the legitimacy of the result is undermined. We have seen in the SIAC example that certain issues are in fact amenable to be determined in open proceedings, with an open judgment giving the reasons for the determination. It was argued that special advocates have an important transparency role in trying to ensure that open judgments are as detailed and transparent as possible. The second undesirable effect is that closed procedures, even with cleared counsel, may make the courts more willing to accept evidence of a quality which would not be accepted in a public proceeding. The quality of the evidence presented in closed procedures is by definition not susceptible to critical evaluation. Special advocates interviewed in this study had mixed views about the quality of the closed evidence presented in intelligence files. In relation to SIAC, however, special advocates seemed to enjoy some success in being able to challenge closed evidence.

This study suggests that special advocates *can* ameliorate the closed nature of the proceedings by arguing for greater disclosure and transparency and by challenging the quality of the evidence that is presented in closed. But it would seem that a very fact-specific judgement is needed in each case as to whether they are able to ameliorate the deficiencies of closed procedures *sufficiently* to make them acceptable on balance. There is a broader point, however, put by one special advocate interviewed. In the overall scheme of things, the presence of special advocates in closed procedures creates a perverse incentive on the government to expand the role of closed procedures within courts more than would otherwise be acceptable. In this manner, special advocates actually perpetuate and indeed encourage the use of closed procedures.[44] In his view, the question came down to whether the institution of the special advocate played a positive role by keeping Ministers on their toes in closed procedures or whether, on the contrary, special advocates played a negative role by providing legitimacy for an ever more expansive use of closed procedures in the judicial realm.

One particular aspect of this argument is that there may be a temptation for government to abandon criminal proceedings in favour of using closed procedures and special advocates in proceedings that are just as punitive in their effect. Many executive measures that are taken against individuals and made the subject of appeal or review in closed judicial procedures are punitive in nature,[45] yet even with special advocates, the individuals concerned are not getting the quality of justice they would receive in criminal proceedings. The UK experience is that although the primary focus in the immediate aftermath of 9/11 was weighted

43 Cole and Vladeck (n 34) 175–176.

44 SA8, 7 December 2015.

45 L Zedner, 'Preventive Justice or Pre-punishment? The case of control orders' (2007) 59 CLP 174.

towards executive interventions affecting the liberty of the individual rather than court-based prosecution, in more recent years there has been a reversion to criminal prosecution.[46] After the policy of indefinite executive detention of suspected terrorists was struck down by the House of Lords in the Belmarsh decision in 2004,[47] the government responded by resorting to control orders and later to TPIMs. After the terrorist events of 7 July 2005, foreign suspects were subjected to new measures relating to deportation, exclusion and deprivation of citizenship. At the same time, however, there was a general shift away from executive measures towards the use of the criminal courts. A number of terrorist offences and investigative powers, notably 28 day detention without charge (since reduced to 14 days), were enacted in the Terrorism Act 2006. This shift can be seen by comparing the figures for terrorism-related prosecutions brought by the Crown Prosecution Service in England and Wales as against the number of TPIMs in force between 2012 and 2016 (see Table 11.1 below). At least in England and Wales, the argument that special advocates are encouraging the government to resort to executive measures at the expense of using the criminal courts does not seem to be made out.

Civil claims

Irrespective of the use made of special advocates in proceedings challenging executive measures, resort to special advocates has expanded since the Justice and Security Act 2013 permitted closed procedures to be used in any form of civil litigation. Special advocates opposed this move at the time.[48] In this study,

Table 11.1 Number of TPIMs and terrorism-related prosecutions 2012–16

Year April 1 – March 31	*Persons prosecuted**	*TPIMs+*
2012–13	22	8
2013–14	43	8
2014–15	52	1
2015–16	51	3
2016–17	79	7
Total	247	27

* Source: Home Office, *Operation of Police Powers under the Terrorism Act, financial year ending March 2017* (Home Office 2017).
\+ Source: G Allen and N Dempsey, *Terrorism in Great Britain: the statistics* (House of Commons Library 2018).

46 See C Walker, 'Terrorism Prosecution in the United Kingdom' in F Ní Aoláin and O Gross (eds), *Guantánamo and Beyond: Exceptional Courts and Military Commissions in Comparative Perspective* (CUP 2013) 245.

47 *A v SSHD* [2004] UKHL 56, [2005] 2 AC 68.

48 See Chapter 3.

mixed views were expressed by special advocates regarding the justifiability of this expansion. One interviewee considered that he was more comfortable acting as a special advocate in a tribunal such as SIAC where the court is charged with implementing public policy than in ordinary civil claims where the courts are not there to uphold the public interest, but to hold the ring between the parties and where, as he put it, 'we managed God knows how many centuries without closed procedures'.[49] Others, however, took the view that the use of special advocates could be justified exceptionally in certain civil claims. One special advocate cited the Binyam Mohammed case, where an individual is taking action against the state, in this case for disclosure of material which the UK government had in its possession relating to his detention and torture by or on behalf of the US authorities. In a scenario such as this, the involvement of a special advocate is exactly what the claimant wants.[50] As the special advocate explained, he wanted someone to go in and grab the documents and say, 'Look at the content of these documents. I've got to have these for my defence in the US'. Sometimes special advocates can therefore be useful when the claimant is pursuing an aggressive litigation action, acting as a sword rather than as shield, as one open counsel put it.[51]

Another interviewee observed that the use of PII to deal with cases where there is sensitive information had its drawbacks because invariably special advocates were not present during these applications.[52] Judges were left to rule on submissions from one side only and they consequently often made the wrong decision. In the absence of a CMP option, the risk was that the case could not get off the ground as the court could not proceed with information ruled out as a result of a PII application.[53] This interviewee special advocate said he had seen cases which special advocates have won as a result of disclosure work and closed submissions which would have failed if the procedure had been entirely PII-driven without a special advocate. Against this, another special advocate said that it may be better to 'non-suit' a case and admit that justice cannot be done than have a party submit to an unfair process by being unable to be present.[54] Admittedly, there may be cases where closed procedures with a special advocate are justified, but there was a danger that judges were being drawn into acceding to closed procedures too readily in order to view more material and evidence than might be received in regular open or private hearings. As a former President of the Supreme Court has said, the danger is that increasing familiarisation with the use of CMPs will sedate those who use them against the abhorrence that the need to resort to such measures should provoke.[55]

49 SA4, 25 November 2015.

50 SA12, 14 January 2016. See *R (Binyam Mohamed) v Secretary of State for Foreign and Commonwealth Affairs* [2010] EWCA Civ 65.

51 OC4 19, 15 January 2016.

52 SA3, 25 November 2015.

53 See *Carnduff v Rock* [2001] EWCA Civ 680, [2001] 1 WLR 1786.

54 SA12, 14 January 2016.

55 N Phillips, 'Closed Material', *London Review of Books* (17 April 2014) 29, 32.

It is too early to predict how often the courts will resort to CMPs in civil cases. It has been stressed that making a section 6 declaration under the Justice and Security Act that a closed material application may be made to the court merely opens the gateway towards a closed procedure and does not mean that there will necessarily be a CMP at trial.[56] That determination is made the subject of a second stage application under section 8 of the Act where it is assessed and determined whether material should be disclosed and deployed in open or in the closed procedure. At the initial section 6 stage, the court merely has to take a view, on the basis of the sensitive information and its importance as compared with the open material, as to whether the likely result of a PII exercise or stage two evaluation would put sufficient material in open proceedings to meet the justice of the case.[57]

This raises the further question of what is necessary to meet the justice of the case. The courts have accepted that a closed material procedure is a serious departure from the fundamental principles, but have at the same time accepted that it represents Parliament's assessment of how, in relevant civil proceedings, the balance is to be struck between the competing interests of open justice and natural justice, on the one hand, and the protection of national security, on the other.[58] Incursion on these principles is the price which Parliament has determined should be paid in cases where the non-disclosure of material which would damage national security would otherwise make it impossible to have a trial at all.[59] The assumption that Parliament has made and that the courts have to respect, in other words, is that the fair and effective administration of justice is better served by a closed procedure than by refusing to try the case or by trying the case in the absence of the closed material. To recall the assertion in the government's Green Paper, it is fairer in terms of outcome to seek to include the relevant material in a closed hearing rather than to exclude it from the court altogether.[60] But the unspoken assumption here, as Lord Kerr put it in *Al Rawi v Security Service*,[61] is that because the judge sees everything, she is bound to be in a better position to reach a fair result. In his lordship's view, this assumption was misplaced because '[t]o be truly valuable, evidence must be capable of withstanding challenge'; indeed to go further, '[e]vidence which has been insulated from challenge may positively mislead'.[62] The question then becomes one of whether the special advocate procedure can compensate effectively by being able to challenge the

56 *R (Sarkandi) v Secretary of State for Foreign and Commonwealth Affairs* [2015] EWCA Civ 687 [19], *Belhaj v Straw* [2017] EWHC 1861 (QB) [23].

57 *XH v SSHD* [2015] EWHC 2932 (Admin) [18–19]; *Belhaj v Straw* [2017] EWHC 1861 (QB) [24].

58 See eg *R (Sarkandi) v Secretary of State for Foreign and Commonwealth Affairs* [2015] EWCA Civ 687 [57]–[58].

59 *Belhaj v Straw* [2017] EWHC 1861 (QB) [26].

60 Ministry of Justice, *Justice and Security Green Paper* (Cm 8194, 2011) [2.2].

61 *Al-Rawi v The Security Service* [2011] UKSC 34, [2012] 1 AC 531 [93].

62 ibid.

evidence in the closed procedure. One of the safeguards built into section 8 of the 2013 Act is that where the court gives permission to the Secretary of State to withhold sensitive material, it can require her to provide summaries to the claimants and their open representatives, failing which she is not to rely on the material or must make concessions.[63] The public interest in disclosure informs this approach. It may also be necessary to provide minimal disclosure in order to comply with a party's ECHR Article 6 rights.[64]

Even if these mechanisms enable the special advocate to make an effective challenge to the closed material, there is the further question whether the special advocate can compensate for the lack of party participation in the closed procedure. Applicants who take actions against the state for alleged abuses against them are often not merely seeking compensation for wrongs committed, on the model of an ordinary civil claim. They are seeking an opportunity to hold those accountable for the harm allegedly done to them. Thus when Abdul Hakim Belhaj, together with his wife Fatima Boudchar, took a civil action against the UK Government for its alleged complicity in their extraordinary rendition from Thailand to Libya in a joint MI6–CIA–Libyan intelligence operation, he said from the beginning that all he wanted was an apology rather than compensation.[65] When it was ruled that allegations over the role played by the former Foreign Secretary and a senior intelligence officer could be determined in closed procedures,[66] he reportedly asked: 'What kind of a trial is it when we put in a mountain of evidence and government officials can simply refuse to answer us?'[67] In the end, Belhaj and his wife received a public apology from the Prime Minister after the case was settled.[68] But if the case had proceeded in closed procedure, these litigants would have been deprived of the satisfaction of personally seeing alleged wrongdoers called to account.

The further element extending beyond a claimant's lack of participation in the closed procedure is the public interest in open justice. In contesting the government's claim for a section 6 declaration, Belhaj's counsel argued that the more serious the allegations made against the state, the stronger the public interest in such allegations being tried in an open forum with the greatest transparency.[69] The court considered that this argument cuts both ways. If the state could not defend its claim without reference to material that could not be disclosed publicly, there was a risk that there might be no trial at all. The more serious the case, the greater the imperative to avoid this result, which would be the antithesis of

63 Justice and Security Act 2013, s 8 and CPR r 82.14(7)(8).

64 See *R (Sarkandi) v Secretary of State for Foreign and Commonwealth Affairs* [2015] EWCA Civ 687 [59]; *Belhaj v Straw* [2017] EWHC 1861 (QB) [25].

65 See *The Guardian* (London, 11 May 2018) 7.

66 *Belhaj v Straw* [2017] EWHC 1861 (QB).

67 'Renditions case against Jack Straw must be held in secret, judge rules', *The Guardian* (London, 21 July 2017).

68 See *The Guardian* (London, 11 May 2018) 1.

69 *Belhaj v Straw* [2017] EWHC 1861 (QB) [27].

the fair and effective administration of justice. The court here was reflecting the intention of the legislature in enacting section 6 that if there is a considerable amount of relevant sensitive information in the case that cannot be disclosed openly, the interests of justice would seem to require a closed procedure. But again, it is debatable whether the fair and effective administration of justice does indeed require this result. For if CMPs rob courts of their ability to command public confidence, then untold damage might be done to the administration of justice in the longer term and the inability to do justice in individual cases may be a price that has to be paid to offset such a damaging prospect.

All this is not to deny that there may be a place for special advocates in certain civil procedures. We have seen that special advocates may be used exceptionally in criminal cases when PII applications are made in order to have defence interests represented when judges are deciding whether to uphold the application. A similar practice has developed in civil cases of employing special advocates, sometimes referred to as 'PII advocates', to represent the interests of a party excluded from a PII hearing.[70] Under section 6(7) of the Justice and Security Act the court must not consider an application by the Secretary of State for a declaration under section 6 unless it is satisfied that he or she has considered whether to make a claim for PII in relation to the material on which the declaration is based. One special advocate said that where the Secretary of State goes through a PII exercise as a prelude to potentially making an application under section 6, a special advocate should be there as a check on any tendency to put closed material before a possibly inexperienced judge without it being properly scrutinised with a view to possible disclosure.[71] Although the legislation does not state that a CMP must only be used as a last resort, this interviewee argued that special advocates have an important role in testing whether a section 6 declaration is really necessary. We have also seen that where there is statutory provision for a closed procedure and the excluded party wishes to appeal or judicially review a closed judgment that emerges from it, there is a strong case for the appellate or judicial review court being able to scrutinise the closed judgment in a closed hearing with special advocates appointed to represent the interests of the excluded party in such a hearing.[72]

Apart from ordinary civil claims, we have seen special advocates being used in a number of specialist tribunals where CMPs are deemed necessary to protect information in the public interest and in other proceedings where there is a strong public interest involved, such as family proceedings where the interests of the child are paramount. One issue that was considered in the Green Paper preceding

70 SASO, *A Guide to the Role of Special Advocates & the Special Advocates' Support Office* (2nd edn Government Legal Department 2019) [150]-[153].

71 SA11, 14 January 2016.

72 See *R (Haralambous) v Crown Court at St Albans* [2018] UKSC 1, [2018] AC 236. On the question whether there can be a judicial review of a closed judgment of the IPT notwithstanding an ouster clause in s 67(8) of RIPA, see *R (Privacy International) v Investigatory Powers* [2019] UKSC 22 under appeal to the Supreme Court.

the Justice and Security Act was whether CMPs should be employed in inquests where sensitive material is relevant, with provision for families to receive a gist of sensitive material and to be represented by special advocates when sensitive information is presented to the inquest.[73] The Green Paper referred in particular to the limitations of the arrangements in the Northern Ireland 'legacy inquests' from the perspective of bereaved families whereby relevant sensitive information may have to be excluded from the process altogether under PII.[74] Questions also arise as to whether their inability to rely on such information makes inquests unable to comply with the UK's procedural obligation under Article 2 of the ECHR (right to life) to investigate any death implicating agents of the state. New arrangements have recently been proposed which envisage creating a new Historical Inquiries Unit (HIU) to complete all outstanding investigations into Troubles-related deaths, with a specific mandate to provide family reports on each death that is investigated.[75] Under the proposals, special advocates would be appointed to represent the interests of families in appeals before the Northern Ireland High Court against the Secretary of State's decision to withhold permission for the HIU to include certain information in these reports on the grounds that its release would damage national security.[76] This proposal is a good example of special advocates being deployed to advance the public interest that as much information as possible should be made available to family members about how their loved ones met their deaths during the Troubles.

Special advocate procedures

Whilst the kinds of cases in which closed procedures should be deployed remains controversial, we have seen that special advocates play an important role in furthering the interests of parties who are excluded from such procedures, in terms of disclosing more information to such parties, representing their interests in those parts of the substantive case that are held in closed procedures and ensuring greater transparency in the reasons that are given for decisions that are reached. If a positive case can be made for their deployment in various types of proceedings and they are going to be with us for the foreseeable future, a further question is whether there should be greater clarity surrounding the procedures they are subject to. We have seen that there are rules relating to special advocates in the various types of proceedings in which special advocates operate. This is especially the case where their appointment is specifically provided for by statute. But special advocates may also be appointed in the absence of statutory authority and the question is whether there should be a more comprehensive set of 'best practice'

73 Ministry of Justice (n 60) [2.15].
74 ibid [2.23].
75 See Northern Ireland Office, *Addressing the Legacy of Northern Ireland's Past* (Consultation Paper 2018).
76 ibid 38–39.

guidelines, that would apply in all cases, governing their appointment, their communications with the excluded party and the kind of supports they can expect to carry out their functions. SASO's *Open Manual* provides very helpful guidance on many of these matters, but throughout this study we have across areas where special advocates and other practitioners considered that there could be greater certainty and clarity.

As far as the appointment of special advocates is concerned, we have seen that there are transparent recruitment processes in place for appointment to the Special Advocates' panel in England and Wales and in Northern Ireland. Excluded parties are now permitted to select from the panel whom they would like appointed to represent their interests, although they have no absolute right to have their choice of special advocate appointed. One matter on which there could be greater clarity relates to the appointment of special counsel in criminal cases and of so-called 'PII advocates' in civil cases where the government chooses to make a PII application in parallel with, or instead of, an application for a section 6 declaration under the Justice and Security Act. In practice, it seems that such counsel are appointed from the Special Advocates' panel but where the sensitive material does not reach the threshold of closed material that requires developed vetting, there is no reason why the choice of counsel should be so restricted.

Another area in need of clearer guidelines concerns the situations when a conflict of interest may arise and when a special advocate may become 'tainted' if they were to act for an excluded party. As we saw in Chapter 5, the first edition of SASO's manual appeared to consider that this was largely a matter for special advocates to regulate themselves, but the latest edition sets down the procedures to be followed when the 'information owner' asserts that a particular special advocate cannot be considered for nomination because of a conflict of interest or because the special advocate is tainted. There is still lacking, however, a clear statement as to when a conflict of interest may arise.

Although the appointment processes put in place by the Attorney General's Office put the Attorney General's impartiality in respect of *who* should be appointed as a special advocate beyond question, *whether* to appoint a special advocate, special counsel or PII advocate in a case where there is no statutory provision for one to be appointed is a different question. There is an obvious conflict of interest when this matter is left to the Attorney General because the purpose of any appointment is to support the interests of a party opposing the government side.[77] We have seen that the appointment of special counsel in criminal cases is particularly rare, and yet they can provide judges with much needed assistance in cases of complexity. Where the court requests the appointment of a special counsel in complex cases, it would seem that the court is in a better position to reach an impartial view on whether such an appointment is necessary in the interests of justice than the Attorney General's Office, and that the court's view should prevail. There should also be an established principle that the party making the

77 JUSTICE, *Secret Evidence* (JUSTICE 2009) [404].

PII application or the application for closed material to be viewed by the court should bear the costs of appointing a special advocate and of any witnesses whose evidence the special advocate wishes to adduce.

Once special advocates have been appointed and are in receipt of closed material, we have seen that there are very strict rules governing any communications between them and excluded parties. But there are also areas of uncertainty about the parameters of their role vis-à-vis the excluded party before they are in receipt of closed material. For example, it would help if it were made unambiguously clear that communications between the excluded party, the party's legal representatives and special advocates are privileged. How is the special advocate to act in the interests of the excluded party, if there cannot be frank and full discussions between them because clients and their lawyers are worried that what is said may go beyond the special advocate? There might also be greater clarity as to whether, in their turn, special advocates may give excluded parties and their legal representatives the benefit of any 'special' knowledge in broad terms of how cases are run in a closed procedure. At present, it would seem that special advocates must maintain a 'vow of silence' in respect of all that transpires in closed proceedings. In terms of seeking authorisation to communicate with excluded parties once special advocates are in receipt of closed material, we have seen that in Canada this may be sought on an ex parte basis before a trial judge, and we raised the question whether a judge not involved in hearing the case as a whole could be designated to determine these applications.

One way of circumventing the need for such applications is by ensuring that as much relevant information as can be disclosed about the allegations made against excluded parties is made available so that the special advocate can be given the fullest instructions possible from the excluded party before going into closed. But we have seen that the 'iterative' disclosure process that gets under way once the special advocate is in closed invariably results in greater disclosure with further gists as a result of the submissions that the special advocate makes in closed. This is where the value of two special advocates comes into play: one who goes into closed to argue for greater disclosure of material to the excluded party and the other who stays in open to take instructions from the excluded party when further disclosure is made. Special advocates interviewed in this research both in the UK and Canada also referred to the substantial benefit that is derived from having two special advocates in a case, as this offsets the isolation that special advocates feel in the absence of an instructing solicitor. Although the government would seem to have been fairly generous to date in permitting both a senior and junior special advocate to be appointed in many cases, this does not invariably happen and guidelines could specify that there should be a presumption in favour of appointing both a senior and junior special advocate in CMPs.

Special advocates in this study referred to a number of other ways in which their job could be made easier. They were appreciative of the support that SASO gave them, but considered that SASO needed to be better resourced so as to give them more dedicated support in individual cases. There is a clear need for a database of closed judgments to be developed so that special advocates are made aware of closed judgments in other cases. Special advocates also need the time to carry out their disclosure duties effectively before closed hearings which requires active judicial management of cases. The government has so far resisted any idea that special advocates be provided with some support from the intelligence or ex-intelligence community, in terms of seeking further closed information, making submissions for greater open disclosure or assisting in the substantive representations that are made in closed hearings. At the very least, however, special advocates should be facilitated in calling experts to testify in closed hearings with a pool of security-cleared experts made available who could be put under similar constraints as special advocates not to communicate with the excluded party or open representatives. Finally, in order that special advocates can play an effective role in making submissions to open up aspects of closed judgments, they need access to draft closed judgments as well as draft open judgments as soon as these are issued.

The types of support that this study has uncovered would assist special advocates to perform their functions more effectively are very similar to the kinds of support that any counsel needs to do their job properly. Regular counsel need to have detailed instructions, they need easy access to the relevant law, they need time to carry out any disclosure functions and to prepare for trial and they need to be able to call any witnesses who can assist their case. But this study has also highlighted a number of respects in which the position of special advocates differs from that of ordinary counsel. We have identified how they feel isolated, cut adrift from any client or instructing solicitor and often feeling squeezed (according to one interviewee, like 'the ham in the middle of a sandwich'[78]) between the countervailing pressures of the excluded party and the government party, with no control over the direction of the case. Crucially, where special advocates have been provided by statute, it is invariably stated that they are not responsible to any excluded party. While some special advocates considered that their role was de facto that of acting as the excluded party's counsel in the closed procedures, they accepted that they were not the party's representatives de jure. The very fact that they are unable to share information with their 'clients' and communicate with them without permission placed them in a markedly different position to ordinary counsel.

If special advocates are not responsible to any party, this raises the question to whom they are responsible. In Chapter 10, we differentiated the role of the special advocate not only from that of ordinary counsel, but also from that of an amicus who assists the court. Although they do not represent any particular party to the proceedings, they do have a particular mandate to act in the interests of a party. It is important not to blur the lines between the special advocate role and the amicus role as there can be occasions when the two may conflict. It will be recalled that, in an early case, special advocates took a strong stance against

78 SA12, 14 January 2016.

representing an excluded party in closed proceedings when they considered it was not in the party's interests to be represented, even though SIAC put considerable pressure on them to represent the party in closed proceedings.[79] Ultimately, it was not for the special advocates to do the court's bidding. Special advocates, of course, owe certain duties to the court, as do ordinary counsel. But they do not act as an extension of the court.

Some blurring of the role of special counsel and amicus seemed to occur in a criminal appeal based on anonymity orders made by the trial judge.[80] In this case, the Court of Appeal, in granting leave to appeal, asked for the appointment of special counsel who had appeared at trial, and it considered that this had proved valuable. The special counsel played an important role in the appeal in ensuring that the court saw all the closed evidence that it ought to see. The Court went on to consider various reasons supporting the appointment of special counsel, including 'questions on which the court feels that it needs the assistance of special counsel to do justice'.[81] But the Court also ventured the view, reiterated by the special counsel in this case and later cases,[82] that special counsel's role is not that of an amicus but 'is essentially the same as would be that of the appellant's ordinary counsel if that counsel had been privy to the same information'.[83] It is not difficult to discern a tension between this role and 'assisting' the Court of Appeal 'to do justice', as answering questions of the latter kind may end up not helping the appellant's case. Given the priority that special counsel must give to representing the interests of the defence, it is questionable whether they should be engaged at the appellate stage to assist the court to assess the safety of a conviction. We have seen that special counsel can be put into a difficult position here. It may be that when the Court of Appeal specifically seeks submissions to assist it, it should seek to appoint an amicus rather than a special counsel.

Reconceptualising the role of special advocates in theory and practice

If special advocates are accountable neither to a specific party to the proceedings nor to the court (except in so far as they owe certain duties to the court like any ordinary counsel), this seems to open up a potential accountability gap that needs to be explored further.[84] One way of developing a theory of accountability for special advocates is to see them playing an entirely *sui generis* role, hitherto unknown in adversarial proceedings. In conventional adversarial theory, counsel are there either to act on behalf of a party to the proceedings or, in the

79 See Chapter 6.
80 *R v Chrisholm* [2010] EWCA Crim 258.
81 ibid [46].
82 See also *R v Austin* [2013] EWCA Crim 1028 [84].
83 ibid [47].
84 See E Metcalfe, '"Representative but not Responsible": the Use of Special Advocates in English Law' (2004) 1 *Justice Journal* 11, 30.

case of an amicus counsel, on behalf of the court. But once we stray outside this conventional framework, other possibilities open up. We have discussed the role of 'public interest monitors' who act as public interest advocates in Australia. Drawing on this analogy, JUSTICE has argued that a distinction should be made between the role that special advocates play in PII claims from the role that they play in closed procedures such as SIAC.[85] There is nothing to be gained, it said, by confusing an advocate who argues for *disclosure* in a PII claim with an advocate who helps *determine the substantive facts in issue* in a secret trial.[86] The two functions of disclosure and substantive argument are fundamentally different. Accordingly, JUSTICE recommended that a terminological distinction should be made between *public interest advocates* who represent the interest of defendants in PII applications and in other ex parte applications such as search warrants, surveillance warrants etc. and *special advocates* who act on behalf of defendants in closed procedures and take on a substantive role. The former represent the public interest that the administration of justice shall not be frustrated, while the latter act in a representational role on behalf of defendants in closed sessions.

However, on the evidence of this research study, it is not so easy to draw such a clear line between these two roles. When advocates act in the interests of defendants or potential defendants in search warrant or surveillance cases, they are not playing a disclosure role; they are putting forward substantive arguments in the interests of these parties. We have seen that in PII applications, there can also be a thin line between disclosure and substantive arguments. There is another point here as well. In each case, special advocates are there to act in the interests of parties excluded from the proceedings as best as they can, but it is hard to say that they are acting on their behalf and 'representing' their interests when, as we have repeatedly noted, they do not enjoy unfettered access to them and are unable to take full instructions from them. Throughout this book, we have succumbed to the idea that special advocates play a substantive representational role in closed procedures. This is because it is difficult to conceive of advocacy in the common law world as being anything other than one of representing parties or the court, and of owing corresponding professional duties. But as Lord Bingham put it so vividly in *R v H and C*,[87] by improvising the role of special advocate, we have created an advocate who is acting in a manner hitherto unknown to the legal profession. It is not just the link between representation and responsibility that has been severed; representation in the sense of acting on behalf of a party has also been modified.

Once we move away from the idea that the special advocate represents a party, we can invoke JUSTICE's idea that special advocates are there to act in the public interest of the administration of justice, not only by ensuring that as much information is disclosed to the excluded party as is possible, but also by ensuring

85 JUSTICE (n 77) [445].
86 ibid (emphasis in original).
87 *R v H; R v C* [2004] UKHL 3, [2004] 2 AC 135 [22].

that there is a counterweight to the prosecution or the government's arguments in closed session. The public interest requires that the absent party's interests are protected throughout the proceedings. One special advocate succinctly encapsulated the idea in terms of his job being to hold the state to account:

> That is how I see the crucial role performed by the special advocates. But for the special advocate system, you have to question whether or not that would happen. Is the state going to be held to the same degree of account by the court system, if you don't have special advocates there testing the closed evidence which is going to be relied on anyway. … It's not ideal but it's the art of the possible with what you're dealing with.[88]

On this view, the relationship between the excluded party and the special advocate is not really one of agency. The special advocate is neither required nor, indeed, permitted to give the excluded party an account of what she has done or what she is doing. The relationship is perhaps better characterised as trusteeship. The special advocate is appointed to act as a trustee for the benefit of the absent party but is not bound by their instructions, and even entitled to act against their wishes if it is perceived to advance their interests to do so.

This is not a well-developed role for an advocate in the adversarial tradition. It is a role, however, that lawyers play in other procedural systems where lawyers maintain an independence from their clients and assist rather than represent their client's cause.[89] In Germany, for example, defence counsel does not represent the accused but acts only as an adviser. According to Wohlers, this means having to protect the interests of the accused against law enforcement agencies and prosecutors, ensure that the prosecution is pursued in a fair manner and that all circumstances favourable to the accused are taken into consideration.[90] Defence counsel in Germany must develop a strategy together with the accused with the aim of building a basis of trust that allows the accused to put the conduct of the defence in the hands of counsel. In this research, special advocates similarly emphasised the importance of trying to work as closely as possible with the excluded party and his legal representative and the open representatives interviewed recognised the importance of working closely with special advocates. It is not a case of the party having two legal representatives, each acting independently in the open and closed proceedings respectively. Instead, the special advocate must try within established institutional frameworks to develop strategies with the party's legal representative, in a supporting and advisory role. As one interviewee put it, the

88 SA7, 3 December 2015.

89 See, eg J Leubsdorf, 'On the History of French Legal Ethics' (2001) 8 *University of Chicago Law School Roundtable* 341, 344–345.

90 W Wohlers, 'The Role of Counsel in Criminal Proceedings' in J Jackson and S Summers (eds), *Obstacles to Fairness in Criminal Proceedings: Individual Rights and Institutional Forms* (Hart 2018) 127, 145.

special advocate should try as hard as possible to make her own position redundant, putting as much material as possible into open so that the open representatives can make the case they wish.[91] To boil it down:

> the more they get, the better they'll be able to decide the case or advance their case – I mean the ideal scenario is for them to do all the work.

Of course, there may come a point when the special advocate must make her own submissions on the closed material with or without instructions from the absent party's legal representative. But even then, the role is not one of *representing* that party but acting with independent judgement in the party's interest.

The need to maintain a close working relationship with a party's true legal representative raises practical questions, such as whether certain types of less sensitive material might be disclosable on a 'counsel to counsel' basis to the excluded party's legal representative if the representative can obtain the consent of her client to do so. Alternatively, the special advocate might ask permission to communicate with the legal representatives on a 'counsel to counsel' basis. Whilst precluded from disclosing sensitive information, special advocates might thereby be able to maintain some communication after examining the closed material for the purpose of elucidation, seeking further information or assisting in strategy. We have seen that security-cleared counsel acting for a court or an inquiry can retain contact with open legal representatives after being privy to closed material. Why should special advocates not also be able to do so?

All this serves to underline that the developing role of the special advocate has some way to go before it can be said that the duties are fully established and understood within the legal profession and by the wider public. In addition to the disclosure and representational roles performed by special advocates, there is also merit in emphasising the contribution to transparency that special advocates make in ensuring that the open judgments that emerge from proceedings involving CMPs are as detailed and fully reasoned as possible. Reconceptualisation of the special advocate's role helps to foster creativity and new thinking. If, as we have argued, the special advocate's role is best formulated in terms of acting in the interests of the administration of justice as a whole, how are they to be held accountable for their conduct? One response might be to say that as they are appointed by the Attorney General to serve the interests of justice, the reality is that special advocates are responsible to the government which is their client.[92] This was not the way in which any of the interviewees viewed their role. Indeed, as we have seen, far from acting *for* the government, there was a view that the whole raison d'être of special advocates was to hold government to account. While they may not be responsible to the excluded party, they were certainly not responsible

91 SA14, 5 February 2016.

92 A Boon and S Nash, 'Special Advocacy: Political Expediency and Legal Roles in Modern Judicial Systems' (2006) *Legal Ethics* 101, 121.

to the government, except in anything other than the formal sense that they were appointed by the government to act in the excluded party's interest. At this point it is useful to invoke a distinction Waldron has made between 'agent' accountability and 'forensic' accountability.[93] Agent accountability denotes the duty owed by an agent to her principal, whereby the principal may demand from the agent an account of the work that the agent has been doing in the principal's name or on the principal's behalf.[94] The traditional lawyer–client relationship is one of agency in terms of structure, however far removed this may be from institutional and sociological realities. The client directs the professional as to the broad remit of the task to be performed and the professional has to answer to the client for her performance. Forensic accountability, by contrast, denotes the liability of a person to have her actions assessed by a tribunal on the basis of some established norm.[95] Waldron argues that in a trust relationship, neither the settlor nor the beneficiary of the trust has the right to control or to demand an account from the trustee.[96] If they do demand an account, they have to do it on the basis that the trustee has breached some established norm. The kind of accountability that a trust involves much more resembles forensic accountability. If the special advocate's relationship towards an excluded party in legal proceedings is more akin to that of a trustee than an agent, then they can only be held accountable by reference to an established normative framework.

Of course, special advocates, like other legal professionals, remain bound by the codes of ethics observed by their professional bodies. But the question is whether, as the role expands to encompass greater numbers of advocates, there should be a tailored ethical code for the special advocate setting out the standards that are required. Special advocates interviewed in this study did not themselves seem to think this was necessary, and special advocates were praised by ordinary counsel for unstinting conscientiousness in their efforts to represent the interests of excluded parties. But if the only manner in which special advocates can be made accountable for the work they do is by means of adherence to a set of rules rather than by adhering to the instructions of those whose interests they represent, then in the interests of greater transparency and the rule of law there is an argument for a special set of rules being drawn up to govern their conduct, enforceable by their professional body. Special advocates may not be responsible to a client or an instructing solicitor, but they are ultimately responsible to their professional body for the work that they do. This in turn behoves the professional body to set out what standards are to be expected and how these are to be enforced. This proposal would require the Bar to become more engaged with the role of special advocates than hitherto. Other than assisting in the appointment of special advocates to the panel, the profession's collective engagement with special

93 See J Waldron, *Political Political Theory: Essays on Institutions* (Harvard UP 2016) 167–168.
94 ibid 168.
95 ibid 167.
96 ibid 178.

advocates has been limited. We saw in Chapter 5 that the latest SASO manual also envisages a role for the profession in resolving disputes over questions of conflict of interest which arise when 'information owners' assert that a special advocate cannot be considered for nomination due to a conflict of interest. As special advocates appear to have become a permanent feature of the legal system, it is perhaps time for the professional bodies to take greater responsibility for developing their role and monitoring their performance.

This book has argued that, although the role of the special advocate remains controversial, special advocates play a valuable role in the administration of justice by importing a degree of adversariality into processes where it would otherwise be lacking. There is further work to do in developing the role, both conceptually as a departure from orthodox adversarialism and pragmatically in terms of special advocates' day-to-day activities. By trying to bring to life the work of special advocates in their own words, and by looking comparatively at other models, it is hoped that this book provides a starting point for future work on how the traditional roles that lawyers play within adversarial systems are being modified as these systems cope with the increasing demands of having to deal with secret evidence. In all of this, it is essential that we maintain respect for core underlying values that underpin the rule of law, but equally important that in doing so we pay close attention to the mechanisms through which these values are institutionalised. Political and legal philosophers have argued that normative theorists have paid insufficient attention to the importance of the institutional structures and operations that have been created to achieve systemic objectives such as justice, liberty, security and equality.[97] The adversarial system with its emphasis on testing versions of events that are put forward by disputatious parties has long been instrumental in our conception of how justice is achieved, and the roles assigned to key participants are vital in contributing towards this aim. The special advocate is a new participant, invented to play a novel professional role alongside established professional and judicial players. The role that these new advocates play needs to be understood in terms of its relationship with other participants, and assessed in terms of the contribution it makes to the administration of justice as a whole. Whether special advocates continue to exist will depend on how that contribution is judged.

97 See, eg, Waldron (n 93), R A Duff, 'Fairness in Criminal Proceedings' in J Jackson and S Summers (n 90), 301, 309–310. Cf L Farmer, *Making the Modern Criminal Law: Criminalisation and Civil Order* (OUP 2016).

Index

Page numbers in **bold** denote tables.

For Product Safety Concerns and Information please contact our EU representative GPSR@taylorandfrancis.com
Taylor & Francis Verlag GmbH, Kaufingerstraße 24, 80331 München, Germany

www.ingramcontent.com/pod-product-compliance
Ingram Content Group UK Ltd.
Pitfield, Milton Keynes, MK11 3LW, UK
UKHW022012180926
475701UK00003B/327
* 9 7 8 0 3 6 7 7 2 6 8 5 0 *